275 RECIPES

❖

APPETIZERS
THROUGH
DESSERTS

Serve with Champagne

Hilde Gabriel Lee

with Allan E. Lee

TEN SPEED PRESS

1☉
Ten Speed Press
Post Office Box 7123
Berkeley, California 94707

First Edition

Cover, interior design and typography by Fifth Street Design, Berkeley, California
Cover photography by Walter Swarthout, San Francisco, California

Library of Congress Cataloging-in-Publication-Data

Lee, Hilde Gabriel
Serve with Champagne

Includes index.

1. Cookery.
2. Champagne (Wine)   I. Lee, Allan E., 1923— .   II. Titl.
TX714.L44   1988   641.5   88-50976

ISBN 0-89815-262-3
ISBN 0-89815-274-7 (pbk.)

Manufactured in the United States of America

88 89 90 91 92 — 5 4 3 2 1

TABLE OF CONTENTS

LIST OF RECIPES

HORS D'OEUVRES 39

FIRST COURSES 61

SOUPS 101

SORBETS 127

MAIN COURSES 137

BREADS 237

SALADS 249

DESSERTS 269

BRUNCHES 307

INTRODUCTION

THIS IS A COOKBOOK ABOUT FINE FOOD AND CHAMPAGNE — American style food and American style champagne. While my underlying purpose in writing this book is to establish that champagne is a wine for food in addition to being a wine for celebration, I wanted to do so in the context of American food and the American approach to champagne making. Just as American food is a mélange of ethnic heritages from many countries, so American champagne is created from a wide array of grape varieties, in differing climates, and with a variety of champagne-making styles. Both are different from any other styles of food or champagne in the world. Matching champagne style to American food, therefore, requires a winemaking approach that acknowledges American eating habits and culture.

In developing the concept of this book, I solicited the help of ten of the leading American makers of champagne. They were chosen to represent a cross section of American champagne-making styles and *cuvées*; as a group, the ten companies provide 70 percent of the champagne made by the *méthode champenoise* in the United States. Each in some fashion has been a pioneer in the development of the American champagne industry. While Northern Californian producers predominate, other major wine-growing regions are represented, including the Finger Lakes region of New York, the mid-Atlantic states, the Pacific Northwest, and Southern California.

Each champagne maker has a full time, professional culinary director on its staff. I felt it important that each participant took the interaction of food and champagne seriously enough to have a program of matching food with champagne. Several of the champagne makers selected operate excellent restaurants in connection with their wineries. The backgrounds of the culinary directors are as varied as the *cuvées* of champagne with which they work.

Every one of the ten firms that I approached with the concept enthusiastically accepted the invitation to participate. They agreed with the premise that the American public would benefit from becoming more knowledgeable about matching food and champagne. Each offered to provide at least twenty-five recipes. The culinary directors worked closely with me to coordinate the various recipes within each category — hors d'oeuvres, first course, soup, sorbet, main course, vegetable, salad, dessert, and brunch — to avoid duplication and overemphasis. They each spent many hours carefully creating the original recipes that have been included in this book.

The participating American champagne makers and their culinary directors are, in alphabetical order:

Biltmore Estates Winery, Asheville, North Carolina
Culinary director: Steve Wenger
Chateau Ste. Michelle, Woodinville, Washington
Culinary director: Karen Mack
The Great Western Winery, Hammondsport, New York
Culinary director: Edna Tears
Hanns Kornell Champagne Cellars, Napa Valley, California
Culinary director: Marilouise Kornell
John Culbertson Winery, Temecula Valley, California
Culinary Director: Martha Culbertson

Korbel Champagne Cellars, Guerneville, California
Culinary Director: Sheryl Benesch
Mirassou Vineyards, San José, California
Culinary Director: Ruth Wiens
S. Anderson Vineyard, Napa Valley, California
Culinary Director: Tracy Wood Anderson
Schramsberg Vineyards and Cellars, Calistoga, California
Culinary Director: Jamie Davies
Wente Bros. Sparkling Wine Cellars, Livermore, California
Culinary Director: Fred Horton

The selection does not include any of the growing number of subsidiaries of foreign companies. This is not meant to slight their fine products nor to display an anti-foreign bias. It is simply that I have chosen to focus on the match between American food and the American approach to champagne making. It is not possible to ignore the fundamental contribution the French have made to the development of this wonderful beverage over the centuries. In fact, it was Moët-Hennessy's decision to create Domaine Chandon in the Napa Valley in 1973 that gave legitimacy, in the eyes of the American public, to America's fine champagnes.

The use of the term *champagne* for American sparkling wines raises a controversial issue. The French believe, with considerable justification, that the word should apply only to the sparkling wine produced in the Champagne region of France. Most Americans, however, use the term *champagne* in referring to almost all sparkling wine, irrespective of how or where it is made. With no desire to take up the issue, I have chosen here to use the term more freely than the French would prefer, but not as freely as it is generally used in North America.

In this book, the term *champagne* refers to sparkling wine wherever made, but only if it is made by the process developed in the Champagne region of France over 150 years ago and called *la méthode champenoise*. This decision is in no way intended as a slight to the views of the people of Champagne, nor to their product. Rather, it is made in deference to the predominantly American readers of this book. It is to the credit of the Champenois and to the French language that champagne has come to be associated with the most treasured moments of our lives and that no other word can quite convey this association.

I only hope that the American champagne makers who have contributed their wonderful recipes to this book will accept my viewpoint. As a group, they are divided in their feelings about the appropriate use of the term *champagne* so I have decided to take my own position. In the descriptions of the products of the individual participants, however, I have used the term preferred by the firm.

As I stated at the beginning, this book is a cookbook about food and champagne that is designed to enhance both. To enjoy food fully, we go to great lengths to prepare and present it as artistically as possible. We enjoy learning about and trying exotic ingredients so that we can savor them in conversation as well as on the palate. Similarly, I believe, we can savor and enjoy champagne more when we know something about how it came into being and has developed over the years. There is much more to champagne than the momentary sensual pleasure to be derived from drinking it.

For those readers who wish to enjoy champagne in its broader sense, I have included a brief history of French champagne — how it all started and where it is today. This is followed by a similar review of the development and status of American champagne. As a preamble to these two historical reviews, I have included a section on the wine itself, to describe how champagne is made, the differences between champagne and sparkling wine, and the variations in style of the final product.

I have included a brief history of each of the participating champagne makers and the backgrounds of the culinary directors. These histories appear in the book chronologically, according to the date on which champagne was first produced. Some of the ventures go back to the late eighteen hundreds.

My deep appreciation goes to the culinary directors who created the wonderful assortment of recipes in this book. These ten individuals have melded a wide array of ingredients into fascinating and elegant recipes. Without Sheryl Benesch, Karen Mack, Martha Culbertson, Ruth Wiens, Jamie Davies, Fred Horton, Steve Wenger, Tracy Wood Anderson, Edna Tears, and Marilouise Kornell, this book would not have been possible.

This book also would not have been possible without the cooperation and effort of key members of the management of the ten firms. Although they were not directly involved in creating recipes, they supported the effort and made valuable comments. I wish to acknowledge the contributions of Jerome Douglas, Manager of Marketing and Sales, and Phillipe Jordain, Winemaker at Biltmore Estates; Robert Betz, Vice-President of Public Relations, of Chateau Ste. Michelle; Michael Doyle, President, and William Fox, Director of Consumer and Community Services, of Taylor Wine Company (Great Western); Hanns Kornell and his daughter Paula, Director of Marketing, for Hanns Kornell Champagne Cellars; John Culbertson, co-owner with his wife, Martha, of the John Culbertson Winery; Gary Heck, President, Robert Stashak, Winemaker, and William Batkin, Vice-President of Marketing, at Korbel; Daniel Mirassou, President, and Tom Stutz, Winemaker, of Mirassou Vineyards; Stan and Carol Anderson, owners of S. Anderson Vineyard; Jack Davies, President and co-owner along with his wife, Jamie, of Schramsberg Vineyards and Cellars; and Carolyn Wente, Vice-President of Marketing, for Wente Bros.

Many others contributed at these firms and elsewhere. Among those are Jean Dubois, Directeur-Général of Sagrera & Cie, in Épernay, France, who acted as our host during our visit to the Champagne region of France, and Frances Bowles, my editor, who worked so meticulously on the text.

I also appreciate the patience and contributions of my husband, Allan, who wrote the history section and the description of the champagne-making process. His comments and suggestions were invaluable during the testing of the recipes and the preparation of the manuscript. This truly has been a joint effort.

WHAT IS CHAMPAGNE?

SIMPLY PUT, CHAMPAGNE IS A SPARKLING WINE made by the *méthode champenoise*. Every step in the process of making champagne is critical since the winemaker is dealing with a delicate and complex living thing from the picking of the grapes to the capping of the bottle. Making champagne is like making two separate wines, the base wines resulting from the first fermentation and the champagne derived from the blended *cuvée* in the second fermentation. An understanding of this complex process can contribute immeasurably to the enjoyment of fine champagne.

La Méthode Champenoise

The *méthode champenoise* is the traditional process for making champagne as developed by the winemakers in the Champagne region of France during the seventeen and eighteen hundreds. Today in Champagne it is the legally prescribed method of making champagne and is strictly enforced. The finest sparkling wines throughout the world are made by this labor-intensive process. While various steps of the process have been mechanized, the basic process has remained the same for over 150 years. The individual steps in the process are described in this chapter.

Harvesting and Pressing the Grapes

The process starts with the harvesting of the grapes in the vineyard. Harvesting begins when the grapes have ripened to the proper balance of sugar and acid. When ripening, the grape increases its sugar content and decreases its acid level. Premium champagne requires a high-acid base wine, so the grapes are picked when they have developed a sugar content of between 17 and 20 percent — several percentage points of sugar below that of the fully ripened grapes required for still wine. Bunches of grapes are carefully picked and placed in small containers to protect them from breaking open and causing the juice to oxidize. Even small amounts of oxidation can be detected in the final champagne.

The grapes are then either crushed in the field or rushed immediately to the nearest pressing house. They are pressed and the juice (the must) is stored in cooled tanks as soon as possible to avoid oxidation. Only the juice from the first pressing is used since further pressings pick up unwanted color and tannins from the grapes. When pressing Pinot Noir and other red grapes, the juice is separated quickly from the skins to avoid picking up unwanted color. Champagne grapes, unlike those for still wines, are pressed in whole bunches as the use of a crusher-stemmer would also release unwanted pigments and chemicals.

The First Fermentation

The must from each individual vineyard is fermented completely dry, meaning that all of the sugar in the must is converted to alcohol. The fermentation of the base wines is usually carried out in large steel tanks, although a few of the French champagne houses still believe that fermentation in barrels improves the final product. At the completion of this fermentation, the unblended base wines are tested and analyzed. Based on this analysis and past experience, the champagne maker creates an appropriate blend (*cuvée*) of base wines that he or she believes will create the style of champagne desired.

The French call this blending process *l'assemblage*. It is the most critical and challenging step in the process of making fine champagne. More than thirty different base wines from different vineyards may go into the final *cuvée*. For a nonvintage champagne, which constitutes three-quarters of the champagne produced in France, the *cuvée* may include base wines from a dozen different harvest years.

The Second Fermentation

The precise steps of the *méthode champenoise* process begins with the second fermentation. A solution of wine, sugar and yeast (*liqueur de tirage*) in precisely measured quantities is added to the blended wine for the second fermentation. The *cuvée* is bottled with a temporary cap and the bottles stored on their sides in large stacks in the cellar. This storage arrangement, called *sur lattes*, consists of horizontal layers of bottles with slats between each layer. The arrangement was designed to avoid a chain reaction should one bottle in the stack accidently explode during the second fermentation. Stacks can contain over half a million bottles, so multiple explosions are costly.

In the stacks, the wine goes through the second fermentation, which usually takes between thirty and ninety days depending on the temperature of the cellar and the type of yeast used. During fermentation, the bottles are shaken and restacked periodically to prevent the dead yeast from sticking to the inside of the bottle. Upon completion of the fermentation, the bottles are left on their sides to allow the wine to age on the dead yeast, *sur lies:* on the lees. The process of fermenting the *cuvée* the French call *prise de mousse:* creating the sparkle.

The second fermentation in the bottle creates the carbon dioxide bubbles in champagne. (The carbon dioxide generated in the first fermentation is allowed to dissipate.) There are two reasons for having two fermentations. The first is that they permit the champagne maker, when blending the base wines, to better foretaste the final product. While Dom Pérignon apparently was highly skilled at blending unfermented grape juices from individual vineyards in 1700, few winemakers today have that skill. The second purpose is to have a sugar-free *cuvée* so that the precise amount of *liqueur de tirage* is added to achieve the desired effervescence in the bottle — too much and the bottle explodes; too little and the champagne is flat. In the days of only one fermentation, between twenty and fifty percent of the bottles exploded. Today, the pressure in a bottle of champagne is kept within a narrow range of between seventy-five and ninety pounds per square inch (5 — 6 atmospheres).

The second fermentation adds approximately 1 percent to the alcohol content of the wine. To achieve 12.5 percent in the final champagne, therefore, the first fermentation must yield about 11.5 percent. Frequently in France, the normal grape sugar is not sufficient to produce even that much alcohol and sugar must be added at the start of the first fermentation — a process called *chaptilization*. In warm climates such as California's, the reverse is a problem. If the grapes are not picked soon enough, there is too much natural grape sugar and the first fermentation must be stopped prematurely, before all of the sugar has turned to alcohol. In this case, this residual sugar must be taken into account when the amount of sugar needed in the *liqueur de tirage* is calculated.

Aging Sur Lattes and Sur Pointes

Aging can take between one to six years depending on the *cuvée*, the style of champagne, and the quality desired. Generally speaking, the longer the champagne ages on the lees, the more subtle and delicate will be the final product. During aging, the bottles are stored *sur lattes* and moved periodically. Some champagne houses riddle the bottles part way through the aging process while others wait closer to disgorgement. If aging of the wine is to continue after riddling, the bottles are stored head down, a position the French call *sur pointes*.

Riddling or Remuage

The purpose of riddling (*remuage*) is to bring the dead yeast down to the neck of the bottle so that it can be removed. If it were not, the finished champagne would be cloudy, have a yeasty taste, and would certainly be inelegant to drink. In riddling, the bottle is slowly tipped down to the vertical position over a period of four or five weeks and slightly turned once each day to work the sediment down to the cap. Most champagne makers still riddle by hand; an experienced *remueur* can turn fifty thousand bottles in a working day. Increasingly, however, computer-controlled mechanical riddling machines, which riddle 405 bottles in a two-week cycle, are being used. Some huge machines are can riddle over four thousand bottles in a cycle.

Disgorging, Dosaging and Finishing

After riddling, the dead yeast must be removed (disgorged) from the neck of the bottle and the champagne prepared for shipping. While riddling may be done at any time during aging, the final steps of the process — disgorging, dosaging, and finishing — are usually done within a few months of the champagne's being shipped. Disgorging is performed by removing the bottles, with their necks down, from the riddling racks or the *sur pointes* storage area to a cold bath of glycol or brine maintained at 0° F. The neck of the bottle is kept in the bath until the plug of dead yeast has almost frozen. The bottle is then set upright and the temporary cap removed. The pressure in the bottle has been lowered by the cold bath, but it is still sufficient to push the plug out without an appreciable loss of champagne.

Before the freezing technique was first employed around 1890, a very skilled *dégorgeur* was needed who could deftly remove the temporary cork with the bottle held downward, disgorge the sediment, and then quickly bring the bottle upright, all without losing an excessive amount of champagne. The modern technique is called *dégorgement à la glace;* the old system is called *dégorgement à la volée*, or on the fly.

As soon as disgorging is complete, a mixture of wine and sugar is added, called *liqueur d'expédition,* which translates from the French as "sweet wine for shipping." This dosage of wine and sugar replaces the liquid lost during disgorging and brings the sweetness of the champagne up to the desired level. For completely dry champagne, no sugar is added and only enough wine to replace the liquid lost during disgorging. A few champagne makers still use cognac or brandy in the dosage to provide both sugar and a stronger taste. In years past when champagnes were not fermented completely dry and alcohol levels were correspondingly lower, cognac was used more extensively for providing sugar, as it also augmented the alcohol level. After dosaging, the bottle is capped, washed, dressed (labelled), and boxed for shipping.

The riddling and disgorging steps of the *méthode champenoise* are used primarily for standard-sized 750 ml bottles, although some producers riddle and disgorge 1,500 ml magnums. Quarter bottles or splits (187 ml) and bottles larger than magnums are filled, in a pressurized transfer process, from standard-sized bottles after disgorgement.

The Base Wines

The character of the base wines is extremely important in establishing the quality and style of the final product. Champagne made solely from Chardonnay is called *blanc de blancs;* made solely from Pinot Noir is called *blanc de noirs;* and a blend of the two is called *blanc de noirs et blancs.* On a spectrum of taste from *blanc de blancs* to *blanc de noirs,* the latter is the most fruity while *blanc de blancs* is the most delicate. In France, champagne is typically a blend of Pinot Noir and Chardonnay in ratios ranging from 1:2 to 2:1, as the blend has proved to be the most satisfying champagne for general consumption.

The champagne houses of France blend grapes from a number of vineyards and from up to a dozen vintages. The blending of vintages provides consistent characteristics from year to year while the blending of wines from various vineyards balances the characteristics of the base wines. Only in an exceptional year does a French champagne house create a vintage champagne — perhaps in three years out of ten. Few people are aware that over one-third of the grapes grown in Champagne are from a variety called Pinot Meunier. A red grape used for blending in conjunction with Pinot Noir, it is more productive and more resistant to severe cold, although it lacks the intense flavor of the Pinot Noir.

Although champagne producers in France are limited to the use of base wines made from the three varieties of grapes mentioned above, American champagne makers work with a much broader range of grape varieties. The Americans are also producing more sparkling red wines than do the French. They tend to experiment more with unique *cuvées* and styles than do their French counterparts because they do not have the tight controls over grape growing and wine production that have been established in France. While the lack of standardization in America has its drawbacks, it does provide the consumer with a wider range of flavors and styles.

Other Processes for Making Sparkling Wine

Over the years, alternatives to the traditional *méthode champenoise* have been developed, mainly to reduce labor costs and shorten processing time. The sparkling wines made by these alternative processes can be good, but they lack the subtleties of those produced by the classical method. The two principal alternatives are the transfer method and the Charmat or bulk method. Neither is allowed to be used in the Champagne region of France.

The transfer method was developed to eliminate the costly riddling and disgorging steps. The *cuvée* does go through the second fermentation and the aging in the bottle as in the *méthode champenoise*, but the yeast is not disgorged from the bottle in the traditional manner. After aging, the wine is transferred from the bottle to a tank, filtered, and then rebottled in different bottles — all under sufficient pressure to retain the bubbles.

The Charmat or bulk method was developed in France in the early nineteen hundreds by Eugène Charmat and his father, M. Maumené-Charmat, to reduce the cost of the second fermentation. The second fermentation and the dosing take place under pressure in large tanks. The fermented sparkling wine is then filtered and finally bottled. This process involves very little aging, only that which takes place on the lees in the tank. In America, bottles of sparkling wine made by the bulk process are frequently sealed with plastic caps which are cheaper than corks.

American producers of sparkling wine are required to state clearly on the label of the bottle which of the three processes was used. If the *méthode champenoise* were used, the label will state that or indicate that the sparkling wine was "naturally fermented in *this* bottle." The transfer method does not require a special designation on the label, but no reference can be made to the *méthode champenoise*. Most producers using the transfer process will state on their label that the sparkling wine was, "naturally fermented in *the* bottle." The distinction between the two statements is that the *méthode chempenoise* champagne must be fermented and disgorged in the same bottle in which it is sold to the customer. If the Charmat process were used, the label will state that or indicate the "bulk process."

Styles of Champagne

In matching sparkling wine with food, it is important to know the style of the wine you wish to serve — that is, the approximate amount of sugar in the champagne. *Brut* champagne, which is on the dry side, is the most popular champagne in both Europe and America, although dryer champagnes, receiving essentially no dosage, are becoming more popular. Typically, these extremely dry champagnes are labelled Natural in the United States. In France, they are labelled: *brut zéro, brut non-dosage, ultra brut, naturel* or *natur*, or *sans sucre*. This very dry champagne must be crafted carefully since it requires a delicate balance of acid, sugar, and fruitiness. Historically, imbalances have been masked by the addition of sugar.

The following table summarizes the label designations used in France, Germany, and America for the various styles of champagne and the approximate sugar content for each. The ranges of sugar content shown are only approximate as each champagne-producing nation and each producer, at least in America, has its own interpretation of these definitions.

CHAMPAGNE STYLES

FRENCH	ENGLISH	GERMAN	SUGAR CONTENT
Naturel	Natural	Brut de Brut	0.0 — 0.6%
Brut	Brut	Herb or Brut	0.5 — 1.5%
Extra-sec	Extra Dry	Sehr Trocken	1.0 — 2.0%
Sec	Dry	Trocken	1.7 — 4.0%
Demi-doux or Demi-sec	Semi-dry	Halbtrocken	3.3 — 6.0%
Doux	Sweet	Mild	5.0% and above

Today, these terms may be confusing since they were created many years ago when sweet champagne was in vogue in most countries of Europe. The designations came into common use before champagne-making technology had developed so that a truly dry champagne was a pleasurable drink. Hence, what was termed a *dry* champagne at the time still had over 2 percent sugar. The term *extra dry* came along when English champagne drinkers demanded a champagne drier than *dry*. As tastes continued to move toward drier and lighter champagnes, the market asked for completely dry champagne. To meet this demand, the champagne houses started to offer champagne with very little sugar in the dosage and called it *brut*, which in French translates roughly as, unaltered. A small dosage was still needed to take the rough edges off the wine. Finally, in recent years, the producers have become able to make a balanced champagne and the drinking public has begun to accept a completely dry champagne.

What Is Fine Champagne?

Sparkling wine can be enjoyed at all levels of price and quality, but only that made by the *méthode champenoise* can be classed as having the elusive character of fine champagne. The best French champagnes are currently used as the standard of excellence throughout the world. However, French champagnes can vary considerably in quality, depending on the quality of the grapes, the *cuvée* selected, and the length of aging. American champagne makers are also producing excellent champagne. It varies in style and quality even more than does French champagne because of the wide variations in climate, soil, and grape variety from one wine-growing region to another throughout America. For the same reasons, American and French champagnes are not directly comparable. As the Champenois themselves state, "We do not say we make better sparkling wine than you do in America, merely that yours is different because you have different soil and climatic conditions."

Since bubbles are what make champagne unique, high quality champagne must, above all, exhibit a single steady and long-lasting stream of bubbles rising from the bottom of the glass. More than one writer has likened it to a string of pearls. An important attribute of the *méthode champenoise* is that the gas becomes well integrated into the wine. This produces smaller bubbles than those from other processes and also causes them to be released more slowly and for longer. Except when the champagne is first poured into the glass, the bubbles should not foam or percolate as they do in a soft drink.

Bubbles aside, adequate acidity of the champagne is also critical. Champagne is a high-acid wine. Acid imparts freshness to the champagne and, as in still wine, extends its life. Because the Champagne region of France is one of the most northerly grape-growing regions in the world, the grapes typically do not ripen fully and the acidity remains high at the time of harvest. Champagne from fully ripened grapes is flabby and short-lived since the acid level typically is low. Champagne made from grapes grown in warm climates, such as southern Europe and the San Joaquin Valley of California, exhibit these characteristics.

The term *style* has a specific meaning to champagne makers. Sweetness is only one of the variables. Others are: light- or full-body, fruitiness or austerity, youth or maturity, simplicity or complexity. Wines fermented in the bottle tend to have more individuality than do those fermented in tanks or casks. Consequently, bottle fermentation brings out both the strong and the weak points of any given *cuvée*. The winemaker is challenged to use all of his or her skills and resources to create a finished product with the proper characteristics and without noticeable rough edges. In years past, these rough edges could be hidden in the sweet champagnes that were popular, but this is no longer possible with today's dry champagnes.

Notes on the Care and Selection of Champagne

There are many excellent books and pamphlets on how to buy, store and serve champagne and the information need not be repeated here. A few notes of reminder, however, may be useful.

Champagne is meant to be drunk young and will not improve with age after it has been disgorged — although a high quality champagne can maintain its vitality for a number of years. The champagne being sold in any reputable store should be ready to be enjoyed. Non-vintage champagnes, however should have been aged for at least one year before being disgorged and bottled. Vintage champagnes in France are required to be aged for at least three years before being disgorged, or taken off the lees, and this is a good rule of thumb for the best American vintage champagnes.

Champagne should always be stored in a cool place with a constant temperature. The latter is more important than the coolness since bottles breath in air and breath out aroma if subject to temperature variations. Always store a bottle of champagne on its side so that the cork stays moist.

Champagne should be served chilled, around 45 – 50° F., which gives it a crispness and allows the bubbles to be released slowly as the glass warms. In an ice bucket the bottle will chill in about 20 minutes. Champagne is best drunk from a flute-shaped glass; its narrow form encourages creation of a single stream of bubbles and slows down the loss of effervescence. A tulip-shaped wine glass can be used in a pinch, particularly if it curves in at the top, but it is not quite as effective as the bubbles tend to dissipate quickly. Use of the saucer-shaped *coupe* glass is to be avoided.

When opening a bottle, tip it at a 45 degree angle and twist the bottle downward away from the cork, easing the cork out slowly. You should not frighten your guests nor disrupt their conversation by creating a loud "pop." Do not remove the wire hood until you are ready to remove the cork; the hood is there for a reason. It is quite correct to grip the cork through a towel so as to avoid spraying your guests from a rogue bottle. (Keep in mind that the inside of the bottle is under a pressure of 90 pounds per square inch.) When the bottle is empty, never turn it upside down in the ice bucket — that is, unless the champagne was so terrible that you wish to insult the champagne maker.

THE HISTORY OF CHAMPAGNE IN FRANCE

TRADITION HAS IT THAT SPARKLING WINE was invented by Dom Pérignon, a monk and the winemaker at the Abbey of Hautvillers, near Épernay in the Champagne district of France. While this version of history provides a romantic background to the enjoyment of champagne, it is not supported by historical evidence. Sparkling wine is a natural phenomenon produced by the chemistry of fermentation, needing only to be commercialized by man. Records mentioning sparkling wine date back to biblical times, while its first commercialization actually occurred in England in the mid-sixteen hundreds — thirty or forty years before it appeared in France. This, of course, is not the whole story.

The Romans had developed sophisticated methods of winemaking at least several hundred years before Christ. They brought their grape varieties and knowledge of winemaking to the Champagne region in the first century A.D. When the Roman influence in France waned in the fourth and fifth centuries, the church began to take over the growing and making of wine. As each new abbey was started, the monks planted vineyards and, over time, acquired others through bequests. It was the custom, for example, for the crusaders to give their vineyards to the church upon leaving for the Holy Land. By the time of the French Revolution in 1789, the church owned over half of the vineyard land in Champagne.

Lovers of champagne should perpetually toast the efforts of succeeding generations of monks at the abbeys. They kept wine growing alive in Champagne for twelve hundred years — all during the Dark and Middle Ages and up until the secularization of the vineyards in the sixteenth and seventeenth centuries.

No records are available to indicate that sparkling wine was much more than a curiosity in Europe until the middle of the sixteen hundreds, although Italian documents show that a *spumante* or foaming, wine was being sold in the late fifteen hundreds. The abbey of St. Hilaire in southern France is also reported to have made a sparkling wine over a hundred years before Dom Pérignon's success at Hautvillers. At St. Hilaire, sparkling wine was, and still is, made by the "rural method," which involves only a single fermentation and leaves the sediment in the bottle.

The challenge in the commercialization of sparkling wine in the seventeenth century was to developed containers and stoppers strong enough to hold the gas pressure as it developed during fermentation.

Containers

Glass containers were developed around 1500 B.C. in the Middle East. The Romans brought glass technology to Europe, but the art died out in France with the decline of the Roman Empire. The Greeks and Romans generally used earthenware containers, called *amphorae*, for storing and shipping wine. Wooden casks were predominant in France and northern Europe. Neither was strong enough, however, to store sparkling wine. Until the early sixteen hundreds, glass was used mainly for the decanters in which wine was brought from cask to table; even then, they were held in straw baskets because they were so fragile.

Glass sufficiently strong to be used for storage containers was developed in England in the first half of the seventeenth century and first used for wine containers around 1660. Since

France prohibited the export of wine in less than cask lots, English wine merchants developed the custom of bottling French wine in England. It was at the urging of Dom Pérignon that the English glass technology was brought to the Champagne region of France around 1700. Louis XV finally permitted the Champenois to export bottles of wine in 1728.

Stoppers

The other essential ingredient required to commercialize sparkling wine production was the cork. The stoppering of wine containers had been a problem for centuries. In olden times, olive oil was poured onto the surface of the wine to prevent spoilage and evaporation. The common type of stopper in Europe up to the sixteen hundreds was a wooden plug wrapped with hemp on which oil was poured when the plug was inserted into the bottle. The English started using corks to stopper a variety of glass containers in the early seventeenth century, but the Champagne region was isolated from this innovation, as it was from glass bottles, until the beginning of the eighteenth century.

The cork did not arrive in the Champagne region until Dom Pérignon introduced it, also around 1700. Cork had been used for stoppers by the Portuguese and Spanish for hundreds of years. Tradition has it that in the late sixteen hundreds the monks at the Hautvillers Abbey observed cork stoppers in the water containers made of gourds that were carried by traveling Spanish monks stopping at the abbey. They conveyed this information to Dom Pérignon and he immediately ordered a supply of Spanish corks. While there are other versions of the story, it is generally accepted that he was the first in Champagne to use cork stoppers.

Dom Pérignon

Dom Pérignon was born in 1638 at Sainte-Ménehould in the Marne district. He entered the Benedictine Order at the age of nineteen and became cellar master at Hautvillers at the age of thirty in 1668. He continued in that position until his death in 1715 at the age of seventy-seven. Dom Pérignon became blind during his later years but carried on his duties and remained creative until the end.

The most important element in the production of fine champagne is the quality of the still, or base, wine. Dom Pérignon's contributions are truly significant in this area. During his forty-seven years as cellar master at Hautvillers, Dom Pérignon steadily improved his mastery of winemaking and grape growing. His wines acquired such renown that they were referred to as *vins de Pérignon* and sold for many times the price of other wines of the region.

He is reported to have been an extremely intelligent and meticulous man who gave attention to the most insignificant details in both his religious and secular duties. Several years after Dom Pérignon died, his successor, Dom Pierre, published a detailed treatise on the vineyard and winemaking practices employed by Dom Pérignon. Dom Pierre states that his mentor was "scrupulously concerned with details that to others appeared insignificant . . ." and that he performed tasks that to other growers seemed ". . . impossible, even ridiculous."

He is best known for his improvements of the quality of the still wines of Champagne. At that time, 80 percent of the wine made in Champagne was red and tended to be thin and pale. In years of exceptionally warm weather, which occurs only every third to fourth year in the Champagne region, Dom Pérignon was able to develop the first truly red wine. He also developed the first white wine from black grapes — the basis for today's *blanc de noirs* champagnes. Both of these developments took careful attention to detail at each stage of the winemaking process, from planting the vines to aging and storing the wines.

Dom Pérignon designed the traditional champagne press, still in use today, that extracts the minimum of color from the black grapes. He planted the Pinot Meunier grape for its productivity and hardiness against frost and winter cold, and carefully selected his vineyard sites. He was also the first to recognize the importance of cellaring and is reported to have enlarged the caves at Hautvillers for that purpose.

Dom Pérignon also contributed to the overall quality of the wines of Champagne by raising to a fine art the technique of blending wines from different vineyards. This is necessary in order to produce elegant champagne that maintains consistency of style year after year. Apparently, Dom Pérignon had an innate ability to select the appropriate vineyard and its individual proportion of the blend in order to arrive at a fine balance of acid, sugar, and fruitiness. Most of the winemaking practices he developed are still in use today.

The Vineyards of Champagne

The vineyards of Champagne, along with those in Germany along the Rhine and the Moselle Rivers, are among the most northerly in the world. Consequently, the climate in the region is not conducive to the growing of outstanding wine grapes. Most summers are not hot enough to ripen the grapes properly. There is always the risk of spring frosts that can ruin the year's crop just as the vines are sprouting and the chance of fall rain, or even early frost, that can ruin the grape crop before harvest. The average summer temperature is around 70° F. However, the area experiences a fairly mild winter, with temperatures seldom going below 0° F. These moderate summer and winter temperatures are the result of France's being surrounded by water on three sides — giving it a maritime climate.

Dom Pérignon's development of sparkling wine capitalized on the one real strength of the Champagne region's wine industry, its weather. The chilly climate of the region typically prevents the grapes from ripening fully, so that they are low in sugar, color, body, and fruitiness, while high in acid. These characteristics do not create fine still wines but do provide ideal base wines for champagne. The chalky soil of northern France and the southern coast of England is believed by French vineyardists to make a major contribution to the quality of French champagne.

The main virtue of Champagne as a wine growing region, prior to the introduction of sparkling champagne, was its location rather than its wine. The champagne-growing region was, and still is, at the crossroads of France, where routes between southern and northern Europe cross the main arteries between Paris and eastern Europe. The Champagne Fairs of the Middle Ages were famous gathering places for merchants from the north and south of France and from neighboring countries. Consequently, knowledge of the wines of Champagne spread sooner than that of wines grown elsewhere.

The Kings of France, starting with Clovis in 496, were traditionally crowned in Rheims. Philip the Fair in 1285 designated champagne as the official wine of his coronation, as did many kings after him. The wines of Champagne received special recognition by the royal courts because of their use at coronations and the proximity of Champagne to Paris. Until the eighteenth century, transportation of wine to Paris from Burgandy, and particularly Bordeaux, was arduous and expensive.

The Champagne Region

Because of its location and history, the Champagne region holds a special place in the hearts of the French. The region lies between Lorraine to the east and the area around Paris (the former Île-de-France) to the west. It reaches to the Belgian border in the north and the Burgandy region to the south and includes the political *départéments* of Ardennes, Marne, Aube, and Haute-Marne.

The name *Champagne* comes from *compania,* a Latin word for an open expanse of countryside. Aside from the vineyard lands, the region is flat and has been described as the bleakest spot in Europe. According to the eighteenth-century French historian, Michelet, it is "an expanse of white chalk, dirty, poor . . . a sea of stubble stretched across an immense plain of plaster." This flat land was long considered too dry for any agriculture but the raising of sheep. Fortunately, it proved suitable for grain and since the 1920s has become the wheatland of France, but it is still sparsely populated.

Champagne as a viticultural appellation constitutes only a small portion of the Champagne region. The wine-growing area is shaped like an opened umbrella and lies in the center third of the region. It is bounded by the city of Rheims in the north at the tip and the village of Bergères-les-Vertus, twenty-five miles to the south at the "handle." The lower edge of the umbrella is formed by the Marne River, from Dormans in the west to the A-4 motorway in the east, with Épernay in the center — a distance of forty-five miles. This very compact hilly area, bisected by the Marne, was created by an upheaval in the earth's surface, many millennia ago. The upheaval crumbled this portion of the thick chalk beds that underlie northern France and southern England.

It is this crumbled chalk that has distinguished the wines of Champagne. The vines must work their way into the chalk to find sustenance and water. The soil on top of the chalk is so thin, only six inches deep in some places, that for centuries the vineyard workers of Champagne have had to replenish it by hauling sand and soil from the bottom lands of the valley back up to the vineyards on the hillsides. The Romans used the chalk for building material and their quarries provided the start for the famous champagne cellars of Rheims.

In developing their wines over the centuries, the Champenois have had to cope with more than just weather and soil. For good reason the Champagne region is also known as the battleground of France. Since 500 A.D. it has been in the direct path of invasions of France from the east and has been the site of most of the country's critical battles from those against Attila the Hun in 451 to the Nazi invasion in 1940. Rheims, in particular, was a lightning rod for the hordes of Asia. It was sacked every fifty years between the fifth and the tenth centuries and was besieged, shelled, and occupied periodically by the Prussians, Germans, Austrians, Russians, and even the British, right through World War II.

The vineyards on the north side of La Montagne de Rhiems were within a hundred yards of no-man's-land during the four-year stalemate of World War I. There are many heartrending stories about vineyard workers tending and harvesting the vines at night and on foggy days to avoid being shelled. Some were killed in the process, but the vineyards continued to produce. During the siege, the citizens lived in the champagne cellars underlying Rheims, coming out only during the day to work.

The dominant physical features of Champagne are the two ranges of hills, the Côte des Blancs and the Montagne de Rheims, separated by the Marne River. The two major cities of the region are Rheims and Épernay. Châlons-sur-Marne was once an important champagne producing center but now serves mainly as the capital of the Marne district.

All but a few of the important champagne houses are in either Rheims or Épernay. Rheims is dominated by the famous cathedral built around 400 A.D. and by the Butte Saint Nicaise, which contains the ancient Roman caves and on whose slopes stand many of today's champagne houses. Épernay is backed by the Côte des Blancs and faces the Montagne de Rheims across the Marne. Crossing the Marne into Épernay, one is captivated by the quaint Moorish-style tower of the champagne house of de Castellane, which was started by a Spanish family in 1890. North from Épernay, the picturesque abbey of Hautvillers is visible across the Marne half way up the south-facing slope of the Montagne de Rheims.

The Caves

The caves beneath the principal cities and towns of Champagne are undoubtedly the most extensive anywhere in the world. The chalk deposits, which average a thousand feet in thickness throughout the region, make an ideal material for champagne cellars. It is easy to excavate, is strong enough to be tunneled without extra support, and does not deteriorate over time if not subject directly to weathering.

The Romans quarried the chalk for building materials during their occupation of Rheims by opening small holes at the top and then expanding the cavern down to depths of between two and three hundred feet. As the need for cellaring capacity expanded during the eighteenth and nineteenth centuries, the champagne producers connected and extended the underground quarries. Producers in Épernay and other towns in the region started their own excavations. The digging of cellars went on continuously for well over a hundred years. Today, these tunnels extend for several hundred miles in the Champagne region, with 120 miles of tunnels under Rheims and sixty miles under Épernay.

The chalk caves are undoubtedly one of the key resources of the region. They provide constant humidity and a constant temperature of 55° F. all year round. Large enough to store and age over 600 million bottles of champagne at any one time, the caves are essentially small villages with all of the necessary utilities and transportation facilities. Electricity was not introduced until the late eighteen hundreds, before which candles and later gas were employed for lighting. According to Patrick Forbes, one of the major firms in Épernay consumed sixty thousand pounds of candles each year during the mid-eighteen hundreds.

The Acceptance of Sparkling Champagne

While broad acceptance of sparkling wine in France was slow in coming, England took to it immediately. References to sparkling champagne started appearing in London magazines and theatrical productions around 1660. It appears likely that the English purchased the wine in barrels from France during the winter and then bottled and corked it in the spring before fermentation started up again. There is at least one indication that they added sugar to the wine to encourage more aggressive bubbles as well as raise the alcohol level. A Dr. Merret, in a speech to the Royal Society in London in 1662, stated, "our wine-coopers of recent times use vast quantities of Sugar Molasses to all sorts of wines to make them drink brisk and sparkling and to give them Spirits." The practice of adding sugar to induce a second fermentation was not adopted in France for another hundred years.

Apparently, the wines of Champagne were introduced to the royalty and wealthy of England by the Marquis de Saint-Evremond several years after the restoration of Charles II to the throne of England in 1660. Saint-Evremond had been in the party sent by Louis XIV to the English king's restoration. Then, having incurred Louis's wrath a year later, fled to England for the rest of his life to avoid the Bastille. With his wit and knowledge, he was an immediate hit with Charles II and the court.

The Marquis became an adviser to the upper crust of England on good taste and manners. He taught the court to appreciate the red wines of Champagne after they were aged, but to drink the whites immediately in the spring to enjoy the *pétillance* (sparkle). Having many friends in Champagne, he undoubtedly had wine shipped to him in London. During the seventeen hundreds, the still wines of Champagne continued to be more in demand than the sparkling. The red wines of Champagne also continued to be more popular in England than those of Burgundy during this period as they were considered the more fashionable.

The practice of shipping barrels of new wine to England for subsequent bottling continued until 1728, when the Mayor of Rhiems prevailed upon Louis XV to let the merchants ship in bottles. The mayor's main argument was that "people who drink *champagne gris* (near-white) prefer it sparkling . . . besides which no *vin gris* can be sent . . . without losing completely its quality if sent in casks." By the end of the seventeen hundreds, sparkling champagne was being shipped in bottles to most of the countries of Europe and to the America, although the trade was disrupted from 1789 to 1790 by the French Revolution. The wine was popularized in America by George Washington, who served it at the White House.

Not everybody appreciated the increased popularity of sparkling champagne. One of the principal merchants in Épernay at the time, Bertin de Rocheret, complained in a letter written to a customer in 1713 about "this abominable drink . . . which destroys the flavor of the individual growths." He also referred to it as *vin du diable*, attributing the bubbles to unwholesome causes. As demand increased, Rocheret was forced to sell more sparkling champagne at higher and higher prices, although probably grumbling all of the way to the bank.

He complained to one English customer who had ordered some that the only merit of sparkling wine was the gas, referring to it as *saute-bouchon*, a cork-blower, and belonging in the category of beer, chocolate, and whipped cream. The customer wrote back, apologizing for his indiscretion, and promised never to order it again — at least not from M. Rocheret.

The Champagne Houses of the Eighteenth Century

Several of the honored Champagne houses we know today were created within a few decades after the death of Dom Pérignon. Among these were Ruinart, Taittinger, and Moët et Chandon. Others began to appear later in the seventeen hundreds.

Ruinart Père et Fils

The earliest of the pioneers was Ruinart Père et Fils, which was created in 1729. Nicolas Ruinart was a cloth merchant in Épernay who, like many textile merchants, found himself buying champagne for his customers and finally decided to engage in it full time. Nicolas added the Père et Fils in 1764 when his son Claude joined the firm. Its principal period of growth was in the 1950s when Baron Philippe de Rothschild made a substantial investment in the firm. Ruinart was acquired by Moët et Chandon in 1963 and has continued to grow, still remaining as an independent producer. The firm has always been active in the export market and today exports 60 percent of its 1.3 million bottles of annual production. Ruinart purchases 80 percent of its grapes from independent growers.

Taittinger

Taittinger was founded in 1734 by Jacques Fourneaux, the son of a vineyard owner in Rilly-la-Montagne. The Taittinger family acquired the firm after World War I, at which time the name was changed to Taittinger. In 1934, the firm moved its headquarters from its original location in Mailly-Champagne to Rheims. Taittinger currently produces 3.5 million bottles, of which 55 percent is for export. The firm grows approximately 50 percent of its grapes and still ferments a quarter of its production in wooden casks. Taittinger was, however, one of the first to adopt computer-controlled mechanical *remuage* (riddling). The company is currently developing a vineyard and winery in the Carneros region of California.

Moët et Chandon

Moët et Chandon, another of the early pioneers, is today the largest champagne producer in the region. The firm was started in 1743 by Claude Moët, a descendent of an influential family that had lived in Rheims for three hundred years. Claude Moët owned substantial vineyard property near Épernay and had become a *courtier en vin* in 1716. The term, *courtier en vin*, refers to a wine broker, originally appointed by the king, who sold the wine of the vineyard owner. Gradually these brokers purchased vineyards and started making their own wine, even though it was illegal until 1776. They were the forerunners of today's wholesalers, in the United States, or *négociants*, in France.

Moët et Chandon became firmly established under the guidance of Jean-Remy, Claude's grandson, who took over the firm from his father in 1792. Jean-Remy became an acknowledged leader in both the company and the community of Épernay. He purchased the abbey at Hautvillers, which had been secularized in 1790, was Mayor of Épernay for some years, and was a close friend of Napoleon I. Napoleon would rest briefly at the Moët villa before many of his successful major battles. He did not stay there before the battle at Waterloo and it is held to this day by the descendents of the Moët family that failure to observe this custom was the cause of his defeat. Jean-Remy built the miniature of the Trianon across the street from his own residence so that Napoleon would have a place to stay when in Épernay. Today the Trianon is used by Moët et Chandon to entertain its guests.

Jean-Remy retired in 1832 and his son Victor and son-in-law, Pierre-Gabriel Chandon de Brailles, took over the firm. A year later the firm's name was changed to Moët et Chandon. During World War I, the firm suffered considerable damage to both its facilities and vineyards, which took over a decade to recover fully. During World War II, the head of the firm, Comte Robert-Jean de Vogüé, was influential in keeping the champagne industry viable. His resistance efforts caused the Germans to imprison the Comte and sentence him to death — although the sentence was never carried out. He continued to head the firm after the war. In 1962, Moët et Chandon went public, the first of the champagne houses to do so.

During the following twenty-five years, the company became involved in a series of acquisitions, mergers and expansions, the most significant being:

1968 — invested in Parfums Christian Dior

1970 — acquired Mercier (founded in 1858 by Eugène Mercier and had became second only to Moët in the domestic market)

1971 — merged with Jas Hennessy, the cognac firm, to establish holding company called Moët-Hennessy

1973 — assumed control of Ruinart

1973 — acquired thirteen thousand acres of vineyard land in Napa Valley in California

1974 — acquired three hundred acres of vineyard land in Brazil

1977 — introduced sparkling wine produced in California and Brazil into domestic markets

1987 — acquired Louis Vuitton, which controlled Parfums Givenchy and the champagne house Veuve Clicquot-Ponsardin

Through growth and acquisition, Moët et Chandon has become the largest of the champagne houses. Its annual production of twenty-four million bottles, of which approximately 75 percent is exported, represents 12 percent of the industry's total sales and 25 percent of its exports. With the addition of Moët et Chandon's sister companies, Mercier, Ruinart, and Veuve Clicquot-Ponsardin, Moët-Hennessy produces over thirty-six million bottles of champagne each year, or over 18 percent of the industry's total sales. Moët-Hennessy provides 35 percent of the industry's total export sales.

Veuve Clicquot-Ponsardin

Veuve Clicquot-Ponsardin, in Rheims, is another of the famous eighteenth-century pioneering firms, having started in 1772. Like Nicolas Ruinart, Philippe Clicquot was primarily a textile trader who provided champagne to his important customers. His son François married Nicole-Barbe Ponsardin in 1798 and took over his father's business in 1801. He proceeded to expand the vineyard and winemaking activities of the firm, but became sick and died suddenly in 1805. Philippe Clicquot was crushed by the event and wanted to sell the business. His widowed daughter-in-law, who was only 27 years old at the time, prevailed upon him to let her take it over — an undertaking almost unheard-of in 1800.

Madame Clicquot-Ponsardin lead the firm into international markets. In 1830 she brought in as partner, Edouard Werlé, to whom she willed her share of the company when she died in 1866. Leadership of the firm has remained in the extended Werlé family as succeeding sons and sons-in-law became head of the firm. Even today, however, Clicquot champagne is referred to as the Widow's champagne, so great was her contribution to the firm, to the industry and, particularly, to the development of the foreign market for champagne. Today the firm is owned by Moët-Hennessy; it produces approximately six million bottles per year, 75 percent of which is exported. Clicquot grows only 30 percent of its own grapes.

Louis Roederer

Another of the major houses formed in the seventeen hundreds was Louis Roederer, founded in 1760. It was originally named Dubois Père et Fils, but after changing hands several times, was acquired by Nicolas-Henri Schreider. In 1827 Schreider brought his nephew, Louis Roederer, into the firm. Roederer became head of the firm in 1833 when his uncle died, at which time he changed its name to Louis Roederer. Roederer is known for having established the firm in the Russian market, particularly with the court of the Tsar. Louis's son, another Louis, took over in 1879. He created a famous sweet champagne, called Cristal, which was bottled in a crystal bottle for the exclusive use of the emperor, Alexander II, and his court. It is still being produced today. The Russian Revolution in 1917 almost destroyed the company, since the new communist government cancelled all orders and refused to pay the outstanding bills of the court.

In 1932, another famous widow of Champagne was created when Madame Camille Orly-Roederer took over the company on the death of her husband. She ran it with great distinction for over forty years. Today Louis Roederer produces approximately 1.5 million bottles annually, of which 60 percent goes to the export market. Roederer is unique among the major houses in that it grows all but 20 percent of its grapes. The firm has also started a vineyard and sparkling wine facility in the Anderson Valley in California to serve the American market.

The Heidsieck Houses

There are three Heidsieck champagne houses, each totally independent of the others. They all stem from the original Heidsieck firm founded in 1785 by Florenz-Louis Heidsieck. His was the first of the champagne houses formed by German immigrants who had been hired originally by French champagne merchants to handle their foreign language problems.

Two of the three Heidsieck firms in existence today, Heidsieck & Co. Monopole and Piper-Heidsieck, were started in 1834, six years after Florenz-Louis died. They were started by two of his nephews who had tried to keep their uncle's firm going but found they could not work effectively together. The third company, Charles Heidsieck, was formed in 1851 by Charles-Camille Heidsieck, who had left Piper-Heidsieck to form a new company with his brother-in-law, Ernest Henriot. Charles-Camille Heidsieck was an active developer of the American market in the mid-eighteen hundreds and during the American Civil War was briefly put in jail by Union forces for helping to provide supplies to the Confederate army.

Today, of the three companies only Piper Heidsieck remains independent. Heidsieck & Co. Monopole was acquired by G. H. Mumm & Co. in 1972, and Charles Heidsieck was acquired by Remy Martin in 1985. Piper-Heidsieck currently produces approximately six million bottles annually, of which 60 percent is for export. Since 1980, Piper-Heidsieck has been involved in a joint venture with Sonoma Vineyards in California to produce sparkling wine for the American market. Charles Heidsieck currently produces 3.5 million bottles; Heidsieck and Co. Monopole approximately 1.8 million. Both export approximately 50 percent of their total sales.

Lanson Père et Fils

Another of the champagne houses created in the seventeen hundreds and still in operation, Lanson was started in 1760 by François Delamotte under his own name. M. Jean-Baptiste Lanson joined the firm in 1828 and, when he took over the firm in 1856, changed the name to Lanson Père et Fils. The company continued in the Lanson family until it was purchased by the Gardiner Group, who subsequently bought Pommery. Both firms were sold to the French food conglomerate, BSN, in 1983. The company currently produces approximately five million bottles of which 55 percent is exported.

The Nineteenth Century

By the start of the eighteen hundreds, sparkling champagne was well established in markets throughout the world. Champagne making, however, continued to be a very risky and speculative business. The unpredictable weather, which produced a few bountiful harvests intermingled with the poor ones, resulted in wide swings in price for both growers and producers.

The biggest problem at the time was the loss caused by breakage, poor corkage, and decanting. Breakage resulted from the bottle makers' inability to control the quality of the bottles and from the champagne makers' inability to control the amount of pressure that built up within them from fermentation. Exploding bottles were extremely dangerous to cellar workers. During certain times of the year, they were required to wear face masks to guard against flying glass. Poor corkage caused the wine to lose its effervescence while aging, or turn to vinegar, or even to leak completely out of the bottle. Spoilage typically ranged from 20 to 30 percent.

The breakage problem was somewhat alleviated in 1836 when M. François, a pharmacist in Châlons-sur-Marne, developed a method to measure the sugar content of the wine. This helped determine how much sugar needed to be added to produce a given level of pressure. In 1856, Louis Pasteur explained the fermentation reaction in precise chemical terms, knowledge of which further reduced the range of likely error. With improvements in the quality of glass bottles, the breakage rate dropped to less than 1 percent by the early nineteen hundreds and today is less than 0.1 percent.

The problem of sediment in the bottle had plagued the makers of sparkling wine ever since they first attempted to finish the fermentation in the bottle. The champagne makers who used the rural method, initially at St. Hilaire, ignored the problem and the drinker accepted the cloudy, earthy-looking result. Until the end of the eighteen hundreds, producers or *négociants* removed the sediment by decanting the sparkling wine from one bottle to another, frequently more than once, accepting a large loss of liquid and effervescence. After taking over her husband's and father-in-law's company in 1805, Madame Clicquot-Ponsardin was able, with help from her *chef de caves*, to develop the *remuage* and disgorging process used to this day.

The demand for sparkling champagne grew by a hundredfold during the eighteen hundreds. In 1785, according to Patrick Forbes, three hundred thousand bottles were sold. By 1890, sparkling champagne sales had reached over twenty-five million bottles. Sales continued to rise to a peak of thirty-nine million bottles in 1909 — a volume not exceeded until 1956. Sales of the still wines of Champagne dropped steadily during the eighteen hundreds and early nineteen hundreds, falling below that of sparkling wine in 1840, and ceasing almost entirely by World War I.

A major issue that arose for the champagne makers during the eighteen hundreds was the question, How much sugar for sweetness? The Russian market, which was second only to that in Great Britain, had a preference for sparkling wine with 10 to 15% sugar. (A noted English academician of the time declared it "only good for savages and children.") The English market preferred a dry champagne. The French market preferred a moderately sweet wine, somewhere between the other two. The producers needed to cater to foreign preferences because, by 1890, export sales of champagne had risen to 80 percent of total sales.

The Russian had acquired a taste for champagne during the Napoleonic wars when Russian troops had joined British, Prussian, and Austrian troops to defeat Napoleon at Leipzig and Waterloo. Russian troops had occupied Rheims and the eastern Champagne region during most of 1814 and 1815. Russians who could afford champagne developed an intense loyalty to that of the Widow Clicquot.

The English continued to be Champagne's most important customer — even today, it is still the largest foreign market. The English had become accustomed to drinking dry champagne as an apéritif and during the meal. They preferred to maintain their long-established custom of drinking sweet still wines with desserts and Port at the end of the meal. The French drank still wine with dinner, including red wine with cheese after dinner, and preferred sweet champagne with the desserts at the end of the meal.

The battle between sweet and dry champagne in England became intense around 1875, and was fought in the press and in high society. The "drys" referred to sweet champagne as "gooseberry juice" and "chorus girl mixture," while the "sweets" contended that, "you cannot trust a man who claims he likes his champagne dry." By the 1880s, the drys had won out. This was a hard blow to those producers in France who had been relying on sugar to hide the imperfections in their base wine. It also required the French producers to increase their cellar stock significantly: dry champagne needed to be aged for at least three years — over three times as long as the sweeter style. Fortunately, the French continued to prefer sweet champagne.

Even by the turn of the century, the Champenois did not approve of the English preference for dry champagne. In the 1903 edition of *The Gourmet's Guide to Europe,* the author, an Englishman, Lieutenant-Colonel Newham-Davis, tells the story of an experience he had in Rheims at a social gathering sponsored by several of the large champagne houses. When asked by the host what style of champagne he preferred, he replied, *"du vin brut."* The host exclaimed, with a smile, "Ah! You are a drinker of the poison?"

England had what can only be called a love affair with French champagne during the nineteenth century. Poems, stage plays, and songs frequently contained some reference to the joys of champagne. Patrick Forbes and other authors recount a story of one song that sparked an advertising war. A favorite London music hall ballad by George Leybourne was a particular hit in 1869:

> *Champagne Charlie is my name,*
> *Champagne drinking gained my fame,*
> *So as of old when on a spree,*
> *Moet and Shandon's the wine for me*

The song's popularity immediately raised cries from Moët's competitors, one of which, Clicquot, prevailed upon another singer, named the Great Vance, to challenge Leybourne to a singing and drinking contest. While Leybourne stood at one side of the stage drinking and singing about Moët et Chandon, Vance was doing likewise on the other side, singing:

> *Clicquot! Clicquot! That's the stuff to make you jolly,*
> *Clicquot! Clicquot! Soon will banish melancholy.*
> *Clicquot! Clicquot! Drinking other wines is folly.*
> *Clicquot! Clicquot! That's the drink for me.*

In 1894, a poem, titled *Ode to Pommery 1874,* was published in *Vanity Fair.* The 1874 harvest in Champagne had been exceptional and this vintage champagne was enjoyed for several decades. The poem, sung to the tune of Old Lang Syne, went, in part, as follows

> *Should auld acquaintance be forgot*
> *'Twixt human friends and wine?*
> . . . .
> *Ah no! my trusted friend;*
> *Thy colour has not paled;*
> *Like Statesman drawing near his end,*
> *The froth, not strength, has failed.*
> *Farewell, then, Pommery Seventy-Four!*
> *With reverential sips*
> *We part and grieve that never more*
> *Such wine may pass our lips.*

Champagne Houses of Nineteenth Century

Most of the significant houses in existence today were started during the booming years of the eighteen hundreds. The best known of these to Americans are Bollinger, Mumm, and Pommery, but there is also a number of fine lesser-known producers worth mentioning.

Laurant-Perrier & Co.

The Laurants were coopers who decided, in 1812, to make wine as well as barrels. The name Perrier, that of the founder's daughter-in-law, was added in 1887. The firm stayed in the Laurant family until the 1920s and was saved from oblivion in 1938 by Marie-Louise de Nonancourt, the sister of Henri Lanson of Lanson Père et Fils, when she bought the *marque*. Laurant-Perrier has grown aggressively since World War II and now produces six million bottles each year, 55 percent of which is sold in the export trade.

G. H. Mumm & Co.

Mumm was founded in 1827 by Peter Arnold de Mumm and a fellow German, Frederick Giesler, who left to form his own company ten years later. The firm stayed in the Mumm family until after World War I when it was confiscated and sold. Unfortunately, as it turned out, the family heads of the firm had never become French citizens over the years. The Dubonnet family took over control and expanded its activities. It was purchased by Seagram in 1969. Mumm had acquired Perrier-Jouët in 1959 (a pioneer champagne house started in 1811 by Pierre Nicolas-Marie Perrier) and, as part of Seagram, acquired Heidsieck & Co. Monopole in 1972. Mumm currently sells more than eight million bottles and exports close to 70 percent. The famous Cordon Rouge line of champagne, which was originated in the 1870s continues to be its most successful *marque*. With Seagrams, Mumm has a joint venture in the Napa Valley of California to make sparkling wine for the American market.

Bollinger

The Bollinger firm was actually started by a gentleman vineyard owner in Aÿ, Athanase-Louis-Emmanuel de Villermont. In 1829, not wishing to have his name associated with a commercial activity, Comte de Villermont arranged to establish Renaudin, Bollinger and Co. The firm, headed by M. Paul Renaudin and M. Joseph-Jacob-Placide (Jacques) Bollinger, was created to sell the wines of the Comte's estate. Jacques Bollinger was born in Germany and was selling champagne in Germany for Müller-Ruinart when approached by Comte de Villermont. In 1837 Jacques Bollinger married Comte de Villermont's daughter and expanded the vineyard holdings. The firm stayed in the Bollinger family until the death of Madame Bollinger in the 1970s.

Madame Bollinger is another of the famous widows of Champagne. She took over the company when her husband, Jacques (grandson of the founder), died in 1941 at the age of forty-seven. He had been serving as the mayor of Aÿ during the German occupation. Madame Bollinger headed the firm for over thirty years. Tom Stevenson, in his excellent book, *Champagne*, states that Madame Lily Bollinger is the only woman vintner in Champagne who can match the accomplishments of the Widow Clicquot. She gave the same degree of attention to detail for which Dom Pérignon was famous. Madame Bollinger significantly increased the firm's vineyard holdings and champagne production to today's 1.5 million bottles. Through her direct efforts, the firm is selling 70 percent of its output in the export market. Bollinger is one of the few firms that continues to ferment its vintage wines in wooden casks.

Pommery & Greno

Although known throughout the world as Pommery, the firm actually started out before 1836 as Dubois-Gosset, which was acquired by Narcisse Greno with the help of Louis

Alexandre Pommery in that year. Pommery died in 1858 and his widow, Madame Jeanne Alexandrine Louise Pommery took over the company at the age of thirty-nine. She proceeded to expand its activities, becoming another of the famous widows of Champagne. One of her first moves was to shift the emphasis of the company from red still wine to sparkling wine and to concentrate on the English market.

Following the occupation of her home by the German governor of Rheims during the Franco-Prussian War of 1870 — 71, Madame Pommery proceeded to expand by acquiring the Butte Saint Nicaise, outside Rheims, which contained 120 abandoned chalk pits. She had the cellar chambers decorated with wall carvings and Gothic arches. Having already developed the English market, she had the winery buildings designed to give the impression of an English castle and manor house. Madame Pommery died in 1890. Her son took over until his death in 1907, at which time her grandson, Melchior, the Marquis de Polignac, became head of the firm. Being an avid sportsman, he constructed a sports center for the employees of Pommery and the citizens of Rheims. Much of the park, sports center, and winery buildings had to be rebuilt after World War I, having been shelled repeatedly by the Germans, whose trenches were only fifteen hundred yards away.

The Marquis de Polignac retired in 1947 and was succeeded in 1952 by Prince Guy de Polignac. In 1979 the Gardiner Group purchased the firm but sold it a year later, along with Lanson Père et Fils, to the French food conglomerate, BSN. Pommery currently produces four million bottles annually, of which 70 percent enters the export market. Around 50 percent of the firm's champagne is produced from the company's own vineyards.

Other Nineteenth-Century Champagne Houses

While it is not practical to mention all of the champagne houses created in the nineteen hundreds, several are worth mentioning. The oldest of these is Deutz & Geldermann, which was founded by these two gentlemen in 1838. It is a smaller winery with annual production of less than a million bottles, but has diversified internationally by opening a facility in Germany to produce *sekt* and one in California near San Luis Obispo to produce sparkling wine for the American market. Probably the most well known of the smaller international champagne houses is Krug & Co., which was founded by Joseph Krug in 1843 and currently produces approximately half a million bottles a year. Krug is one of the few houses that continues to ferment still wine in wooden casks.

Another champagne house that has focused on the export market is Pol Roger, which was founded in 1849 and currently produces around 1.5 million bottles of champagne. Pol Roger has always been strong in the English market and was Winston Churchill's favorite champagne. Once asked how important champagne was to England, Churchill replied, "In victory we deserve it, and in defeat we need it."

The Twentieth Century

The closing years of the nineteenth century and the opening years of the twentieth were very prosperous for champagne growers, producers, and shippers. This prosperity did not last. The phylloxera disease hit the region in 1890 and became epidemic by 1905. Around this time, the weather caused several years of bad harvests and producers began to bring in base wines from other grape-growing regions. Growers faced bankruptcy and loss of their vineyards. They rioted in 1908 and again in 1911. The government responded by establishing boundaries for the Champagne viticultural region and restricting the use of grapes that were not grown in Champagne. The controversy over boundaries was not fully resolved until 1935.

Today, almost 80 percent of the vineyards within the appellation lie in the Marne district. The vineyards of Pinot Noir are north of the Marne River, extending east from Épernay. The Pinot Meunier is planted mainly at the western end of the appellation. The Pinot Noir and the Pinot Meunier each represents 37 percent of the total acreage planted in the region. Plantings of Chardonnay grapes constitute the remaining 26 percent of the total and extend south from the Marne River for ten miles on the eastern slopes of the Côte des Blancs. The entire Champagne wine region can be circumnavigated in one day. It is one-third the size of the Burgandy wine region and one-seventh that of Bordeaux, yet the wines of the Champagne region are as famous throughout the world as those of its larger cousins.

As the boundary issue lessened in intensity in the late 1930s, growers and producers of champagne focused on restricting the use of the name *Champagne* for both still and sparkling wines of the region. The first court battle over use of the name was won in 1824 against a producer of sparkling wine in Vouvray who was using the word *champagne* on his label. Various court and legislative battles fought during the following hundred years led up to the major changes that were made in the law in 1935.

The law passed in 1935 prohibited any use of the word on labels for sparkling wine produced outside the delimited area of Champagne. Other producers of sparkling wine were required to use the term *vin mousseaux*. Restaurants in France were required to have separate categories on their wine lists for champagne, *vin mousseaux*, and any foreign sparkling wines such as *spumante* (Italian) or *sekt* (German). The still wines of the Champagne region had also to be shown separately on the wine list from the sparkling. The law placed a number of restrictions on growers and producers, specifying, for instance, the density of vine plantings, the method of pruning, the quantities of grapes harvested per acre, and the quantity of juice extracted from each press.

The law set up an enforcement mechanism by establishing a Commission Spéciale de la Champagne Viticole. This commission was abolished in 1941 during the Nazi occupation and replaced by the Comité Interprofessionel du Vin de Champagne (CIVC). The CIVC handled all of the negotiations with the Office of the *Führer* of Champagne established by the Germans during the four years of the occupation. The CIVC's more fundamental role, however, is to set the price of grapes to be paid the growers by the producers each harvest.

In setting price, the CIVC first sets it for grapes from the vineyards in the finest locations, the *grand cru* vineyards. The *grand cru* price is based on the average price of a bottle of champagne early in the harvest year. Grapes from all other classified vineyards, called *premiere cru* and *deuxième cru*, are then set at a predetermined percentage, ranging from 80 to 99 percent, of the *grand cru* price. The term, *cru*, means growth. A *cru* is defined as the local area around a village and carries the name of the village (e.g., Bouzy, Dizy, Sillery, Verzy). There are currently seventeen *grand cru* villages comprising 10,700 acres. The thirty-eight *premier cru* villages receive price ratings of between 90 and 99 percent and comprise fifteen thousand acres. The remaining thirty-seven thousand acres, rated between 80 and 89 percent, are called *deuxièmes crus*.

The percentages of the three varieties of grapes planted in the vineyards of Champagne — Pinot Noir, Chardonnay, and Pinot Meunier — vary considerably among the three levels of *cru*. Almost all of the vineyards of *grand cru* rating are planted to either Chardonnay or Pinot Noir, with Pinot Meunier constituting only 2 percent. The *premiers crus* are almost evenly divided among the three varietals, while the *deuxièmes crus* are almost half Pinot Meunier, a third Pinot Noir, and relatively little Chardonnay.

World War II and After

During World War II, the industry was under considerable strain. The champagne houses had cemented up the cellars holding the premium *cuvées* before the Germans arrived, but they were still required to ship between three hundred and four hundred thousand bottles per week to German troops throughout the world. The Germans prohibited the champagne houses from selling champagne to civilians or to export, although these restrictions were later relaxed somewhat. By the time the armistice was signed, the region was suffering, having been deprived of adequate food, equipment, chemicals, and workers for over four years.

Immediately following the war, the industry devoted itself to re-establishing the export market and the vineyards. During the 1930s, export sales had dropped from 60 percent of the total to 30 percent and then the war essentially eliminated all exports. By 1948, however, exports had reached the prewar share of 30 percent and have fluctuated around 30 percent ever since (37 percent in 1986). Acreage under commercial production at the end of the war had dropped to twenty-seven thousand acres. By 1966, productive acreage had risen to forty thousand and is currently approaching sixty-five thousand acres out of the maximum authorized 86,500 acres.

Since World War II, the CIVC has continued to control the growing and making of champagne, and of the use of the term *champagne* on labels. It established as law that neither grape juice nor still wine produced in Champagne can be exported from France. Before World War II, German producers had been buying still wine from the Champagne producers, making it sparkle, and then labelling it *"sekt* from Champagne."

In 1987, the CIVC was successful in obtaining a ruling from the Common Market High Court that prevents European sparkling wine producers from even stating on their label that their wine was made by the *méthode champenoise*. However, the CIVC was not as successful in Canada. The Supreme Court of the province of Ontario recently ruled that Canadian producers of sparkling wine could label their product "Canadian Champagne" without misleading consumers into believing that they are drinking the French product. The official policy of the United States is that the word *champagne* has become a generic term and can be used with appropriate geographic designation, such as "California Champagne."

Champagne production in Champagne continues to grow substantially. From its modest start of three hundred thousand bottles of sparkling champagne in 1785, the industry has grown to produce a record 205 million bottles in 1986. The initial stages of growth took place in the eighteen hundreds and peaked in 1909 at thirty-nine million bottles. World War I, Prohibition in the United States, the Great Depression, and World War II kept annual production below the 1909 record until 1956 when production reached forty-four million bottles. Growth has been achieved almost every year since.

Historically, the appreciation of champagne was not a French-inspired phenomenon. As mentioned earlier, England was enjoying sparkling champagne for fifty years before the Champenois discovered their own gold mine. Even then, they were forced to rely mainly on the foreign market all during the nineteenth century. During the eighteen hundreds and up to World War I, the foreign market consumed between 60 and 80 percent of annual production. It was not until the Great Depression, in 1930, that the French domestic market expanded sufficiently to consume 50 percent of the champagne produced.

The French Champagne Industry Today

Today, France consumes approximately two-thirds of the total production of champagne, with Great Britain being the next largest consumer at a distant 8 percent, and the United States following closely at 7 percent.

The growers and producers in the Champagne region, with the support of the French government, have been phenomenally successful in developing their industry. The producers are profitable and the growers enjoy a standard of living that would not have been possible without strong controls. The product provides the standard by which sparkling wines throughout the world are judged. While conformity to the tight regulations of the CIVC suggests that the industry is structured into a few large companies, this is not the case. Close to nineteen thousand growers own 87 percent of the vineyard acreage. The sixty major champagne houses own only 13 percent of the vineyard acreage while producing over 50 percent of the champagne.

Most of the thousands of growers sell their grapes each harvest to the champagne houses that grow only a small portion of their needs. Conversely, over four thousand of the growers produce champagne from their own grapes, selling only the excess grapes to the major champagne houses. In recent years, these grower-producers have produced and sold under their own labels a third of the total champagne sales. Most of their sales are to the domestic market, of which they supply almost half, frequently selling directly from the cellar door.

Included among the four thousand grower-producers are 150 cooperatives which, by pooling the grapes from a group of growers, can achieve enough volume to sell through established national and international distribution channels. The largest of these cooperatives is Centre Vinicole de la Champagne in Chouilly, which produces ten million bottles of champagne annually, second only to Moët et Chandon. It was formed in 1972 by seventy grower-cooperatives to serve their four thousand members. The next largest cooperative is La Co-opérative Régionale des Vins de Champagne (Jacquart) in Rheims, whose members include 680 growers and fourteen grower- cooperatives. It produces eight million bottles annually. The oldest of the cooperatives is Co-opérative Générale des Vignerons (Raoul Collet), which was formed in 1921 in Aÿ and produces approximately two million bottles of champagne each year.

While not a cooperative, Marne et Champagne is another champagne producer worth mentioning because next to Moët et Chandon it is the largest single-owner champagne house, with annual production of ten million bottles. Marne et Champagne was started in 1933 by Gaston Burtin who is still the owner. It is little known in the marketplace because, while it has close to three hundred labels, they are mostly the private labels of the buyers. The firm's own label, representing somewhat over 10 percent of the total, is A. Rothschild. According to Tom Stevenson, Marne et Champagne is referred to as the "life support system" of Champagne, since it also sells untold numbers of yet-to-be-disgorged bottles of champagne without labels to the more famous houses so that they may balance their supply and demand. Marne et Champagne owns no vineyards.

The concept of control of production by a consortium of producers, growers, and the government has proved to be very effective in maintaining the profitability and product quality of the champagne industry. The general concept has now been applied to over thirty other wine regions or commodities in France. It is also being applied in other countries of Europe but has not as yet spread to the United States or other parts of the world.

Vin Mousseaux

The French champagne houses are prevented by CIVC regulations from experimenting with unusual *cuvées*. Since they cannot use grapes from outside the Champagne region, they are limited to Chardonnay, Pinot Noir, and Pinot Meunier. The other regions of France, however, are free to produce sparkling wine, called *vin mousseaux*, using a wide range of local grape varieties. Crémant d'Alsace made from Riesling and Pinot Blanc grapes, as well as Pinot Noir or Chardonnay, is one example. Some of the best *vin mousseux* of France is produced in the Loire Valley where Chenin Blanc and Sauvignon Blanc are used as base wines. The Crémant de Burgandy uses a wide range of grape varieties in the *cuvée*, including Pinot Gris, Pinot Noir, Pinot Blanc, Chardonnay, Gamay, and Aligote. Many of these sparkling wines are entitled to use an *appellation d'origine contrôlée (AOC)* designation, which requires that they use the *méthode champenoise* technique and observe some restrictions similar to those imposed by the CIVC on grape productivity, aging, and so forth.

THE HISTORY OF CHAMPAGNE IN AMERICA

IN CONTRAST TO THE STEADY DEVELOPMENT of French champagne, that of the American counterpart occurred in fits and starts. Champagne making blossomed briefly in the second half of the nineteenth century, came to an abrupt halt due to Prohibition, languished during the 1930s, was resurrected in the forties and fifties, and finally began to take off again in the late 1960s. After Prohibition, sparkling wine made by the Charmat process became very popular in the United States. Only a few pioneers persevered in making champagne by the classical *méthode champenoise* during the three decades following the repeal of Prohibition. Only since the 1970s has the American public learned to appreciate American-produced champagne.

The Birthplace of American Champagne

Champagne was first made in America on the Ohio River near Cincinnati by Nicholas Longworth in 1842 — apparently by accident. As had happened in France, Longworth, having bottled partially fermented wine in the early spring from the previous fall's harvest, discovered his wine sparkled when he later opened a bottle. Fermentation had stopped during the cold winter months and as the weather warmed it started up again in the bottle. Mr. Longworth immediately recognized the value of his accident and started producing sparkling wine commercially. He used the American hybrid grape, the Catawba, from his twelve-hundred-acre vineyard. According to Longworth's own written record, he proceeded to hire a "skilled wine cooper" from France, but the first one he hired "drowned in the Ohio [River] a few days after his arrival."

Longworth hired a second "wine cooper" and started making champagne by the *méthode champenoise*, using rock candy for the *dosage* — cane sugar being far too expensive and not readily available. By 1858, Longworth's fame reached London where *The Illustrated London News* reported that his "Sparkling Catawba, of the pure, unadulterated juice of the odoriferous Catawba grape, transcends the Champagne of France." This may well have been an overstatement, but Mr. Longworth's pride in his product caused him at one point to complain to several New York hotels that they were substituting French champagne for his Sparkling Catawba.

Other grape growers along the Ohio in the Cincinnati area soon followed Mr. Longworth's lead and started making champagne from Catawba and from Isabella grapes — another native American hybrid. By 1850, the growers were producing 135 thousand bottles annually and, by 1855, close to three hundred thousand bottles. Unfortunately, the success of Mr. Longworth and the other growers did not last, as the vineyards around Cincinnati were destroyed by disease in the 1860s.

From that humble beginning, American champagne production started to grow in other regions of America until hit by Prohibition in 1919. Following Repeal, the Charmat process took over and it was not until the 1960s that the classical French method of champagne making again began to be practiced extensively in the United States. Since then, its use has grown phenomenally. By 1987, the production of champagne by the *méthode champenoise* in the United States approached thirty million bottles annually. This is still only 15 percent of the 205 million bottles produced each year in the Champagne region of France but is double the quantity of champagne currently being imported into the United States from France.

The Finger Lakes Region of New York

Following the developments at Cincinnati, the next significant American venture into champagne was made in Hammondsport, New York, at the south end of Keuka Lake in the Finger Lakes region. Three famous wineries were founded at Hammondsport: Great Western, Gold Seal, and Taylor Wine Company. The Finger Lakes region has been a center for commercial grape growing in New York since the 1830s. Until after World War II, grape growers in the region grew American hybrids such as Concord, Catawba, Isabella, and Aurora. After the war, with the encouragement of the wineries in the region, grape growers planted French hybrids such as Chelois, De Chaunac, Vidal Blanc, and Seyval Blanc. It was believed that the French hybrids were better suited to the sophisticated tastes being developed by the wine-drinking public than were the strong-flavored American hybrids. Both types of hybrids continue to be used in champagne and sparkling wine to this day, however.

Great Western started out in 1860 as the Pleasant Valley Winery, created by Charles Champlin and a number of other local farmers in the Finger Lakes region. In 1865 they started to make champagne, calling it Sparkling Catawba, the same name that Longworth had used — perhaps not surprisingly since the French-trained winemaker, Joseph Masson, had come from one of the champagne producers in Cincinnati. Champlin and his associates changed the name of the champagne to Great Western around 1870 when a Boston wine connoisseur decreed that Pleasant Valley's champagne "will be the great champagne of the Western World!" Great Western champagne won medals at East Coast wine tastings and in Europe — a gold medal at a Paris Exposition in 1867 and another in Vienna in 1873.

Gold Seal was initially created as the Urbana Wine Company, which also started making champagne in 1865 at Hammondsport. Its first label used the name Imperial but it was changed to Gold Seal in 1887. Throughout its 118-year history, the winery hired French winemakers. The most famous of these winemakers was Charles Fournier, who, in 1934, was hired away from Veuve Clicquot-Ponsardin in Rheims, where he had been chief champagne maker.

From 1953 into the 1970s, Charles Fournier, who by then had become president of Gold Seal, fostered a major advancement in New York wine-growing technology. He hired Dr. Konsantin Frank, a Russian emigrant and enologist, and assigned to him the task of commercializing the growing of European grape varieties, particularly Chardonnay and White Riesling, in the Finger Lakes region. Despite political resistance and numerous technical problems, Fournier and Frank succeeded, and these two varieties now provide excellent still wines and the base wines for fine champagnes — Great Western's Blanc de Blancs and Hermann Weimer's Brut being good examples.

Both Great Western and Gold Seal continued to make champagne by the *méthode champenoise* until Prohibition. After Repeal, both firms started making *méthode champenoise* champagne again, but later used the transfer process. In 1983, Great Western again started making champagne by the *méthode champenoise*. A year later, the aged Gold Seal facility was closed down and the operations shifted to the Taylor Wine Company facility. By that time, Taylor, Great Western, and Gold Seal were all part of Seagram's wine operations — later sold to a newly formed company called Vintners International.

Taylor had been founded in 1880 by Walter Taylor, a cooper who had come to Hammondsport to make wine barrels. This family-owned company became famous for its still wines, particularly after Prohibition. Taylor did not start making sparkling wine until 1939, at which time the *méthode champenoise* was used. However, it shifted production to the transfer process in 1968. With its acquisition of Great Western in 1961 and its merger with Gold Seal in 1979 (by Seagram), Taylor now has the largest winemaking facility in America outside California.

Champagne in St. Louis

Another famous champagne of the eighteen hundreds was started in St. Louis when a Chicago entrepreneur and politician, Isaac Cook, bought the Missouri Wine Company around 1858. He changed the name to the American Wine Company and started producing Cook's Imperial champagne. Also made from the Catawba grape, it won many awards in the United States and abroad. The winery was closed by Prohibition, reopened after Repeal by Adolf Heck, Sr, and then disbanded during World War II. Mr Heck's sons, Adolf Jr. and Paul, later went to California and purchased Korbel in 1954. Today, the Cook's Imperial label is owned by the Guild Winery in Lodi, California, and is used on a line of sparkling wine made by the bulk process.

Adolf Heck, Jr. had been sent by his father to the Geisenheim Institute in Germany to study champagne making and, upon his return to St. Louis in 1936, became champagne maker. He continued in that position until 1943. During that period, Heck developed the first automatic riddling machine. He installed these machines at Korbel after he and his brother, Paul, acquired the company in 1954. During the ensuing thirty years, Adolf Heck continued to improve upon the equipment and by the time of his death in 1985, had developed a highly mechanized system that performed the riddling in twelve-bottle cases.

Early Developments in California

Efforts to make champagne in California were started in the 1850s at San Gabriel in Southern California by Benjamin Davis Wilson and the Sainsevain brothers, Pierre and Jean Louis. The latter named their champagne Sparkling California, and reached an annual production of 150 thousand bottles by 1858. Champagne making in Southern California died out in the 1880s and 1890s as the vineyards succumbed to Pierce's disease and the plantings of the Mission grape were eclipsed by the European grapes being grown in Northern California. Champagne was not made in Southern California again until John Culbertson started producing champagne by the *méthode champenoise* in 1980 on his property in Fallbrook, near Temecula.

By the 1860s, the center of champagne development in California had moved north to Sonoma County. In 1862, General Mariano Guadalupe Vallejo, with the help of a French winemaker, developed a champagne, although it apparently was not a commercial success. Agoston Haraszthy and his son Arpad were the next to make California champagne, at Agoston's Buena Vista vineyards in Sonoma in the 1860s. The Haraszthys were close friends of Vallejo, Agoston's two sons having married Vallejo's daughters in a double wedding. Unfortunately, the Buena Vista venture was not a financial success either.

These early efforts to make champagne yielded little commercial success, due mainly to inexperience and the use of the inferior Mission grape. The Mission grape is low in acid and has little flavor, but was used until around 1880 because, until then, it was the only grape available in any quantity in California.

Arpad Haraszthy started his own champagne-making company in San Francisco in 1868. By then, he had given up on the Mission grape and had begun to experiment with Riesling, Muscatel, and several other European grape varieties. His Dry Eclipse became famous in the United States and, to a limited extent, in Europe until World War I, when Haraszthy stopped production. The name Eclipse came from a famous race horse.

Between 1875 and 1885, three other pioneer California winemakers started to make champagne: Charles Lefranc at Almaden in 1876; the Korbel brothers in 1883; and Paul Masson (Charles Lefranc's son-in-law) in 1884. The Korbel brothers soon became internationally famous for their Grand Pacific champagne, although the others were also successful. All of these champagnes were made from white grape varieties by the *méthode champenoise*.

The market for artificially carbonated wine as a less expensive alternative to champagne also began to grow in the 1880s . (The Charmat, or bulk, process was not developed until around 1910 in France and was not used in America until after Prohibition.) For several decades California wine producers shipped still wine in tank cars to New York where it was bottled and carbonated before being corked. The market for both champagne and artificially carbonated wine continued to grow until stopped by Prohibition in 1919.

The Aftermath of Prohibition

Following the repeal of Prohibition, the California wineries that started to use the *méthode champenoise* included Almaden, Paul Masson, Italian Swiss Colony, and Korbel. However, the American consumer was not ready to enjoy American-made fine champagne in the 1930s. Consequently, the bulk process of making sparkling wine came into vogue. Those who preferred fine champagne continued to pay a premium price for the French product.

The first Charmat facility installed in the United States after Repeal was actually built by a Canadian winery. During Prohibition in the 1920s, Chateau Gai of Ontario, Canada, had installed Charmat equipment to produce sparkling wine for the Canadian market. With the repeal of Prohibition, the company built a Charmat plant in New York State to serve the market for sparkling wine in the United States. Soon after that, several large bulk wine producers in the San Joaquin Valley of California also built Charmat facilities.

During the 1930s, government regulations were passed preventing producers of artificially carbonated wine from using the word *champagne* on their labels, its use being restricted to champagne produced by either the *méthode champenoise* or its modification, the transfer process. The regulations required Charmat producers to so label their bottles, and required *méthode champenoise* producers to specify the region or country in which their champagne was produced. The regulation applying to Charmat producers was subsequently relaxed to permit them to use the term *champagne* on their labels as long as they also stated that it was produced by the Charmat, or bulk, process. As a consequence of these regulations, the production of artificially carbonated wine was all but abandoned in the United States until the advent of the wine cooler in the 1980s.

World War II brought an increased demand for champagne and sparkling wine. Weibel and Mirassou entered the *méthode champenoise* market in 1938 and 1945 respectively. Weibel also built a Charmat facility in 1945, as did the Christian Brothers. By 1946, production of all types of sparkling wine in California had increased over six times since Repeal, from three quarters of a million bottles to almost five million bottles. Immediately after the end of the war, however, France started exporting champagne to the United States again and domestic production of all types of sparkling wine dropped to half of its 1946 peak. During the 1950s and early 1960s, the market for sparkling wine grew slowly.

In the decades following the war, the transfer technique became a popular method for producing sparkling wine as a result of improvements made in the equipment by several German firms. Although the process is more expensive than the Charmat process, it produces a sparkling wine more nearly comparable to true champagne. The transfer process involves fermentation and aging in the bottle, which permits aging on the lees and creation of a more complex wine. A number of California producers, including Paul Masson, Almaden, and Weibel, switched to this new process from the *méthode champenoise* around 1960.

California Champagne Today

The consumption of sparkling wine exploded in the 1960s, going from ten million bottles annually to eighty million. Most of this increase was provided by Gallo, who entered the market in 1965 when it built a huge Charmat facility to produce sparkling wine under the Eden Rock label. By 1971, Gallo was producing almost half of the entire United States production of sparkling wine — thirty-eight million bottles. The Christian Brothers and Weibel had been the largest Charmat producers until Gallo entered the market.

In the early 1960s, American champagne made by the *méthode champenoise* was an insignificant portion of the total sparkling wine consumed. Interest in fine champagne was stimulated, however, by the growing interest in sparkling wine generally. Korbel had been the only pre-Prohibition producer to continue to rely on the classical process after Repeal. Weibel and Mirassou had started during World War II. Hanns Kornell, who had emigrated from Germany to the United States in the early stages of World War II, started his *méthode champenoise* facility in the Napa Valley in 1952. Aside from these four, very few others were producing true champagne. The next pioneers to further the cause of the *méthode champenoise* in America were Jack and Jamie Davies, who purchased the defunct Schramsberg winery in the Napa Valley and started making champagne under the Schramsberg label.

When the Jack and Jamie Davies started, in 1965, only seven hundred thousand bottles (sixty thousand cases) of *méthode champenoise* were produce in the United States — essentially all of them in California. Their considerable marketing expertise added to that of the already established producers was sufficient, finally, to engender public recognition that the American producers were making fine champagne.

The biggest stimulus to the recognition of America's potential, however, came from a French company. In 1973 Domaine Chandon was started by Moët-Hennessy in the Napa Valley. Daniel Mirassou remarked at the time that, "the entrance of the largest French champagne producer into Napa Valley establishes the legitimacy of California as a source of fine champagne." Within eight years, Domaine Chandon was producing five million bottles of *méthode champenoise* champagne annually, thereby stimulating the consumption of champagne made by American-owned wineries.

Dozens of wineries in almost every wine-growing state in the Union have followed the lead of these modern pioneers. Chateau Ste. Michelle in Woodinville, Washington, was the first large winery outside California to start producing sparkling wine by the classic method. It started a *méthode champenoise* facility in 1974, using Pinot Noir and Chardonnay grapes from its own vineyards in eastern Washington.

Currently, over one hundred American wineries in twenty-three states now claim to be producing champagne by the classic method. Almost half of these wineries are in California. New York State is the second largest after California, with approximately fifteen producers using the *méthode champenoise*. The leading ones in New York besides Great Western are: Hermann J. Weimer in the Finger Lakes region, Gary Woodbury of Woodbury Vineyards on Lake Erie, and Marc Miller at his Benmarle Wine Company in the Hudson River Valley. While many of the wineries currently making champagne are small, with little more than garage-sized facilities, their proliferation does indicate that American consumers now widely appreciate the fine champagnes made by American producers.

A number of European champagne houses, observing Moët-Hennessy's success, started to acquire land and build *méthode champenoise* facilities in California. In 1980, Piper-Heidsieck and Sonoma Vineyards formed Piper Sonoma Cellars. Freixenet, the giant Spanish producer of champagne, started Gloria Ferrar in 1982, and Codorniu, the other large Spanish producer, purchased land near San Luis Obispo. These two Spanish firms are the largest *méthode champenoise* champagne makers in the world, each producing half as much again as Moët et Chandon, the largest French producer. Several other French champagne houses are now following Moët to California, including Taittinger, Roederer, Deutz, Laurent Perrier, Lanson, and Mumm.

Today, American production of champagne by the *méthode champenoise* is approximately 2.3 million cases, or twenty-seven million bottles. This currently constitutes close to 15 percent of the two hundred million bottles of all types of sparkling wine produced in the United States. The principal producers are listed below in descending order of annual production.

The figures are only approximations as actual production can vary significantly from year to year.

COMPANY	PRODUCTION (BOTTLES)
Korbel Champagne Cellars	15,500,000
Domaine Chandon	5,500,000
Piper Sonoma Cellars	900,000
Hanns Kornell	750,000
Gloria Ferrar (Freixenet)	700,000
Schramsberg Vineyards	600,000
John Culbertson Winery	360,000
Wente Bros.	360,000
Chateau St. Jean	300,000
Great Western (Vintners International)	250,000
Paul Mirassou Vineyards	250,000
Shadow Creek	250,000
Domaine Mumm	200,000
All others	1,100,000
TOTAL	**27,000,000**

The Grapes

French champagne is made from only three grape varieties, Chardonnay, Pinot Noir, and Pinot Meunier. American producers are free to use whatever variety they believe will make good champagne. In the western United States, these include Gewürztraminer, Riesling, Sémillon, French Colombard, Muscat Cannelli, Pinot Blanc, and Chenin Blanc, in addition to Pinot Noir and Chardonnay. In the eastern United States, American and French hybrids, such as Catawba, Delaware, Aurora, and Niagara and Seyval Blanc, Verdelet, and Vidal Blanc, are used. Chardonnay, Riesling, and Pinot Noir are becoming more common in the east as techniques have been developed to grow these more delicate varieties in the harsh summer and winter climates of such states as New York and Virginia.

Attempts to compare the quality of American and French champagnes are futile. They are inherently different champagnes and can only be compared in terms of personal preference and price. While the techniques for making the champagnes are the same, the climate, soil, and grape characteristics are unique to each region. The same distinctions can even be made about the champagnes from the eastern and western United States. The West Coast has a maritime climate in which European grape varieties thrive — dry, warm summers and mild winters. The East Coast, in contrast, has a continental climate — hot, humid summers and very cold winters — unsuited to European grape varieties. Soil conditions also vary widely. The Champagne region of France depends on its famous chalk beds; the Finger Lakes region has deposits of slate; and California has a wide range of soils varying from volcanic deposits to alluvial fills.

Some champagnes available in the United States are made from unusual *cuvées*. David Colman at Adler Fels, for example, produces a champagne he calls Ménage à Deux, made from a *cuvée* of Gewürztraminer and Johannisberg Riesling. Both Hanns Kornell in the Napa Valley and Hermann Weimer in the Finger Lakes region of New York make a champagne entirely of Johannisberg Riesling grapes, in the German *sekt* style. John Culbertson makes a dessert champagne he calls Cuvée de Frontignan, which is a blend of Muscat Canelli, Chenin Blanc, and Pinot Blanc. Schramsberg has developed a *crémant* style of champagne using the Flora grape, a cross between Gewürztraminer and Sémillon, developed by the University of California at Davis. One of the most interesting champagnes is produced on the island of Maui in the state of Hawaii by Tedeschi Vineyards. Emil Tedeschi makes a *blanc de noir* from the

Carnelian grape, a red hybrid developed at the University of California at Davis for use in hot climates. The Carnelian is a multiple cross of Carignan, Cabernet Sauvignon, and Grenache grapes.

During the past forty years, technology and experience have produced significant improvements in both the grapes used in the base wine and in the process of making champagne. Two of the most important developments, the introduction of temperature-controlled fermentation and improvements in filtration, have yielded fresher and crisper base wines. Mechanical harvesters have helped reduce the cost of picking the grapes. The computer-controlled gyropallet, developed in France, has helped reduce the cost of riddling by processing 405 bottles at one time. Automatic disgorging and capping machines have also been developed to reduce costs further. These and other techniques have now brought the cost of a bottle of fine American-made champagne within the price range of excellent still wines.

California-style champagne tends to emphasize the fruit flavor. As Bob Stashak, winemaker at Korbel, has remarked, "The fruit flavor is available in California-grown grapes because we can typically harvest when the Brix (sugar content) is 3 to 4 points higher than in France. We try to take advantage of that. The fresh, crisp fruitiness of California champagne fits the California and American lifestyle." Korbel has developed its own yeast strains that minimize the yeasty, or bread dough, bouquet that is characteristic of many French champagnes. Korbel also ages its champagne with the bottle in the upright position to minimize further the transfer of yeast flavors to the wine. A number of California champagne makers use such wines as Green Hungarian in the *cuvée* to give added flavor and acidity.

American champagne makers are still experimenting and steadily improving their product. This trend will undoubtedly go on for many years as they learn which grapes and what locations for vineyards are best suited for champagne making. Ultimately, grape varieties will undoubtedly be developed specifically for champagne. The diversity of varieties currently being used will continue to increase as the association of champagne and food is better understood and appreciated. In time, there will be "a champagne for all seasonings."

CHAMPAGNE AND FOOD

THE PURPOSE OF THIS BOOK IS TO DEMONSTRATE that champagne is not merely a celebration wine but is also a food wine. Like two close friends, food and champagne support each other and create truly memorable experiences.

There has always been a certain aloofness and mysticism associated with champagne, but for no valid reason. Cost is no longer a factor since the price of a bottle of premium champagne is comparable to that of a premium wine. Champagne does not have to be restricted to special occasions; it is an enjoyable drink at any time from breakfast to lunch, as an apéritif, and right through dinner to dessert. There is a style of champagne not only for any occasion, but as an accompaniment to any type of food — from *foie gras* to Chinese stir-fry. The styles can range from very dry to semisweet, from delicate in taste to fruity, and from red in color to golden or light straw.

What is it that makes champagne unique among beverages? The obvious answer is: the effervescence — the bubbles. They create a sensation on the palate that gives champagne sufficient zestiness not only to stand up to such still-wine killers as smoked oysters or caviar, but to enhance such dishes. Because champagne's effervescence, taste, and aroma are so delicate, the wine mingles well with the taste, texture, and aroma of a wide range of foods.

The dryer champagnes are best served as apéritifs and with food; the sweeter champagnes go best with dessert — and, naturally, with wedding, anniversary, and birthday cake. Champagne made primarily from red grapes has a fruitier taste and goes better with heavier foods than does champagne made primarily from white grapes. The latter has a more delicate taste and goes best with first courses and light foods.

The bubbles and the acidity in champagne give it the ability to match many foods and flavors that would overpower or conflict with still wines. Champagne holds up to bland, spicy, and salty foods — hence its close association with caviar. These same attributes make champagne an excellent palate-cleanser between courses.

A surprise to many people is that champagne is an appropriate accompaniment to spicy ethnic foods such as the hot foods of Szechuan, Hunan, and other regions of the Far East. It also goes well with Mexican dishes, even tacos, *chiles rellenos*, and refried beans. Since champagne stands up to acidic foods, it can be a delightful accompaniment to a pasta dish made with a lightly herbed fresh tomato sauce. Champagne goes with pizza and with tunafish sandwiches, as well as with gourmet entrées and desserts.

Obviously the list can go on for ever, but these examples will, I hope, trigger your own imagination as to what can be served with champagne. I challenge you to find something that will not go with champagne. This is not to imply that food goes better with champagne than with a fine red or white still wine, or some other beverage. I mean merely to suggest that when a glass of champagne fits the mood or occasion, do not stop drinking it simply because the meal is ready.

I hope you will enjoy trying the recipes contained in this book. Champagne is a state of mind, perhaps even a way of life for some, and can enhance the enjoyment of practically any food just as it can enhance the enjoyment of practically any occasion. The recipes in this book were specifically designed by makers of American champagne to ensure that enhancement. Each recipe, except those for sorbets, vegetables, and breads, is accompanied by suggestions about the type and style of champagne best suited to it.

KORBEL CHAMPAGNE CELLARS

KORBEL CHAMPAGNE CELLARS, also known as F. Korbel & Bros., is one of America's oldest producers of premium champagne. It has been producing champagne by the *méthode champenoise* for over one hundred years — since 1882.

The firm was not started as a winery, however. The three Korbel brothers, Francis, Anton, and Joseph, came to San Francisco in 1860 from their native Bohemia. Two years later the brothers moved to the Russian River area in Sonoma County to make their fortune in the lumber business. They established a lumber mill near the town of Guerneville to cut the huge redwoods into large timbers for further processing. The Korbel brothers also erected a factory to cut and craft the wood into cigar boxes.

Needing labels for the cigar boxes, the brothers founded a printing company. This printing company, in turn, gave them the opportunity to publish a political news magazine which they called *The Wasp*. In addition to news and editorials, it was liberally spiced with political cartoons. The magazine became popular throughout Northern California and lasted for several decades.

In order to transport their lumber to market, in 1876 the Korbels persuaded the Northwestern Pacific Railroad to build a rail line from Santa Rosa to the Russian River Valley. The small railroad station at Korbel still stands and was used at one time as the Korbel tasting room. Once the large stands of redwoods along the Russian River near the mill had been cleared, the Korbels looked for other uses for the land. From a farming expert at the University of California they learned that the soil and climatic conditions were ideal for the growing of European *vinifera* grapes for wine.

The Korbels planted vines among the redwood stumps and constructed a small winery. They had huge wine casks shipped by boat around the Horn from Europe. By 1886, they had completed the present brick winery building from timbers cut on the property and bricks also made on the property. A brandy tower was constructed in 1889 and is said to resemble the prison in Bohemia where one of the brothers had spent some time as a political prisoner. The Korbels were unique among California wineries at the time in that they concentrated from the start in making only champagne and brandy.

Company records show that the first Korbel champagne was shipped in 1882. A few years later, a winemaker from Prague, Franz Hazek, was hired as champagne maker. He brought with him choice European vine cuttings and made one of the first dry sparkling wines in California, which the Korbels labelled Sec. Later he made a sparkling Burgundy which the brothers called Korbel Rouge. Today Korbel still makes a Sec champagne and only recently discontinued the Rouge. The early success of Korbel champagnes reaffirmed to the brothers that they should concentrate on the production of fine champagnes rather than still wines. By the turn of the century, Korbel champagnes had become well known throughout the United States, as well as internationally.

The Korbel family operated the winery until 1954. By then, Anton Korbel, the third generation Korbel, had lost interest in the business and put the winery and the vineyards up for sale. However, he wanted to sell the operation to someone who would carry on its tradition of producing fine champagne by the *méthode champenoise*. Adolf Heck was the ideal person to carry on this legacy. The Heck family purchased the winery and operate it to this day.

Adolf Heck was a third generation descendent of winemakers from Alsace-Lorraine. He initially learned his winemaking skills from his father, Adolf, Sr., who had brought the family from Strasbourg to the United States in the early nineteen hundreds. After Prohibition, the elder Adolf Heck reopened the Cook's Imperial Champagne Cellars in St. Louis for the American Wine Company. When young Adolf was in his teens he worked part time at the St. Louis winery. After graduating from high school he was sent to the Geisenheim Wine Institute in Germany for training in winemaking. Upon his return, his father appointed Adolf as champagne master at Cook's.

Adolf operated wineries in Ohio for National Distillers during the 1940s. In 1950, at the age of thirty-six, he came to California and became president of Italian Swiss Colony — at that time the largest winery in the United States. At Swiss Colony, Adolf created the "Little Old Winemaker" theme, probably the best-known wine commercial of the 1950s. Adolf, however, dreamed of owning a small champagne cellar in California where he could create his own style of champagne, which he liked to describe as "California-style." In 1954 his dream came true when he learned that Korbel Champagne Cellars was up for sale. Adolf mortgaged his house, arranged for additional financing, and at one minute after midnight on the day the winery went on the market, made an offer for the property. Anton Korbel accepted it immediately.

In 1956, Adolf introduced his *brut*-style champagne, a lighter and dryer style than that of any American champagne on the market at the time. Korbel Brut was the first champagne specifically designed for American tastes. The *cuvée* used in Korbel Brut was (and still is) a blend of California grape varieties, including Chardonnay and Pinot Noir, the traditional French champagne grapes. Subsequently Adolf introduced additional *cuvées:* the Korbel Natural produced from a blend of classic champagne grapes; the blush Blanc de Noirs made entirely from Pinot Noir grapes; and the Blanc de Blancs entirely from Chardonnay. He also developed all of his own champagne yeasts, which are still used at Korbel for the second fermentation.

Adolf Heck was not only a creator of champagne *cuvées*, he was constantly improving the production and technical aspects of the business. He invented and patented one of the first automatic riddling machines. The original idea has continued to be improved upon and today provides Korbel with a highly automatic riddling, bottling, and packaging line. It is a patented process that is exclusively used at Korbel.

In thirty years winery production under Adolf Heck's leadership grew manyfold. New buildings were added and the staff enlarged. Unfortunately, Adolf Heck died suddenly in 1984. He was succeeded by his son, Gary, who now serves as president and chairman of the board of F. Korbel & Bros.

Korbel has continued to grow under Gary Heck's leadership. Today Korbel is the largest American producer of champagne made by the *méthode champenoise* with a production of 1.3 million cases per year. This constitutes over 50 percent of the premium champagne produced in America. Korbel continues to win many awards. One of the most important was received in 1985 at the New York Wine Experience, where Korbel was designated as one of the sixty-eight great wineries of the world.

Although Korbel owns six hundred acres of vineyards near the winery, it purchases a substantial quantity of its grapes from independent growers. Long-term contracts have been established with growers in the Alexander Valley and near Santa Barbara, regions in which the fruit is similar in quality to that grown in the Russian River Valley.

Robert M. Stashak is the Champagne Master at Korbel Champagne Cellars. Under his watchful eye and trained palate, the *cuvées* are blended for the seven types of Korbel champagne. Bob joined Korbel in 1973 after graduating from the University of California at Davis with a degree in fermentation science. He learned the art of champagne making under the late Adolf Heck. In 1977 Bob became the assistant winemaker, and was promoted to assistant vice-president in 1983. When Adolf Heck died in 1984, he assumed the title of Korbel Champagne Master.

"Champagnes are delicate wines. The grapes are picked young and we here at Korbel try to protect their delicate flavor," says Bob Stashak. Bob is following Adolf Heck's style of California champagne with the accent on the fruit, not on the yeastiness, of the champagne. "This region of the world, with its coastal climate, gives us excellent fruit. Not only is the fruit delicate, but it also has good acidity, which is critical in premium champagne," Bob emphasizes.

The grapes for Korbel champagnes are all hand picked about the middle of August, usually when the sugar content has reached 18 Brix. The grapes are delivered to the winery in two-ton gondolas and then transferred to the crusher-stemmer for a light pressing. After the still wine is made, it is aged in oak for between four and eight weeks before being blended into the champagne *cuvée*.

After the second fermentation, the champagne is aged on the yeast for periods ranging from twelve months to six years. The longer aging periods are used for the vintage champagnes, such as Korbel's 1981 Private Reserve Blanc de Blancs. During aging the bottles are stored cap-up in the case and kept in a temperature-controlled environment. "This aging with the bottles in an upright position subdues the tendency toward a yeasty taste," says Bob. After aging, the champagne bottles are mechanically riddled, also while in the case. The riddling is timed by a computer. The disgorging, dosaging (with sugar syrup and still wine), finishing, and packaging are all performed by mechanical equipment.

Over the years, Korbel has discontinued some of its champagne styles, such as the Korbel Rouge, but added others. Korbel Brut Rosé, made entirely from Pinot Noir grapes, is a popular addition. This champagne has a lovely color, achieved by modest skin contact during pressing, and a fruity, slightly sweet taste. The Blanc de Blancs, the Blanc de Noirs, and the Natural are carefully crafted in limited quantities.

All of the complexities created in champagne by the *méthode champenoise* take place in the same bottle purchased by the consumer. The process requires an uncompromising attention to detail and standards of quality, at Korbel, traditions that date back to its early days of champagne making and that have only been enhanced by the technical advances since then.

Korbel Champagne Cellars produces seven champagnes, from dry (0.5 percent residual sugar), to medium dry (1.0 to 1.5 percent residual sugar):

Blanc de Blancs — 100 percent Chardonnay; dry

Blanc de Noirs — 100 percent Pinot Noir; dry

Natural — a blend of Chardonnay and Pinot Noir; dry

Brut — a blend of Chardonnay, Pinot Noir, French Colombard, and Chenin Blanc; medium dry

Extra Dry — a blend of Chardonnay, Pinot Noir, French Colombard, and Chenin Blanc, with more Chenin Blanc than there is in the Brut; medium dry

Sec — Chardonnay, Pinot Noir, French Colombard, and Chenin Blanc with more French Colombard in the blend than there is in the Brut; medium dry

Brut Rose — 100 percent Pinot Noir; medium dry

Culinary Director: Sheryl Benesch

A native of Los Angeles, Sheryl was a biology major at Santa Rosa College when she decided to make food preparation her full-time career. After enjoying a Thanksgiving dinner in 1979 at River's End, a local restaurant on the Russian River, she decided to become an apprentice there. Starting in food service, she soon progressed to making salads and desserts. The more opportunities she was given to work with food, the better she liked it. After four and a half years at River's End, Korbel asked her to join its staff in 1984 and take over all food preparation.

Sheryl prepares all the executive lunches, special dinners, and meals at special company events. Whether it be a lunch for twelve or a dinner for eighty, she is always ready to create exciting dishes to complement Korbel champagnes. "I have to be flexible, since I often have more people for a meal than I had planned on. I just add a dish or two," she says. Often Sheryl is asked to create special recipes to complement the Korbel champagnes. These are used for in-house events and have appeared in national publications.

Mexican and Asian cuisines are of special interest to Sheryl. She particularly likes to use the ingredients of these cuisines with traditional European or American dishes. "However, I am very careful when using spices, so as not to overpower the champagne that is to accompany the food," Sheryl adds.

Korbel Champagne Cellars — F. Korbel & Bros.
13250 River Road
Guerneville, California 95446
(707) 887-2294

Visits: 9:00 A.M. to 5:00 P.M. daily
Principal: Gary Heck
Champagnes produced: Blanc de Blancs, Blanc de Noirs, Natural, Brut, Extra
Dry, Sec, and Brut Rosé
1988 champagne production: 1,300,000 cases

HORS D'OEUVRES

LITERALLY TRANSLATED AS "OUTSIDE THE WORK," hors d'oeuvres, in the context of cooking, are dishes that provide an introduction to the meal. In France, the term applies to small appetizers usually eaten with a fork at the table, as a prelude to the meal, and served with an apéritif. In America, the term describes bite-sized appetizers, canapés, spreads, and finger food. More generally, it refers to the type of food served at cocktail parties and consumed while standing.

In the United States, cocktail parties became popular after Prohibition when, with the decline in the number of household servants, entertaining became more casual. Such parties suited the American style and provided an outlet for the American love of snacking. Hors d'oeuvres were eaten as a buffer to counterbalance the intake of alcohol. This was not a new innovation: centuries earlier Burgundian wine tasters had found the *gougère*, a delicate little cheese puff, complemented the taste and the effect of the wine.

Modern cocktail interludes feature drinks and finger food — food that can be eaten in one or two bites without dribbling all over clothing, furniture, or rugs. Over the years an amazing variety of finger food has been developed — some variations borrowed from European and Asian cuisines, others using American ingredients and ingenuity. Today cocktail parties often become cocktail buffets, at which more substantial food is offered and small plates are used.

Champagne has become a popular beverage at cocktail time. Its effervescence matches the occasion and enhances the appetite. Styles of champagne have expanded to accommodate various types of food and styles of entertaining. Consequently, a host or hostess may match the champagne with the hors d'oeuvres selected. All of the following hors d'oeuvres recipes are especially designed to complement champagne and most of them are easy to prepare.

❖ Buckwheat Blinis and Caviar ❖

Martha Culbertson, John Culbertson Winery
Accompanying champagne *Culbertson Brut*

Makes about 40 two-inch blinis

The blini is a centuries-old Russian version of the pancake. Historically, blinis were especially popular during Shrovetide, which is pancake time throughout Europe. From the noblest house to the humblest cottage, blinis were served twice a day during this festival period just before Ash Wednesday. Blinis are usually small, made with buckwheat flour, and use yeast as a rising agent. Filled with various stuffings such as salmon, cottage cheese or, best of all, elegant caviar, they are served as hors d'oeuvres.

BLINIS

½ tablespoon dry yeast
3 cups milk
1 cup buckwheat flour
1 cup all-purpose flour
2 teaspoons sugar

½ teaspoon salt
3 egg yolks, slightly beaten
3 egg whites
2 tablespoons butter, to grease griddle

FILLING

8 ounces of the best caviar you can buy, for example, Russian Sevruga
1 cup sour cream
1 medium white onion, minced

2 hard-boiled eggs, yolks separated from whites and sieved into a small dish, whites finely chopped and placed in another dish

In a large bowl dissolve the dry yeast in 1½ cups warm milk (105 to 115° F.). In another bowl mix together ½ cup buckwheat flour, ½ cup all-purpose flour, 2 teaspoons sugar, and ½ teaspoon salt. Add the egg yolks and the flour mixture to the yeast mixture. Mix well. Cover bowl and let the batter rise until double in bulk, about 1 hour.

Mix the remaining ½ cup of buckwheat flour with the remaining ½ cup all-purpose flour and add, alternately with 1½ cups lukewarm milk, to the risen yeast mixture. Again cover the bowl and let batter rise until double in bulk, about 45 minutes.

Beat the 3 egg whites to soft peaks and gently fold them into the batter. Drop 2 tablespoons of batter onto a hot, lightly buttered griddle. Cook for 40 seconds, turn, and cook until lightly browned on second side.

Serve the blinis warm with the caviar, sour cream, onion, egg yolks, and egg whites each in separate bowls. Let everyone help themselves.

❖ Caviar Mold ❖

Steve Wenger, Biltmore Estate
Accompanying champagne *Biltmore Estate Brut*

Serves 12 to 16; makes a 1-quart mold

Caviar has always been regarded as a perfect combination with champagne. The rich cheese mixture of this recipe highlights the caviar, whether it is an elegant imported one or a fresh local variety. A layer of gold and a layer of black caviar would make an attractive contrast to the cheese mixture. For a slightly different taste, substitute *crème fraîche* for the sour cream.

16 ounces farmer's cheese
8 ounces cream cheese
4 ounces sour cream
1/2 medium red onion, chopped

1 teaspoon Worcestershire sauce
1/8 teaspoon Tabasco sauce
3 ounces caviar; reserve 2
teaspoons for garnish

Oil a 1-quart mold. If the mold is decorative, you may want to line it with cheesecloth to ensure easy unmolding.

Place all ingredients except the caviar in the bowl of a food processor and process until well mixed. Place one-third of the cheese mixture in the mold. Spread half of the caviar on top, to within 1/2 inch of the edge. Place another third of the cheese mixture on caviar, pressing gently to smooth out air pockets. Repeat the caviar procedure and finish with the last third of the cheese mixture.

Chill the mold in the refrigerator for several hours or overnight. Unmold on a serving platter and garnish with lettuce leaves and tiny lemon wedges. Place the 2 teaspoons of caviar on top of the mold. Serve with crackers.

❖ Caviar Mousse D'or ❖

Ruth Wiens, Mirassou Vineyards
Accompanying champagne *Mirassou Au Naturel*

Makes 1¹/₂ cups

Mousse, a French culinary term meaning "froth," denotes a light, spongy dish. Mousses may be made from fish, meat, vegetables, fruit, or sweet confections. The latter two are served as dessert. Lightened with gelatin, egg whites, or whipped cream, mousses are usually served cold — chilled, not frozen. Inexpensive and simple to prepare, this delicate mousse provides several textures that complement the effervescence and tartness of the Au Naturel champagne.

2 teaspoons unflavored gelatin
¹/₄ cup Mirassou Au Naturel
  champagne
2 hard-boiled eggs
¹/₄ cup mayonnaise
¹/₄ cup sour cream

1 tablespoon grated shallot
4 ounces golden caviar, drained
2 teaspoons lemon juice
A pinch of freshly ground white
  pepper
¹/₃ cup whipping cream

Sprinkle the gelatin over the champagne in a small saucepan. Let the mixture sit for 10 minutes and then place over low heat to dissolve gelatin. Set aside to cool.

Sieve the hard-boiled eggs and gently combine them with the mayonnaise, sour cream, shallot, caviar, and lemon juice. Add the gelatin mixture and blend to combine ingredients. Add pepper, seasoning to taste. Whip the cream until stiff and gently fold into caviar mixture.

Lightly oil a 1¹/₂ cup decorative mold. Spoon caviar mixture into the mold and chill for at least 4 hours. Quickly dip mold into hot water and unmold onto a bed of lettuce leaves arranged on a platter. Serve with toast points or crackers.

❖ Potato Pancakes and Caviar ❖

Frederick Horton, Wente Bros. Sparkling Wine Cellars
Accompanying champagne *Wente Bros. Brut*

Serves 6 to 8

Caviar, one of the most expensive foods, was once so abundant in the Hudson River area that it was a regular free lunch item on the counters of the local New York saloons. A five cent glass of beer allowed the drinker to partake of all the caviar he desired.

For these delicate pancakes, use a good quality caviar, such as American Spoombill, a medium grain, pearly gray-black variety; or try the golden, small textured caviar from the whitefish. For a beautiful contrast mix the two, being careful to drain any excess juice from each.

1 very large new potato, to make
  1¼ cups grated
1½ cups water
½ teaspoon lemon juice
1 small boiled potato, mashed
1 egg, beaten

1 tablespoon milk
¼ teaspoon salt
¼ teaspoon black pepper
¼ teaspoon garlic powder
Vegetable oil, for frying

GARNISH
½ cup sour cream
4 ounces caviar

Chives, finely chopped

Grate the raw potato into the water to which lemon juice has been added. Place grated potato mixture into a strainer or cheesecloth and drain off the liquid thoroughly.

Beat the raw and cooked potatoes with the egg, milk, salt, pepper, and garlic powder until the mixture forms a batter.

Cover bottom of a large skillet or griddle with a thin layer of vegetable oil. Drop spoonfuls of the potato mixture onto the hot oil and press them into pancakes. The pancakes should be about the size of a silver dollar. Turn the pancakes when the underside is golden brown and crisp. Brown the other side.

To serve, garnish each pancake with a teaspoon of sour cream; place a teaspoon of caviar on top of the cream and garnish with chopped chives.

❖ Eggplant "Caviar" ❖

Marilouise Kornell, Hanns Kornell Champagne Cellars
Accompanying champagne *Hanns Kornell Blanc de Blancs*

Serves 6 to 8

Eggplant, a native of southeast Asia and a staple of Middle Eastern cuisine, was brought to Europe during the Middle Ages. There are many varieties, colors, and sizes of this vegetable. The first variety to reach Europe resembled a hen's egg, thus the name *eggplant*. This particular dish is an old Italian favorite and is a pleasant hors d'oeuvre to serve on a warm day. For a more spicy version, add the optional chile peppers.

*1 eggplant, weighing about 2
  pounds
Juice of 1 lemon
1 tablespoon dry white wine
2 tablespoons olive oil
2 tablespoons capers, chopped*

*1 clove garlic, mashed
Salt and pepper to taste
1 tablespoon chopped chile
  peppers (optional)
2 tablespoons chopped parsley*

Place the eggplant in a shallow baking dish and bake in a preheated 350° F. oven for 1 to 1½ hours or until the pulp is soft and the skin is shriveled. Peel off the skin and squeeze out the excess moisture.

Put the pulp through a food mill or mash well in a bowl. Do not use a blender or food processor because there should be some distinct pieces in the purée. Stir in the lemon juice, wine, olive oil, capers, garlic, and salt and pepper. Add the chile peppers, if desired. Taste and correct the seasonings. Stir in the parsley.

Refrigerate the mixture for at least a day so that the flavors can blend together. Remove from the refrigerator 1 hour before serving.

Serve with pieces of French bread or toast points, slices of jicama, or pieces of celery.

❖ Oysters on the Half Shell ❖

Marilouise Kornell, Hanns Kornell Champagne Cellars
Accompanying champagne *Hanns Kornell Blanc de Blancs*

Serves 4

The human race has had a continuous love affair with oysters. In Europe, in the seventeenth and eighteenth centuries, the nobility ate oysters, not by the dozen, but by the hundreds. From the first discovery of America, European settlers enjoyed native oysters that were reported to be a foot long in New York Bay. Oysters and champagne are a pleasing combination. One of the best ways to serve them is simply on the half shell. If serving other hors d'oeuvres, allow three oysters per person; if serving them as a first course, allow six.

*12 oysters on the half shell
1 small tin caviar*

1 lemon, cut in wedges

Top each oyster on the half shell with ½ teaspoon caviar. Serve on a bed of ice garnished with lemon wedges.

❖ Smoked Oyster Pâté ❖

Steve Wenger, Biltmore Estate
Accompanying champagne *Biltmore Estate Brut*

Serves 8; makes 1$^1/_2$ cups

Pâté is commonly used today to describe a paste or spread made from minced or ground ingredients, such as meat, liver, seafood, or vegetables. In this Smoked Oyster Pâté, the ingredients do not have to be baked in the oven as is customary with the traditional French pâtés.

*2 cans (3$^1/_2$ ounces each) smoked
  oysters, well drained
Juice of half a lemon*

*8 drops Tabasco Sauce
$^1/_2$ cup whipping cream*

Combine all the ingredients in the bowl of a food processor. Process until smooth, stopping frequently to scrape down the bowl and blend the ingredients. Pack the mixture into a 2-cup container or crock, and chill overnight.

For pâté, serve cold with crackers. To pipe onto canapés or into miniature *choux* pastry puffs, soften before use.

❖ Smoked Salmon Mousse in ❖ Belgian Endive

Frederick Horton, Wente Bros. Sparkling Wine Cellars
Accompanying champagne *Wente Bros. Brut*

Serves 6; makes approximately 32 hors d'oeuvres

Belgian endive is one of the most difficult vegetables to cultivate. Originally grown only in the flatlands that surround Brussels, small quantities are now being raised in the United States. An endive requires several growing stages — all done in the dark. First, seeds are planted. Six weeks later, the seedlings are replanted in a mixture of sand and soil. When the small endives are formed they are replanted again and covered with mounds of loamy earth. Weeks later the plants are harvested, washed, spin dried, and packaged. In this recipe, the delicate bitter flavor of endive is contrasted with the slightly salty flavor of the salmon mousse. When arranged in a sunburst pattern on a tray, this dish makes a beautiful display.

*8 ounces cream cheese, at room
  temperature
4 ounces smoked salmon
Few drops of lemon juice
3 tablespoons whipping cream*

*White pepper to taste
4 heads Belgian endive, pulled
  apart into petals,
  approximately 32 petals
Watercress leaves, for garnish*

Combine the cream cheese, smoked salmon, lemon juice, cream, and pepper in the bowl of a food processor and blend until the mixture is smooth. Chill for at least 30 minutes.

Assemble the hors d'oeuvres no more than an hour before serving. Soften the mousse with a wooden spoon and put it into a pastry bag with a star tip. Pipe mousse in each endive leaf and garnish it with a watercress leaf.

❖ Marinated Salmon ❖

Sheryl Benesch, Korbel Champagne Cellars
Accompanying champagne *Korbel Natural*

Serves 8 to 10; makes about 40 crackers

Salmon was once so plentiful that servants specified as part of their contracts that they would not be served salmon more than three to five times a week. Times have changed and the fish today is not the staple item it used to be. Marinated salmon, or *gravlax* is a Swedish delicacy. It is simple to prepare and may be served with crackers or small slices of bread. The slices of *gravlax* may also be served on lettuce with a sour cream sauce for a first course. Any leftovers are excellent in an omelet or a frittata.

1 pound salmon fillet, tail end, skin still attached
2 teaspoons black peppercorns, cracked
2 teaspoons granulated sugar

2 teaspoons kosher salt
2 sprigs fresh dill
2 sprigs fresh tarragon
2 teaspoons vodka

GARNISH

Sour cream
Capers

Green onion or fresh dill, finely chopped

Slice the salmon fillet in half lengthwise. Place 1 slice of salmon, skin-side down, on a plate. Sprinkle the fish with 1 teaspoon each of the peppercorns, sugar, and salt. Top with dill and tarragon, spreading the herbs evenly. Sprinkle the remaining salt, pepper, sugar, and the vodka over the herbs. Lay the other half of the salmon, skin-side up, on top, creating a sandwich. Weigh it down by placing a plate on top and refrigerate overnight.

To serve, remove the herbs. Place the salmon, skin-side down, on a cutting board and slice the fish approximately 1/8-inch thick. Slice away from the skin at an angle. Place the slices of salmon on crackers or pumpernickel. Spoon 1/2 teaspoon sour cream on top; add some capers and chopped green onion or chopped fresh dill.

❖ Crab-Stuffed Smoked Salmon ❖

Karen Mack, Chateau Ste. Michelle Winery
Accompanying champagne *Domaine Ste. Michelle Blanc de Noir*

Makes 24 appetizers

The delicate flavor of crabmeat cooked in a mild wine and cheese sauce balances the smoked salmon. These attractive salmon rolls are enhanced with the addition of parsley and dill.

1 tablespoon unsalted butter
Juice of 1 lemon
¼ pound mushrooms, finely
*   chopped*
3 green onions, finely chopped
3 tablespoons all-purpose flour
¼ cup whipping cream
4 ounces cream cheese

¼ cup blanc de noir sparkling wine
8 ounces cooked Dungeness
*   crabmeat, all leg meat if possible*
¼ teaspoon white pepper
12 slices smoked salmon, each cut
*   in half*
Finely chopped fresh parsley and
*   dill, mixed*

Melt the butter in a medium saucepan. Add 2 teaspoons of the lemon juice. Then add the mushrooms and onions and sauté for 2 to 3 minutes. Add flour and stir until thickened, about 1 minute. Add the cream, cream cheese, and sparkling wine, stirring constantly until thickened. Add the crab, pepper, and more lemon juice to taste. Continue stirring and cooking over very low heat until crab is heated through, about 3 to 4 minutes. Let the mixture cool.

Place a little of the crab mixture on the narrow end of a slice of salmon and roll it up. Dip each end of the roll into fresh herbs and place on platter seam-side down. Continue to fill and roll the other salmon slices. Garnish plate with lemon roses and serve.

❖ Shrimp in Blanc de Noir ❖

Karen Mack, Chateau Ste. Michelle
Accompanying champagne *Domaine Ste. Michelle Blanc de Noir*

Serves 6 to 8

The shrimp shells impart an additional flavor and support the shrimp as they are broiling.

1 pound large shrimp
1½ to 2 cups, plus 2 tablespoons,
*   blanc de noir sparkling wine*
½ cup freshly grated Parmesan
*   cheese*

½ cup bread crumbs
1 tablespoon fresh, minced parsley
1 teaspoon fresh, minced garlic
1 tablespoon olive oil

Clean, devein, and split each shrimp down the center, not quite cutting through the body. Leave them in the shell. Place shrimp in a bowl and add enough sparkling wine to cover them. Refrigerate the shrimp for a minimum of 2 hours.

In a small bowl combine the Parmesan cheese, bread crumbs, parsley and garlic. In another small bowl combine the 2 tablespoons sparkling wine and the olive oil.

Remove the shrimp from the sparkling wine marinade and drain them. Place shrimp on a baking sheet and brush them with the oil mixture. Then sprinkle them heavily with the cheese and crumb mixture. Broil 6 to 8 inches from the heat for 5 to 8 minutes, depending on the size of the shrimp.

❖ Seafood en Brochette ❖

Jamie Davies, Schramsberg Vineyards and Cellars
Accompanying champagne *Schramsberg Blanc de Noirs*

Serves 4

These seafood morsels may be eaten off the skewer or placed on a plate and eaten with a fork. The Asiago cheese melts easily into the sauce and its piquant flavor goes well with the seafood. If serving the dish as a first course, place some of the sauce on individual plates and top with seafood. Garnish with parsley or watercress.

8 medium prawns, peeled and
    deveined
8 scallops
4 pieces lobster or 1 lobster tail
½ cup chopped clams

¼ cup clam juice
½ cup sour cream
2 tablespoons crumbled Asiago
    cheese

Arrange the prawns, scallops, and lobster on small skewers.

Place the clams and clam juice in a blender and purée, allowing some texture to remain. In a small saucepan, combine the clam purée, sour cream, and cheese and heat gently until the cheese melts. Keep sauce warm.

Grill seafood over hot coals or under a broiler for 3 to 5 minutes until done. Do not overcook. Serve with warm sauce.

❖ Seafood Hearts ❖

Karen Mack, Chateau Ste. Michelle Winery
Accompanying champagne *Domaine Ste. Michelle Blanc de Noir*

Serves 8 to 10

The artichoke was first introduced into the United States by the French and the Spaniards. Today this thistlelike plant is cultivated primarily in the foggy coastal regions of California. The heart or bottom is the tenderest part of the plant and forms a base for this tasty creamed seafood. Butter clams are small tender clams prevalent in the Pacific Northwest. Any variety of small clams, such as littleneck, may be used in this recipe. Since the seafood hearts are very tender, serve them on small individual plates, allowing two or three per person.

4 tablespoons unsalted butter
1 cup minced onion
4 cloves garlic, minced
Juice of half a lemon
1/8 teaspoon red pepper flakes
2 pounds mussels, shells scrubbed and beards removed
2 pounds butter clams, shells scrubbed
2 cups blanc de noir sparkling wine

2 pounds jumbo prawns, shelled and deveined
1 package (8 ounces) cream cheese, softened
2 cans (16 ounces each) artichoke hearts (not marinated), thoroughly drained
1 bunch fresh parsley, washed and chopped fine

Melt the butter in a large non-aluminum soup pot with lid. Add the onion, garlic, lemon juice, and red pepper flakes and sauté slowly for 4 to 5 minutes. Add the mussels and clams and stir to coat. Add the sparkling wine and stir again. Turn heat to high. Cover and steam for 2 minutes. Add the prawns. Cover and steam for 1 to 2 more minutes longer until prawns are no longer translucent and the mussel and clam shells are open. Remove from heat and remove shellfish with slotted spoon. Reserve the liquid, letting any sand settle.

Remove the mussels and clams from their shells. Cut the mussels, clams, and prawns in half. Mix all the seafood with the cream cheese and 2 tablespoons reserved liquid (carefully avoiding any sand) until the seafood is thoroughly coated.

Place a large spoonful of the seafood mixture on each artichoke heart. Place under broiler for 4 to 5 minutes until bubbly. Sprinkle with chopped parsley and serve immediately.

❖ Bay Shrimp Canapés ❖

Ruth Wiens, Mirassou Vineyards
Accompanying champagne *Mirassou Au Naturel*

Makes 36 canapés

Canapés, small open-faced sandwiches, do not have to use baked dough as a base. Cucumber slices provide a crispy texture to complement the spicy shrimp mixture. Extra lemon juice will turn this canapé mixture into an excellent dip for an assortment of fresh vegetables.

3/4 pound cooked bay shrimp
4 ounces garlic and herb cream cheese (such as Rondelé)
1 tablespoon lemon juice (1 to 2 tablespoons more if making as a dip)

1/4 teaspoon dill weed
1/4 teaspoon Tabasco sauce, or to taste
1 unpeeled English cucumber, cut into 1/4-inch slices

Pick over the shrimp, removing any cartilage or pieces of shell. Reserve 36 shrimp for garnish. Place the remaining shrimp, cheese, lemon juice, dill weed, and Tabasco sauce in the bowl of a food processor and process until smooth and creamy. Using a pastry bag, pipe the mixture onto cucumber rounds. Place a shrimp in the center. Chill canapés until serving time.

❖ Crab-Stuffed Mushrooms ❖

Edna Tears, The Great Western Winery
Accompanying champagne *Great Western Natural*

Serves 4 to 6

Select large firm mushrooms for stuffing. The thick white sauce adds richness to the filling. Use only enough sauce, however, to bind the ingredients together lightly. Because mushrooms exude moisture when cooking, an overabundance of sauce can make the hors d'oeuvres too soggy.

16 large mushrooms
8 ounces fresh cooked, or 1 can (7 1/2 ounces), crabmeat
2 teaspoons chopped chives
1 tablespoon semisweet sherry
1 teaspoon Worcestershire sauce
1/4 teaspoon salt

Dash of white pepper
2 tablespoons butter
1 1/2 tablespoons all-purpose flour
1/3 to 1/2 cup milk
1/3 cup grated Parmesan cheese
Paprika

Remove the stems from the mushrooms. Wipe the caps with a damp cloth or clean under running water with a brush and then dry the mushrooms with a cloth.

Pick over the crabmeat to remove any cartilage and break up any large pieces. Combine crabmeat, chives, sherry, Worcestershire sauce, salt, and pepper. In a small saucepan melt the butter, add flour, and mix well. Slowly add the milk, salt, and pepper. Cook, stirring over medium heat until thickened. Add the sauce by tablespoons to the crabmeat, adding only enough to bind the mixture lightly. Fill the mushroom caps with the crabmeat.

Place the caps in a 9- by 13-inch glass baking dish and sprinkle with grated Parmesan cheese and paprika. Bake in a preheated 350° F. oven for 10 to 12 minutes or until bubbly.

❖ Stuffed Nasturtiums ❖

Tracy Wood Anderson, S. Anderson Vineyard
Accompanying champagne *S. Anderson Tivoli*

Serves 4

Similar to watercress in taste, nasturtium leaves were once a popular salad ingredient. Native to America, nasturtiums have once again gained popularity for their edible flowers. They add color to salads and are frequently stuffed for hors d'oeuvres. Nasturtiums are not readily available commercially, but they can be easily grown in the garden. The sweet flavor of chutney in the nasturtium filling pairs well with the slight sharpness of the flowers.

8 ounces cream cheese　　　　　　　*12 to 15 freshly cut nasturtiums*
3 tablespoons chutney

Combine the chutney and the cream cheese in the bowl of a food processor. Process only until smooth. Do not overwork as the mixture will become soupy.

Put cheese mixture in a piping bag fitted with a medium star tip. Pipe about 1 to 2 teaspoons of the filling into the middle of each flower. Place in refrigerator until ready to serve.

❖ Almond Phyllos ❖

Jamie Davies, Schramsberg Vineyards and Cellars
Accompanying champagne *Schramsberg Blanc de Blancs*

Makes 12 pieces

These dainty phyllo packages can be prepared and frozen, then baked just before serving; or they can be kept covered in the refrigerator for up to twenty-four hours before baking. If they are to be frozen, place them on an unbuttered baking sheet, freeze overnight and then store them in a freezer bag. Bake as needed. Refreeze any unused phyllo dough.

1 package (1 pound) phyllo leaves　　*into 12 squares, each measuring*
3 tablespoons butter, melted　　　　*¹/₂- by ¹/₂- by ¹/₄-inch*
24 hickory-smoked almonds　　　　*12 long chives, blanched*
6 ounces Monterey Jack cheese, cut

Unfold the phyllo leaves and, working with 4 sheets at a time (cover the remaining leaves with a damp cloth to prevent them from becoming brittle), brush each sheet with melted butter and cut into 3¹/₂ inch squares. Stack 4 squares slightly askew. Gently press each stack into a miniature muffin tins and place 1 piece of cheese and 2 almonds in the center. Gather tops together and tie loosely with a piece of blanched chive. The packages may be frozen at this point.

Bake in a preheated 375° F. oven for 4 minutes or until phyllo is light brown. If previously frozen, bake for 1 to 2 minutes longer.

❖ Smoked Mussels in Phyllo ❖

Ruth Wiens, Mirassou Vineyards
Accompanying champagne *Mirassou Au Naturel*

Makes about 2 dozen

Phyllo, the Middle Eastern version of strudel dough, is thin like an onion skin. Basically made from flour and water, the leaflike baked dough is reminiscent of puff pastry. Phyllo dough is available in the freezer section of the grocery store. Simple to assemble, especially if you buy pre-buttered phyllo, these flavorful triangles can be made ahead. If frozen, they should go directly from freezer to oven and a little extra baking time should be allowed.

> 2 cans (4 ounces each) smoked mussels
> 2 tablespoons unsalted butter
> ¼ cup water
> 1 cup (packed) finely julienned leeks, white part only
> 8 ounces cream cheese
>
> 2 tablespoons balsamic vinegar (red wine vinegar may be substituted)
> ¼ teaspoon salt, or to taste
> ¼ teaspoon cayenne pepper
> 1 pound phyllo leaves
> 4 ounces unsalted butter, melted

Thoroughly drain mussels on paper towels.

Melt the 2 tablespoons of butter in a heavy saucepan. Add the water and leeks. Cook slowly over low heat, stirring often until leeks are very soft but not brown, and all of the water has evaporated, about 15 minutes. Stir in the cream cheese and continue cooking until it is very soft. Blend in the vinegar, salt and cayenne pepper. Remove the mixture from the heat; fold in the drained mussels.

After the mixture has cooled, cut the phyllo sheets into rectangles measuring about 4 by 9 inches. Peel off a strip, brush with the melted butter and top with another strip. Keep remaining phyllo strips covered with a damp cloth to prevent them from becoming brittle. Place 1 tablespoon of the filling one inch from the bottom end of a strip and slightly left of center. Holding the left corner, fold the right corner over filling to form a triangle. Then continue to fold from side to side as if you were folding a flag. Continue until entire strip is folded, turning excess dough under. Place the triangle on a buttered baking sheet and brush top with melted butter. Continue until filling is all used. Remaining phyllo should be tightly wrapped and frozen.

Bake triangles in a preheated 350° F. oven for about 15 minutes, until they are golden and puffy. Serve hot.

❖ Phyllo Triangles with Apples and ❖ Goat Cheese

Sheryl Benesch, Korbel Champagne Cellars
Accompanying champagne *Korbel Brut*

Makes 40 triangles

The tangy flavor of goat cheese is complemented by the tartness of apples. The cheese triangles may be prepared up twelve hours before serving and baked at the last minute. When working with the phyllo dough, keep the sheets covered until used, otherwise the dough dries out.

*1 cup chopped, peeled tart apple
  (approximately 1 large apple)
1/2 cup chopped pecans*

*5 1/2 ounces chèvre (goat cheese)
8 tablespoons butter, melted
10 sheets phyllo dough*

Toss the chopped apple with 1/4 cup of chopped pecans. Reserve other 1/4 cup of pecans to sprinkle over the top of the phyllo triangles.

    Lay 2 sheets of phyllo dough, one over the other, on a work surface. Cut the sheet with a knife down the shorter width into 8 equal strips. Brush cut edges with melted butter. One inch from the bottom of each strip, place 1 teaspoon *chèvre* and top it with 1 heaping teaspoon of the chopped apple mixture. Fold the phyllo and the stuffing up the length of the strip in a triangular form — as you would fold a flag, folding from corner to corner. Repeat the filling and folding with the other strips of phyllo in the same manner. Brush the triangles with melted butter. Place them on a cookie sheet and sprinkle with the remaining chopped pecans. Repeat the process with the remaining 8 sheets of phyllo. The triangles can be prepared to this point and kept covered overnight in the refrigerator.

    Just before you intend to serve them, bake the triangles on the middle shelf in a preheated 350° F. oven for about 8 minutes or until golden brown. Serve hot.

❖ Cheese Crisps ❖

Ruth Wiens, Mirassou Vineyards
Accompanying champagne *Mirassou Au Naturel*

Makes 50 to 60 slices

This recipe was originally developed as a means of using odds and ends of cheese. Cheeses other than Camembert or Brie that are of a similar consistency may be substituted. The dough can be frozen and baked later.

*8 ounces ripe Camembert or Brie,
    at room temperature
4 tablespoons unsalted butter, at
    room temperature
1 cup unbleached all-purpose flour*

*⅛ teaspoon cayenne pepper
½ teaspoon seasoning salt
Sesame or poppy seeds
Paprika (optional)*

Trim any rind from the cheese. Place all ingredients except sesame seeds and paprika in the bowl of a food processor. Process with metal blade until mixture forms a ball. Remove dough from the bowl and divide it into 2 equal portions. On a sheet of waxed paper, form each portion into a log 1 to 1½ inches in diameter. Roll the logs in sesame or poppy seeds and sprinkle with paprika if desired.

    Wrap logs well and refrigerate them overnight. (They may be frozen at this point.)

    Just before serving, remove logs from the refrigerator (frozen logs should be thawed but still firm) and cut them into ¼-inch slices. Place slices on ungreased baking sheet and bake in preheated 400° F. oven for 10 to 12 minutes. Serve hot.

❖ Cheese and Bacon Puffs ❖

Edna Tears, The Great Western Winery
Accompanying champagne *Great Western Blanc de Blanc*

Makes 30

Small pieces of toast or crackers are topped with a cheese and bacon mixture for canapés. The literal translation of the French word *canapé* is couch. Used as a culinary term, it denotes tasty bits of food resting on small pieces of bread or crackers.

*1 cup mayonnaise
½ cup grated medium-sharp
    Cheddar cheese
2 teaspoons prepared horseradish,
    drained of liquid*

*1 teaspoon semisweet sherry
½ cup cooked, crumbled bacon
Toast cut-outs or crisp crackers
Paprika*

Combine the mayonnaise, cheese, horseradish, sherry, and bacon. Fold the ingredients together, but do not beat or whip. Spread the mixture on toast cut-outs or crackers. Sprinkle with paprika and place on a baking sheet. Broil until bubbly and brown, about 3 to 4 minutes.

❖ Tartlets of Savory Cheese ❖

Martha Culbertson, John Culbertson Winery
Accompanying champagne *Culbertson Brut*

Makes 16 tiny tarts

Tartlets, or small tarts, date back to the sixteenth century. Appetizer tartlets are unusually small so that they may be eaten in no more than two bites. Ready-made puff pastry dough makes this recipe easy to prepare. Puff pastry dough is widely available in the freezer section of the grocery store.

1 pound puff pastry dough, purchased
¼ cup brut champagne
1 clove garlic
7 ounces California goat cheese, cut into small pieces

3½ ounces Gruyère cheese, shredded
1½ tablespoons unsalted butter
1½ tablespoons Dijon mustard
Dash of freshly ground pepper
Sprigs of fresh thyme or savory for garnish

Roll out the puff pastry into a sheet ½-inch thick. Cut into small circles to fit tiny tartlet pans. Prick the dough with a fork. Bake in preheated 375° F. oven for 5 to 7 minutes or until lightly browned.

Place the champagne and garlic in a small saucepan, bring to a boil, and reduce by half. Remove the garlic. Add the goat cheese and let it melt over low heat, stirring occasionally. Add the Gruyère cheese and butter, and stir over low heat until the cheeses are melted and well blended.

Remove from the heat and stir in the mustard and pepper. The mixture can be kept at this point in a warm *bain-marie* (water bath).

Put a spoonful of the cheese mixture in each warm pastry shell and garnish the tiny tarts with a fresh sprig of thyme or savory.

❖ Sausage Rolls ❖

Martha Culbertson, John Culbertson Winery
Accompanying champagne *Culbertson Brut*

Serves 8

These sausage rolls are best served with either a champagne mustard or a hot sweet mustard.

1 pound commercial puff pastry, from the freezer section of the grocery

12 small, skinless breakfast sausages
1 to 2 eggs, beaten

Roll half of the puff pastry into a rectangle measuring 3 by 12 inches. Place 6 of the sausages along the wide edge and roll up. (You might want to place the puff pastry on a piece of waxed paper and use the paper to help you roll.)

Cut the roll into 2-inch diagonal pieces. Place each piece, seam-side down, on an ungreased cookie sheet and brush with beaten egg.

Repeat with the other half of the puff pastry and the rest of the sausages. Bake sausage rolls in a preheated 375° F. oven for 8 to 10 minutes or until they are nicely browned.

❖ Pork Tenderloin with Oregano ❖

Tracy Wood Anderson, S. Anderson Vineyard
Accompanying champagne *S. Anderson Blanc de Noirs*

Serves 10

The pork tenderloin as well as the mayonnaise is prepared in advance. The Oregano Mayonnaise may also be used with other cold meats.

*2 cups loosely packed fresh
    oregano*
¹/₂ cup Italian parsley (optional)
4 medium cloves garlic
¹/₃ cup olive oil

¹/₂ teaspoon garlic salt
1¹/₂ pounds pork tenderloin
1 slim loaf French bread (baguette)
*Oregano Mayonnaise (recipe
    follows)*

In the bowl of a food processor combine the oregano, parsley, if desired, and garlic. Pulse a few times to combine ingredients. Add the oil and garlic salt and process to a smooth paste.

Lather the pork with the oregano mixture, pressing it into the meat. Place in a shallow roasting pan. Insert a meat thermometer into the meat and roast in a preheated 375° F. oven until the meat thermometer registers 160° F., about 1 to 1¹/₄ hours.

Let the pork cool, then slice ¹/₄-inch thick. Also slice the *baguette* ¹/₄-inch thick. Spread each slice with the Oregano Mayonnaise. Place a slice of pork on top of each bread slice and garnish with a rosette of Oregano Mayonnaise and a sprig of oregano.

OREGANO MAYONNAISE

3 egg yolks
2 tablespoons Dijon mustard
2 tablespoons lemon juice
¹/₄ teaspoon salt

¹/₈ teaspoon white pepper
2 cups vegetable oil
*1 tablespoon fresh, finely chopped
    oregano*

In the bowl of a food processor, mix the egg yolks, mustard, lemon juice, salt and white pepper. With machine running, add the oil in a slow thin stream. Add oregano and process 30 seconds longer. Adjust salt and lemon juice to taste.

HANNS KORNELL
CHAMPAGNE CELLARS

WINE AND CHAMPAGNE MAKING HAVE ALMOST ALWAYS been a part of Hanns Kornell's life. At the age of four, he helped clean bottles in his grandfather's winery in the Rhine Valley in Germany; at five he helped in his grandfather's vineyards; and during his school years he learned the art of tasting from his father who was an independent winery owner.

After graduating from school, Hanns studied enology at the University of Geisenheim. To gain practical experience, he worked in wineries in Italy and France, including the champagne cellars in Épernay. He also spent some time in England to learn bottling techniques. In 1938 Hanns was ready to take over the family winery business, but was prevented from doing so. Being Jewish, he was imprisoned in Dachau, the infamous Nazi concentration camp. After eight months of diplomatic appeals by the British Consul to Germany, Hanns was finally released and given forty-eight hours in which to leave the country. His father was not as fortunate and perished in the death camp at Theresenstadt.

In 1939 Hanns fled to England where he was almost interned as an unfriendly alien. To gain a legal status he had to appear before a judge. Fortunately, the judge was a wine fancier and granted him a work permit in exchange for information about an old bottle of port he possessed. For over a year, Hanns worked as a bottler in order to save enough money to come to the United States.

When he arrived in New York, Hanns could not find work and he decided to hitchhike across the country with only two dollars in his pocket. He came to the wine country of Northern California. After working for a while in a service station, Hanns got his first real job as the champagne maker at Fountain Grove vineyard in Santa Rosa, north of San Francisco. From that position he went east to become the champagne maker for the Gibson Wine Company in Cincinnati and Kentucky. Hanns later moved to St. Louis where he made Cook's Imperial Champagne for the American Wine Company.

In 1952, Hanns took his savings and a small loan from a friend and drove back to California to establish his own champagne business. He leased a small winery in Sonoma for a hundred dollars a month. At night Hanns blended the *cuvées*, did the riddling, and bottled his champagnes. By day he sold his champagnes from a small panel truck to wine stores, restaurants, hotels, and the cruise lines in the San Francisco Bay Area. "It was a hand-to-mouth existence and for the first two years I lived on six hundred dollars a year," he recalls.

By 1958 he had accumulated an inventory of five thousand bottles and enough savings to purchase the Larkmead Cellars in the Napa Valley. The winery had been built in 1884 on property originally owned by Lillie Hitchcock Coit, an enthusiastic supporter of the San Francisco Fire Department and the namesake of Coit Tower in that city. The Larkmead winery changed hands several times until, in the early 1890s, the Saliminas, a well-known winery family in the valley, purchased the property. They added stone cellars to the winery and built a beautiful residence behind it. The cellars are still part of Hanns Kornell Champagne Cellars and have been placed on the National Register of Historic Places. The residence now serves as the administrative office of the winery.

In the same year that Hanns Kornell purchased the winery, he married Marilouise Rossini, the granddaughter of a Napa Valley wine pioneer. She had a varied career in music and education, but upon her marriage joined her husband in the operation of the winery.

Each year his champagne production grew, but Hanns Kornell would not increase production to the extent that he was sacrificing quality for quantity. Hanns has continuously refused to take in any investors for the purpose of expansion, since he wants to keep control of his family winery. "You don't sell diamonds by the carload," he says.

The Kornell children, Paula and Peter, have joined the winery. Paula, who received a degree in marketing from the University of the Pacific, became vice-president of marketing in 1982. Peter received a degree in business administration from Fresno State University and has joined his father in the winemaking.

Hanns Kornell is an unusual champagne vintner. He does not own any vineyards and he does not make his base wines. "If your own grapes turn out bad, which can happen even in California, or your wine is faulty, you're stuck with it," he says. Hanns has long-term contracts with growers and wineries and uses their base wines to make the blends for his champagne *cuvées*. It takes several weeks of tasting and blending to determine the *cuvée* for each of the Kornell champagnes.

Hanns does not limit his *cuvées* to the Pinot Chardonnay and Pinot Noir grapes of the classic French champagnes. The German grape, Johannisberg Riesling, provides the *cuvée* for the Sehr Trocken, which is the driest of the Kornell champagnes with less than one-half of one percent residual sugar. Hanns also uses such unconventional grapes as Chenin Blanc and Muscat of Alexandria for his *cuvées*. The deep red sparkling burgundy known as Rouge, however, is made entirely from Pinot Noir. Character Champagne, named after a poster created for the winery by Stephen Haines Hall, a well-known West Coast artist, is a fruity and young-of-spirit champagne made primarily from Chenin Blanc grapes.

After fermentation the champagne is aged for between two and five years. All of the riddling is done by hand. "We tried the gyropallets, but they did not work for our *cuvées*," says Marilouise Kornell. A blend of cognac and sugar syrup is used for the *dosage*. The amount of sugar depends on the sweetness of the champagne desired.

The figures on the Kornell label have been used on the family wines for centuries. This symbol of two Israelites carrying a huge cluster of grapes on a branch between them comes from a story in the Bible told in the thirteenth chapter of the Book of Numbers. As the story goes, the Israelites, after a long journey across the wilderness, came to Canaan, the promised land. Instructed by God, Moses sent out teams of two distinguished men from each of the tribes to see what they could find. One of the teams brought back huge delicious grapes from this fruitful new land. The story has a special meaning for Hanns Kornell. The two men of Canaan continue to be a symbol of a new and joyful promised land — America — where he had the opportunity to start life anew in his chosen profession of champagne making.

Hanns Kornell Champagne Cellars produces eight champagnes: dry, off-dry, semidry, and a dessert champagne with 2 percent residual sugar:

Sehr Trocken — Johannisberg Riesling; dry
Blanc de Noirs — 100 percent Pinot Noir
Blanc de Blancs — 100 percent Chardonnay
Brut — Pinot Blanc
Extra Dry — Chenin Blanc
Muscat Alexandria — Muscat of Alexandria
Character — primarily Chenin Blanc
Rouge — 100 percent Pinot Noir; a sparkling burgundy

Culinary Director: **Marilouise Kornell**

Marilouise Kornell is a native Californian. Her grandfather was one of the earliest winemakers to settle in the Napa Valley and his vineyards were some of the first on the east side of the valley. Marilouise grew up appreciating good wines and Swiss-Italian family cooking.

From an early age, Marilouise was interested in music and had pursued a singing career. Her maternal grandfather was one of the founding members of the San Francisco Symphony Orchestra. She performed professionally with both the San Francisco Symphony and the San Francisco Opera. Marilouise toured Europe, giving recitals in France, Italy, and Switzerland. At about the same time, she was deeply involved in establishing the first program in California for physically impaired students. Marilouise gave up her singing career for this educational program and, when she married Hanns Kornell, she devoted her energies to the winery.

Not only did Marilouise Kornell work in the administration of the winery, but also she created foods to complement the Hanns Kornell champagnes. It is her Swiss-Italian food background and some of Hanns's German food preferences, combined with American influences, that enabled her to create recipes that blend well with the Kornell California champagnes. The Kornells' love of international travel has added to Marilouise's culinary repertoire. On these travels, however, she is never too busy to attend a recital, see an opera, or do what she can to show her support for the arts that she loves.

Hanns Kornell Champagne Cellars
1091 Larkmead Lane
St. Helena, California 94574
(707) 963-1237

Visits: daily, 10:00 A.M. to 4:30 P.M.
Principal: Hanns J. Kornell
Champagnes produced: Sehr Trocken, Blanc de Blancs, Brut, Extra Dry, Muscat
  Alexandria, Character, Blanc de Noirs, and Rouge
1988 champagne production: 80,000 cases

FIRST COURSES

FIRST COURSES, ALSO KNOWN AS APPETIZERS, are served at the table. Dishes for a first course range from meat, seafood, and pastas, to salads and vegetable preparations. First courses are a part of almost every national cuisine — as *antipasti* in Italy, *smörgåsbord* in Scandinavia, *zakuska* in Russia and Eastern Europe, *vorspeisen* in Germany, and *hors-d'œuvres* in France.

The preparation of the first course gives the host or hostess a chance to combine several of his or her cooking talents into such dishes as pâtés, terrines, quenelles, puff pastry creations, soufflés, and various other out-of-the-ordinary creations. Many first courses reflect an international influence, either in the dish itself, or in the seasonings used. A great number of appetizer dishes, such as the Spicy Chard and Smoked Mussel Roulade in this section, offer a combination of ingredients that are not typically used in everyday cooking.

Research has shown that first courses in colonial days were substantial. In Virginia, for instance, dinner consisted of three courses — first, second, and dessert. Each of the first two courses was composed of two fewer dishes than the number of diners. For example, if there were ten diners at the table, eight dishes would be served. A typical first course might have consisted of soup, ham, mutton, a game pie, one or two vegetable puddings, stewed vegetables, pickles, relishes, and preserves. These would all have been placed on the table at the same time and diners could chose some of whatever they fancied. The second course, similarly served, would consist of entirely different dishes with the soup usually being replaced by fish. The dessert course, too, had numerous dishes.

Today, first courses are much smaller and many dinner parties consist of three or four courses served sequentially. The soup, particularly if it is a clear soup, may precede the first course. The order of service is a matter of individual preference.

In this section is a range of first courses including pâtés, salads, pastas, cheese tarts, mushroom timbales and seafood dishes. Many may be prepared in advance. All have been especially designed to complement champagne.

❖ Mushroom Tarts ❖

Karen Mack, Chateau Ste. Michelle
Accompanying champagne *Domaine Ste. Michelle Blanc de Noir*

Serves 12

Blanched mushrooms and asparagus decorate large puff pastry squares that have been filled with herb mayonnaise and a mushroom spread. Frozen puff pastry dough simplifies the preparation of these tarts.

PUFF PASTRY SQUARES

1 package ($17^{1}/4$ ounces; 2 sheets)
puff pastry

1 egg yolk
1 teaspoon water

Thaw the puff pastry sheets according to the package directions and roll each sheet into a $12^{1}/2$ inch square about $1/8$-inch thick. Whisk together the egg yolk and water and brush the pastry with the mixture. Fold over $1/4$ inch of the pastry all the way around to form a rim. Brush the edges again. Place the two tart shells on an ungreased baking sheet and prick the bottom of each shell thoroughly. Bake in a preheated 400° F. oven for 12 to 15 minutes until golden brown. Cool slightly, remove shells from the sheet, and cool completely before filling.

HERB MAYONNAISE

$1/4$ cup mayonnaise
1 tablespoon minced fresh
rosemary

1 tablespoon minced fresh thyme
1 tablespoon minced parsley

Combine all of the ingredients and stir until well blended.

MUSHROOM SPREAD

2 tablespoons unsalted butter
1 green onion, chopped
$1^{1}/2$ cups chopped fresh mushrooms

$1/4$ cup blanc de noir sparkling wine
$1/2$ teaspoon fresh lemon juice

Melt the butter in a sauté pan over medium heat. Add the onion and mushrooms and sauté for 7 to 8 minutes. Place the mixture in the bowl of a food processor and add the sparkling wine and lemon juice. Process until well blended.

GARNISH

8 large mushrooms, washed,
    trimmed, and sliced evenly
8 thin asparagus spears, washed
    and peeled, if necessary

1 tablespoon fresh lemon juice
1 cup blanc de noir sparkling wine

Place the mushrooms, asparagus, lemon juice, and sparkling wine in a saucepan, bring to a simmer, and simmer for 3 to 4 minutes, cooking until the asparagus is crisp-tender. Remove from heat and drain the vegetables well. Slice the asparagus into 1-inch pieces.

To assemble the tarts, pipe alternate strips of herb mayonnaise and mushroom spread diagonally across the cool tart shells. Place the sliced asparagus on the herb strips and the sliced mushrooms on the mushroom spread stripe. Make the glaze (recipe follows) and immediately spoon over the garnished tarts. Cool tarts to room temperature and then chill them until serving time. To serve, cut into squares using a long sharp knife, pressing down to make clean cuts. Do not use a sawing motion.

TART GLAZE

1 teaspoon firmly packed
    cornstarch

⅓ cup blanc de noir sparkling wine

Whisk together the cornstarch and sparkling wine in a small saucepan over medium heat until the mixture boils, stirring constantly. Immediately spoon over the assembled tarts.

❖ Gratin of Brie and ❖ Wild Mushrooms

Frederick Horton, Wente Bros. Sparkling Wine Cellars
Accompanying champagne *Wente Bros. Brut*

Serves 4

Gratin is a term used to describe a thin, golden-brown crust on the surface of a dish. The crust, usually of cheese or bread crumbs, is formed when the dish is placed either under a broiler or in a very hot oven. In this dish the gratin is formed by the Brie cheese.

*4 ounces golden chanterelle
    mushrooms*
*4 ounces orange porcini
    mushrooms*
4 ounces shiitake mushrooms
6 ounces Brie cheese, rind removed

3 tablespoons butter
1 tablespoon minced shallots
1 cup whipping cream
1/2 cup brut sparkling wine

Wash, towel dry, and slice the mushrooms. Cut the Brie into 12 slices. Divide the mushrooms and cheese evenly among into 4 ovenproof bowls.

In a sauté pan melt the butter over medium heat. Add the shallots and sauté until they are transparent; do not brown them. Add the cream and sparkling wine to the pan, reduce by two-thirds, and pour over the mushrooms. Bake for 30 minutes in a preheated 350° F. oven. Serve hot.

❖ Blue Cheese Mold ❖

Karen Mack, Chateau Ste. Michelle
Accompanying champagne *Domaine Ste. Michelle Blanc de Noir*

Serves 8

Stilton, a soft blue-veined cheese, is considered by many to be the "king of English cheeses." Although not made in the village of Stilton, it was first produced in Leicestershire, England, and supplied to the Bell Inn at Stilton, hence the name. The blue veins are a penicillin mold that has been allowed to grow in the cheese. This same mold also grows in Roquefort, Gorgonzola, and Danish Blue. Both Stilton and Danish Blue are rich and creamy cheeses and combine well with other ingredients, as they do in this Cheese Mold.

*8 ounces cream cheese, at room
    temperature*
*2 tablespoons blanc de noir
    sparkling wine*

*8 ounces Stilton or Danish Blue
    cheese*
1/3 cup coarsely chopped walnuts

In a bowl combine the cream cheese and the sparkling wine and beat until smooth. Crumble in the blue cheese and beat gently with a fork until well blended. The mixture will still be slightly lumpy. Spoon the cheese mixture into a 6-inch springform pan and chill until well set, about 2 hours.

Twenty minutes before serving, toast the walnuts on a baking sheet for 10 minutes in a preheated 350° F. oven. Allow them to cool. Unmold the cheese and garnish it with the walnuts. Slice the Cheese Mold into individual wedges and serve with slices of *baguette*.

❖ Brie Baked in Phyllo ❖

Marilouise Kornell, Hanns Kornell Champagne Cellars
Accompanying champagne *Hanns Kornell Sehr Trocken or Extra Dry*

Serves 10 to 12

Cheese has been made by French farmers in Brie since the eighth century. Brie, a flat cheese with a white and brown outer crust and a creamy yellow interior, has been likened by many poets to the moon. The white powdery crust of the cheese is caused by the mold, *Pencillium candidum*, which has been sprinkled over the cheese. To ripen Brie, the cheese is sprinkled with mold, then placed on straw mats in a controlled temperature for four months, during which time the whitish outer crust is formed. Depending on its ripeness, Brie can vary from firm and almost chalky, to creamy, to butter-gold and very soft. The apricot flavor in this phyllo-encased Brie complements the slightly fruity taste of the cheese.

¼ cup apricot chutney
1 wheel (2 pounds) Brie cheese
10 sheets frozen phyllo dough, thawed

16 tablespoons (2 sticks) butter, melted
Red and green grapes, and slices of apples and pears, for garnish

Leave the rind on the cheese and spread the apricot chutney on top of the Brie. Keeping the unused phyllo sheets covered with a damp cloth, wrap the cheese in the phyllo dough, one sheet at a time, brushing each sheet with melted butter. Keep turning the cheese as it is being wrapped to distribute the dough evenly. Continue wrapping and brushing with butter until all of the sheets of dough have been used. Cover the cheese and refrigerate until almost ready to serve.

Twenty-five minutes before serving, place the cheese in a shallow baking pan and bake it in a preheated 425° F. oven for 8 to 12 minutes or until golden brown. Remove from oven and let the cheese stand for 10 minutes. Place on a platter and garnish with grapes, and apple and pear slices. Serve wedges of cheese with pieces of fruit.

❖ Tiny Smoked Salmon Tarts ❖

Martha Culbertson, John Culbertson Winery
Accompanying champagne *Culbertson Brut Rosé*

Serves 6 to 8; makes 16 two-inch tarts

These miniature quiches are flavored with smoked salmon and dill. The recipe may also be used for a 10-inch tart pan, in which case the baking time should be increased to 25 to 30 minutes.

PASTRY

1³/₄ cups all-purpose flour
¹/₄ teaspoon salt

8 tablespoons (1 stick) butter
¹/₄ cup cold water

Place the flour, salt, and butter in the bowl of a food processor. Process until the dough resembles meal. (A pastry cutter may be used instead of the food processor.) Add water and process until the dough forms a ball on the blade. Roll the dough out ¹/₄-inch thick and cut into 2-inch rounds. Line miniature tart pans with the dough rounds.

FILLING

4 ounces smoked salmon
5 ounces Gruyère cheese, shredded finely
4 eggs, beaten

1¹/₂ cups milk
¹/₂ cup whipping cream
¹/₄ teaspoon salt
¹/₄ teaspoon pepper

Blot the smoked salmon slices with a paper towel to remove excess moisture and then cut the slices into 1-inch slivers. Divide the slivered salmon among the tart shells and sprinkle the cheese over each. Mix the eggs, milk, and cream with the salt and pepper and pour into each tart shell. Bake the tarts (place individual tart pans on a baking sheet) in a preheated 400° F. oven for about 15 minutes. Keep checking during baking since the tarts are small and take much less time than would a larger tart.

❖ Eggplant Crêpes ❖

Sheryl Benesch, Korbel Champagne Cellars
Accompanying champagne *Korbel Brut*

Serves 8

The eggplant crêpes may be prepared a few hours ahead of serving time and stored in the refrigerator. If they are refrigerated, increase the baking time by 5 to 10 minutes. This dish may also be used as an accompaniment to a main course such as veal or chicken prepared with an Italian accent.

CRÊPES

2 large eggplants
Salt
Olive oil

4 ounces Mozzarella cheese, thinly
sliced

Cut the ends off of the eggplants and cut into 1/8-inch slices from top to bottom. Discard the first and last slice. Sprinkle each slice lightly with salt, lay the eggplant on a towel, and cover with another towel to absorb the moisture. Weight this down with a cutting board or books for 30 minutes. Then place the eggplant slices on a cookie sheet, brush lightly with olive oil, and broil until golden brown, about 2 to 4 minutes.

Lay the broiled side of the eggplant slices down on a work surface and spoon approximately 3 tablespoons of filling (recipe follows) down one of the longer sides of the eggplant. Roll up the crêpe and place it seam-side down in a long flat casserole dish. Place a small slice of Mozzarella cheese diagonally across each rolled-up crêpe. Bake in a preheated 350° F. oven for 15 to 20 minutes (20 to 25 minutes if crêpes have been refrigerated).

FILLING

2 cups ricotta cheese
1 cup fresh Pesto (recipe follows)
*   or purchased pesto*
2 egg yolks

1/4 teaspoon nutmeg
1/4 teaspoon white pepper
1/2 teaspoon dry oregano leaves

Combine all filling ingredients.

PESTO

4 cups packed fresh basil leaves
1/3 cup olive oil

8 cloves garlic
1 cup grated Parmesan cheese

Blend the basil, oil, and garlic in a food processor until smooth. Add the cheese. Any leftover pesto may be frozen and used in other dishes.

❖ Escargots in Roquefort Cream ❖

Steve Wenger, Biltmore Estate
Accompanying champagne *Biltmore Estate Brut*

Serves 6

Snails have been a gourmet food since Roman times, particularly in France and Italy. In France vineyard snails are the most prized. Snails have very little taste and serve as a vehicle for highly flavored sauces, usually of garlic and butter. Canned snails imported from France are widely available in the United States. In recent years commercial producers of snails have emerged in America, particularly in California. This recipe for escargots, with Roquefort cheese in the sauce, does reflect the influence of France.

36 escargots   *Roquefort Cream (recipe follows)*

Place 6 escargots in each of 6 individual ovenproof ramekins. Pour an equal amount of the Roquefort Cream over each serving. Broil until bubbly and golden and serve immediately.

ROQUEFORT CREAM
2/3 cup whipping cream
6 ounces Roquefort cheese

*2 teaspoons cornstarch dissolved
in 2 tablespoons water*

In a small saucepan combine the cream and cornstarch. Bring to a boil over medium-high heat, whisking until thickened. Reduce the heat and simmer for a few minutes. Add the Roquefort cheese, whisking until smooth. Remove the sauce from the heat.

❖ Chicken Liver Pâté ❖

Marilouise Kornell, Hanns Kornell Champagne Cellars
Accompanying champagne *Hanns Kornell Blanc de Blancs*

Serves 6 to 8

The most famous pâté is the *pâté de foie gras* — goose liver pâté. Chicken livers are often substituted in home cookery since goose livers are not readily available. The oregano in this recipe adds an interesting flavor.

4 tablespoons butter
1 large onion, thinly sliced
1 pound chicken livers
2 cloves garlic, chopped
1/2 teaspoon oregano

*Salt and freshly ground pepper, to
taste*
1 to 2 tablespoons brandy
Clarified butter, for sealing

Melt the butter over medium heat in a sauté pan. Add the onion and sauté until golden. Add the livers and garlic, and sauté lightly until cooked but not brown or dried. Add the oregano and salt and pepper. Place the liver mixture in a food processor and process until smooth. Remove from processor and add the brandy to smooth out the mixture. Pack into a small bowl and top with clarified butter. Chill in the refrigerator for at least 4 hours before serving.

To serve, place rounded mounds the size of a scoop of ice cream on lettuce leaves and accompany with toast points.

❖ Chicken Quenelles with ❖ Roquefort Sauce

Tracy Wood Anderson, S. Anderson Vineyard
Accompanying champagne *S. Anderson Brut*

Serves 4 to 6

A wonderful first course, these light chicken quenelles are served with a basic hollandaise sauce that has been enriched with Roquefort cheese.

QUENELLES

*1 pound boneless chicken breast,
 skin removed*
1 egg white
3 cups whipping cream
1½ teaspoons salt

1 quart chicken broth
Roquefort Sauce (recipe follows)
Parsley, for garnish
*½ cup toasted walnut halves, for
 garnish*

In making the quenelles, start with cold ingredients and keep the mixture as cold as possible. Cut the chicken into small pieces and process with the egg white in a food processor until smooth. Add the cream and mix only enough to blend. Do not overmix or the mixture will break down. Add salt to taste.

Have the chicken broth hot and barely simmering. Shape the chicken mixture with a soup spoon into quenelles and drop carefully into the simmering broth. Cook about 5 minutes, turning the quenelles carefully. Drain the quenelles on paper towels and keep them warm.

To serve, place 2 quenelles on small individual plates and spoon some Roquefort Sauce over each quenelle. Garnish with parsley and toasted walnut halves.

ROQUEFORT SAUCE

3 egg yolks
2 tablespoons lemon juice
1 tablespoon hot water
*16 tablespoons (2 sticks) melted
 butter*

*4 to 6 tablespoons whipping
 cream, whipped*
*3 tablespoons crumbled Roquefort
 cheese*
Salt, to taste

Combine the egg yolks, lemon juice, and water in the top of a double boiler. Whisk over simmering water, stirring constantly until the mixture is thick, but not lumpy. Add the butter in a slow stream, whisking constantly. The mixture should be the consistency of a thick hollandaise sauce. Carefully fold in the whipped cream and then the crumbled Roquefort cheese. Add salt to taste.

❖ Veal and Ham Pâté en Croute ❖

Steve Wenger, Biltmore Estate
Accompanying champagne *Biltmore Estate Brut*

Serves 6 to 8

In French the word *pâté* is used like our word *pie*. This pâté is made in the traditional French style and is a beautiful presentation. It has not only a pastry crust, but also an aspic veil encasing the filling. A pâté pan is essential for this recipe. Serve the pâté with a homemade mayonnaise to which fresh dill has been added.

2 ounces lean veal, cut into strips
2 ounces lean ham, cut into strips
½ cup dry red wine
½ cup sliced carrots
¼ cup sliced onions
5 peppercorns
¼ teaspoon poultry seasoning
1 bay leaf
Pastry dough for a 2-crust pie
1½ pounds veal, ground fine

4 strips bacon, diced
1 tablespoon fresh chopped parsley
1 shallot, chopped fine
¼ teaspoon salt
3 tablespoons whipping cream
1 large egg
½ cup shelled pistachio nuts
1 egg beaten with 1 teaspoon water to make an egg wash
Aspic (recipe follows)

In a bowl mix together the veal and ham strips, wine, carrots, onions, peppercorns, poultry seasoning, and bay leaf. Marinate in the refrigerator overnight.

Grease an 8½-inch pâté pan. Roll the pastry to ⅛-inch thickness and line the sides and bottom of the pan. Reserve the remainder of the pastry to make the top crust.

In a bowl mix together the ground veal, diced bacon, parsley, shallot, salt, cream, and egg. Spread one-third of the mixture in the pastry-lined pâté pan. Remove veal and ham strips from the marinade and dry them on paper towels. Press alternating rows of veal and ham strips (2 rows of each) into the mixture. Place pistachios between each row of meat. Cover with another one-third of the mixture and repeat the process with the veal and ham strips and pistachios. Finish with the final third of the veal mixture. Cover with the top crust and seal with egg wash.

Insert two piping tips, points down, to form vents in the top pastry crust. These will enable steam to escape and will later be used to pour the aspic mixture into the pâté. Bake pâté in a preheated 350° F. oven for about 1 hour and 20 minutes. The internal temperature of the pâté should be 170° F. Cool the pâté to room temperature and refrigerate for several hours. Then pour the liquid aspic into the pâté through the piping-tip vents. Refrigerate the pâté overnight before removing it from the pan. Slice and serve cold.

ASPIC

1 tablespoon (1 envelope) plain gelatin

3 tablespoons white wine
1 can (14 ½ ounces) beef consommé

Soften the gelatin in cold wine. Bring the consommé to a boil and add the wine mixture. Cool several minutes before using.

❖ Vineyard Pâté ❖

Frederick Horton, Wente Bros. Sparkling Wine Cellars
Accompanying champagne *Wente Bros. Brut*

Serves 10 to 12

The word *pâté* also refers to a ground meat filling enclosed in strips of fat or bacon, instead of a pastry crust, and baked in the oven. This Vineyard Pâté uses a combination of meats and seasonings. It will keep about a week in the refrigerator.

1 medium onion, chopped
4 bay leaves
1 tablespoon vegetable oil
2¹/₂ pounds pork butt
³/₄ pound veal
¹/₄ pound ham
¹/₄ pound pork backfat
3 shallots
2 garlic cloves
¹/₂ teaspoon thyme
¹/₄ teaspoon sage
1 teaspoon rosemary

¹/₈ teaspoon nutmeg
2 teaspoons salt
1 teaspoon black pepper
¹/₂ cup dry red wine
¹/₂ cup brandy
1 egg
3 tablespoons minced parsley
1 sheet caul fat for lining the
   terrine (strips of bacon may
   be substituted)
3 bay leaves

Sauté the onion and 1 bay leaf in the tablespoon of oil just until the onion is transparent. Set aside to cool. After the onions have cooled grind them with the pork, veal, ham, backfat, shallots, and garlic. (Use a meat grinder or grind in small batches in a food processor.) Add the seasonings, wine, brandy, egg, and parsley and mix well.

Line a 2-quart terrine or loaf pan with the caul fat or bacon strips. Fill with the ground meat, packing it down to eliminate air pockets. Place the 3 remaining bay leaves on the top and enclose with caul fat or bacon. Trim off excess fat and tuck in the ends. Refrigerate overnight. Remove from the refrigerator 1 hour before baking.

Place the pâté in a baking dish filled with warm water to reach half-way up the sides of the pâté pan. Bake in a preheated 325° F. oven for 1³/₄ hours or until an instant-reading meat thermometer registers 165° F. Remove the pâté from the oven, cool it to room temperature, and refrigerate it overnight to allow flavors to blend.

To serve, unmold the pâté, cut into ¹/₄-inch thick slices, and accompany with Dijon mustard, *cornichons*, and slices of French bread.

❖ Vitello Tonnato ❖

Marilouise Kornell, Hanns Kornell Champagne Cellars
Accompanying champagne *Hanns Kornell Brut*

Serves 8

Vitello tonnato, cold veal with a tuna sauce, is a well-known Italian dish of the Lombardy and Piedmont regions. For this recipe, use a tender piece of veal and, in cooking, only enough water to cover otherwise the veal will be dry. To retain the meat's juiciness do not add salt to the cooking water and allow the veal to cool in its own broth. A simple homemade mayonnaise is the best base for the sauce.

2 pounds boned leg of veal, fat and tendons removed, rolled, and firmly tied
2 medium carrots, cut into 1-inch pieces
2 stalks celery, cut into 1-inch pieces

1 medium yellow onion, sliced
4 sprigs parsley
1 bay leaf
Tuna Sauce (recipe follows)
Lemon slices, capers, olives, and parsley sprigs, for garnish

Place the veal, carrots, celery, onion, parsley, and bay leaf in a pan. Add just enough water to cover the meat and remove the meat. Cover the pan, bring the water and vegetables to a boil, add the meat, and bring gently to a boil again. Simmer, covered, very gently for 2 hours. Remove the pan from the heat and allow the meat to cool in its broth.

When the meat is quite cold, remove the strings and cut into thin, uniform slices. Cover the bottom of a small serving platter with some of the Tuna Sauce, arrange the slices of veal over this in a single layer, edge to edge. Cover the layer with sauce, place another layer of veal over this, and cover again with sauce. Save enough sauce to cover the top layer just before serving.

Refrigerate for 24 hours covered with plastic wrap. Before serving, cover the top of the veal with the remaining Tuna Sauce and garnish with lemon slices, capers, olives, and parsley sprigs.

TUNA SAUCE

1 can (7 ounces) Italian tuna in olive oil
4 anchovy fillets
1 cup olive oil

3 tablespoons lemon juice
3 tablespoons capers
1/2 to 1 cup mayonnaise

In a food processor, mix the tuna, anchovies, olive oil, lemon juice, and capers until the mixture is a creamy consistency. Blend the tuna mixture into enough mayonnaise to make a sauce that is easily spread, but is not runny.

❖ Chicken Terrine ❖

Steve Wenger, Biltmore Estate
Accompanying champagne *Biltmore Estate Brut*

Serves 6 to 8; approximately 12 slices

Terrine, a word derived from the Latin *terra*, meaning earth, was originally the name for an earthenware cooking dish in which meat, fish, or vegetables were cooked. Pâtés were also cooked in terrines. The term eventually was extended to designate the food cooked in such dishes. Terrines, although baked, are eaten cold. In this terrine, chicken and vegetables are combined for a first course that appeals to the eye as well as the palate.

*3 pounds skinless boned chicken
    breasts, ground*
1/2 cup whipping cream
1/4 cup Chardonnay wine
1 teaspoon salt
1 teaspoon ground white pepper

1 teaspoon powdered thyme
*1 large carrot, peeled, cut into
    1/4-inch sticks and blanched*
*4 to 6 stems asparagus, cleaned,
    trimmed, and blanched*

Thoroughly combine the ground chicken, cream, Chardonnay, salt, pepper and thyme. If using a food processor, do this in two batches and frequently scrape the bowl to ensure an even mix. (The chicken may also be ground in the food processor in several batches.)

Place one-third of the mixture in the bottom of a greased loaf pan, spreading evenly. Taking care not to arrange the vegetables too close to the edge, place 3 rows of carrot sticks lengthwise on the chicken, pressing them gently into the mixture. Spread another third of the chicken mixture over the carrots, being careful not to displace them. Place 3 rows of asparagus lengthwise, cutting them to fit if necessary, and pressing them gently into the mixture. Carefully spread the last of the chicken mixture over the asparagus.

Place the loaf pan in a water bath *(bain-marie)* and bake in a preheated 325° F. oven for about 1 hour and 30 minutes; internal temperature should be about 170° F. Bring the terrine to room temperature, then chill overnight before slicing.

❖ Watercress, Endive and ❖ Goat Cheese Salad

Frederick Horton, Wente Bros. Sparkling Wine Cellars
Accompanying champagne *Wente Bros. Brut*

Serves 4

Watercress, so named because it grows in cold running water, has since Greek and Roman times been a favorite salad ingredient. Until the seventeenth century, watercress was also used for medicinal purposes and it was believed that eating watercress was like taking a drink from the fountain of youth. Even today, watercress is considered a health food because of its high vitamin and iron content. The pungent flavor of watercress and the slight bitterness of Belgian endive are a pleasing combination in this salad.

2 heads Belgian endive
2 bunches watercress
6 ounces white goat cheese

16 Nicoise olives
¼ cup toasted pine nuts

DRESSING

Juice and zest of 1 lemon
2 tablespoons walnut oil
½ cup peanut oil

1½ teaspoons fresh thyme, chopped
Salt and pepper, to taste

Wash the endive and watercress.

Whisk the salad dressing ingredients together and toss with the endive and watercress. Arrange the mixture on 4 individual plates. Garnish each plate with the goat cheese, olives, and pine nuts.

❖ Warm Goat Cheese Salad ❖ with Seasonal Greens

Martha Culbertson, John Culbertson Winery
Accompanying champagne *Culbertson Brut*

Serves 6

Slices of small rounds of goat cheese are dipped in olive oil and fresh bread crumbs, baked to a golden-brown, and served on a bed of seasonal greens. The *chabis* called for in this recipe are cylinders of cheese, packaged when the cheese is less than a week old, and weighing five ounces each. They have a fresh, mild taste.

*2 California goat cheese chabis
  (about 5 ounces each), each
  chabis sliced into 3 pieces
  horizontally*
¹/₂ cup olive oil
1 cup fresh bread crumbs
*6 bunches watercress, cleaned, and
  leaves removed from the stems*

*4 heads Butter lettuce, washed,
  dried, and torn into bite-sized
  pieces*
*2 cups large sprouts, such as
  sunflower or clover seed*
Vinaigrette (recipe follows)

Dip the slices of goat cheese in the olive oil and then roll them in the bread crumbs until well covered. Place the cheese slices on a baking sheet and refrigerate until ready to serve.

Put the goat cheese into a preheated 400° F. oven for 3 to 5 minutes or until lightly browned.

Toss the lettuce, watercress and sprouts with the Vinaigrette and place the greens on individual plates. Top with warm goat cheese slices.

VINAIGRETTE

2 teaspoons Dijon mustard
2 teaspoons fresh minced tarragon
2 tablespoons brut rosé champagne
2 egg yolks

¹/₄ teaspoon salt
Ground pepper, to taste
2 cups salad oil, such as safflower

Whisk all of the ingredients together, except the oil. Slowly add the oil in a stream, whisking constantly.

❖ Flaked Salmon in Lettuce Leaves ❖

Jamie Davies, Schramsberg Vineyards and Cellars
Accompanying champagne *Schramsberg Blanc de Noirs*

Serves 6

Poached salmon provides a tangy filling for lettuce cups that are rolled and eaten as finger food. As a first course several of the lettuce cups may be served on individual plates.

1 head Iceberg lettuce
2 cups water
Juice of 1/2 lemon
5 cracked peppercorns
3 green onions, chopped
1 salmon steak (about 8 ounces)
1 egg boiled for 5 minutes, cooled,
*   and peeled*

1/2 cucumber, finely chopped
1/4 cup cornichons, or dill pickle,
*   chopped*
1 tablespoon pistachios, coarsely
*   chopped*
1 tablespoon mayonnaise
Red pepper flakes, to taste
1 tablespoon chopped cilantro

Remove the core from the lettuce and separate the leaves. Place small cup-shaped leaves in ice water to crisp.

In a medium saucepan, heat the water with the lemon juice, green onions, and peppercorns. Simmer for 2 to 3 minutes and add the salmon. Simmer for 2 minutes and remove from the heat. Cover and let the fish stand for 5 minutes. Remove the salmon from the water, drain it, and discard the skin and bones.

Flake the salmon into a bowl. Chop the egg (the yolk will be runny) and add to the salmon along with the rest of the ingredients. Arrange drained lettuce leaves in a bowl or on individual plates. Spoon the salmon mixture into the lettuce cups, roll, and eat with the fingers.

❖ Lettuce Packages ❖

Martha Culbertson, John Culbertson Winery
Accompanying champagne *Culbertson Blanc de Noir*

Serves 8

Several Chinese cooking classes taught by Gerrie Storm gave Martha Culbertson the idea for these lettuce packages. The filling, which includes not only the usual pork, but also smoked oysters, is placed on top of lettuce leaves and crisp bean-thread noodles. These Lettuce Packages may also be served for a light lunch.

2 heads Boston lettuce
1 cup safflower oil
1 ounce bean-thread noodles
⅓ cup walnuts
1 teaspoon minced garlic
2 green onions, cut into pea-sized pieces
12 ounces ground pork

1 can (3¾ ounces) smoked oysters, drained and chopped
1 cup water chestnuts, chopped into pea-sized pieces
1 cup coarsely chopped fresh bean sprouts
2 teaspoons cornstarch mixed with 1 tablespoon water

SAUCE

1 tablespoon thin soy sauce
2 tablespoons oyster-flavored sauce
¼ teaspoon sugar

¼ teaspoon cayenne pepper
1 teaspoon pale dry sherry or Chinese rice wine
1 teaspoon sesame seed oil

Detach the lettuce leaves, wash and dry them, and arrange in a circle around the edge of a large serving platter.

Heat the safflower oil in a wok and loosen the bean-thread noodles by pulling them apart. When the oil is hot enough for frying, plunge the noodles into the oil. Turn the noodle nest over and fry on the other side, then remove, and drain on paper towels.

Using the same oil, fry the walnuts, and drain them on paper towels. Crush the walnuts into small pieces.

Slightly break the noodles into pieces and put them in the center of the platter.

Mix together all of the sauce ingredients and set aside.

Remove all except 2 tablespoons of oil from the wok. Reheat the oil, then slightly brown the garlic and green onions. Add the ground pork and stir-fry until the pork is no longer pink. Add the oysters and stir-fry for another minute. Add the water chestnuts and bean sprouts. Swirl in the sauce mixture and mix well. Stir in the cornstarch mixture and cook for 1 minute.

Place the pork mixture over the noodles on the platter and then top with the walnuts.

To eat, put 2 or 3 spoonfuls of meat with the noodles in the center of a piece of Boston lettuce. Fold the lettuce into a package and eat as if it were a burrito.

❖ Avocado and Smoked Oyster Salad ❖

Ruth Wiens, Mirassou Vineyards
Accompanying champagne *Mirassou Brut*

Serves 6

A mélange of textures and flavors combines in this salad to provide an excellent complement to *brut* champagne. Served in avocado shells, this salad is also an ideal entrée for lunch or a summer brunch. Tomato cups may be substituted for the avocado shells.

1 unpeeled red apple, cored and diced (about 1½ cups)

2 tablespoons lemon juice

3 medium potatoes, cooked (about ¾ pound)

3 large avocados, ripe but firm

½ cup finely diced sweet red onion

1 cup lightly toasted walnuts, coarsely chopped

1 can (3¾ ounces) smoked oysters, well drained on paper towels

½ cup mayonnaise

3 tablespoons coarse grain mustard

Salt and pepper, to taste

Salad greens, washed and well dried

Toss the apple cubes with lemon juice to prevent discoloration.

Peel the cooled potatoes and cut into small cubes; place them in a large bowl. Cut the avocados in half lengthwise and remove the pit. Using a large spoon, scoop the flesh out of the skin and cut into cubes. Reserve the skins for serving. Add the avocado cubes to the bowl along with the onion, apple cubes, walnuts, and oysters. Combine the mayonnaise and mustard, and pour over the salad, tossing to coat evenly. Add salt and pepper to taste. Place plastic wrap directly on top of the salad to seal well and prevent darkening. Refrigerate for several hours so that the flavors meld.

To serve, mound the salad into the reserved avocado shells and place them on individual plates on a bed of salad greens.

❖ Warm Mussel Salad ❖

Karen Mack, Chateau Ste. Michelle
Accompanying champagne *Domaine Ste. Michelle Blanc de Noir*

Serves 6

The light sparkling wine sauce and the fresh spinach provide a good foil for mussels. Fresh mussels are available in local seafood markets throughout the year, so this dish may be served as a first course for dinner in winter or as a salad for lunch in summer.

2½ pounds mussels
3 tablespoons butter
4 tablespoons minced shallots
3 cups blanc de noir sparkling wine

1 small carrot, minced
½ cup whipping cream
Shredded spinach leaves
Butter lettuce leaves

Scrub and debeard the mussels and set them aside.

Melt the butter in a saucepan over medium-low heat. Add 2 tablespoons of the minced shallots. Sauté for 5 minutes. Add the sparkling wine and the mussels. Cover and cook over medium-high heat until mussels open, about 3 to 4 minutes.

Remove from heat and take the mussels from the pan with a slotted spoon. When cool enough to handle, shell the mussels and set them aside.

Strain the cooking liquid through a fine sieve into a frying pan. Add the minced carrot and the remaining 2 tablespoons of minced shallots. Cook over medium-high heat until reduced by half, approximately 15 minutes. Add the cream and simmer until thickened, about another 15 minutes.

Five minutes before serving, add the mussels and simmer to warm them. Place a bed of shredded spinach in each of 6 lettuce cups. Spoon mussels and sauce equally onto each bed of shredded spinach. Serve at once.

❖ Seafood Pasta Salad ❖

Karen Mack, Chateau Ste. Michelle
Accompanying champagne *Domaine Ste. Michelle Blanc de Noir*

Serves 8

Scallops, named for their shells, are delicately flavored bivalves that are found primarily along the European and American Atlantic coasts. In America only the muscle that opens and closes the shell is eaten. In Europe the coral-colored roe is also used. There are two varieties, the tiny bay scallop and the large deep-sea scallop. The bay scallop is also found on the Pacific coast of America. In this salad, small bay scallops, combined with other seafood and pasta, are accompanied by a Red Pepper Dressing. *Fusilli* are spiral spaghetti. Other medium-sized, shaped pasta such as shells, bows, or wagon wheels, may be substituted.

1 pound salmon fillet
1 cup blanc de noir sparkling wine
1 pound medium-sized raw shrimp, shelled and deveined
1 pound bay scallops, rinsed
8 ounces cut fusilli
1 cup shelled fresh peas (frozen may be substituted, if defrosted and drained thoroughly)

1 cup fresh asparagus, cut into 1-inch pieces (if not available, use canned lightly pickled asparagus, well-drained)
½ cup red onion, finely chopped
1 cup black olives
2 tablespoons lemon juice
Red Pepper Dressing (recipe follows)

Skin and bone the salmon fillet. Place it in a noncorrosive pan with sparkling wine and poach in a 325° F. oven until the salmon starts to flake, approximately 12 to 15 minutes. Remove the salmon, drain, and cool it.

Bring a large pot of salted water to a boil, add the shrimps and scallops and cook for 1 to 2 minutes until they are no longer opaque. Drain and cool.

Bring another pot of salted water to a boil and cook the pasta until tender. Do not overcook it. Drain and cool.

When the seafood, pasta, and vegetables are well drained, lightly toss them together in a large bowl. Add the onion, olives, and lemon juice and toss again. Serve at room temperature on a bed of salad greens with Red Pepper Dressing.

RED PEPPER DRESSING

2 medium red bell peppers, core and seeds removed
1 clove garlic
2 tablespoons fresh basil

¼ teaspoon salt
⅛ teaspoon white pepper
¼ cup blanc de noir sparkling wine
Dash of lemon juice

Place the red pepper, garlic, basil, and salt and pepper in a food processor and purée. Add the sparkling wine and the dash of lemon juice, a little at a time until the desired consistency is reached. Drizzle over the salad.

❖ Sea Fruit Salad ❖

Ruth Wiens, Mirassou Vineyards
Accompanying champagne *Mirassou Brut*

Serves 6

This refreshing shellfish salad, served in a melon half with a citrus dressing, is the creation of Mirassou Vineyards' former chef, Janie Corby, who was in charge of the Sunset Dinners at the winery. The salad may also be served as a luncheon entrée.

2 cups brut champagne
1 pound scallops
1 pound raw medium-sized prawns

½ pound crabmeat
3 small ripe cantaloupes

Bring the champagne to a boil in a skillet. Add the scallops and poach them gently for about 3 minutes (less if scallops are small). Remove them from the pan with a slotted spoon. When cool, slice the scallops into ¼-inch medallions. Bring the wine back to a boil, add the prawns and cook until they have just turned pink. Drain and allow them to cool. (The poaching liquid may be saved for use as a fish stock.) When the prawns are cool, peel and slice them in half lengthwise, removing any dark veins. Combine all of the seafood in a large bowl and refrigerate while making the dressing.

DRESSING

1 lime
1 lemon
Half an orange
½ teaspoon salt
⅛ teaspoon white pepper
1 garlic clove, minced
*¾ cup grape-seed, walnut, or light
    olive oil*

*2 to 3 tablespoons chopped fresh
    tarragon (or 1 tablespoon dried
    tarragon)*
*½ cup chopped pimiento (water
    packed)*
2 tablespoons capers
½ cup thinly sliced celery

Use a vegetable peeler to remove the zest (colored part of the skin) from the lime, lemon, and half orange. Cut into very fine julienne. Keeping the flavors separate, place 2 teaspoons of each type of zest into one cup of boiling water and blanch for 30 seconds. Drain, rinse with cold water, and drain again. Squeeze the juices from the lime, lemon, and orange into a bowl, add salt, pepper, and garlic and whisk until the salt is dissolved. Whisk in the oil in a slow stream. Stir in the remaining ingredients including the blanched zest. Pour the dressing over the seafood and fold until evenly mixed. Refrigerate for at least an hour before serving.

To assemble, cut the melons in half, making a decorative zigzag pattern. Scoop out the seeds and cut a small slice off the rounded bottom so that the melon will not roll on the plate. Fill the melon halves with the seafood salad and serve on plates lined with green leaf lettuce.

❖ Angel Hair Pasta with ❖ Fresh Tomato Sauce

Martha Culbertson, John Culbertson Winery
Accompanying champagne *Culbertson Blanc de Noir*

Serves 6

Pastas in their many varieties may be served at various stages of a meal. This delicate angel hair pasta with a fresh tomato and basil sauce is a delicious start to a summer meal. It may also be served as an accompaniment to a grilled meat entrée, such as Marinated Leg of Lamb (page 199).

1 white onion, minced
4 tablespoons olive oil
2 cloves garlic, minced
8 fresh tomatoes, peeled, seeded, and chopped
1 bunch fresh basil (about 1 cup of leaves)

1 pound angel hair pasta (capellini), homemade or bought fresh
Freshly grated Parmesan cheese, if desired

In a large skillet, sauté the onion in the olive oil until it is transparent, then add the garlic, and cook for a few more minutes. Add the fresh tomatoes and cook on medium-low heat for about 15 minutes or until the mixture has reduced to the consistency of a sauce.

Place 4 to 6 basil leaves on top of one another. Roll them from the long side and cut into diagonal pieces, to make a *chiffonnade*. Cut up the rest of the basil in the same manner. Add the basil to the sauce just before serving. Stir to heat through but do not cook the basil.

Toss the sauce with the pasta, which has been cooked al dente. Sprinkle with Parmesan cheese, if desired.

❖ Angel Hair Pasta with Caviar ❖

Ruth Wiens, Mirassou Vineyards
Accompanying champagne *Mirassou Au Naturel*

Serves 6

Decadent and impressive, this dish is made affordable because it uses delicate American golden caviar, which is the roe of white fish. If you want luxury, sturgeon caviar may be substituted.

1 pound angel hair pasta (capellini)
2½ cups whipping cream
2 egg yolks, beaten
1 tablespoon lemon juice
1 cup freshly grated Parmesan
  cheese

Salt and freshly ground white
  pepper, to taste
4 ounces golden caviar
2 ounces salmon roe
2 tablespoon chopped fresh chives

To cook the pasta, bring 8 quarts of salted water to a boil in a large pot.

Bring the cream to a boil in a large heavy saucepan. Lower heat and simmer the cream for 10 minutes until it is slightly reduced. Whisk the egg yolks and lemon juice together, add a little hot cream, then whisk the egg mixture into the cream. Remove the saucepan from the heat. Stir in the Parmesan cheese and salt and pepper; mixing well. Keep the sauce hot.

Cook the pasta in the boiling water for 3 minutes or until al dente. Drain well. Add the cooked pasta to the sauce; toss until well coated. Divide the pasta among 6 heated serving plates. Spoon an equal amount of golden caviar in the center of each serving. Sprinkle with salmon roe and chopped chives. Serve immediately.

❖ Fresh Pasta with Truffles ❖

Jamie Davies, Schramsberg Vineyards and Cellars
Accompanying champagne *Schramsberg Reserve*

Serves 4 to 6

Pâté de foie gras, of French origin, is considered one of the most prized foods in the world. It basically consists of the liver of a well-fattened goose. The pâté may also contain duck liver, pork, eggs, spices, and truffles. Some are made by chopping the ingredients, in others, they are puréed. Although the goose has contributed a lot, it has been man's ingenuity that has created this buttery, silken taste. The higher the goose liver content, the more expensive the pâté. In this elegant first course, angel hair pasta is tossed with a cream sauce enhanced with truffles and *pâté de foie gras*. If fresh truffles are not available, canned ones may be used. The quantity of truffles used in this dish depends on how much you want to invest.

1 pound fresh angel hair pasta
   (capellini)
2 shallots, chopped
1 tablespoon butter
1 cup whipping cream
Fresh black or white truffles,
   chopped (canned ones may be
   used)

1 tablespoon brandy
2 egg yolks, beaten
1 can (2 ounces) pâté de foie gras,
   cut into cubes
Salt and pepper, to taste
Freshly grated Parmesan cheese

Cook the pasta until al dente in a large quantity of boiling water and drain. Keep warm.

Sauté the shallots in the butter in a large sauté pan. Add the cream and reduce for 2 minutes. Stir the pasta into the cream and reheat. Mix in the truffles and the brandy. Remove from heat. Add the egg yolks, the *pâté de foie gras*, and salt and pepper to taste; toss. Serve on heated plates. Sprinkle with freshly grated Parmesan cheese.

❖ Fresh Pasta with Prawn Sauce ❖

Tracy Wood Anderson, S. Anderson Vineyard
Accompanying champagne *S. Anderson Blanc de Noirs*

Serves 6

The secret of this dish lies in the sautéing and cooking of the prawn shells that impart a wonderful flavor to the sauce. The flavor is enhanced by tomatoes, onion, garlic, champagne, and cream. Fresh ready-made pasta may be substituted.

PASTA

2 cups all-purpose flour
2 eggs
2 tablespoons oil

½ teaspoon salt
Cold water, if necessary

Combine all of the ingredients, except the water, in the food processor and process until crumbly, but moist. Add the water if necessary to reach the right consistency. The dough will be stiffer than bread dough and a little rubbery, but not so rubbery that you cannot knead it a little. Let the dough rest for 10 minutes, then cut it into quarters. Run one-fourth of the dough through a pasta machine at the thinnest setting. Cut into spaghettini or angel hair lengths, about 12 to 15 inches.

PRAWN SAUCE

1 tablespoon olive oil
30 medium prawns, shelled and
  deveined, shells reserved
1 carrot, finely chopped
1 celery stalk, finely chopped
1 small onion, chopped
2 shallots, chopped
2 garlic cloves, minced
1 cup dry champagne
1 tomato, chopped

2 tablespoons tomato paste
¼ cup brandy
1 tablespoon fresh tarragon,
  lightly chopped
1 cup whipping cream
8 tablespoons (1 stick), plus 2
  tablespoons, butter
Salt and white pepper, to taste
Black caviar, for garnish if desired

Heat the olive oil in a saucepan over medium-high heat until almost smoking. Reduce heat to medium and add the prawn shells, stirring quickly for a few minutes. They should turn dark red and brown in spots. Cook the shells for a few minutes. Then add the carrot, celery, onion, and shallots. Cook and stir a few more minutes. Add the champagne to deglaze the pan and reduce the liquid by half. Then add the tomato, tomato paste, brandy and tarragon and simmer the mixture for 20 to 25 minutes.

Remove from the heat and place the sauce in a food processor. Process until smooth and the shells are in very fine pieces. Press the mixture through a fine sieve, extracting all of the juices possible. Return the sauce mixture to a saucepan, add the cream, and simmer for 10 minutes. Add 8 tablespoons of the butter, a little at a time, whisking until thoroughly combined. (It is not necessary to use all of the butter called for, although the full measure makes the sauce rich and tasty.)

To assemble the dish, heat the remaining 2 tablespoons of butter in a sauté pan over high heat. Add the prawns to the pan and sauté until deep pink, but not rubbery, about 4 minutes. Remove the prawns from the pan and keep them warm.

Cook the pasta al dente, about 3 minutes, in boiling salted water with a little olive oil in it to keep the strands from sticking together. Drain the pasta and add it to the sauce.

Place the pasta on warm plates, pour a little extra sauce over each serving, and arrange 5 prawns on each plate. Garnish with black caviar, if desired.

❖ Tortellini with Scallops ❖ and Prawns

Frederick Horton, Wente Bros. Sparkling Wine Cellars
Accompanying champagne *Wente Bros. Brut*

Serve 6 to 8

This simple dish of scallops and prawns in a cream sauce enriched with a little garlic and parsley emphasizes the delicate flavors of the seafood. It is served with tortellini for an interesting texture.

8 ounces scallops
8 ounces prawns
1 pound tortellini
8 tablespoons (1 stick) butter
2 cloves garlic, finely chopped

1 cup whipping cream
3 tablespoons chopped parsley
Salt and white pepper, to taste
Freshly grated Parmesan cheese

Wash the scallops in cold water and dry them well. Shell and devein the prawns and wash and dry them.

Cook the tortellini in boiling salted water until they are tender but firm to the bite. Drain and keep the tortellini warm.

While the tortellini are cooking, melt the butter in a large skillet. When the butter foams, add the scallops, prawns and garlic. Cook for about 4 minutes over medium heat until lightly colored, stirring occasionally. Stir in the cream, parsley, and salt and pepper. Cook 1 minute longer or until cream begins to thicken. Add the tortellini to the sauce and toss over low heat until the sauce coats the pasta, 20 to 30 seconds. Serve immediately with grated Parmesan cheese.

❖ Prawns with Cilantro and Tequila ❖

Tracy Wood Anderson, S. Anderson Vineyard
Accompanying champagne *S. Anderson Tivoli*

Serves 6

A spicy sauce of Mexican influence highlights this easily prepared prawn appetizer.

1 pound medium prawns, shelled
    and deveined
2 tablespoons butter
4 tablespoons tequila

2 medium tomatoes, peeled,
    seeded, and chopped
2 tablespoons chopped cilantro
A few dashes Tabasco sauce

In a sauté pan melt the butter over medium-high heat. Add the prawns and sauté for a few minutes until they are almost done. Deglaze the pan with the tequila. Add the tomato and cilantro and sauté just until heated through. Add a few dashes of Tabasco sauce and serve immediately.

❖ Oysters in Puff Pastry Boxes ❖

Jamie Davies, Schramsberg Vineyards and Cellars
Accompanying champagne *Schramsberg Reserve*

Serves 4

Champagne-poached oysters topped with a lightly herbed sauce are served in puff pastry boxes garnished with watercress. The presentation makes an interesting first course.

*1 package (17¼ ounces) frozen puff
    pastry, thawed*
*1 egg beaten with 1 tablespoon
    water*
1 cup chicken broth
1 cup watercress leaves (packed)
*1 cup sorrel leaves (packed), stems
    and center ribs removed*
½ cup fresh basil leaves (packed)
1½ cups whipping cream

1 egg yolk
3 shallots, chopped
1 tablespoon butter
1 cup champagne
24 medium oysters and their liquor
*Beurre manié (1 tablespoon butter
    and 1 tablespoon flour kneaded
    together)*
*Small bunches of watercress for
    garnish*

Preheat the oven to 450° F.

    Carefully unroll one piece of the puff pastry and cut into 4 rectangles, each measuring 5 by 3½ inches. Place the rectangles on a baking sheet. Cut another 4 rectangles of the same size into 3 long strips each. Using the egg and water as glue, paste two long strips on each long side of the rectangles and two short strips on the ends, making a shallow box. Take care that no egg drips over the edges or the dough will not rise. Prick the bottom of each box with a fork. Bake in the preheated 450° F. oven for 20 to 25 minutes or until golden brown. Remove the boxes from the oven and keep them warm.

    Heat the chicken broth in a large saucepan. Wilt the watercress, sorrel and basil in the broth, about 3 to 4 minutes. Purée the mixture in a food processor. Return to the saucepan, add the cream, and simmer to reduce and thicken slightly. Remove from heat and stir in the egg yolk and keep warm. Do not reheat.

    In a large skillet, sauté the shallots in the butter until translucent. Add the champagne and bring to a simmer. Slip in the oysters and their liquor. Poach gently just until the edges of the oysters begin to curl. Thicken the liquid with the beurre manié and mix to a light sauce.

    To assemble, place a warm puff pastry shell on each 4 individual plates. Carefully remove the bottom crust from the boxes and use them for lids. With a slotted spoon, remove the oysters from their sauce and distribute them among the 4 boxes. Quickly combine the oyster sauce and the herb sauce and spoon over the oysters. Place the lids on the top. Garnish with small bunches of watercress.

❖ Oysters Poached in Champagne ❖ on Fennel Purée

Jamie Davies, Schramsberg Vineyards and Cellars
Accompanying champagne *Schramsberg Blanc de Blancs*

Serves 4

Although native to the coasts of Europe and America, the best oysters have come from cultivated beds. Olympias from the West Coast and bluepoints from the East Coast are among the better-known oysters of this country. In this recipe, poached oysters are paired with the anise flavor of fennel — an interesting combination with champagne.

FENNEL PURÉE

2$^1/_2$ to 3 pounds fennel (sweet anise)
2 cups chicken broth

2 tablespoons lemon juice

Clean the fennel, reserving the feathery green leaves. Cut the fennel in wedges and cook it in the combination of chicken broth and lemon juice until tender, about 8 to 10 minutes. Drain the broth and purée the fennel in a food processor, then rub through a sieve to remove any strings. The purée should be smooth and have a creamy consistency. If it is too stiff, add some of the broth. Keep the purée warm.

POACHED OYSTERS

2 shallots, minced
1 tablespoon butter
2 cups champagne
12 medium oysters freshly
    shucked, reserve oyster liquor

Beurre manié (1 tablespoon butter
    kneaded together with 1
    tablespoon flour)
12 toast points, for garnish

In a medium sauté pan, cook the shallots in butter until limp. Do not brown. Add the champagne and bring to a simmer. Slip in the oysters and their liquor and poach gently until they are plump and their edges curl. Do not overcook. Remove the oysters and keep them warm. Turn the heat to high and reduce the liquid to 1$^1/_2$ cups. Gradually whisk in the beurre manié until the desired consistency is reached.

To serve, put some fennel purée in the center of each of 4 plates, top with 3 oysters, spoon sauce over the oysters, and sprinkle with green fennel leaves. Place 3 toast points around the edge.

❖ Hot Crabmeat in Pastry Shells ❖

Edna Tears, The Great Western Winery
Accompanying champagne Great Western Blanc de Blanc

Serves 6

The water chestnut grows under the water, while its leaves are visible on the surface. The Chinese water chestnut, or *pi tsi*, is the most familiar of the species and is used as a vegetable in Oriental cooking. Another variety, *ling*, is dried, ground, and used as a thickener for sauces. Mostly cultivated in China, Japan, and the East Indies, the plant has also been very profuse in the Potomac River, where at one time it was reputed to be so dense that it stopped river traffic. In this recipe, the crunchiness of water chestnuts and the tanginess of black olives are combined with delicate crabmeat in a warm sauce served in puff pastry shells.

6 frozen puff pastry shells
1 pound crabmeat
2 cups coarsely chopped celery
1 can (8 ounces) water chestnuts, drained and sliced
½ cup sliced pitted black olives
2 tablespoons chopped onion

4 tablespoons chopped green pepper
¾ cup mayonnaise
¾ cup sour cream
¼ cup dry white wine
¼ teaspoon garlic salt
¼ cup slivered almonds, toasted

Bake the puff pastry shells according to the package directions. If two ovens are available, the puff pastry shells and the crabmeat may be baked at the same time. Otherwise, keep the pastry shells warm while preparing the filling.

In a 1½-quart casserole combine the crabmeat, celery, water chestnuts, olives, onion, and green pepper. In a small mixing bowl combine the mayonnaise, sour cream, wine, and garlic salt. Fold the mayonnaise into the crab mixture. Bake in a preheated 350° F. oven for 30 to 35 minutes or until bubbly.

Spoon the hot crabmeat into the puff pastry shells and sprinkle with almonds. Serve immediately.

❖ Spicy Chard and ❖ Smoked Mussel Roulade

Ruth Wiens, Mirassou Vineyards
Accompanying champagne *Mirassou Brut*

Serves 8

Resembling a jelly roll, this roulade may be made ahead and reheated, or it may be served at room temperature. *Salsa* can be found fresh in the delicatessen section or in jars in the ethnic food section of the supermarket. Additional *salsa* may be served as an accompaniment. This dish will also serve four as a luncheon entrée.

2 pounds fresh red or green chard, cleaned and coarse ribs removed
5 eggs, separated
½ teaspoon salt
½ teaspoon freshly ground black pepper
1 teaspoon lemon juice
½ cup grated Parmesan cheese
4 tablespoons unsalted butter

1 large sweet red onion, finely chopped (about 1½ cups)
3 tablespoons all-purpose flour
1 cup salsa
½ cup sour cream
2 cans (4 ounces each) smoked mussels, drained on paper towels and chopped

Preheat oven to 375° F. Butter a 10- by 15-inch jelly roll pan. Line the bottom and sides of the pan with parchment paper or aluminum foil. Butter the paper or foil.

Cook the chard until tender. Drain, cool, squeeze it dry, and chop it finely. Beat the egg yolks; add the salt, ¼ teaspoon of the pepper, and the chard. Mix well. Beat the egg whites with the lemon juice until they hold soft peaks. Mix about one-third of the egg whites into the chard mixture. Then fold in the remaining egg whites. Turn the mixture into the lined baking pan, spread out evenly, and sprinkle with Parmesan cheese. Bake in the preheated 375° F. oven for 12 to 15 minutes, until set and firm to the touch. Remove from oven and allow to cool in the pan.

While the roulade is baking, melt the butter in a large sauté pan. Add the onion and sauté over medium heat until tender, about 8 to 10 minutes. Do not allow the onion to brown. Sprinkle the flour over the onion and stir well. Mix in the *salsa* and sour cream. Cook and stir for 5 minutes. Stir in the mussels and the remaining ¼ teaspoon pepper. Remove from heat.

To assemble, invert the roulade onto another piece of parchment or foil, with the cheese-side down. Peel off the paper on top and discard. Spread the roulade with the mussel filling. Starting with one short edge, roll up, using the paper to lift the roulade. Roll the paper or foil around the roulade and allow it to rest, seam-side down, for 5 minutes before cutting it into 8 slices with a serrated knife. To serve warm, wrap roulade, already sliced, in foil and place in a preheated 400° F. oven for 5 to 10 minutes.

❖ Bay Scallops ❖
and Fresh Strawberries
in Champagne Sauce

Marilouise Kornell, Hanns Kornell Champagne Cellars
Accompanying champagne *Hanns Kornell Brut*

Serves 6

The sweetness of strawberries, orange marmalade, and honey provides an interesting contrast to delicate bay scallops. For additional flavor and color, the seafood is served on a bed of spinach that has been poached in champagne.

8 cups spinach leaves, coarsely chopped
1½ cups dry champagne
2 tablespoons walnut oil
2 cloves garlic, minced
3 tablespoons chopped shallots
3 cups bay scallops
⅔ cup Hanns Kornell Muscat Alexandria champagne
2 tablespoons brandy

2 tablespoons orange marmalade
1 tablespoon chopped thyme
1 tablespoon chopped basil
1½ cups whipping cream
1¼ cups firm, ripe, small strawberries
1 tablespoon honey
Salt and pepper, to taste
4 tablespoons soft butter, cut in 4 pieces

Place the 8 cups of spinach and the 1½ cups of dry champagne in a large saucepan. Bring to a slow boil and simmer for 2 to 3 minutes until just tender. Remove from heat and drain well. Keep the spinach warm.

Heat the walnut oil in a large sauté pan over medium-high heat and add the garlic, shallots, and scallops. Cook for 1 to 2 minutes to sear the scallops. Set aside. In a separate sauté pan, combine the ⅔ cup of Muscat Alexandria champagne, brandy, marmalade, thyme, and basil and cook until the liquid is reduced by half. Add the cream and cook until thick, about 10 minutes, Drain the scallops and add to the champagne mixture. Add the strawberries and poach for 1 to 2 minutes. Then add the honey and salt and pepper to taste. Quickly whisk in the butter, a piece at a time.

Divide the spinach among 6 individual plates and top with the scallops and the sauce.

❖ Butter Clams and Leeks ❖

Karen Mack, Chateau Ste. Michelle
Accompanying champagne *Domaine Ste. Michelle Blanc de Noir*

Serves 4

Clams have been eaten since prehistoric times and various species of them are found all over
the world. The tiniest clams abound in the seas around Japan; the largest, weighing almost
500 pounds, are found in the Indian Ocean. On the East Coast littleneck and cherrystone
clams are often called by their Indian name, *quahog*. Any of the smaller varieties of clams,
such as littlenecks or Pacific white Venus may be used for the butter clams in this recipe.

*4 leeks, washed, trimmed, and
    sliced ⅓-inch thick
2 cups chicken broth
4 tablespoons unsalted butter
3 cups blanc de noir sparkling wine
4 tablespoons fresh cilantro, finely
    chopped*

*4 tablespoons fresh parsley, finely
    chopped
1 clove garlic, minced
4 cups small butter clams, rinsed
    thoroughly*

Combine all of the ingredients except the clams in a large noncorrosive saucepan. Bring to a
gentle simmer, cooking leeks until almost tender, 5 to 7 minutes. Add the clams and simmer
until the shells open, about 2 to 3 minutes. Do not overcook the clams.

Ladle into 4 soup bowls with a generous quantity of the cooking broth. Serve with warm
slices of crusty French bread.

❖ Sautéed Prawns in ❖ Lemon Thyme Sauce

Sheryl Benesch, Korbel Champagne Cellars
Accompanying champagne *Korbel Blanc de Blancs*

Serves 4

In this easy and elegant first course, prawns are sautéed and served with a rich champagne
and lemon thyme sauce.

*3 tablespoons clarified butter
20 large prawns
½ cup blanc de blanc champagne*

*2 tablespoons fresh lemon thyme,
    minced
1 golden tomato, inside removed,
    remainder of tomato julienned
6 tablespoons chilled butter, cubed*

Heat the clarified butter in a sauté pan. Add the shelled, deveined prawns and cook on
medium-high heat until they are pink. Add the champagne, cover, and cook for 1 minute.
Remove the prawns to a heated platter. Lower the heat and add the lemon thyme and tomato
to the pan. When the liquid is reduced to 1 to 2 tablespoons, add the chilled butter. Whisk
until the butter is incorporated. Spoon the sauce over the prawns and serve.

❖ Shrimp Quenelles ❖ with Nantua Sauce

Steve Wenger, Biltmore Estate
Accompanying champagne *Biltmore Estate Brut*

Serves 6 to 8

Crayfish, fresh-water crustaceans, are found primarily in the South and are used in Creole and Cajun cooking. They are also popular in France and the Scandinavia. Nantua sauce, named after the city in France where it originated, is a butter sauce garnished with crayfish. In this recipe for the sauce, the crayfish meat is used as an ingredient.

SHRIMP QUENELLES
(Makes 24 to 30 quenelles)

1½ pounds shrimp
8 tablespoons (1 stick) butter, softened
1 cup very fine bread crumbs

3 eggs, beaten
1 cup hot milk
Nantua Sauce (recipe follows)

In a food processor, process the shrimp to a smooth paste. Add the butter and process until thoroughly blended. Add the bread crumbs and then the eggs, processing after each addition. Add the hot milk and process again. Let the mixture stand for a few minutes to absorb the liquid.

Poach the quenelles by easing 1 rounded teaspoonful of the shrimp mixture into gently boiling water, using two teaspoons to guide the quenelle. Cook for about 1 minute, then roll it over and cook for a few more seconds. Remove the quenelles, drain them on paper towels, and keep them warm. Serve warm with Nantua Sauce.

NANTUA SAUCE

4 tablespoons butter
¾ cup cooked crayfish meat (about 1½ to 2 pounds whole crayfish), minced or puréed

1 cup whipping cream
½ teaspoon cayenne pepper

Melt the butter in a saucepan, add the crayfish, cream, and cayenne pepper. Cook gently until slightly thickened. Serve warm.

❖ Seafood Cakes with Shrimp Sauce ❖

Sheryl Benesch, Korbel Champagne Cellars
Accompanying champagne *Korbel Brut*

Serves 8

Similar to the famous Eastern crab cakes, these fried Seafood Cakes are served with a light shrimp-flavored cream sauce. They may also be served as a luncheon entrée.

1/2 pound prawns, peeled, deveined, and diced (shells reserved)
1/2 pound bay shrimp
1/2 pound snapper (or similar fish), bones removed, chopped fine in a food processor
1 stick celery, finely chopped
1 tablespoon diced red onion
1/4 cup green onions, finely chopped
1/4 cup parsley, finely chopped

1/2 teaspoon thyme
1 tablespoon brandy
1/4 teaspoon salt
1/4 teaspoon white pepper
3/4 cup Shrimp Sauce mixture (recipe follows)
Bread crumbs (about 3 to 4 cups white or French bread, chopped fine in a food processor)
Peanut oil, for frying

Mix all of the ingredients, except the bread crumbs and peanut oil, together in a bowl.

Using a standard-sized ice-cream scoop as a measure, shape the seafood mixture to form a patty 1/2- to 3/4-inch thick. Encase the patty in a layer of bread crumbs. Sprinkle a cookie sheet with bread crumbs and place the assembled patties on it until ready to cook.

Heat 1 to 2 inches of peanut oil in a frying pan over medium heat and fry the patties until brown on both sides, about 3 to 4 minutes. Serve with warm Shrimp Sauce.

SHRIMP SAUCE

2 tablespoons butter
Reserved shrimp shells
1 tablespoon chopped shallot
2-inch piece of carrot, finely diced
3 tablespoons all-purpose flour
1/2 teaspoon paprika

2 cups fish stock, heated
Salt, white pepper, and cayenne pepper, to taste
3/4 cup whipping cream
1 teaspoon brandy

Heat the butter in a saucepan and cook the shrimp shells until they are a toasty brown. Add the shallot and carrot and cook 2 minutes longer. Add the flour and paprika and cook another 2 minutes. Add the fish stock, mixing well; season to taste with salt, pepper and cayenne pepper. Cook for 15 minutes. Strain the mixture through a sieve. This should yield 1 1/4 to 1 1/2 cups. Reserve 3/4 cup for the sauce and mix 3/4 cup into the seafood cake mixture.

To finish the Shrimp Sauce, add 3/4 cup whipping cream and the brandy to the reserved sauce. Heat and serve with Seafood Cakes.

❖ Mushroom Timbales ❖ with Truffle Sauce

Ruth Wiens, Mirassou Vineyards
Accompanying champagne *Mirassou Brut or Brut Reserve*

Serves 8

These individual timbales make an elegant first course. They may also be served without the sauce as a side dish for a beef or lamb entrée. If you wish to omit the truffles, make a black olive sauce by substituting four tablespoons of chopped black olives for the truffles.

2 tablespoons unsalted butter
1/4 cup chopped shallots
1 large clove garlic, minced
1 1/2 pounds fresh mushrooms,
    sliced, preferably 8 ounces each
    of shiitake, oyster, and white
    domestic mushrooms

1/2 sweet red pepper, finely julienned
3/4 teaspoon salt
1/2 teaspoon white pepper
4 eggs, beaten
1 1/2 cups milk
1/2 cup whipping cream

Butter eight 1/2-cup molds.

In a large pan over medium heat, melt the butter and sauté the shallots for about 1 minute. Add the garlic and mushrooms and continue cooking, stirring often, for 5 minutes. Add the sweet red pepper, salt, and white pepper. Continue cooking until all the liquid released by the mushrooms has evaporated. Spoon the mixture into the molds.

In a bowl combine the eggs, milk, and cream. Pour the egg mixture over the mushrooms. Place the molds in a baking pan and add warm water to come halfway up the sides of the molds. Cover the molds with buttered parchment paper. Bake in a preheated 350° F. oven for about 45 minutes, or until a knife inserted in the center comes out clean.

To serve, unmold the mushroom timbales onto individual serving plates and coat them with the sauce.

❖ Truffle Sauce ❖

3 cups rich beef broth
3 tablespoons unsalted butter
2 tablespoons chopped shallots

1/2 cup brut champagne
Salt and pepper, to taste
2 tablespoons chopped truffles

In a wide saucepan reduce the beef broth to 1 1/2 cups and set aside.

In a small sauté pan melt 1 tablespoon of the butter over medium heat. Add the shallots and sauté for 1 minute. The add the champagne and boil until almost evaporated. Add the brown stock and boil until reduced to about 1 cup. Strain the sauce and return to the pan. Season to taste with salt and pepper. Add the truffles and swirl in the remaining 2 tablespoons of butter.

MIRASSOU VINEYARDS

THE MIRASSOU FAMILY IS CONSIDERED TO BE the oldest winemaking family in America. Today the fifth generation of Mirassous, Daniel, James, and Peter, are at the helm of one of America's few remaining family-owned makers of premium wines. Although the family has made wine since the 1850s, the Mirassou label was established as recently as 1966 when the fifth generation took over operation of the winery. Until then, Mirassou wines were sold in bulk to other wineries to be marketed under various labels. Only small quantities were sold exclusively under the Mirassou name through the tasting room at the winery.

Pierre Pellier, the great-great-grandfather of the present owners of Mirassou Vineyards, came from France to San José, California in 1853. He brought with him wine-grape cuttings that had been ordered by his brother Louis, who had founded the City Gardens nursery in San José three years previously. The Pellier brothers had probably come to California in search of gold. Instead of gold, however, they found that fresh grapes of any kind brought high prices in San Francisco. Food was scarce in the city at the time and many discovered that there was more money to be made in supplying the daily necessities of life than in searching for gold in the mountain streams.

In 1858, Pierre Pellier went back to France for more grape cuttings. On his return voyage, the ship was stranded at sea due to the lack of wind and the water supply ran low. In order to keep the vines alive, Pellier purchased the entire cargo of potatoes on board. He then slit the potato ends and inserted the cuttings, and so kept them alive until the end of the journey. Pellier is credited with the first importation into California from France of Pinot Noir and French Colombard grapes.

The demand for fresh grapes in San Francisco was not long lived, and soon there was competition from the Southern Californian grape growers who brought their fruit to San Francisco by ship. With the glut of grapes on the market, the Pellier brothers turned to commercial winemaking. In the late 1850s, Pierre Pellier moved to the Warm Springs district of San José. In 1862 he moved to the Evergreen district, nestled against the foothills southwest of San José. This is still the area where the family resides. Today the original property includes the winery and the family home built by the third-generation Mirassous in 1924.

In 1881, Pellier's oldest daughter, Henrietta, married a neighboring vintner, a young Frenchman named Pierre Huste Mirassou. Pierre joined his father-in-law in the family wine business and together they expanded the vineyards and produced some of the finest early California wines. Tragedy, however, struck the family when Pierre Mirassou died suddenly in 1889 at the age of thirty-three. Henrietta was left, with three young sons, Peter, Herman, and John, to run the winery and the vineyards. Through determination and a love of the art of fine winemaking and grape growing she persevered in carrying on the family business. Even after phylloxera destroyed her vineyards in 1894, Henrietta and her sons replanted the vineyards with native American rootstock. She was following the example set by the "champagne widows" of France.

Eventually her son, Peter Mirassou, took over the vineyard and winery operations and continued selling bulk wine to other wineries who bottled it under their own labels. In 1912 Peter married Justine Schreiber who, with her family, had emigrated from Alsace-Lorraine. When Prohibition took effect, Peter continued growing grapes, selling them to home winemakers in the East. He also taught his sons, Edmund and Norbert (the fourth generation), the art of grape growing and winemaking. When Prohibition ended in 1933, the two young brothers chose to replant the vineyards with premium varietals such as Cabernet Sauvignon, Johannisberg Riesling, Gamay Beaujolais, and Pinot Blanc. They felt that the wine market was becoming more sophisticated.

As urban development began to encroach upon the Evergreen area of San José, it became evident that there was no room for vineyard expansion. Edmund, Norbert, and Peter (Edmund's oldest son) decided to plant vineyards in southern Monterey County. They were the first to plant grapes in an area that until then had only supported cattle and dry-farmed grains. Since then, the area has proven to be one of the most desirable viticultural regions of California.

When Daniel, James, and Peter — the fifth generation — took over the winery in 1966, they decided that after 112 years of winemaking the time had come for a change. Although small quantities of wine had been sold under the Mirassou label at the winery, the new generation wanted to produce and market premium wines under the Mirassou label. They were proud of their family's heritage, including the many innovations the family had made in the wine industry, and wanted to capitalize on the family's accomplishments.

In 1952 Max Huebner, the winemaker at Mirassou, began experimenting with making champagne by the *méthode champenoise*. Blends of Pinot Blanc and French Colombard were among the first *cuvées*. Although there were only a few hundred cases, the first Mirassou champagnes were released in 1954 on the hundredth anniversary of the family's winemaking in California. Two years later, the Pinot Blanc *cuvée* was served at a Wine and Food Society dinner at the Palace Hotel in San Francisco. Over the years since then, the Mirassous have planted Pinot Noir, Pinot Blanc, and Chardonnay in their Monterey vineyards specifically for making champagnes. Over thirty years after the initial release of Mirassou champagne, production has grown from a few hundred cases to twenty thousand cases a year.

In the ensuing years, the Mirassous experimented with various blends, and with various types of yeast in the second fermentation. By the late 1970s, with the matching of particular strains of yeast to specific characteristics in the grapes, Mirassou's champagne style had emerged. In 1982, Tom Stutz joined the winery as winemaker and champagne master. Tom, who has a Master's degree in viticulture from the University of California at Davis, has worked in the Champagne district of France and in the Napa, Sonoma, and Monterey grape-growing regions. He believes that the slower ripening of grapes in the Mirassou's Monterey vineyards caused by the cooler climate adds interest and depth to the champagne *cuvées*. The varietal character of the grape, however, is still evident in a subdued way in his champagnes. "We at Mirassou have benefited from the technology developed over the years and make champagne as good as the French, but with a slightly different character," he says.

A mechanical harvester is used to pick the grapes late at night when the temperatures are cooler, a practice essential for champagne grapes in warm climates. For the harvest of 1983, Mirassou was the first to use a specially designed mobile vineyard press for the champagne and white wine grapes. The Mirassou press is easily transported from station to station in the vineyard and quickly but gently presses the grapes. Stationary field presses are used in the Champagne district of France, but they could not handle the large amounts of grapes harvested by Mirassou.

Tom Stutz has found that Pinot Blanc and Pinot Noir from Monterey go well together in Mirassou's Au Naturel champagne. He has also developed his own yeast cultures for the five Mirassou *cuvées*, all of which are vintaged. Before blending the *cuvées*, the still wines are aged for at least six months. Depending on the *cuvée*, the bottles of champagne, after the second fermentation, are aged for between two and four years on the yeast. All of the riddling is done by hand and the disgorging is also done manually, *à la glace*.

Mirassou produces a total of about 330 thousand cases of wine, both still and sparkling, annually. Like their forefathers, the three Mirassou brothers continue to make wine according the old-world traditions but with the latest techniques. Like their ancestors they, too, are passing the family winemaking heritage along to their children — the sixth generation — of which there are thirteen.

Mirassou produces four types of champagne, in the dry or off-dry style:

Blanc de Noir — 100 percent Pinot Noir

Au Naturel — a blend of 60 percent Pinot Noir and 20 percent each of Chardonnay and Pinot Blanc

Brut — a blend of Pinot Noir, Chardonnay, Pinot Blanc, and some Pinot Gamay

Brut Reserve — the same blend as the Brut, but with a different yeast strain that allows the complexity of the champagne to develop more slowly

Culinary Director: Ruth Wiens

Ruth Wiens was born and raised in Winnipeg, Canada. She acquired her early love of cooking from her mother who entertained frequently and whose repertoire of recipes included specialties of many countries. Upon graduation from college, Ruth taught school for five years, until she moved with her husband to Munich, Germany.

While in Germany, Ruth and her husband, Jack, toured the neighboring countries on weekends and holidays, sampling foods and gathering recipes. After a year and a half in Germany, the Wiens moved to San Francisco, where Ruth's interest in wines was intensified. She joined Mirassou in 1971.

Stimulated by the natural association of wine and food, Ruth began taking cooking classes from Bay Area and visiting chefs. Over a period of ten years, she studied under such renowned teachers as James Beard, Marcella Hazan, André Daguin, and Jacques Pépin.

In the early 1970s, Ruth Wiens started a series of highly successful food and wine programs at the Mirassou Winery. These include Sunday brunches and Sunset and Candlelight Dinners. She also instituted the program of fall and spring cooking classes featuring guest chefs from the San Francisco Bay Area. Ruth develops the winery recipes and does food styling for the food and wine photography. In addition, she consults with the winery chef and caterers on menus and tests and edits recipes for publication. Her style of cooking focuses on the use of fresh ingredients creatively combined, simply prepared, and with an international influence. In addition to her duties at Mirassou, Ruth Wiens serves as food consultant to The Seagram Classic Wine Company, marketers of Mirassou wines.

Mirassou Vineyards
3000 Aborn Road
San Jose, California 95135
(408) 274-4000

Visits: 10:00 A.M. to 5:00 P.M., Monday through Saturday; 12 noon to 4:00 P.M. on Sundays

Principals: Daniel, James, and Peter Mirassou

Varietal wines produced: Chardonnay, White Burgundy (Pinot Blanc), Fumé Blanc (Sauvignon Blanc), Gewürztraminer, Johannisberg Riesling, Chenin Blanc, Cabernet Sauvignon, Zinfandel, Gamay Beaujolais, Petite Sirah, and Pinot Noir

Champagnes produced: Blanc de Noir, Au Naturel, Brut, and Brut Reserve

1988 champagne production: 20,000 cases

SOUPS

SOUPS HAVE LONG BEEN PART OF THE WORLD'S CUISINE. No doubt early man and woman filled an animal skin bag with meat, bones, green plants, and water and dropped in hot stones to cook the mixture. Although the result was probably more like a stew, this method of cooking was improved upon through the ages in all parts of the world. The next stage of cooking soups and stews occurred with the invention of metal pots that could be placed directly over the fire.

In Roman times, soups became very complicated and were served in great variety at banquets for the wealthy and the nobility. Soups presented in gold dishes were laced with precious stones. It is imagined that the rule "finders keepers" prevailed. For the common folk more hearty soups provided the sustenance needed for daily existence.

During the Dark and Middle Ages, soups consisted of anything and everything that could be foraged simply to sustain body and soul. It was also during this time that the first soup kitchens came into existence. The monasteries fed countless numbers of unfortunate people with soup. Such soup kitchens have been revived many times through the centuries — not only in the monasteries, but by a variety of charitable organizations and governments — to counteract famine and depression.

Catherine de Médicis, the young Italian princess who married the future French king, Henry II, is reputed to have contributed much to French cooking. It is said that among her accomplishments was the popularization of the modern version of soup in France. She drastically altered the dining habits of the French nobility by declaring that all meals should consist of only three courses. However, she defined the first course as including between four and six soups, in addition to pâtés and terrines. Louis XIV later refined this tradition by decreeing that soups should constitute a separate course and be limited to two — one clear and one thick. The French chefs of the eighteenth century enhanced the flavors of soup by devising certain standards for stocks and seasonings. Like the overture to a light opera, soup sets the tone for the rest of the meal. To this day soup has remained a staple dish of rural France. Until the twentieth century, soup was served at every French meal including breakfast.

In America, the Indians prepared soup with local ingredients such as corn, beans, potatoes, squash, wild game, poultry, and fish. They also used flowers, roots, and leaves. The early settlers would have been lost without soups. In colonial days, the black kettle hanging in the open hearth was invariably filled with a soup or a souplike stew. The Indians taught the settlers how to make a concentrated essence of soup that could be used, not only at home, but also while traveling. This colonial version of the bouillon cube was made by boiling meat and local vegetables to a mushy stew. After the liquid had boiled off, the mixture was allowed to sit until dry, like cake. Since then, Americans, too, have created soups are associated with particular regions — New England's chowders, Louisiana's gumbos, and San Francisco's cioppino, to name a few.

Through the years soups have become lighter in texture and appearance. They have become easier to prepare and most are made with fresh, quickly cooked ingredients. These lighter soups that are ideal complements to the effervescence of champagne. The following recipes have been designed as light beginnings for the main part of the meal. Many of these fruit soups, consommés, cream soups, and bisques — both hot and cold — could also be served as light luncheon entrées.

❖ Oyster Soup with Brie ❖ and Champagne

Martha Culbertson, John Culbertson Winery
Accompanying champagne *Culbertson Brut*

Serves 8

Brie, in addition to being the name of a French cheese, was also the name of an ancient French province, east of Paris and partially in what is today the province of Champagne. Brie is still being produced around Meaux in the western part of Champagne. This Brie soup is quite rich and champagne complements, not only the oysters, but also the cheese. Use fresh oysters to obtain the full flavor of the juices.

24 small oysters (save the juices)
8 tablespoons unsalted butter
½ cup coarsely chopped onion
½ cup all-purpose flour
3 cups water with the oyster juice added

1 pound Brie cheese, cut into small cubes
2 cups whipping cream
½ cup champagne
Salt and pepper to taste

Shuck the oysters, reserving the juice. Melt the butter in a saucepan and sauté the onions until they are translucent. Sprinkle in the flour and whisk until the mixture is smooth and the flour slightly cooked. Slowly add the water and oyster juices, whisking constantly to keep the mixture smooth. Add the cheese and keep stirring. Cook for about 5 minutes or until the cheese is melted. Strain the soup. Put it back into the pot and over high heat bring it quickly to a simmer. Stir in the cream and bring the soup back to a simmer. Add the champagne.

Remove the pot from the stove and add the oysters. The heat of the soup will be sufficient to cook them. Season to taste with salt and pepper. Ladle the soup into warm shallow bowls, allotting 3 oysters per person.

❖ Dungeness Crab Chowder ❖

Frederick Horton, Wente Bros. Sparkling Wine Cellars
Accompanying champagne *Wente Bros. Brut*

Serves 4

There are over four thousand species of crab in the world — all edible. They range in size from those, as large as a small pea, that live inside the shells of mollusks to the giant Tasmanian crab that can weigh as much as thirty pounds. Land crabs are prevalent in the Caribbean Islands and are widely used there for food. The west coast of the United States is famous for the Dungeness crab. Its delicate taste has made it preferable to many other varieties.

Cauliflower combined with crabmeat in this recipe provides an interesting combination of flavors.

1 small head cauliflower
2 cups milk
2 tablespoons sliced green onion
2 tablespoons diced pimiento
½ teaspoon salt
1 cup half-and-half

3 tablespoons flour
10 ounces Dungeness crabmeat
3 ounces cream cheese, cut into
  cubes
Salt and white pepper, to taste

Clean the cauliflower and cut into small florets. In a 3-quart saucepan steam the cauliflower with a small amount of water. When done, cut up any large pieces. Do not drain off the water. Stir in the milk, green onions, pimiento, and salt. Heat and stir until just boiling.

Combine the half-and-half and the flour so that no lumps remain and add to the hot milk and cauliflower mixture. Cook, over medium heat, stirring until thickened. Reduce heat to simmer. Add crabmeat and cubed cream cheese. Heat and stir until cream cheese melts and soup is heated through. Season to taste with additional salt and white pepper.

❖ Lobster Bisque ❖

Sheryl Benesh, Korbel Champagne Cellars
Accompanying champagne *Korbel Blanc de Blancs*

Serves 4

A bisque, as we know it today, is a fairly thick soup based on a purée of shellfish. In the eighteenth century, bisques were made from poultry or game and contained pieces of meat, along with bread crumbs. Usually these soups were highly spiced. In this Lobster Bisque, the spices are subtle companions to the lobster.

1 lobster tail
1 tablespoon melted butter
3 tablespoons clarified butter
2 tablespoons diced celery
2 tablespoons diced onion
2 tablespoons diced carrot
3 tablespoons flour
½ teaspoon paprika
1 cup fish stock, heated

Pinch of each of the following:
  dried thyme, salt, white pepper,
  and cayenne pepper
2 sprigs fresh parsley
2 tablespoons blanc de blanc
  champagne
1 cup whipping cream
1 cup half-and-half
1 teaspoon brandy

With a sharp knife slit the translucent shell of the lobster tail. Drizzle with the tablespoon of melted butter and broil the lobster tail until done. Cut the reserved lobster meat into small cubes or slices and reserve it. Chop the shell.

In the clarified butter sauté the celery, onion, and carrot in a saucepan. Add the lobster shell and cook for a few minutes. Add the flour, paprika, thyme, salt, white pepper, and cayenne pepper. Cook for 2 minutes. Slowly add the heated fish stock, parsley, and champagne, stirring well. Cook over low heat for 20 minutes. Remove from heat and blend the mixture in a food processor. Strain the mixture into a saucepan through a fine mesh sieve, pressing down on the mixture to extract as much liquid as possible. Heat the soup over low heat and add the whipping cream, half-and-half, and brandy.

Serve the bisque garnished with the lobster meat.

❖ Seafood Bisque ❖

Karen Mack, Chateau Ste. Michelle
Accompanying champagne *Domaine Ste. Michelle Blanc de Noir*

Serves 10 to 12

The secret to this soup is to simmer the seafood and the liquid over very low heat — and only just long enough to thicken the soup slightly. Be careful not to overcook the seafood. This recipe will serve 6 for dinner.

6 tablespoons unsalted butter
2 tablespoons finely chopped green
　　onion
2 shallots, finely chopped
2 cloves garlic, minced
1/2 pound fresh medium shrimp,
　　shelled and deveined
1/2 pound fresh scallops
1/2 pound fresh mussels

1/8 teaspoon white pepper
2 cups chicken broth
2 cups blanc de noir sparkling wine
2 cups half-and-half
1/2 pound freshly cooked Dungeness
　　crabmeat
Freshly chopped parsley, for
　　garnish

Melt the butter in a 3-quart saucepan. Sauté the onions, shallots and garlic until they are limp. Add the shrimp and scallops and sauté for 2 minutes. Add mussels and sauté an additional minute. Remove seafood from pan and set aside on a warm, not hot, plate. Add the pepper, chicken broth, and sparkling wine to the onion mixture in the saucepan and cook over low heat until the liquid is slightly reduced. Add the half-and-half, the seafood, and the crabmeat and continue to simmer very gently until the soup is heated through and begins to thicken.

Serve in warm bowls, sprinkled with chopped parsley.

❖ Green Pea and Clam Bisque ❖

Ruth Wiens, Mirassou Vineyards
Accompanying champagne *Mirassou Brut*

Serves 8; makes about 2¹/₂ quarts

Brightly colored and flavored with a hint of the sea, this soup is topped with a froth of champagne at the last minute. The soup is best if made a day in advance and reheated just before serving.

3 slices bacon, chopped
1 cup chopped onion
¹/₂ cup chopped carrot
3 cups chicken broth
1 teaspoon salt
¹/₄ teaspoon white pepper
¹/₂ teaspoon thyme, crumbled

3 cups (1 pound) frozen baby peas, thawed
¹/₂ cup chopped parsley
2 cups whipping cream
2 cans (10 ounces each) baby clams, with juice
1 cup brut champagne

In a soup pot sauté the bacon until the fat is rendered. Add onion and carrot and sauté over medium heat for 5 minutes. Do not allow the vegetables to brown. Add the chicken broth, salt, pepper, and thyme. Cover and bring to a boil. Reduce heat and simmer for 10 minutes. Add the peas and the parsley. Stir the mixture a little to incorporate the peas.

Remove from heat and purée in several batches in a food processor or a blender. (A blender will yield a finer purée.) Return the mixture to the soup pot and bring to a boil. Add the cream and the clams with their juice. Taste and adjust seasonings if necessary. (If making soup ahead, cool and refrigerate at this point. Just before serving, reheat carefully, stirring often.) Continue heating until very hot, but do not allow to boil. Just before serving, stir in the champagne. Serve with slices of crusty *baguette* and unsalted butter.

❖ Apple and Onion Soup ❖

Marilouise Kornell, Hanns Kornell Champagne Cellars
Accompanying champagne *Hanns Kornell Sehr Trocken*

Serves 4 to 6

Simple to prepare, this is a hearty and tasty soup. When carried in a Thermos flask, it is excellent for a fall football tailgate party or a winter picnic.

2 large Pippin or Granny Smith apples, peeled, cored, and sliced
1 Bermuda onion, sliced
2 tablespoons butter

1 teaspoon curry powder
5 cups beef broth
¹/₂ cup half-and-half, or whole milk

In a large saucepan sauté the apples and onion in melted butter until limp. Add the curry powder and sauté a few minutes longer. Then add the beef broth and bring to a simmer. Cover and simmer for 25 minutes. Remove from heat and purée in several batches in a blender. Return the soup to the saucepan, add the half-and-half, and reheat slowly.

❖ Carrot Velvet Soup ❖

Ruth Wiens, Mirassou Vineyards
Accompanying champagne *Mirassou Brut*

Serves 8

Ginger and curry powder give this carrot soup a pleasing oriental flavor. Developed by Marcy Lessack, Mirassou Vineyards' chef, the soup may be served hot or cold.

8 tablespoons unsalted butter
1 large onion, chopped
2 leeks (white part only), chopped
2 cloves garlic, chopped
1/3 cup fresh ginger, peeled and chopped
2 teaspoons oriental (toasted) sesame oil

8 cups chicken broth
1 1/2 cups dry white wine
2 pounds carrots, peeled and cut into chunks
Curry powder, to taste
Salt and pepper, to taste
Fresh, snipped chives, for garnish (optional)

Melt the butter in a large stock pot. Add the chopped onion, leeks, garlic, ginger, and sesame oil and cook over low heat until onion and leeks are limp and transparent, about 20 minutes. Stir the mixture often. Add the chicken broth, wine, and carrots and continue to cook until carrots are very soft, about 25 to 30 minutes. Purée the soup in batches in a food processor until very smooth and velvety. Return the soup to the stock pot and heat; then season with curry powder and salt and pepper to taste. Ladle into individual soup bowls and garnish with chopped chives.

❖ Chilled Carrot Soup ❖

Steve Wenger, Biltmore Estate
Accompanying champagne *Biltmore Estate Dry*

Serves 6 to 8

One culinary tale gives King Louis IX of France credit for popularizing cold soups. Apparently afraid of being poisoned while dining, he had a staff of tasters to sample each dish before he ate it. Many soups were cool or cold before they reached him. On more than one occasion, the king sent back a tepid soup because it was not as cool as it had been previously — although it was supposed to be a hot soup. As a result, cold soups were often served at royal banquets and became popular in France. Their popularity spread to England in the late eighteenth century.

The orange juice in this recipe enhances the sweet flavor of the carrots.

2 pounds carrots, peeled and sliced
3 cups water
1 teaspoon dried cilantro
1 1/2 cups fresh orange juice

3 to 3 1/2 cups half-and-half, depending on how thick a soup is desired
Salt and pepper, to taste

Combine the carrot slices, water, and cilantro in a large saucepan. Bring to a boil, reduce heat, and simmer until carrots are tender, about 20 minutes. Remove from heat and allow to cool.

When cool, purée the carrot mixture in a food processor or blender. Add the orange juice, half-and-half, and salt and pepper to taste. Chill for at least 4 hours before serving.

❖ Cheddar Cheese Soup ❖

Edna Tears, The Great Western Winery
Accompanying champagne *Great Western Blanc de Blanc*

Serves 4 to 6

Until the early 1900s, most American cheese was made in New York State where surroundings and conditions were ideal — fine pastures, a good water supply, good climate, and healthy cattle. Although the cheese industry has spread throughout the country, New York State is still known for its fine Cheddar. Do not use processed cheese in this recipe. It will cause the soup to be sticky and lumpy.

4 tablespoons butter
½ cup diced onions
½ cup diced carrots
½ cup diced celery
¼ cup all-purpose flour
2 cups chicken broth
1 cup dry white wine

2 cups whipping cream
⅛ teaspoon baking soda
2 cups medium Cheddar cheese,
   grated
Salt and pepper to taste
Dash of freshly ground nutmeg

Melt the butter in a stock pot and add the onions, carrots, and celery. Sauté the vegetables until soft, but do not brown. Add flour and stir well to incorporate and make a pale roux. Pour the mixture into a blender or food processor and process until a smooth paste is formed. Return mixture to stock pot. Add the chicken broth, wine, and cream. Stirring constantly, cook until smooth and heated through. Add the baking soda and grated cheese and stir until cheese melts completely. Season to taste with salt and pepper and add a dash of nutmeg. Cook over low heat for 5 minutes and serve.

❖ Cream of Chicken Soup ❖

Steve Wenger, Biltmore Estate
Accompanying champagne *Biltmore Estate Brut*

Serves 8

This is an old-fashioned Southern soup that is simple to prepare. Care should be taken not to make this soup too thick or it will overpower the accompanying champagne.

*1 chicken (3½ to 4 pounds), cut in
  pieces
2 stalks celery, chopped
2 medium carrots, chopped
1 medium onion, chopped
½ teaspoon poultry seasoning
½ teaspoon garlic powder
1 teaspoon salt*

*½ teaspoon freshly ground pepper
Half a green pepper, diced
1 medium carrot, diced
1½ cups milk
1 cup half-and-half
8 tablespoons butter, softened
½ cup all-purpose flour
½ pound mushrooms, thinly sliced*

Place the chicken, celery, carrots, onion, poultry seasoning, garlic powder, salt, and pepper in a stock pot and add cold water to cover. Bring to a gentle boil, reduce heat and skim the surface. Slowly simmer for 1 hour. Remove the chicken pieces and strain the stock. Remove the meat from the bones; dice and set aside.

Place the green pepper, diced carrots, and 2½ cups of the chicken broth in a large saucepan. Heat to a gentle boil. Add milk and half-and-half and reduce the heat. Continue cooking over low heat for about 5 minutes.

Make a roux by melting the butter and adding the flour. Cook over medium-low heat until flour is incorporated and the mixture resembles a cream colored paste. Do not let it brown. Remove from the heat and add the roux, a little at a time, to the soup, stirring constantly. Add only enough of the roux to thicken the soup to your liking. Continue simmering soup for about 15 minutes. Add the diced chicken meat and sliced mushrooms. Heat through and serve.

❖ Chicken Quenelles in a Light ❖ Garlic Broth with Radicchio

Sheryl Benesh, Korbel Champagne Cellars
Accompanying champagne *Korbel Brut*

Serves 4 to 6

Quenelle, according to *Larousse Gastronomique*, is a name derived from the Anglo-Saxon word, *knyll*, meaning to pound or grind. These delicate dumplings are made from forcemeat usually of fish, chicken, or veal. They are light and fluffy and formed with the aid of an oval-shaped soup spoon.

Radicchio, the red Italian chicory, is a welcome addition to salad bowls. In this recipe, its bittersweet flavor provides a good contrast to the sweetness of the roasted garlic.

1 head garlic
Olive oil
Quenelles (recipe follows)
1 head radicchio
Salt
Pepper
Nutmeg

6 cups rich chicken broth
1 medium to medium-hot chile,
  sliced into very thin rings, seeds
  removed
Worcestershire sauce
Cayenne pepper

Heat oven to 400° F. Place the head of garlic on aluminum foil, drizzle with olive oil, and roast in the oven for 30 minutes. While garlic is roasting, prepare the quenelles.

Cut the *radicchio* into quarters, drizzle with 1 tablespoon olive oil and sprinkle with salt, pepper and nutmeg. Grill on the barbecue or under the broiler for 2 to 3 minutes. Remove from the grill, julienne, and set aside.

Bring the 6 cups of chicken broth to a boil. Add the head of roasted garlic, chile rings, dash of Worcestershire sauce, small dash of cayenne pepper, and salt to taste. Simmer the mixture for 5 minutes for a light garlic flavor or longer for a stronger garlic flavor. Remove the garlic.

To serve, ladle the broth into bowls. Add a few chile rings. Place julienned *radicchio* decoratively into the bowls along with the quenelles.

QUENELLES

1 boneless skinned chicken breast
  with the tendons removed
1 egg white
Dash each of salt, pepper, nutmeg,
  and cayenne pepper

2 tablespoons whipping cream
2 cups rich chicken broth, for
  poaching
2 cups water

Cut the chicken breast into several small pieces and process in food processor until fine and smooth. Add the egg white, cream, salt, and spices and continue to blend until well mixed.

Bring the chicken broth and water to a gentle boil. Using an oval soup spoon, scoop out a smooth level spoonful of the chicken forcemeat and, with your fingers, form it into an oval dumpling shape. Poach each quenelle for 3 to 5 minutes, continuing until all are prepared. Keep the quenelles warm. (Reserve the poaching liquid for another use.)

❖ Potato, Basil and Chive Soup ❖

Ruth Wiens, Mirassou Vineyards
Accompanying champagne *Mirassou Brut*

Serves 8; makes 3½ quarts

This unusual soup was created by Marcy Lessack, Mirassou Vineyards' chef. The slight sharpness of the watercress and sour cream is a good contrast to the waxiness of the potatoes. Little flecks of the red potato skins floating on the surface add color to the green soup. Any leftovers may be frozen.

6 cups chicken broth
2 pounds red potatoes, unpeeled and cut into chunks
1 large yellow onion, coarsely chopped
6 tablespoons unsalted butter
4 leeks, cleaned and coarsely chopped (about 4 cups)
½ cup watercress leaves, packed

1 cup fresh basil leaves, loosely packed
¾ cup fresh chopped chives
1 cup milk
½ cup whipping cream
1 cup sour cream
Salt and white pepper, to taste

Combine the chicken broth, potatoes, and onion in a stock pot. Bring to a boil, lower heat, and simmer until potatoes are tender. Meanwhile, melt the butter in a large sauté pan, add the leeks and sauté until soft, about 10 minutes. Do not brown. Add the basil, watercress, and chives and cook 5 more minutes.

Add the leek and herb mixture to the stock pot. Simmer 5 minutes to blend flavors. Purée the soup in batches in a food processor or blender until very smooth. Return mixture to the stock pot and add the milk, cream, and sour cream. Season to taste with salt and pepper. Continue heating until hot but do not allow the soup to boil again. Additional chicken broth or milk may be added if the soup is too thick.

❖ Pumpkin Soup ❖

Edna Tears, The Great Western Winery
Accompanying champagne *Great Western Natural*

Serves 6

Native to Central America and the Caribbean, the pumpkin was a mainstay of the diet of early settlers in what is today Florida. Grown originally by the native Indians, it soon traversed the United States. The Indians dried the pumpkin and ground it into meal similar to corn meal. In the mountains of Virginia, dried pumpkin was used as a substitute for molasses. Traditionally pumpkin pie is associated with fall and Thanksgiving. However, the vegetable has been a soup ingredient in the Caribbean and South America for centuries and there it is served throughout the year. Freshly cooked and mashed pumpkin may be substituted for the canned pumpkin in this recipe.

4 tablespoon butter
¼ cup finely chopped green onions
*2 large white potatoes, peeled and
    cut into cubes*
*1 can (1 pound 13 ounces) cooked,
    mashed pumpkin*

4 cups chicken broth
2 cups half-and-half
⅓ cup semisweet sherry
*Salt, pepper, and freshly grated
    nutmeg to taste*

Melt the butter in a stock pot over medium-low heat. Add the onions and cook them until transparent and wilted; do not brown. Add the cubed potatoes and 1 cup of the chicken broth. Cover and simmer until the potatoes are tender, 20 to 25 minutes. Place mixture in a food processor or blender and purée until smooth. Return mixture to the stock pot and add remaining chicken broth, pumpkin, cream, and sherry. Stir until well blended. Season to taste. Heat, but do not boil.

❖ Sorrel Soup ❖

Tracy Wood Anderson, S. Anderson Vineyard
Accompanying champagne *S. Anderson Blanc de Noirs*

Serves 8

Sorrel still grows wild in Asia, Europe, and certain parts of North America. Today the herb is used primarily by French and northern European cooks, although in the seventeenth and early eighteenth centuries it was popular in England. It seems that cuisines that favor sweetness do not readily make use of sorrel. In central France where sorrel grows wild, it is used not only as a soup ingredient but also as an herb in fish sauces. This recipe for sorrel soup is similar to the French version. Sorrel is available in the produce section of gourmet markets, or can very easily be grown in the garden.

2 tablespoons butter	*3 cups chicken broth*
1 large onion, diced	*1 cup whipping cream*
4 medium shallots, minced	*Salt, to taste*
4 cups loosely packed sorrel leaves	*Lemon juice, if desired*

Melt the butter in a large saucepan over medium high heat. Add the onion and shallots and sauté them until soft, but not brown Then add the sorrel and sauté until just tender. Add the broth and heat to boiling. Remove the mixture from the heat and purée in a blender. Return the soup to the saucepan, add the cream and salt, to taste. Heat the soup and adjust seasonings. Add lemon juice if desired.

❖ Green Pea Soup with Custards ❖

Jamie Davies, Schramsberg Vineyards and Cellars
Accompanying champagne *Schramsberg Blanc de Blancs*

Serves 4

The tiny custards, baked in miniature muffin pans, enhance the flavor of this green pea soup and add texture. The soup may also be served cold — an ideal starter for a summer dinner.

1½ quarts freshly shelled peas	*¼ cup sour cream*
6 green onions, chopped	*1 tablespoon butter, if soup is*
5 cups chicken broth	* served hot*
2 eggs	*Fresh mint leaves, for garnish*

Cook the peas and green onions in 1½ cups chicken broth until tender. Purée the mixture in a food processor and then press through a sieve.

Butter a miniature muffin tin (12 muffins). Beat the eggs to blend. Add 1 cup of the pea purée and the sour cream to the eggs. Divide the mixture equally among the muffin cups. Place muffin tin in a pan of hot water. Water should be half the height of the molds. Bake in a preheated 350° F. oven for 10 to 12 minutes or until a knife inserted in center of custard comes out clean.

While custards are baking, combine the remaining pea purée with the chicken broth and heat. If soup is to be served hot, enrich it with 1 tablespoon of butter. Unmold custards and place 3 in each soup plate. Top with soup and garnish with finely chopped fresh mint. If soup is served cold, the custards are also served cold.

❖ A Spring Soup ❖

Jamie Davies, Schramsberg Vineyards and Cellars
Accompanying champagne *Schramsberg Blanc de Blancs*

Serves 6

Spring vegetables are served in a chicken broth accompanied by oriental-style ravioli. Ready-made wonton skins simplify the "ravioli" preparation.

8 cups chicken broth
8 baby carrots, or thin regular-sized carrots, cut in long diagonal slices
1 cup green beans, cut in diagonal pieces
1 cup asparagus, cut in diagonal pieces
1 cup small green peas, shelled
1 cup finely shredded green cabbage

1 cup green onions, cut in diagonal pieces
1 cup zucchini, cut in medium dice
1 cup mushrooms, quartered
1 cup spinach leaves, cut in ribbons
1 tablespoon fresh dill, or 1 teaspoon dried dill
Pesto Wontons (recipe follows)

Bring the chicken broth to a simmer in a large stock pot. Add the vegetables in the order given above, allowing the broth to come to a simmer again after each addition.

Add pesto-filled wontons and cook gently until they are tender, about 5 to 8 minutes. Serve in warmed soup plates.

PESTO WONTONS

12 wonton skins
¾ cup pesto sauce

1 egg yolk, beaten

Arrange each wonton skin on a board so that it looks like a diamond, and place 1 teaspoon of pesto in the center. Put a dot of egg yolk, to act as glue, on the topmost corner and fold up the bottom corner to make a triangle. Again placing a dot of egg yolk on the topmost point of the triangle, fold the right-hand point over and up, to meet the glued point. Fold the left-hand point likewise, so that the two edges of the points meet in the middle of the top point. Glue these edges down as well, so that you now have a pesto-filled square.

❖ Tomato and Basil Summer Soup ❖

Martha Culbertson, John Culbertson Winery
Accompanying champagne *Culbertson Blanc de Noir*

Serves 8

Tomatoes, native to Central and South America, were brought back to Europe in seed form by the Spanish explorers in the early sixteenth century. Although the Spaniards and Italians used tomatoes primarily in sauces, the English considered the fruit poisonous. Thomas Jefferson was one of the first to introduce the tomato as an edible fruit to the United States. Used with basil in this recipe, the tomatoes create a delightful summer soup that may be served hot or cold.

4 carrots, peeled and diced
4 stalks celery, diced
3 medium onions, minced
¼ cup olive oil
4 tablespoons butter
14 large tomatoes, peeled and
  chopped
¼ cup chopped fresh basil

Salt and pepper, to taste
½ cup half-and-half
1 cup tomato juice or enough to
  thin soup to desired consistency
  (optional)
½ cup sour cream
8 basil leaves, for garnish

In a large saucepan cook the carrots, celery, and onions in the oil and butter until very tender. Add the tomatoes and basil and cook covered over moderate heat for 30 minutes.

Remove from heat, strain soup, pressing all the soft ingredients through the sieve. Season the mixture with salt and pepper to taste and cool.

Just before serving, heat the soup and stir in the half-and-half. If the soup is too thick, add some of the tomato juice. Heat through, but do not bring to a boil. Ladle into bowls, top with a dollop of sour cream and place a basil leaf on top. If serving the soup cold, do not reheat it. Simply add the half-and-half and the optional tomato juice.

❖ Cream of Zucchini Soup ❖

Sheryl Benesh, Korbel Champagne Cellars
Accompanying champagne *Korbel Brut*

Serves 6 to 8

Zucchini squash, originally an Italian vegetable, has become an integral part of our American cuisine. In this recipe it is the basis for a delicate soup with Italian herbs and is enhanced by a carrot purée. This fresh-tasting and lovely looking soup can easily be prepared in 30 minutes.

1/2 cup chopped green onions	*1/4 cup chopped parsley*
2 cloves garlic, minced	*1 teaspoon Italian seasonings*
3 tablespoons olive oil	*Dash of cayenne pepper*
5 cups sliced zucchini	*Salt and white pepper, to taste*
2 cups chicken broth	*2 cups half-and-half*
1 cup peeled and diced potatoes	*Carrot Purée (recipe follows)*

In a saucepan sauté the onions and garlic in olive oil until the onions are translucent. Add the zucchini and cook for about 2 minutes. Then add the chicken broth, potatoes, parsley, Italian seasonings, cayenne pepper, and salt and pepper to taste. Bring to a boil, reduce heat to medium and cook about 15 minutes or until vegetables are tender. Remove from heat and purée the soup in a blender or food processor. Return the soup to the saucepan, add the half-and-half, and heat but do not boil. Adjust seasonings, if necessary. Ladle soup into bowls and swirl Carrot Purée into the zucchini soup. Serve.

CARROT PURÉE

1 1/2 cups chopped carrots (approximately 5 small or 2 large carrots)	*Dash of nutmeg*
	2 cardamom seeds
	Salt and white pepper to taste
1 cup water, enough to cover carrots	*1/2 cup whipping cream*
1 teaspoon sugar	

In a small saucepan bring all ingredients except the cream to a boil. Turn heat to medium-low and cook until carrots are soft, about 10 to 15 minutes. Remove the cardamom seeds and purée the carrots and liquid in a food processor. Return the mixture to the saucepan, add the cream and bring to a boil. Remove from heat and use to garnish the zucchini soup.

❖ Chilled Avocado Soup ❖ with Salsa Ice

Frederick Horton, Wente Bros. Sparkling Wine Cellars
Accompanying champagne *Wente Bros. Brut*

Serves 4

Avocados, native to Mexico, are said to have been brought north to California by the Spanish padres. It seems that on their journey north, the padres would stop along the way and eat avocados. Wherever they threw away the seeds, so the story goes, trees eventually grew. Today the fruit is widely grown, not only in California, but also in Florida. This simple soup is a refreshing starter to a summer meal. Make the Salsa Ice the day before.

2 avocados, diced
1/2 cup sour cream
2 tablespoons chopped green onions
2 tablespoons canned diced chiles, drained

1 tablespoon lemon juice
1/4 teaspoon minced garlic
1/2 teaspoon seasoned salt
2 cups chicken broth

In a blender or food processor, purée the avocados, sour cream, green onions, chiles, lemon juice, and garlic. In a medium-sized bowl combine the avocado purée, seasoned salt, and chicken broth. Chill until ready to serve.

To serve, pour the soup into a tureen or individual soup bowls. Garnish with small balls of Salsa Ice (recipe follows).

SALSA ICE

2 small tomatoes, peeled
1 jalapeño chile
1 small green bell pepper
1/4 small onion, finely grated
1 clove garlic, minced

1/2 teaspoon dried oregano leaf, crushed
1 teaspoon lime juice
1/2 teaspoon salt

Dice the tomatoes into 1/4-inch pieces and set them aside to drain. Dice the unpeeled jalapeño chile and the bell pepper. Combine the diced jalapeño, green pepper, and tomatoes with the onion, garlic, oregano, lime juice, and salt. Cover the mixture and place in the refrigerator overnight before freezing.

Put *salsa* in the freezer 30 minutes to 1 hour before serving the soup, stirring it with a fork every 15 minutes. *Salsa* is ready when it can be scooped out with a small ice-cream scoop and formed into a 1-inch ball.

❖ Gazpacho ❖

Marilouise Kornell, Hanns Kornell Champagne Cellars
Accompanying champagne *Hanns Kornell Brut*

Serves 6 to 8

Before the Spanish explorers brought tomatoes and green peppers to Spain from the New World, gazpacho was a white soup made of milk, garlic, almonds, and white grapes. It is still prepared this way in parts of Spain. The soup was originally eaten with bread that had been soaked in it, and the name of the soup is derived from an Arabic word referring to bread. The tomato version of gazpacho was also known to be a salad served on bread. This version has a chicken broth base for extra heartiness. Make the chicken broth ahead of time and let it jell in the refrigerator. In keeping with tradition, croutons are served with this soup.

2 cups gelatinous chicken broth
3 cups water
1 large red onion, sliced
½ cup green pepper, minced
2 cloves garlic, minced
3 large tomatoes, peeled, seeded, and finely chopped
2 tablespoons finely minced green or red pepper
2 cucumbers, peeled, seeded and finely minced

1 clove garlic, finely minced
½ cup celery, finely minced
2 tablespoons finely minced red onion
1½ tablespoons lemon or lime juice
3 tablespoons olive oil
2 to 3 drops Tabasco sauce
¼ teaspoon ground cumin
Chilled brut champagne

GARNISH

2 avocados, cut in thin rings
2 cups herbed croutons

Freshly chopped parsley

Bring the chicken broth, water, sliced onion, minced green pepper and garlic in a large saucepan or stock pot and bring to a boil. Simmer gently for 10 minutes. Cool, strain, and chill the mixture. Then gently stir in the tomatoes, the finely minced green or red pepper, cucumber, garlic, celery, minced red onion, lemon or lime juice, olive oil, Tabasco sauce, and cumin. Chill thoroughly and adjust seasonings to taste.

Serve in well-chilled bowls and add a splash of chilled champagne to each serving to provide an extra nuance and thin the soup slightly. Garnish with avocado rings, herb croutons, and chopped parsley.

❖ Jellied Mushroom Consommé ❖

Jamie Davies, Schramsberg Vineyards and Cellars
Accompanying champagne *Schramsberg Blanc de Noirs*

Serves 4 to 6

A great variety of both fresh and dried mushrooms is available in local grocery stores. *Shiitake* mushrooms, originally from Japan and Korea, are now grown in Vermont, Maine, Virginia, and Washington State. They are available fresh in many gourmet markets. Dried, the *shiitake* mushroom is better known as the black Chinese mushroom. The flavor of this jellied soup depends on the variety of mushrooms used. Although it takes time, the preparation is very simple and is perhaps best done over a period of several days.

JELLIED VEAL STOCK

6 veal bones	2 ribs of celery with leaves, cut in pieces
4 chicken backs	
1 onion stuck with 2 cloves	4 cracked peppercorns
1 carrot, cut in pieces	1 bay leaf

Place the veal bones, chicken backs, vegetables, and spices in a large stock pot and cover with water. Bring to a boil and remove the scum that forms on the top. Cover the pot, reduce heat, and simmer gently for 3 hours. Strain the stock and chill.

Remove the fat that has congealed on the surface. Reheat the stock before proceeding with the recipe.

JELLIED MUSHROOM CONSOMMÉ

1 pound white domestic mushrooms, coarsely chopped	6 to 8 morels, if available
2 to 3 tablespoons butter	4 egg whites and 4 crushed egg shells, for clarifying the soup
6 to 8 fresh or dry shiitake mushrooms	Fresh herbs, for garnish
8 fresh or dry porcini mushrooms	Croutons browned in butter, for garnish

Sauté the white domestic mushrooms in 2 to 3 tablespoons butter. Add them to the broth along with all of the other mushrooms. Cover and simmer for 30 minutes. Strain the soup through a large sieve lined with several layers of dampened cheesecloth. Press down on the mushrooms to extract all of the liquid.

To clarify the consommé, beat egg whites slightly, add the crushed shells and whisk the mixture into the soup. Stirring constantly, bring the soup to a boil. Reduce heat to simmer and cook for 10 minutes. Remove the scum that forms. Let the consomme stand for 15 minutes and then strain again through several thicknesses of cheesecloth.

Chill the consommé until jellied. Chop it up and serve garnished with a sprinkling of fresh herbs and croutons.

❖ Cold Papaya Soup ❖

Ruth Wiens, Mirassou Vineyards
Accompanying champagne *Mirassou Brut*

Serves 4

Cold fruit soups are traditional in Scandinavian cuisine. In this recipe the flavor of a tropical fruit is accented with cinnamon and ginger. The density of the soup is governed by the amount of papaya flesh, which in turn, dictates the amount of cream added at the end. Since papaya has a very delicate taste, do not add too much cream or it will be overpowering.

6 ripe papayas
2 cups brut champagne
6 tablespoons fresh lime juice
1 teaspoon cinnamon
1/3 cup honey

1/2 teaspoon ground ginger
4 tablespoons brandy
1 to 1 1/2 cups half-and-half
Mint leaves, for garnish

Cut off the neck end of 4 papayas. Scoop out the seeds, and discard them. Scoop out most of the meat, being extremely careful not to puncture the skin. (Leave a layer of papaya meat in the skin as support for the soup.) Place the papaya meat and all other ingredients except the cream and mint in a blender or food processor. Blend until smooth. Add 1 cup of cream and blend again. Add more cream if mixture is too thick. Return this mixture to the hollowed papayas. Chill for several hours.

To make the garnish, peel the remaining two papayas, cut them in half lengthwise, and remove the seeds. Cut the halves into fan shapes by making 4 or 5 lengthwise cuts from the neck to the base.

To serve the soup, place the whole papayas containing the soup onto plates. Garnish with papaya fans and mint leaves. The soup may also be served in soup bowls, similarly garnished with papaya fans and mint leaves.

❖ Cold Pea Soup ❖

Karen Mack, Chateau Ste. Michelle
Accompanying champagne *Domaine Ste. Michelle Blanc de Noir*

Serves 8

There is nothing more refreshing on a warm day than a chilled soup. A cold soup is also ideal before a heavily spiced main course. Karen Mack suggests serving the soup in a *radicchio*- leaf bowl, which is an attractive presentation. One large, crisp, outer *radicchio* leaf makes a bowl. It may also be served in a regular soup bowl.

*2 pounds snow peas (Chinese sugar
    peas), washed, strings removed,
    and chopped
2 bunches green onions, washed
    and sliced
8 tablespoons butter
1 bottle blanc de noir sparkling
    wine*

*3 cups chicken broth
½ teaspoon dried tarragon
1 tablespoon minced fresh mint
3 tablespoons lemon juice
1 large head radicchio (optional)
Fresh mint leaves, for garnish*

Sauté the chopped snow peas and onions in 1 to 2 tablespoons melted butter until just cooked through. Add more butter as needed. Purée the mixture until smooth.

Combine the remaining butter, sparkling wine, chicken broth, tarragon, mint, and lemon juice in a large saucepan and bring to a simmer. Add the purée and simmer until the soup thickens and begins to reduce.

Remove from heat and chill. Serve chilled, with a sprig of fresh mint for garnish.

❖ Peach Soup ❖

Karen Mack, Chateau Ste. Michelle
Accompanying champagne *Domaine Ste. Michelle Blanc de Noir*

Serves 4 to 6

Peaches are said to have originated in China over 2,000 years ago. Today they grow in the warmer climates of Europe, Asia, and the Americas. Simple to prepare, this soup is very refreshing as a starter for a summer meal.

*2 cups fresh peaches, peeled and
    sliced
1 tablespoon lemon juice
¼ to ⅓ cup sugar, depending on
    tartness of peaches*

*2 cups blanc de noir sparkling wine
1 cup whipping cream
Fresh mint leaves, for garnish*

Immediately after slicing peaches sprinkle them with the lemon juice. Place the peaches, sugar, and sparkling wine in a medium-sized saucepan. Slowly bring mixture to a simmer and simmer for 6 to 8 minutes or until peaches start to soften. Add cream and continue to simmer slowly for another 10 minutes. Place mixture in a food processor and process until smooth. Chill. Garnish each serving with a mint leaf.

❖ Vichyssoise ❖

Tracy Wood Anderson, S. Anderson Vineyard
Accompanying champagne *S. Anderson Brut*

Serves 4

Vichyssoise is a leek and potato soup with a French name. It was created in America by Louis Diat while he was the *chef des cuisines* at the Ritz-Carlton in New York early in the nineteen hundreds. The soup was actually a recreation of a soup of his childhood. He added cream to the original and, since it was first being served for the opening of the roof garden at the Ritz on a hot summer's day, he decided to serve it cold. It has been served that way ever since. However, this version is equally delicious warm.

2 tablespoons butter
3 leeks, white part only, sliced
1 medium onion, chopped
1 medium white potato, cut into
   cubes
1½ cups water
1½ cups chicken broth
¾ cup whipping cream

Lemon juice to taste, about 1
   tablespoon
Dash of white pepper
3 or 4 drops Tabasco sauce
Salt to taste
Chopped chives or lemon thyme,
   for garnish

Melt the butter in a medium-sized saucepan. Add the leeks and onion and cook very gently over medium-low heat for about 15 minutes or until the vegetables are wilted. Do not brown. Add the potato, water, and chicken broth. Bring to a boil and gently simmer, covered, until potato is tender, about 20 minutes.

Add the cream and simmer, uncovered, another 5 minutes. Purée the mixture in a blender. Strain and rub through a sieve to ensure that there are no large pieces of vegetable in the soup. Add lemon juice, white pepper, Tabasco sauce, and salt to taste. Chill thoroughly. Serve garnished with chopped chives or lemon thyme leaves.

Champagne made by the méthode champenoise is the result of a delicate, complex process that takes a considerable time. Every step is critical because the winemaker is dealing with a living organism. Some of the procedures, as they are followed at Mirassou Vineyards in California, are shown in these pictures.

Because fermentation is less easily controlled in hot weather, Mirassou began, in 1983, to harvest at night, when temperatures are cooler. (1) The grapes are pressed immediately in the vineyard, in a mobile press. (2) After the first fermentation is completed, the base wines are blended to create the particular styles of champagne. Sean Lin, the oenologist at Mirassou, uses base wines of Pinot Noir, Pinot Blanc, and Chardonnay. (3) To initiate the second fermentation, *liqueur de tirage* — a mixture of wine, a cane sugar syrup, and yeasts — is added. (4) A crown cap is placed on each bottle, which is then laid on its side. During this time, the second fermentation occurs and the champagne ages on the lees of the yeasts for between two and five years. (5) After the wine has aged for the required time, the bottles are placed in A-frame riddling racks where they are slowly turned and gently elevated until they are standing upside down and all the yeast sediment has collected in the neck. (6) The champagne is then chilled and the bottles inserted, still upside down, into a dry-ice solution to freeze the yeast sediment. (7) The bottles are turned slightly in one direction at each step of the riddling procedure. The white lines on the base of the bottles guide the riddler. (8) The champagne is then disgorged: the crown cap is popped off and natural pressure in the bottles forces out the plug of frozen yeast sediment and a very small quantity of wine. (9) A second dosage — the *liqueur d'expédition* — to replenish the wine lost during disgorgement and to balance the flavor is added. (10) Finally, the bottles are "dressed," with the familiar cork and wire hood covered with lead foil, labels applied, and the bottles laid in cases to rest for another two or three months before being sold. (11)

According to tradition, champagne was discovered, perhaps even invented, by Dom Pérignon, a monk and the cellarmaster at the Abbey of Hautvillers near Épernay, France. Tradition errs a little, but it is true that Dom Pérignon was a very skillful winemaker and his wines commanded premium prices. He pioneered many of the practices still used in the champagne making industry.

*I*n acknowledgement of his life's work, a statue of Dom Pérignon stands outside the winery of Moët et Chandon in Epernay. The company sells much of its champagne under the "Dom Pérignon" label — a continuing tribute to the Father of Champagne. (1) ■ In keeping with the extravagant cachet of champagne is the Pommery winery, modelled after a Scottish castle and seemingly quite at home in the cool damp climate of Rheims. (2) ■ The vineyards of the Abbey of Hautvillers. First planted over 300 years ago, the ancestors of these Pinot Noir vines provided the grapes for the original champagnes and the vineyards are still in full production today. (3)

■ Épernay across the River Marne. The fanciful tower is that of the de Castellane winery, established in 1890 by champagne makers who had come to France from Spain. (4) ■ The sanctuary of the abbey church at Hautvillers, the monastery at which Dom Pérignon made still wines and champagne for forty-seven years — from his appointment in 1668 until his death in 1715. (5) ■ Bottles of champagne in the iron riddling racks in the caves of Moët et Chandon in Rheims. On the left are regular bottles, in the middle the magnums, and on the right the salmanazars and nebuchadnezzars. (6) ■ Vineyards of Pinot Noir grapes on the slopes of the Montagne de Rheims. The windmill was used as a French observation post during World War I. (7) ■ An oak barrel in the caves of the Moët et Chandon winery. (8)

Vineyards near Rheims planted with Chardonnay grapes. (1) ■ *The bottling line at Pommery. The bottles are receiving their corks and wire hoods. (2)* ■ *Hand riddling of champagne in the underground cellars of Moët et Chandon. (3)* ■ *The headquarters of the Bollinger winery in Aÿ. (4)* ■ *Cork making at Segrera in Épernay. (5)* ■ *A cooper repairing a barrel at the Bollinger winery. (6)* ■ *Inspecting the barrels at the Bollinger winery. (7)* ■ *Magnums of champagne aging in the Bollinger cellars in Aÿ. (8)* ■ *An iron grape press used at Bollinger. (9)*

4

5

6

8

9

7

*A*lthough much of the champagne produced in America comes from California, the industry has developed, over the past 100 years, in various parts of the country. Since the repeal of Prohibition, the quality and quantity of the American champagnes have been improving steadily. The industry is not as rigidly controlled as it is in France and American winemakers have been innovative. Champagne here is made with numerous varieties of grape and many champagne makers have developed their own strains of yeast.

*T*he Korbel Champagne Cellars, in Guerneville, California. (1) ■ *Traditional A-frame riddling racks at the Hanns Kornell Champagne Cellars in the Napa Valley, California. (2) ■ This stone building, part of the Kornell winery, is listed on the Register of Historic Buildings in California. (3) ■ The original buildings at Korbel were built in the 1880 and the Victorian gingerbread has been carefully preserved. (4) ■ The automated bottling line at the Korbel winery. (5) ■ Barrels of still wine — the base wines from which champagne will be made — aging in the Korbel cellars. (6) ■ An elegant landmark, the brandy tower at Korbel. (7)*

*S*outh of San Francisco, the lush vines of the Mirassou Vineyards contrast strangely with the bare, summer-brown hills that evidence the area's Mediterranean climate; very different from the cool, damp plains of the Champagne region in France. (1)　■　*Pinot Noir grapes shortly before being harvested in the Monterey County vineyards of Mirassou. (2)*　■　*To pick the grapes a mechanical harvester is used. The machinery was designed by Peter Mirassou, of Mirassou Vineyards, and the Up-Right Harvester Company. (3)*　■　*The winery buildings of the Mirassou Vineyards, San José, California. (4)*　■　*Final decisions on the blend of base wines for the cuvées that will become champagne are made by Peter, Daniel, and Jim Mirassou, owners, and Tom Stutz, the winemaker, at Mirassou. (5)*

*T*he Chateau Ste. Michelle winery, in Woodinville, Washington. The climate of Washington State is more like that of the Champagne district of France than is the climate of California. (1) ■ Traditional, familiar barrels hold wine aging in the cellars of the Chateau Ste. Michelle winery. (2) ■ Riddling racks in the caves of the Schramsberg winery in Calistoga, California. (3) ■ The Schramsberg vineyards at sunrise. (4) ■ A truckload of champagne grapes in front of the caves at Schramsberg. (5) ■ The Victorian house at Schramsberg was built in 1875 by Jacob Schram, who had a winery on the property, and has been restored by the present owners. (6)

© Bob Peterson

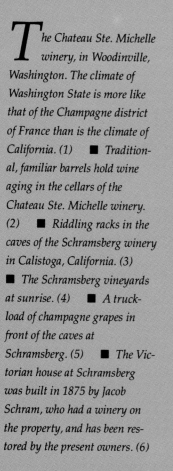

5

© Fred Lyon

4

© Fred Lyon

6

The dramatic caves carved out of the hillside at the S. Anderson Vineyard in the Napa Valley, California. (1)

■ The setting for the S. Anderson winery and its vineyards. (2)

■ The unexpectedly contemporary design of the aging caves at the John Culbertson Winery, in Fallbrook, California. (3)

■ The entrance to the S. Anderson aging caves. (4)   ■ The old Cresta Blanca champagne cellars, now used by the Wente Bros. winery, in Livermore, California. (5)   ■ A vineyard of Pinot Noir grapes belonging to S. Anderson. American champagnes have been made of a much wider variety of grapes than is permitted in France, but Pinot Noir still provides one of the mainstays. (6)   ■ The Wente Bros. Sparkling Wine Cellars, in Livermore, California. (7)

4

5 6

7

One of the eight large Tiffany-style stained glass windows in the Biltmore winery. (1)   ■   The Biltmore House, commissioned in 1890, by the grandson of Cornelius Vanderbilt, and its newly established vineyards. (2)   ■   The vineyards at Biltmore slope down to a manmade lake on the estate. (3)   ■   Wrought iron gates at the entrance to the aging cellars of the Biltmore winery. (4)   ■   The refurbished dairy is now the Biltmore Estate Winery, in Asheville, North Carolina. (5)

5

*T*he oldest bonded winery in the United States is the Great Western Winery in Hammondsport, New York. Champagne has been made here since the 1860s. (1) ■ Part of the original buildings of the Great Western Winery, then known as the Hammondsport and Pleasant Valley Wine Company. (2) ■ The vineyards of the Great Western Winery are planted on land that slopes down to Lake Keuka, one of the Finger Lakes of upper New York State. (3)

SCHRAMSBERG VINEYARDS AND CELLARS

WHEN JACK AND JAMIE DAVIES PURCHASED the defunct Schramsberg winery near Calistoga a little over twenty years ago, their goal was to make American *méthode champenoise* champagne equal in quality to the best French ones. Most critics say that they have achieved that goal. Today, Schramsberg is recognized as one of the finest champagnes in this country and overseas.

Schramsberg champagne has graced the tables of five summit conferences, and has been used by the last four American presidents to toast numerous heads of state, including Queen Elizabeth, the Emperor of Japan, and the presidents of France and Mexico.

Jamie Davies and her husband Jack have helped pioneer the modern American champagne industry using the traditional French *méthode champenoise*. They were among the first vintners to produce only champagne. "When we started there were only a few American champagne producers who grew their own grapes, made their own wines, and produced sparkling wines from them — and produced nothing else," says Jack Davies.

In 1965, Jack and Jamie Davies purchased the Schramsberg property, which included an old defunct winery, wine aging caves, and a hundred-year-old house. It was a challenge to them both, not only to make this ghost winery and house a working entity, but also to establish and pioneer a new aspect of the California wine business. It was their goal to produce champagne by the *méthode champenoise* as close to the French product as possible, not only in the method of production, but also in the grapes used.

A native Californian, Jack Davies is a graduate of Stanford University and the Harvard Business School. At the age of forty-two, Jack Davies had already had a successful business career with such companies as Kaiser Aluminum, McKinsey & Co., Fibreboard Corp., and Ducommun, Inc., where he was a vice-president. Although he had been successful in the world of business administration, Jack felt he wanted to be involved in an industry where he could make a major contribution. "We had a desire to have our own business — to do things that we could influence ourselves," said Jack Davies. He believed that the wine business offered him an opportunity to produce a single unique product and put into practice his own theories on business management. Jamie Davies, an art major, operated her own art gallery before they moved to the Napa Valley.

Over the years Jack and Jamie Davies had developed an interest in wines fostered by their membership in the San Francisco Wine and Food Society. They had also developed an excellent wine cellar. In the early 1960s, they joined a group of investors in buying a winery near Saratoga in the Santa Cruz Mountains south of San Francisco. At the same time, they purchased an adjacent plot and started planting grapes. They had now progressed from being casual wine lovers to serious participants in the industry. However, after several years, their interest diminished; they liquidated their investment in the winery and sold the adjoining vineyard. The episode, however, did pave a way to their future desire to be vintners.

When Jack and Jamie finally decided to become full-time vintners, they looked at several wineries that were for sale in the Napa Valley. They saw the old Schramsberg property, overgrown with weeds and the buildings in disrepair, and immediately wanted to buy it. Jack and Jamie thought it had great potential for the type of winery they had envisioned. Earlier Jack had enlisted a college friend as a partner in the proposed winery — each contributed $40,000 — and the negotiations for the property were soon concluded. In August of 1965 the final papers were completed and Jack and Jamie Davies owned Schramsberg.

Schramsberg winery was started in 1862 by Jacob Schram and his wife Annie, immigrants from Germany. Jacob Schram originally made his living as a barber. With the help of Chinese laborers, he planted one of the first vineyards in the Napa Valley and, a few years later, established a winery. Chinese laborers dug tunnels 175 feet deep into the side of the mountain to provide aging cellars which are still used today. Schram's wines became renowned all over the United States. After Jacob Schram's death, his son operated the winery until it closed on the advent of Prohibition. Between the end of Prohibition and the time Jack and Jamie Davies purchased the property, several attempts had been made to revive the Schramsberg winery. All ended in failure.

The first years of operation were not easy ones for Jack and Jamie. The winery equipment was old and run-down, the grounds and existing vineyards needed lots of work and the house was in need of repair. "We had to acquire knowledge fast. Jack took short courses in winemaking," says Jamie. She made the old Victorian house habitable again and also took over the renovation of the grounds.

Jack, who was the winemaker for the first seven years, learned very quickly. He knew what he wanted to produce — a champagne that would go with food, from hors d'oeuvres to dessert. "From the beginning we vintaged our wines and focused on their wineness, their individuality," he says. Jack also supervised the planting of forty acres of vineyards with Chardonnay and Pinot Noir grapes on the property. The remaining sixty acres of the original Schram vineyards remained in forest land. By 1967, the first vintage of 250 cases of Blanc de Blancs was released.

Gradually the winery has been expanded. The cellars have been enlarged by two-thirds, and all new equipment was purchased. Today Schramsberg produces fifty thousand cases a year. Due to the aging time, production continues to exceed sales.

Not only does Jack Davies use grapes from the estate vineyards, but he also purchases grapes from about ten different growers with whom he has long-term contracts. Until fairly recently Schramsberg's production was limited by the availability of Chardonnay grapes. However, as more of that variety has become available, Schramsberg have been able to increase production.

Alan Tenscher is now the winemaker at Schramsberg and works closely with both Jack and Jamie. The *méthode champenoise* is strictly followed. Jack and Alan believe that the preparation of the blend of still wine, the *cuvée,* is most important in creating the individual style of the champagne. They must first make the finest table wine before they can ever ferment it into champagne.

After the primary fermentation, the wines remain in stainless steel tanks for between one and six months. They are then filtered and blended to make the *cuvée.* Jack, Jamie, Alan Tenscher, and Dan Holm, the production manager, hold tastings for the blend from October through December. To start the second fermentation, a precise amount of sugar and yeast is added to the dry wines, depending on which champagne is being made. The wine is next poured into bottles that are sealed with stainless steel caps. For the second fermentation and aging, the bottles are laid down in the caves for two to five years.

Jack Davies is a problem solver as well as a champagne maker. Finding that tin caps corroded in the damp caves, he switched to stainless steel ones, which he imports from France. He also uses some mechanical riddling machines. A great deal of the riddling, however, is still done by hand. Jack feels that some *cuvées* do better with hand riddling. "There is no substitute for the human touch," he says.

He also designed a new vacuum system to deliver the grapes from the trucks to the presses, minimizing damage to the grape skins. The wines also flow by gravity from the winery located on the hill to the bottling line in the cellars several hundred yards below the winery.

Jack Davies has not only used the traditional methods and *cuvées* of the French *méthode champenoise*, but he has also been innovative in creating new ones. The Cuvée de Pinot, for example, is unusual in that it is a salmon-colored champagne, completely dry. Most rosé still wines and champagnes are off-dry or slightly sweet. The Cuvée de Pinot combines the fruitiness of the Pinot Noir and the Napa Gamay grapes.

The Crémant Demi-sec is a unique dessert champagne made from the Flora grape — a hybrid grape developed at the University of California at Davis. It is a cross between the Gewürztraminer and Sémillon grapes and has a delightful floral bouquet. "The Crémant is made especially to complement sweet desserts," says Jamie Davies. Crémant contains only half of the effervescence of the usual champagne. The result is a more "creamy" champagne. Crémant, and the use of the Flora grape, are American firsts.

Another innovation of Jack and Jamie Davies is to age their champagne longer. The Reserve, for instance, is aged for between four and six years. Many of the other Schramsberg champagnes are aged for four years.

Both Jack and Jamie are very much involved in all aspects of the winery. Jamie does a great deal of travelling to promote Schramsberg champagnes. She is much in demand as a lecturer on food and champagne and has been the subject of numerous newspaper and magazine articles about her wine and culinary expertise. Jack does all of the marketing and travels widely in this country and abroad. Schramsberg champagnes are sold in Europe and the Far East.

Jack and Jamie Davies have brought their individuality and excellent technical and managerial capabilities to the wine industry. Over the years they have not lost sight of their purpose and goals. They have continued to experiment with new ways to improve their product, always keeping in mind that champagne is the most versatile of wines — especially in the company of food.

Schramsberg produces five types of champagne:

Blanc de Blancs — a blend of Chardonnay and Pinot Blanc, finished as a dry and somewhat austere wine

Blanc de Noirs — a blend primarily of Pinot Noir with some Chardonnay for complexity, aged over three years and finished dry

Cuvée de Pinot — a blend of Pinot Noir and Napa Gamay, finished dry

Crémant Demi-sec — uses the Flora grape and has only half of the effervescence of traditional champagne

Reserve — a limited bottling of each year's choicest harvest and aged for four or more years for maximum complexity

Culinary Director: Jamie Peterman Davies

Jamie Davies grew up the Midwest and has been cooking since she was eight, when her mother died. She attended Boston University and graduated from the University of California with a Bachelor of Arts degree. A long visit to Europe, after graduating from college gave her a basic grounding in new cuisines and ingredients. She has been adding to her culinary repertoire ever since.

Prior to the founding of Schramsberg Vineyards and Cellars, Jamie Davies was a cofounder and operated the Hansen-Peterman Art Gallery in San Francisco. Once involved with the winery, she found it necessary to become accomplished in the pairing of food and wine — champagne in particular. She took courses from some of the leading chefs, including James Beard, Jacques Pépin, and Simone Beck. She also travelled extensively all over the world promoting Schramsberg champagnes, and gathering ideas and information on food and cooking. Shortly after the first release of Schramsberg champagnes, Jamie Davies instigated a series of "Evenings at Home with the Davies" in order to introduce interesting combinations of food with champagne.

Over the years, Jamie and her husband Jack have received many honors in the field of winemaking, including the prestigious Winemaker of the Year Award in 1984 and the Junipero Serra Award for Excellence, also in 1984. Jamie is a member of the Wine Institute and of Women in Wine. She is also a Vice-President and Director of Schramsberg Vineyards and Cellars.

Jamie Davies grows her own herbs, believing in the use of fresh ingredients in her cooking, and plans her recipes around seasonally available fresh produce. She tries to present the components of a meal in a simple manner, so that her guests can enjoy the various flavors with the accompanying champagnes. "Each meal is an experience, an important aspect of family life," she says. Jamie, the mother of three grown sons, has combined a love of cooking and entertaining with the business of being a vintner.

Schramsberg Vineyards and Cellars
Schramsberg Road
Calistoga, California 94515
(707) 942-4558

Visits: Tours by appointment only; no tastings
Principals: Jamie and Jack Davies, managing partners
Champagnes produced: Blanc de Blancs, Blanc de Noirs, Cuvée de Pinot, Crémant Demi-sec, and Reserve
1988 champagne production: 50,000 cases

SORBETS

*S*ORBET IS THE FRENCH ADAPTATION OF THE TURKISH WORD for drink, *serbet*. The origin of this combination of ice and fruit juice or purée dates back many centuries to the courts of China. The Chinese passed on their technique of making ices to the Indians, Persians, and Arabs. By the fourteenth century, Marco Polo had helped spread its popularity to Italy.

Two hundred years later, ices had reached the French court. This occurred in 1553 when the future king, Henry II, took as his bride, the fourteen-year-old Catherine de Médicis. As the story goes, she had been allowed to bring along her Italian chefs who knew the secret of making ices. Sorbets soon became so popular at court that the king decreed they were to be solely the province of royalty.

This court monopoly lasted until 1660, when an Italian chef, named Procopia, opened a restaurant in Paris and featured ices. The Parisians took to the delicacy with gusto and soon hundreds of restaurants and shops were offering them. A number of the shops incorporated and then issued franchises to sell their merchandise. In the eighteenth century, ices molded into fantastic shapes and lavishly decorated became the height of social elegance. By the end of the century, milk, egg whites, and/or cream were being added to the puréed fruits to create sherbets and ice creams.

Today, sorbets are usually soft ices made with a simple sugar syrup base and puréed fruit, fruit juices, wine, or liqueur. Some sorbets also contain egg white. Many modern French sorbets contain some type of milk product — milk, cream, or *crème fraîche* — which gives them a consistency somewhere between those of Italian ices and of ice creams. These sorbets are served for dessert.

At formal dinners, sorbets are served just before the entrée. The tart flavor and lightness of sorbets clear the palate of the taste of the previous courses. Since sorbets are too soft to mold, they are served in glasses or goblets. When served in mid-meal, sorbets are not accompanied by champagne. They may, however, contain champagne as an ingredient. At informal dinners, sorbets or sherbets are served with diced fruit for dessert and may then be accompanied by champagne.

To Freeze

Sorbets are easy to make. They should be served on the day they are prepared, since storage in the freezer gives them a stale taste. Ice-cream makers simplify the production of sorbets, but are not essential. Lacking a machine, freeze the sorbet mixture in ice-cube trays covered with plastic wrap or foil. When the mixture is frozen, process it in a food processor, return to the trays, cover and refreeze. Sorbets containing alcohol take longer to freeze and will defrost quickly. Leave all sorbets in the freezer until ready to serve. Then serve in glasses that have been chilled in the freezer.

❖ Champagne Sorbet ❖

Martha Culbertson, John Culbertson Winery

Serves 6 to 8

The egg white helps to lighten this lovely pink sorbet made with a fruity *blanc de noirs* champagne.

1 cup water
1 cup sugar
Half an egg white

1 bottle (750 ml) blanc de noirs
champagne
Juice of half a lemon

Combine the water and sugar in a small saucepan and bring to a boil. Continue boiling gently for about 5 minutes until the liquid is the consistency of a light syrup. Beat the half egg white lightly until very soft peaks form. Stir together the egg white, 1 cup of the sugar syrup, the champagne, and the lemon juice. Place mixture in ice-cream maker and freeze according to the directions, or in ice-cube trays (for procedure, see page 127).

Serve the sorbet accompanied by a few fresh raspberries or small fresh strawberries.

❖ Citrus Sorbet ❖

Marilouise Kornell, Hanns Kornell Champagne Cellars

Serves 6

The tartness of citrus is an excellent palate cleanser after a first course. Use a dry champagne to balance the citrus. Marilouise Kornell prefers Hans Kornell Brut for this recipe.

2 cups water
1 cup sugar
1 cup orange juice

1/4 cup lemon juice
2 cups plus 6 tablespoons
champagne

Combine the water and sugar in a small saucepan and boil gently for 5 minutes to dissolve the sugar and slightly thicken the mixture. Add the orange and lemon juices. Cool the mixture. Stir in the 2 cups of champagne and freeze in an ice-cream maker according to the manufacturer's directions, or in ice-cube trays (for procedure, see page 141).

Divide the sorbet among 6 chilled sorbet glasses and top each serving with 1 tablespoon of champagne.

❖ Pink Sorbet ❖

Steve Wenger, Biltmore Estate

Serves 6

Deep red grapefruit impart a faint blush color to this sorbet.

2 cups fresh pink grapefruit juice,
strained

2 cups Chardonnay wine
Sugar, to taste

Mix the juice and wine. Add only enough sugar to balance the acidity of the grapefruit juice. Process in an ice-cream maker according to the manufacturer's directions, or freeze in ice-cube trays (for procedure, see page 127).

❖ Sparkling Sorbet ❖

Karen Mack, Chateau Ste. Michelle

Serves 8 to 10

The tartness of fresh pineapple, enhanced by lemon juice, is combined with the fruitiness of a *blanc de noir* sparkling wine.

³/₄ cup sugar
1¹/₂ cups blanc de noir sparkling
wine

³/₄ cup water
1¹/₂ cups puréed fresh pineapple
¹/₃ cup fresh lemon juice

Combine the sugar, sparkling wine, and water in a saucepan. Bring to a simmer over medium-high heat and cook slowly for 5 minutes, stirring constantly. Remove the mixture from the heat, cool, and chill it. Then add the pineapple and lemon juice and blend well.

Place the mixture in an ice-cream maker and freeze according to manufacturer's directions, or into ice-cube trays (for procedure, see page 127).

❖ Peach Sorbet ❖

Marilouise Kornell, Hanns Kornell Champagne Cellars

Serves 6 to 8

This sorbet, a little thicker than usual, depends on natural peach juice and lemon juice for its liquid. Nectarines may also be used.

2 pounds peaches, white if
available

6 tablespoons sugar
3 tablespoons lemon juice

Wash, peel, and pit the peaches. Cut them into small pieces. Place the peach pieces and sugar in a food processor or blender and process until liquefied. Add the lemon juice and process a few seconds longer.

Put the sorbet mixture into an ice-cream maker and freeze according to the manufacturer's directions, or place into ice-cube trays (for procedure, see page 127).

❖ Kiwi Sorbet ❖

Martha Culbertson, John Culbertson Winery

Serves 8; makes 2 quarts

Kiwi fruit, originally called Chinese gooseberry, was introduced to New Zealand from China in the early 1900s. By the 1950s, it was being exported in small quantities to the United States but because of the political situation at the time in China, its name did not help to make it popular. So it was renamed kiwi fruit after New Zealand's native, hairy flightless bird. Today kiwi fruit are grown both in New Zealand and California.

The kiwi's green color and tart-sweet taste make it an attractive and palate-pleasing sorbet ingredient. The taste is reminiscent of strawberry, citrus, and melon. Serve as a refresher between courses or as a light dessert.

2 pounds kiwi fruit
3/4 cup sugar

Slices of peeled kiwi fruit, for garnish

Peel the kiwi fruit and purée it in a food processor. Place half of the puréed fruit in a saucepan. Add the sugar and heat over medium heat to dissolve the sugar, stirring occasionally to blend. Add the remaining purée and chill.

Place the kiwi mixture into an ice-cream maker and freeze according to the directions, or in ice-cube trays (for procedure, see page 127). Store in the freezer until serving time. Serve each individual portion with a slice of fresh kiwi fruit on top.

❖ Mackie's Rose Petal Sorbet ❖

Ruth Wiens, Mirassou Vineyards

Makes about 1 quart

This sorbet is named for the late Max Huebner, Mirassou's champagne- and winemaker for almost forty years. One of his hobbies was experimenting with flavored champagnes, of which perhaps the most unusual was a champagne scented with rose petals. Rose water, available in gourmet or Middle Eastern markets, has been substituted in this recipe to give the effect of rose petals and complements the *brut* champagne.

1/4 cup sugar
1/4 cup water
1 bottle (750 ml) brut champagne, chilled

1 tablespoon rose water
Red and white rose petals, for garnish

Combine the sugar and water in a small saucepan. Bring to a boil, lower the heat, and simmer for several minutes, stirring constantly, until sugar is dissolved and mixture thickens a little. Cool the mixture. Combine the syrup, chilled champagne, and rose water. Mix carefully and place in the freezer. Remove and stir the sorbet several times during the first few hours of freezing. Freezing will take up to 6 hours.

To serve, spoon into chilled stemmed glasses and garnish with several unsprayed rose petals.

❖ Basil Sorbet ❖

Tracy Wood Anderson, S. Anderson Vineyard

Serves 6

This sorbet combines a tangy herb with the tartness of grapefruit juice. Tarragon or lemon thyme substituted for the basil will create other interesting sorbets.

2 cups fresh grapefruit juice
Sugar, if necessary

1 tablespoon finely chopped fresh basil

If the grapefruit juice is not sweet enough, add sugar to taste. Then add the basil to the juice and let the mixture sit at room temperature for 1 hour.

Place the mixture in an ice-cream maker and freeze according to the manufacturer's directions, or in ice-cube trays (for procedure, see page 127).

CHATEAU STE. MICHELLE

EXPERIMENTAL PLANTINGS OF EUROPEAN GRAPE varieties in Washington State during the 1950s and 1960s led to the eventual establishment of Chateau Ste. Michelle. From the winery's small initial production of six thousand cases in 1967, Chateau Ste. Michelle has become the largest winery in Washington. It has helped make that state the second largest producer of premium table wines and the second largest grape-growing state after California.

In 1966, the owners of Chateau Ste. Michelle, then known as American Wine Growers, decided to make premium varietal wines from European types of grapes instead of sweet dessert wines from the *labrusca* varieties. The American Wine Growers had been formed by the merging of several smaller wine companies. They brought the famous enologist André Tchelistcheff from California to the Columbia Valley to advise them on the project. Tchelistcheff remains a consultant to Ste. Michelle and, over the past twenty years, has seen the wines evolve into sought-after premium table wines.

Many others also watched the development of the then American Wine Growers. In 1973, a group of investors from Seattle purchased the company and, a year later, resold it to the United States Tobacco Company of Connecticut. U. S. Tobacco invested $100 million in developing the winery, and, as a result, Chateau Ste. Michelle has grown into one of the nation's leading premium wineries.

Chateau Ste. Michelle now consists of two wineries. The 1930s winery in Grandview in eastern Washington's Columbia Valley produces the winery's red wines. The Bordeaux-style chateau set on eighty-seven acres of parkland in Woodinville, outside Seattle, serves as Ste. Michelle's corporate headquarters and is the facility for its white wine and sparkling wine line: Domaine Ste. Michelle. Once the country estate of Fred Stimson, a Seattle lumber baron, the property still contains many of the original buildings. During the summer outdoor concerts, plays, and other events are held on the lawn in front of the chateau on weekends. Chateau Ste. Michelle has always been very involved in the cultural and philanthropic work of the Seattle community.

Columbia Crest, formerly Chateau Ste. Michelle's River Ridge facility, is located south of Prosser, Washington, in the middle of a vineyard overlooking the Columbia River Valley. Built at a cost of $26 million, it consists of 410,000 square feet. Today this sister winery, also owned by United States Tobacco, produces table wines under the Columbia Crest label.

All of Chateau Ste. Michelle's 3,180 acres of vineyards, almost a third of Washington's total *vinifera* vineyards, lie in the Columbia Valley. The region has a unique combination of climate, soil, and geographical location. The geographical latitude lies between the latitudes of the great wine-growing regions of Burgundy and Bordeaux in France. The Cascade Mountains, running north and south in the state, provide shelter from the rainy coastal region. Water for irrigation and frost protection in this semi-arid valley is readily available from the Columbia River. Long warm summer days and cool nights provide the proper temperatures for *vinifera* grapes. To complement the favorable climate, the Columbia Valley has a loamy soil well suited to grape growing. Over the past years, Chateau Ste. Michelle has carefully researched the grape varieties best suited to the microclimates of the Columbia Valley.

Allen Shoup, president of Chateau Ste. Michelle, and his staff have been not only active in promoting their wines, but also in lending their support for research and promotion to other wineries in the state of Washington. Shoup is a great believer in promoting the viticultural region and the wines of Washington State.

Chateau Ste. Michelle's first sparkling wine, a Blanc de Noir, was made in the traditional *méthode champenoise* in Woodinville and was introduced in 1977. Produced entirely from Pinot Noir grapes, the Blanc de Noir is made in a *brut* style. Grown in the cooler Washington climate, the grapes ripen to a lower sugar content and higher acidity than those in warmer climates. The growing conditions in the Chateau Ste. Michelle Pinot Noir vineyards are similar to those of the vineyards in the Champagne region of France. The Blanc de Noir sparkling wine spends between two and three years on the yeast. The bottles are all riddled by hand and topped off with a *dosage* of sugar and Chardonnay or Pinot Noir, depending on the vintage year, to adjust the wine to the proper level of dryness.

Two new *cuvées* have been added to Domaine Ste. Michelle's sparkling wine selection, according to Cheryl Barber, the winemaker in charge of sparkling wine. A Blanc de Blanc, consisting entirely of Chardonnay, is almost completely dry. The new Brut is a blend of Pinot Noir and Chardonnay. Both remain on the yeast for about two years before being disgorged. "We try to handcraft our sparkling wines according to the classic French *méthode champenoise*," commented Ms. Barber.

Cheryl Barber, a native of Washington, grew up in Richland near the vineyards in the Columbia Valley. She received a Bachelor of Science degree in food science and technology from Washington State University in 1976. Later that same year, she joined the winemaking staff at Chateau Ste. Michelle as a Laboratory Supervisor. It was in this position that she learned the entire process of winemaking and was able to analyze each step of the wine's development. During the next five years she carefully studied the Chateau Ste. Michelle style of winemaking. In 1982 Cheryl was promoted to assistant winemaker and the following year to her current position as Winemaker. Still in her early thirties, Cheryl Barber is one of the youngest winemakers of a large premium winery in this country.

Over the past ten years, Chateau Ste. Michelle has become known as one of the premium wineries in the United States. With a production of about five hundred thousand cases a year, attention is still given to the minute details in the making of sparkling wines as well as of still wines.

Chateau Ste. Michelle produces three types of sparkling wine under its Domaine Ste. Michelle label. All are off dry:

Blanc de Noir — 100 percent Pinot Noir
Blanc de Blanc — 100 percent Chardonnay
Brut — a blend of Pinot Noir and Chardonnay

Culinary Director: Karen Mack

Karen Mack, a native of Seattle, Washington, has a deep interest in Pacific Northwest food products. Karen attended the University of Washington, spent thirteen years in the insurance industry, and also assisted her husband in the food service industry.

Karen expanded her food and wine interests as owner and operator of a small restaurant and catering business. This together with a love of travel and years of association with the restaurant industry have long kept Karen involved with the culinary scene.

In 1982, Karen joined Chateau Ste. Michelle in the Special Events department. Under her leadership Chateau Ste. Michelle has become recognized as one of the state's prime tourism assets. She created a summer concert series, which draws visitors from all parts of the country. Karen also developed a culinary program of food and wine research and development. All of these activities have greatly developed the winery's Special Events programs.

Karen is active in the Seattle/King County Convention and Visitors Bureau, the Region V State Tourism Board, the East King County Convention and Visitors Bureau, and actively participates in the Washington Wine Institute, the Enological Society, and the Northwest Culinary Arts Association.

Chateau Ste. Michelle
One Stimson Lane
Woodinville, Wshington 98072
(206) 488-1133

Visits: Daily, 10:00 A.M. to 4:30 P.M.; Memorial Day, Labor Day, Saturdays, and Sundays, 10:00 A.M. to 6:00 P.M.; closed New Year's Day, Easter, Thanksgiving Day, and Christmas Day
Principals: United States Tobacco Company
Varietal wines produced: Chardonnay, Fumé Blanc, Smillon, Sauvignon Blanc, Gewürztraminer, Johannisberg Riesling, Chenin Blanc, Cabernet Blanc, Cabernet Rosé, Cabernet Sauvignon, Merlot, Pinot Noir, Muscat Canelli, and White Riesling
Sparkling wines produced: Blanc de Noir, Blanc de Blanc, and Brut
1988 sparkling wine production: 6,000 cases

MAIN COURSES

SOME THREE THOUSAND YEARS AGO the Egyptians, although limited in their selection of food, managed to dine rather well on such main courses as salmon from the Nile and goose. Later the Greeks and Romans expanded the main course. It was the Romans who chose to recline on sofas while they dined on such delicacies of the day as stuffed peacock, ragout of thrush, and flamingo tongue. They spent hours at their dining tables and the grandeur of gastronomy was probably strongly touched with gluttony.

Dinners became royal feasts for the European nobility of the fifteenth century. The main course at these extravaganzas traditionally consisted of ten dishes. Chefs built entire castles of pastry to present their latest meat creations. One was known to have built, as an extra attraction, a castle of pies that contained live frogs and birds. The quest for spices to preserve and flavor food became so great that fortunes were spent on the explorations to procure them. Columbus, who was sent primarily in the search of black pepper, discovered America instead, and thereby provided many unknown foods to delight the European palate.

The wealthy of Europe marvelled at the new tastes that the explorers had brought back — sweet potatoes, turkeys, and paprika, green peppers, and other pieces to enhance their entrées. Later the discontented poor who fled to the New World would create yet another cuisine. Although, at first, the settlers ate very frugally, they soon learned to use the native pumpkins, corn, and turkey for hearty main courses.

With prosperity in the nineteenth century, this country began to offer new culinary creations to the world and to serve the specialties of other countries as if they were its own. Immigrants had brought with them their native recipes and preferences for ingredients that have found a place in American agriculture as well as in the cuisine.

Americans stationed abroad during two world war, and a new, much-travelled generation have brought more creativity to the dinner table — particularly to the main course. We have the resources and the knowledge to prepare a main course from any of the world's cuisines. After all, in the words of Byron:

> All human history attests
> That happiness of man, — The hungry sinner! —
> Since Eve ate apples, much depends on dinner.

There is a great variety in the main courses in this book. There are recipes for pasta, chicken, seafood, and meat prepared in many different ways. Most of the recipes focus on lighter preparations that are not overly spiced, they will all complement champagne. Fresh ingredients and ease of preparation are also emphasized. These lighter foods are also in keeping with the healthy eating styles that Americans have recently adopted.

❖ Shiitake Mushroom and ❖ Corn Pouches

Ruth Wiens, Mirassou Vineyards
Accompanying champagne *Mirassou Brut or Brut Reserve*

Serves 4; makes 20 to 24 crêpes

Shiitake mushrooms were first grown on the dead and decaying wood of *shi* trees in Japan and China. Hence the name. Today they are also grown on the dead wood of oak trees. The spawn of the mushroom are planted into holes or wedges cut into dead logs and a continuous crop of mushrooms is harvested for between three and six years. With new farming techniques, many mushroom farms use a temperature-controlled environment and artificial logs composed of various plant materials.

In this recipe, *shiitake* mushrooms are the basis of a tasty filling for herbed crêpes. In a novel presentation the crêpes are tied with a ribbon of chives. The crêpes may be prepared ahead and frozen.

Herbed crêpes (recipe follows)
4 tablespoons unsalted butter
½ cup chopped shallots
2 pounds shiitake mushrooms, wiped clean, stems discarded, and caps sliced into strips (or substitute 1 pound white domestic button mushrooms, the latter coarsely chopped, for 1 pound of the shiitake)
¼ cup brut champagne
1 cup whipping cream

½ teaspoon salt
¼ teaspoon freshly ground black pepper
½ teaspoon dried thyme, crumbled
⅛ teaspoon cayenne pepper
1 can (12 ounces) corn kernels, drained
1 cup grated Gruyère or Swiss cheese
24 whole fresh chives (choose long sturdy stems), lightly blanched

Melt the butter in a large heavy pan over medium heat. Add the shallots and sauté for 2 minutes. Add the mushrooms, cooking and stirring for about 10 minutes until all of the liquid has exuded and evaporated. Stir in the champagne, cream, salt, pepper, thyme, and cayenne pepper. Continue cooking until the liquid has almost evaporated, 8 to 10 minutes. Stir in the corn and the cheese. Taste and adjust seasonings, if necessary. Keep the filling warm, or cool and reheat just before serving.

To assemble, place 1 tablespoon of the filling in the center of each crêpe. Gather into a bundle like a drawstring purse and tie with a chive. Use a pair of scissors to snip off any overlong chive ends. Place on a lightly buttered platter and serve immediately.

❖ Herbed Crêpes ❖

2 large eggs
1¼ cups milk
½ teaspoon salt
Pinch of white pepper
2 tablespoons unsalted butter,
   melted

1 cup all-purpose flour
2 tablespoons finely chopped
   chives
Butter, for cooking

Place the eggs and milk in a blender or food processor and whirl for a few seconds. Add the remaining ingredients, except the chives and blend until smooth. Stir in the chives. Pour the batter into a small bowl, cover and refrigerate for at least 2 hours. A little more milk may be added if the batter is too thick after resting.

    Heat a 6-inch crêpe pan over medium heat. Coat the surface lightly with butter. Pour 2 tablespoons of batter into the pan, tilting quickly to cover the surface. Cook each crêpe until golden brown on the bottom and dry on top. Turn and cook about 20 seconds before turning out onto a plate.

❖ Smoked Salmon Hero Sandwiches ❖

Jamie Davies, Schramsberg Vineyards and Cellars
Accompanying champagne *Schramsberg Cuvée de Pinot*

Serves 4

The sandwich takes its name from an eighteenth-century Englishman, John Montagu, the Earl of Sandwich. Reluctant to leave the gambling tables long enough to dine, he had portable meals of cold roast beef between slices of bread brought to him. However the custom of placing food between slices of bread is an old one and workers in the fields had long been fed that way. Today there are various types of sandwiches and breads, with many nations having their own specialties. This sandwich is made from one large loaf of French bread and then cut into individual servings — a great luncheon entrée or picnic dish.

1 large loaf French bread
8 ounces cream cheese, softened
4 ounces smoked salmon, thinly
   sliced
Half a cucumber, thinly sliced

Red onion rings, thinly sliced
Black olives, sliced
Watercress
Freshly ground black pepper

Warm the French bread in the oven. Slice it lengthwise and remove a small amount of bread from each side. Spread each half with the softened cream cheese. Layer the salmon, cucumber, onion rings, olives, and watercress as desired. Grind some black pepper over the filling. Close and slice diagonally into individual servings.

❖ Black Bean Chili ❖

Sheryl Benesch, Korbel Champagne Cellars
Accompanying champagne *Korbel Natural*

Serves: 8 to 10

Chili is as old as the Aztec civilization in Mexico where the dish originated. There are many versions — some with meat and no beans, some with beans and no meat. The black or turtle bean used in this version is oval in shape and smaller than the more familiar red kidney bean. Its off-black skin hides a whitish inside. Black beans are most popular in the South and in South America. The Salsa Cruda, a spicy tomato sauce, may also be used as a dip with tortilla chips. Crusty French bread or corn bread complete this meatless entrée.

3 cups black beans
2 small onions, 1 chopped, 1 diced
3 cloves garlic, chopped
Salt to taste
2 tablespoons olive oil
1 green pepper, diced
2 tablespoons minced garlic
1 can (16 ounces) tomatoes, crushed

1½ cups chicken broth
1 tablespoon sugar
2 teaspoons cumin
1 teaspoon ground oregano
½ teaspoon cinnamon
3 teaspoon blueberry vinegar (or other fruit-flavored vinegar)
Salsa Cruda (recipe follows)

Soak the beans overnight. Drain the water, place the beans in a saucepan and add enough fresh water to cover them. Bring to a boil and boil very gently for 20 minutes. Add the chopped onion, chopped garlic, and salt to taste and simmer, covered, for 1½ hours.

In the olive oil sauté the diced onion, diced peppers, and minced garlic until soft. When the beans have simmered for 1½ hours, add the vegetables to them along with the remaining ingredients. Simmer very gently for another 1½ hours. Serve with sour cream and Salsa Cruda.

SALSA CRUDA

3 to 4 large tomatoes, finely diced
1 small red onion, finely diced
4 green onions, chopped
1 jalapeño pepper, very finely diced

½ cup chopped fresh cilantro
Juice of 1 lemon
1½ teaspoons ground black pepper
Garlic powder and salt to taste

Combine all ingredients in a bowl. Serve with Black Bean Chili.

❖ Linguine With Asparagus ❖

Karen Mack, Chateau Ste. Michelle
Accompanying champagne *Domaine Ste. Michelle Blanc de Noir*

Serves 6

When man first discovered that wheat grains when freed from the chaff had to be cooked to be eaten, he probably mixed them with water to form a paste and made dumplings. From there the paste was flattened, rolled, and cut into strips. By the third and fourth centuries B.C., many cultures were using some form of pasta and, by the Middle Ages, there were various names for this long, stringlike food. In this recipe, linguine, a long, thin, flat pasta, is served with a fresh asparagus sauce. Add the cream cheese very sparingly and only if needed to thicken the sauce, lest it mask the flavor of the asparagus.

2 pounds fresh asparagus, peeled
1 tablespoon butter
1 cup blanc de noir sparkling wine
2½ cups whipping cream

2 to 4 ounces cream cheese, cut in
small pieces
1 pound linguine
Freshly grated nutmeg

Cut the peeled asparagus into 2-inch pieces. Reserve the tips. Boil the asparagus pieces in salted water until crisp-tender, 4 to 5 minutes. Drain and rinse with cold water and drain again. Purée the asparagus in a food processor.

Melt the butter in a large sauté pan and lightly sauté the asparagus tips. Add the puréed asparagus, the sparkling wine, cream, and a few pieces of the cream cheese. Simmer until mixture thickens and reduces by one-third. If a thicker sauce is desired, add a piece or two more of the cream cheese and mix well.

Cook the linguine in boiling salted water. Drain and serve immediately. Spoon the sauce over the pasta and sprinkle lightly with grated nutmeg.

❖ Fettuccine in Cream Sauce with ❖ Goat Cheese and Gorgonzola

Frederick Horton, Wente Bros. Sparkling Wine Cellars
Accompanying champagne *Wente Bros. Brut*

Serves 4

This type of pasta dish is served throughout Italy and varies with the local cheeses available. In this recipe, the tangy flavor of California goat cheese is combined with the piquant flavor of Gorgonzola in an easily prepared sauce for fettuccine. To ensure that the sauce is creamy, buy white, soft Gorgonzola that has recently been cut.

3 tablespoons butter	*1/2 cup chicken broth*
1 1/2 tablespoons all-purpose flour	*1/2 cup white California goat cheese*
1/8 teaspoon ground nutmeg	*1/2 cup Gorgonzola*
Dash of white pepper	*8 ounces fettuccine*
1 cup half-and-half	*Grated Parmesan cheese*

Melt 1 1/2 tablespoons of the butter in a 2-quart pan over medium heat. Stir in the flour, nutmeg, and pepper, stirring until bubbly. Remove the pan from the heat and stir in the half-and-half and the chicken broth. Return the pan to the heat and cook, stirring constantly, until the mixture boils and thickens. Mix in the goat cheese and the Gorgonzola until blended. Place the pan over simmering water to keep the sauce hot.

Cook the fettuccine in a large pot of boiling water until al dente. Drain. Toss the fettuccine lightly with the remaining 1 1/2 tablespoons of butter. Spoon the pasta onto individual warm serving plates, and top with hot cheese sauce. Pass grated Parmesan cheese to sprinkle over each serving.

❖ Fettuccine with Wild Mushrooms ❖ and Champagne

Martha Culbertson, John Culbertson Winery
Accompanying champagne *Culbertson Cuvée de Frontignan*

Serves 4

Any combination of three or more wild mushrooms may be used in this dish. White cultivated mushrooms may be substituted for one of the wild varieties, but the end result will not be as exciting. If fresh mushrooms are not available, use the dried version, soaking it first. Culbertson Cuvée de Frontignan is a fruity, off-dry champagne made from a variety of the Muscat grape. It goes well with the mushroom flavors.

6 ounces wild mushrooms: morels, chanterelles, oyster, shiitake
4 tablespoons unsalted butter
1/4 cup Culbertson Cuvée de Frontignan champagne

1 pound fresh fettuccine
1 1/2 cups whipping cream
Salt and pepper, to taste

Slice the mushrooms into bite-sized pieces, but leave the morels whole. Heat the butter in a medium-sized sauté pan and add the mushrooms. Sauté them until they are just limp. Deglaze the pan with the champagne. Remove from heat and set aside in a warm place.

Bring a large pot of salted water to boiling and cook the fettuccine al dente. Drain and keep warm.

Heat the cream in a large skillet and reduce slightly. Turn the heat to simmering; add the mushrooms and fettuccine. Toss thoroughly. Remove the pan from heat if mixture starts to cook. Season with salt and pepper and serve on warm plates.

❖ Spinach Fettuccine with Prawns ❖ and Oyster Mushrooms

Ruth Wiens, Mirassou Vineyards
Accompanying champagne *Mirassou Au Naturel*

Serves 6

Colored pasta takes little more effort to make than plain pasta. The result is often spectacular. The colors in pasta are achieved by the addition of spinach or chard for green, beets for red, saffron or carrots for orange, and herbs for a speckled green. Many colored pastas are available fresh in the dairy section of the supermarket; some are available dried on the shelf. This recipe not only looks superb with its green pasta, red tomato sauce, and pink prawns, it also tastes delightful.

1 heaping tablespoon chopped shallots
6 tablespoons unsalted butter
1½ cups chopped fresh tomatoes
1 cup chicken broth
1 cup Mirassou Au Naturel champagne
¼ teaspoon dried thyme, crumbled
1 small bay leaf
½ teaspoon salt
¼ teaspoon white pepper

Grated zest of half a lemon
½ cup all-purpose flour
1½ pounds medium prawns, peeled and deveined
2 tablespoons olive oil
1 tablespoon finely chopped garlic
½ pound fresh oyster mushrooms, cut in strips
2 tablespoons chopped parsley
1 pound spinach fettuccine, cooked al dente

In a skillet over medium heat, sauté the shallots in 2 tablespoons of the butter for 1 minute. Add the tomatoes, chicken broth, champagne, thyme, bay leaf, salt, pepper, and lemon zest. Bring to a boil, reduce the heat and simmer for about 5 minutes, and set aside.

Place the flour in a clean plastic bag, add the prawns, and shake to coat them well. In a very large skillet over medium-high heat, combine the olive oil and the remaining 4 tablespoons of butter. When hot, add the prawns, which have been shaken to remove all of the excess flour. Sauté them for several minutes, until the prawns have turned pink and are lightly browned. Add the garlic and mushrooms; sauté for about a minute, stirring constantly. Add the tomato mixture from the other skillet, mix well, and simmer 2 to 3 minutes. Remove the pan from the heat and stir in the chopped parsley. Adjust seasonings if necessary. Cover the skillet to keep the contents warm while cooking the fettuccine.

To serve, divide the cooked fettuccine among 6 heated serving plates. Spoon the prawns and sauce onto the center of each serving.

❖ Spaghettini with Shrimp, ❖ Crab and Scallops

Martha Culbertson, John Culbertson Winery
Accompanying champagne *Culbertson Brut*

Serves 6

Many attribute the origin of pasta to Italy where the Etruscans developed it from a Greek recipe for a dough cake. One of the earliest words for pasta came from the Arabs who periodically invaded Southern Europe during the Dark and Middle Ages. *Tri,* from the Arabic word *itriyah*, meaning string, was used to describe strands, or strings, of pasta and eventually evolved into the name *spaghetti.* Thin spaghetti, called spaghettini, is featured in this recipe with an assortment of seafood in a cream sauce.

3 tablespoons olive oil
1½ pounds fresh medium shrimp, peeled (reserve the shells) and cleaned
1 tablespoon cognac
1 medium carrot, diced
1 onion, diced
1 stalk celery, diced

1 sweet red pepper, diced
½ cup brut champagne
Dash of cayenne pepper
1 cup whipping cream
½ pound sea scallops
½ pound fresh, cooked crabmeat
1 pound fresh spaghettini
Fresh basil leaves, for garnish

In a saucepan heat the olive oil, add the shrimp shells, and sauté them over medium-high heat. Add the cognac and flame the shells. Add the diced carrot, onion, celery and red pepper. Mix well and add the champagne and a dash of cayenne pepper. Then add enough water just to cover the mixture. Bring to a gentle boil and cook on low for 30 minutes. Put the mixture into a blender to chop the shells. Then strain it through a sieve, pressing firmly to remove all of the juices. Put the shrimp juices into a saucepan and reduce to 1 cup.

While the sauce is simmering, cook the shrimp in boiling salted water just until they turn pink. Drain them and set them aside.

Put the cream into another saucepan and reduce it slightly. Add the scallops to the cream and cook for 2 to 3 minutes until they are just done. Then add the shrimp, the reduced shrimp juices, and the crabmeat. Heat through.

While finishing the sauce, cook the spaghettini al dente. Drain and toss with the sauce. Serve on warm plates garnished with fresh basil.

❖ Crab in Pasta Shells ❖

Karen Mack, Chateau Ste. Michelle
Accompanying champagne *Domaine Ste. Michelle Blanc de Noir*

Serves 8

Large pasta shells are stuffed with crabmeat, decorated with pear tomatoes, and served with a rich goat cheese sauce.

*1 pound large pasta shells, cooked
   al dente and drained*
2½ cups crabmeat
4 pear tomatoes, quartered
2 tablespoons butter

2 cloves garlic, thinly sliced
¼ teaspoon red pepper flakes
½ cup blanc de noir sparkling wine
1 cup whipping cream
1 cup goat cheese

Loosely stuff the cooked pasta shells with the crabmeat. Place in a buttered baking dish and place the tomato quarters around the shells.

Melt the butter in a large sauté pan. Add the garlic and pepper flakes and sauté until the garlic is translucent. Then add the sparkling wine and simmer until reduced by one-third. Add the cream and goat cheese and continue to simmer, stirring often, until well blended. The mixture will thicken. Pour the sauce over the stuffed shells and bake in a preheated 425° F. oven for about 15 minutes until golden and bubbling.

❖ Ricotta Ravioli with Sage ❖

Tracy Wood Anderson, S. Anderson Vineyard
Accompanying champagne *S. Anderson Tivoli*

Serves 6 to 8

Ravioli, little packages of fresh pasta, may be stuffed with cheese, vegetables, meat, seafood, or a combination of such ingredients. They are then cooked and served with a sauce. These ravioli are filled with cheese and served with a butter sauce flavored with fresh sage leaves.

FILLING

2 cups ricotta cheese
3 eggs

1 cup freshly grated Parmesan cheese

Blend the ricotta cheese, eggs, and Parmesan cheese together in a food processor until smooth, but not soupy. Store in the refrigerator while preparing the pasta.

PASTA

2 cups bread flour
2 eggs
3 tablespoons olive oil

1 egg mixed with 1 tablespoon water for the egg wash

Blend the flour, eggs, and oil in a food processor until crumbly. Add enough water to make the mixture moist, but still a little crumbly. It should come together when kneaded by hand. Cut dough into 4 pieces and roll out into sheets on the thinnest setting on a pasta machine, or as thinly as possible by hand.

Onto 2 of the pasta sheets, spoon or pipe tablespoons of the filling in rows about 1½ to 2 inches apart. Brush the egg wash on the pasta between the rows of filling. Lay the other 2 sheets on the filled sheets. Press the pasta to seal it between the mounds of filling. Cut into squares and press the edges together. (If you have a ravioli attachment for your pasta machine, the process is much easier.)

To assemble the dish, cook the ravioli in a large pot of boiling salted water with a little oil in it. Boil the ravioli about 4 to 5 minutes and then drain them. Just before serving make the Sage Sauce (recipe follows), heat the ravioli in the sauce, and serve immediately.

SAGE SAUCE

8 tablespoons (1 stick) butter

¼ cup sage leaves

In a large frying pan, melt the butter over medium-high heat. Add the sage leaves and stir until the leaves are wilted, a minute or two.

SEABOOD

❖ **Orange Roughy with Snow Peas** ❖

Ruth Wiens, Mirassou Vineyards
Accompanying champagne *Mirassou Brut*

Serves 6

Orange roughy is a firm-fleshed fish from Australia and New Zealand. Usually shipped in the form of frozen fillets, it is now readily available in the United States. Monk fish or any other dense, firm-fleshed fish can be substituted in this recipe. The lemon-flavored rice gives this dish another pleasing flavor.

*2 pounds orange roughy fillets, cut
    into 1-inch-wide strips
Salt and pepper, to taste
¼ cup all-purpose flour
8 tablespoons (1 stick) butter
2 leeks, white part only, cut into
    2-inch long fine julienne (about
    2 cups)*

*1 cup fish stock or clam juice
1 cup brut champagne
1½ cups whipping cream
2 cups snow peas, cleaned and cut
    in half on the bias*

Season the fish strips lightly with salt and pepper and dust lightly on both sides with flour.

Heat a large skillet over medium-high heat and add 2 tablespoons of butter. Shake the fish strips to remove excess flour before adding them to the pan. Do not crowd them; half of the strips may have to be cooked at a time. Sauté the strips for about 1 minute on each side. Remove from pan and set aside.

Clean the pan, heat, and add the remaining butter. Add the leeks and sauté them over medium-high heat for 3 to 4 minutes, until limp. Do not brown them. Add the fish stock and champagne, bring to a boil, and cook until the liquid is reduced by half, about 10 minutes over medium-high heat. Add the cream and continue cooking about 10 minutes to reduce the sauce until it coats a spoon thickly. Season with salt and pepper to taste. Add the cooked fish, with any juices that have formed, and the snow peas. Cook just until the fish is heated through and the snow peas are softened, about 2 minutes.

Remove from heat and serve with *basmati* (a fine long-grained Indian rice) or regular long-grain rice that has been cooked in chicken broth to which a little grated lemon zest has been added.

❖ Poached Trout ❖

Steve Wenger, Biltmore Estate
Accompanying champagne *Biltmore Estate Brut*

Serves 4

In this recipe, trout is simmered in a champagne court bouillon that is later reduced to a velvety sauce. Serve with parsley-sprinkled boiled potatoes and a green vegetable. The poaching liquid is also excellent for salmon.

1/2 bottle brut champagne
1/2 teaspoon thyme
1 bay leaf
1/4 teaspoon salt
1/4 teaspoon freshly ground pepper

4 shallots, chopped
12 tablespoons (1 1/2 sticks) butter
4 trout, each about 12 inches long,
  cleaned and ready to cook

To make the court bouillon, place the champagne, thyme, bay leaf, salt, and pepper in a saucepan. Bring to a boil, then simmer for 10 minutes. Sauté the shallots in 4 tablespoons of the butter, and then add them to the poaching liquid.

Place the poaching liquid in a large shallow pan. Poach the trout, two at a time if pan is not large enough, until the fish flakes easily. Remove the trout and keep them warm while preparing the sauce.

Return the poaching liquid to the saucepan and reduce it by half. Whisk in the remaining 8 tablespoons of butter, a tablespoon at a time, until the mixture is smooth and the butter is well incorporated. Place trout on individual warm serving plates and spoon sauce over each fish. Serve immediately.

❖ Fillet of Tuna ❖

Steve Wenger, Biltmore Estate
Accompanying champagne *Biltmore Estate Brut*

Serves 6

Found in warmer waters such as the Mediterranean, tuna may well be the oldest food fish. In this recipe, fillets of fresh tuna are marinated in white wine, lemon, and cayenne pepper. They are then baked and served with a sauce of the marinade. The dryness of Chardonnay varies and a sweeter wine will result in a more flavorful sauce.

6 tuna fillets, 6 to 8 ounces each
1 large lemon
1 cup Chardonnay wine

1/4 teaspoon cayenne pepper
2 tablespoons plain yogurt

Rinse the tuna fillets, pat them dry, and place them on a deep platter. Squeeze the lemon juice over both sides of the fish. Combine the wine and cayenne pepper, and pour over the fillets. Cover and let them stand for 20 minutes.

Preheat the oven to 350° F. Place the tuna in a shallow baking dish, reserving the marinade. Bake in the preheated oven for about 10 minutes; fillets should be rare to medium. Do not overcook the fillets or they will dry out.

While the fish is baking, boil the marinade over medium-high heat, reducing its volume by one-third. Remove from heat. When the tuna is done, place the fillets on a warm platter. Add the yogurt to the marinade, heat through, and pour over the tuna.

❖ Snapper with Kale and ❖ Red Pepper Purée

Jamie Davies, Schramsberg Vineyards and Cellars
Accompanying champagne *Schramsberg Blanc de Noirs*

Serves 4

Small fillets of red snapper are steamed in champagne on a bed of kale and potatoes. A purée of red peppers tops the fillets. The red snapper, found principally along the Gulf Coast, is not the same as the Pacific snapper, which is a member of the rock fish family — as is rock cod. Either type of snapper may be used in this recipe, since they are both firm-fleshed, flaky fish.

2 red peppers, seeded and cut into chunks
1½ cups chicken broth
1 tablespoon butter
1 tablespoon vegetable oil
2 potatoes, coarsely grated and squeezed in a towel to remove moisture

1 bunch (about 1 pound) kale, cut into ribbons
½ cup champagne
4 snapper fillets
Lemon juice
Salt and pepper, to taste
Lemon slices, for garnish

Cook the peppers in 1 cup of the chicken broth until they are soft. Purée them in a food processor or blender. Press the pepper mixture through a sieve into a small saucepan. If the purée is too thick to spread easily, add some of the cooking broth. Keep the pepper purée warm.

Heat the butter and oil in a large skillet. Stir-fry the potatoes over high heat for about 2 minutes. Add the kale and toss until slightly wilted. Lower the heat and add the remaining ½ cup of chicken stock and the champagne. Cover and cook about 5 minutes. Sprinkle the snapper fillets with lemon juice, salt, and pepper. Place the fish on top of the kale, cover, and steam the fish until just done, about 4 to 5 minutes.

Reheat the pepper purée. Serve the snapper on a bed of kale and top with a stripe of the red pepper purée. Garnish with lemon slices.

❖ Seafood Ragout ❖

Steve Wenger, Biltmore Estate
Accompanying champagne *Biltmore Estate Brut*

Serves 6 to 8

A ragout is a stew of meat, poultry, or fish cooked in a rich, thick sauce. Since this seafood ragout is only lightly flavored with garlic and saffron, it depends heavily on the stock. The fish should be chosen carefully to provide a variety of flavors. If there are no trimmings to be used for the stock, any fish market will sell fish scraps especially designated for stock.

3 pounds mixed fish (red snapper, whitefish, flounder, bass)
1 medium onion, chopped
1 medium carrot, chopped
1/2 teaspoon thyme
3 to 4 sprigs parsley
1 teaspoon salt
1/2 teaspoon pepper
2 cups Johannisberg Riesling wine
1 pound fresh mussels in the shell

1 leek, rinsed and chopped
1 stalk celery, chopped
2 cloves garlic, minced
6 tablespoon unsalted butter
1 cup whipping cream
Pinch of saffron
1 teaspoon tomato paste
Croutons made from thin slices of French bread fried in butter

Trim the fish and cut into 1 1/2- to 2-inch cubes. Reserve the trimmings; there should be 1 1/2 to 2 cups. Refrigerate the fish chunks. Place the trimmings in a pot with the onion, carrot, thyme, parsley, salt, and pepper. Cover with 3 cups of water and 1 cup of the wine. Bring to a boil, then simmer gently for 30 minutes. Strain the liquid through a sieve, pressing as much of the vegetables through as possible.

Place the mussels in a saucepan with the remaining cup of wine. Cover and cook for about 6 to 8 minutes or until all of the shells are open. Drain, reserving the liquid. Strain the liquid through a fine sieve or cheesecloth to remove any sand. Remove 1 shell from each mussel and set the mussels aside.

In a large saucepan, sauté the leek, celery and garlic in 2 tablespoons of the butter. Add the fish stock and all but 2 tablespoons of the liquid from the mussels. Bring to a boil, then simmer gently for 15 minutes. Add the fish chunks, the remaining 4 tablespoons of butter, and the cream. Simmer over low heat for 12 to 15 minutes or until the fish is done.

While the fish is simmering, place the saffron in 2 tablespoons of the reserved mussel liquid and let it stand.

When the fish is cooked add the mussels, tomato paste, and saffron with its liquid to the ragout. Adjust the seasonings and heat through. Serve in rimmed soup plates with the croutons.

❖ Champagne Salmon with ❖ Sautéed Cucumbers

Ruth Wiens, Mirassou Vineyards
Accompanying champagne *Mirassou Brut*

Serves 8

Having fish stock on hand in the freezer makes this elegant entrée easy to prepare. The salmon fillets are lightly poached in a champagne sauce and garnished with sautéed cucumbers. Serve the salmon with boiled potatoes sprinkled with a little finely chopped dill.

4 tablespoons unsalted butter
1 tablespoon shallots, finely chopped
2 pounds fresh salmon fillet — preferably king (chinook) — in one piece, boned and skinned
Salt and white pepper, to taste

2 cups Fish Stock (recipe follows)
2 cups brut champagne
Parchment paper, buttered, to cover surface of pan
2 cups whipping cream

In a large sauté pan, melt the butter and add the shallots; cook until just translucent, about 2 minutes. Set aside to allow the pan to cool.

Cut the salmon fillet into 8 portions of about 4 ounces each. Arrange the salmon pieces in the sauté pan and season with salt and pepper. Add the fish stock and champagne and cover with the buttered parchment paper. Bring to a gentle boil and simmer until fish is just done, about 3 minutes. Remove the salmon to a heated platter and keep warm. Bring the cooking juices to a boil, add the cream and reduce by half, about 10 minutes. Strain the sauce through a fine sieve. Adjust seasonings, if necessary. Arrange on heated plates with Sautéed Cucumbers.

SAUTÉED CUCUMBERS

4 large cucumbers, peeled, halved, seeded and sliced into ¼-inch pieces

2 tablespoons unsalted butter
Salt and white pepper, to taste

In a large skillet, melt the butter over medium heat. Add the cucumbers, sprinkle with salt, and pepper and sauté until the cucumbers are slightly limp, but still crunchy, about 3 minutes.

FISH STOCK (FUMET)
(Makes approximately 1 quart)

2 pounds fish bones from any white-fleshed fish (sole, halibut, flounder)
1 medium onion, thinly sliced

2 cups dry white wine
Bouquet garni (sprigs of fresh thyme, parsley, and bay leaf, tied together)

Rinse the fish bones in cold water. Place them in a large heavy pot and add the onion. Cook for 10 minutes, covered, over low heat, stirring frequently. This releases the juices. Add the wine, bouquet garni, and enough water to cover. Bring to a boil slowly and skim the surface until there is no scum left. Reduce the heat and cook, uncovered, for 25 minutes. Strain through a very fine sieve. Refrigerate when cool.

❖ Poached Salmon with Black Bean ❖ and Ginger Sauce

Frederick Horton, Wente Bros. Sparkling Wine Cellars
Accompanying champagne *Wente Bros. Brut*

Serves 6

Salmon has probably been eaten since the Ice Age. The Romans, enchanted by the spectacle of hordes of leaping fish in the rivers of Gaul, named them *salmo* which comes from the verb *salio:* to leap. Scientists eventually gave the Atlantic salmon the name *Salmo salar.* There is only one variety of Atlantic salmon but there are five Pacific varieties. Best known are the king (chinook) and silver salmon. There is an Asian influence to this salmon dish which is served with a traditional oriental Black Bean and Ginger Sauce. Black beans are available in oriental markets or in the foreign food section of the supermarket.

5 cups water	*2 whole allspice*
1 cup dry white wine	*1 bay leaf*
3 tablespoons fresh lemon juice	*2½ pounds fresh center-cut salmon*
1 teaspoon salt	*in one piece, with skin*
1 onion, sliced	*Green onion tops and Chinese*
6 whole peppercorns	*parsley, for garnish*

Combine the water, wine, lemon juice, salt, onion, peppercorns, allspice, and bay leaf in an 8-quart saucepan or Dutch oven. Bring to a slow boil and simmer for 20 minutes. Cool this poaching liquid to room temperature.

Wrap the fish in cheesecloth, tying a knot to secure it. Lower the fish into the poaching liquid. Add more water, if necessary, to cover. Bring to a simmer, cover the pan, and poach the fish until just opaque, about 9 minutes per inch of thickness of the fish. Remove the fish and discard the liquid. Unwrap the fish, remove the skin and bones, and cut into 6 pieces. Arrange the salmon on individual heated plates and garnish with the Black Bean and Ginger Sauce (recipe follows), green onion tops, and Chinese parsley.

BLACK BEAN AND GINGER SAUCE

2 tablespoons light soy sauce	*2 teaspoons freshly grated ginger*
4 tablespoons fermented black	*2 tablespoons dry sherry*
beans, rinsed well	*Dash of hot pepper oil or Tabasco*
2 cloves garlic, crushed	*Sauce*

Combine all of the ingredients ahead of time and allow the sauce to stand for about 20 minutes to meld the flavors.

❖ Poached Salmon with ❖ Garlic & Wine Sauce

Karen Mack, Chateau Ste. Michelle
Accompanying champagne *Domaine Ste. Michelle Blanc de Noir*

Serves 8

For a colorful main course, poached salmon fillets with vegetables are served on a bed of crisp spinach topped with an interesting light garlic and wine sauce.

2 bunches fresh spinach
½ pound mushrooms, cleaned and sliced
½ cup sliced onion rings
⅓ cup carrots, sliced diagonally ¼-inch thick
½ cup celery, sliced diagonally ¼-inch thick

3 cloves garlic, peeled and sliced
8 salmon fillets, 6 to 8 ounces each
2 cups blanc de noir sparkling wine
2 tablespoons butter
10 to 12 peppercorns
8 tablespoons chopped parsley

Wash the spinach, discard tough stems, shred into salad size pieces and refrigerate to crisp.

Place the sliced mushrooms, onion rings, carrots, celery, and garlic on the bottom of a large ovenproof pan. Skin the salmon fillets and place them on top of the vegetables. Pour the sparkling wine over the fish. Dot with butter and sprinkle with peppercorns and parsley.

Bake covered in a preheated 375° F. oven for 15 minutes, then uncovered for approximately 10 minutes more or until the salmon flakes easily.

To serve, place a bed of crisp spinach on each serving plate. Lift the salmon out of the baking dish with a slotted server and place on the spinach. Using a slotted spoon, put some of the vegetable mixture over the salmon and spoon 2 or 3 tablespoons of Garlic-Wine Sauce (recipe follows) over the vegetables.

GARLIC-WINE SAUCE

1½ cups mayonnaise
½ cup blanc de noir sparkling wine
2 small cloves garlic
1 tablespoon fresh tarragon

2 hard-boiled eggs, peeled
1 tablespoon Dijon mustard
1 tablespoon fresh parsley

Place all of the ingredients in a blender and blend until smooth. Refrigerate for at least 2 hours before serving.

❖ Salmon Stuffed with Cucumbers ❖

Jamie Davies, Schramsberg Vineyards and Cellars
Accompanying champagne *Schramsberg Reserve*

Serves 4

The rivers of New England and New York were once abundant with salmon, but are no more. Today the East receives most of its salmon, primarily king salmon, by air freight from the Pacific coast. Buttery bread crumbs, cucumbers, and fresh dill are used in this recipe to stuff salmon, which is then oven-poached in champagne.

1 piece (2 to 2½ pounds) salmon, mid-section with cavity
2 cups dried bread crumbs
1 cucumber, peeled, seeded and chopped
3 green onions, chopped
1 tablespoon fresh dill, or 1 teaspoon dried dill weed

Zest of 1 lemon
½ cup chicken broth
3 tablespoons butter, melted
Salt and pepper
½ cup champagne
Watercress for garnish

Place the salmon on a piece of foil large enough to enfold it.

In a bowl combine the bread crumbs, cucumber, green onion, dill, and lemon zest. Toss with the chicken broth and 2 tablespoons of the melted butter. Salt and pepper the fish cavity and stuff with the bread mixture. Brush the remaining tablespoon of butter over the fish and draw the foil up. Pour the champagne around the fish and seal the foil packet. Place on a baking sheet and bake in a preheated 375° F. oven for 20 to 25 minutes, or until the fish is done to your taste. Serve with the juices from the packet spooned over the fish. Garnish with watercress.

❖ Salmon Paupiettes ❖

Sheryl Benesch, Korbel Champagne Cellars
Accompanying champagne *Korbel Natural*

Serves 4 to 6

Paupiettes are usually slices of very thin meat that have been covered with chopped meat or vegetables and then rolled up. Salmon, being a firm fish, may be thinly sliced and used for paupiettes. These salmon rolls, filled with chopped green onions, are quickly poached and served with a champagne sauce enhanced with tarragon.

2 pounds salmon fillet, in 1 piece
3 green onions, finely chopped
4 tablespoons butter
¼ cup sliced yellow onion
2 sprigs fresh tarragon
1 cup fish stock, heated almost to
   boiling (if necessary, substitute
   lightly salted water)

3 cloves
2 bay leaves
½ cup Natural champagne
1 tablespoon whipping cream
Watercress for garnish

Slice the salmon fillet on an angle, making ¼-inch slices. Lightly pound the salmon slices between sheets of waxed paper to a thickness of ⅛-inch or so. Sprinkle finely chopped green onion on salmon slices and roll them up neatly.

In a 12- or 14-inch sauté pan, sauté the sliced onion in 1 tablespoon of the butter over medium heat until the onions are translucent. Remove the pan from the heat and place the salmon rolls into the sauté pan. Sprinkle lightly with salt. Lay a small sprig or a few leaves of fresh tarragon onto each salmon roll. Remove the remaining tarragon leaves from the stems and chop the leaves (there should be about 1 tablespoon); set aside for the sauce.

Add the heated fish stock, or salted water, to the sauté pan with the cloves and bay leaves. Pour the champagne over the salmon. Cover the sauté pan and return to the heat, simmering on low for 8 to 10 minutes. Remove the paupiettes to a platter and keep warm while making the sauce.

To make the sauce, remove ¼ cup of the cooking liquid to a small sauté pan, about 6 inches in diameter. Add the tablespoon of chopped tarragon. Reduce the liquid by half. Whisk in the remaining 3 tablespoons of butter and the tablespoon of cream. Pour the sauce over the paupiettes and garnish with watercress.

❖ Salmon Papillotes ❖

Martha Culbertson, John Culbertson Winery
Accompanying champagne *Culbertson Brut*

Serves 6

In cooking terms, the word *papillote* means something, usually fish, cooked in a buttered paper. Buttered parchment paper is used because it swells with heat allowing its contents to cook in moist heat. In this recipe, the paper encloses fillets of salmon with julienned vegetables.

4 tablespoons butter
2 carrots, peeled and grated
2 leeks, julienned
6 mushrooms, julienned
Salt and pepper
2 teaspoons chopped fresh tarragon

6 circles of parchment paper, each
  14 inches in diameter
6 tablespoons cooking oil
2 pounds salmon fillet
12 fresh tarragon leaves
12 tablespoons brut champagne

Melt the butter and sauté the carrots and leeks for 5 minutes, add the mushrooms, and cook until limp. Season with salt and pepper, add the chopped tarragon and simmer for 2 more minutes.

Brush the parchment circles with the cooking oil, fold each circle in half, then open it again. Lightly brush a baking sheet with oil.

Cut the salmon fillet into 12 thin slices. Place a piece of salmon in each half circle of parchment, top with some of the vegetable mixture, sprinkle with salt and pepper, and add 2 tarragon leaves. Top with another piece of salmon and sprinkle 2 tablespoons of champagne over the fish on each circle.

Fold the circles over and form a package by pleating the edges of the parchment to close them. Starting at one corner, roll a 1-inch section of the edge over onto itself and press it flat. Continue around the half circle to seal.

Place the baking sheet into a preheated 425° F. oven to heat for 5 minutes. Then place the papillotes on the baking sheet and bake for 4 to 5 minutes. The papillote can be sliced open at the table and wonderful aromas will come streaming out.

❖ Oyster Stew ❖

Martha Culbertson, John Culbertson Winery
Accompanying champagne *Culbertson Brut*

Serves 6

In many parts of the country, particularly on the East Coast, oyster stew is traditionally served on Christmas Eve. It dates from colonial times and is not really a stew, since it is barely cooked. There are several methods of preparing this stew, all of them quick and easy: sauté the oysters and add hot milk; or sauté the oysters, heat the milk, and bring the mixture to a boil; or add the oysters to very hot milk and bring just to a boil to cook the oysters. This recipe uses the second method and makes a nice entrée for a Sunday evening supper. To make the stew even richer, substitute whipping cream for the half-and-half.

2 pints fresh shucked oysters
8 tablespoons (1 stick) butter
1/2 teaspoon salt
Pepper, to taste
Dash of Tabasco sauce

3 cups milk
2 cups half-and-half
1 cup whipping cream
Paprika, for garnish
Oyster crackers

Pick over the oysters to remove any shells, drain them, and reserve the liquor.

Melt 6 tablespoons of the butter in a large saucepan. Add the oyster liquor, salt, pepper, and Tabasco sauce and stir to blend well. Cook until heated through. Add the oysters and cook until their edges begin to curl. Do not overcook them.

Stir in the milk, half-and-half, and whipping cream and heat until the mixture comes almost to a boil but do not let it boil. Serve the stew in hot bowls and top each serving with a teaspoon of butter and a sprinkling of paprika. Accompany with small oyster crackers.

❖ Scallops with Pears ❖

Karen Mack, Chateau Ste. Michelle
Accompanying champagne *Domaine Ste. Michelle Blanc de Noir*

Serves 4 to 5

Sea scallops are combined with sliced poached pears in a slightly sweet and sour wine sauce for a light entrée suitable for a luncheon.

3 tablespoons unsalted butter
1 1/2 pounds sea scallops
1 tablespoon brown sugar
2 tablespoons lemon juice
1/2 cup whipping cream

1 cup blanc de noir sparkling wine
3 firm, fresh pears, peeled, sliced,
  and placed in water with 1
  teaspoon of lemon juice
Thin cucumber fans, for garnish

Melt the butter in a large sauté pan. Add the scallops and sauté gently for 3 to 4 minutes until just cooked through. Remove the scallops and set aside. Stir the brown sugar into the pan juices until it is melted and bubbly. Add the lemon juice, cream, and sparkling wine. Stir often until slightly thickened. Drain the pear slices. Return the scallops to the sauce, add the pears, and heat through, 3 to 4 minutes. Serve immediately, garnished with thin cucumber fans.

❖ Scallops in Saffron-Champagne ❖ Sauce

Ruth Wiens, Mirassou Vineyards
Accompanying champagne *Mirassou Blanc de Noir*

Serves 4

Saffron is considered to be the most expensive spice in the world. It is the stigmas of the *Crocus sativus* which now are mainly grown in Spain. The cost of saffron is high because it is necessary to gather the stigmas or "threads" by hand. Each flower produces only three stigma a year and the plant lives for only two years. Between seventy-five thousand and three hundred thousand stigmas are needed to make one pound of saffron. Saffron has been cultivated and used as a spice, as well as a dye, since early times in Egypt and Greece, although it is thought to have originated in Asia. Saffron has been cultivated all over Europe for many centuries and used in many cuisines. It is available either whole (in threads) or ground.

Most chefs pride themselves on their sauces, and Marcy Lessack, Mirassou Vineyards' chef, is no exception. She has created a silky smooth champagne sauce to accompany sautéed scallops. Serve with slices of sweet French bread to scoop up the sauce.

1¹/₂ pounds fresh scallops   *4 tablespoons unsalted butter*

Sauté the scallops in melted butter until warmed through and just opaque, only a few minutes. Using a slotted spoon, divide the scallops onto warmed serving plates and top with the hot Saffron-Champagne Sauce (recipe follows).

SAFFRON-CHAMPAGNE SAUCE
(Makes about 1¹/₂ cups)

3 tablespoons finely chopped shallots

2 tablespoons unsalted butter

2 cups fish stock

1¹/₂ cups blanc de noir champagne

1¹/₂ cups whipping cream

¹/₄ to ¹/₂ teaspoon saffron threads, crumbled

Grated rind and juice of half an orange

Small pinch dried red chile pepper flakes

Salt and white pepper to taste

In a heavy saucepan, sauté the shallots in butter for a few minutes, until they are translucent. Add the fish stock and champagne; boil until reduced by half. Add the cream and reduce by half again, or until the mixture coats the back of a spoon. Strain the sauce and return it to the saucepan. Add the saffron, orange zest and juice, red chile pepper flakes, and salt and pepper to taste. Keep the sauce warm.

❖ Scallops California-Style ❖

Ruth Wiens, Mirassou Vineyards
Accompanying champagne *Mirassou Blanc de Noir*

Serves 6

Fresh mushrooms, tomatoes, garlic, champagne, herbs, and avocado are combined in this recipe with lightly sautéed scallops and served on a bed of rice. The dish needs only a seasonal salad to round out the main course.

6 tablespoons unsalted butter
2 tablespoons minced onion
1 cup fresh tomato, seeded and finely chopped (canned pear tomatoes may be substituted, if good tomatoes are not available)
¼ teaspoon dried thyme, crumbled
½ cup minced fresh mushrooms
2 pounds fresh scallops, well dried (large sea scallops should be quartered)
½ cup all-purpose flour

2 tablespoons olive oil
½ teaspoon salt
¼ teaspoon white pepper
1½ teaspoons very finely chopped garlic
¾ cup blanc de noir champagne
2 tablespoons parsley, finely chopped
1 avocado, peeled and cut into ¼-inch dice
Cooked plain rice

Melt 2 tablespoons of the butter in a small skillet. Add the onion, tomato, thyme, and mushrooms, and sauté for a few minutes. Remove from heat and set aside.

Roll well-dried scallops in flour and shake off the excess. Heat the remaining 4 tablespoons of butter and the olive oil in a very large skillet (use 2 skillets if necessary). Add the scallops and sauté for about 2 minutes, turning to brown lightly on all sides. Season with salt and pepper. Add the garlic and sauté for a few more seconds. Add the champagne and the sautéed vegetables. Simmer for 2 minutes. Stir in the parsley and avocado just before serving over cooked rice.

❖ Sauté of Scallops ❖

Steve Wenger, Biltmore Estate
Accompanying champagne *Biltmore Estate Brut*

Serves 6

Nutmeg is the dark brown nutlike center of the fruit of an evergreen tree native to Southeast Asia and also grown in the Caribbean. The orange lacy husk covering the nutmeg seed is another spice, called mace. They are similar in flavor, but nutmeg is the milder. One of the last spices to reach Europe during the Middle Ages, this "nut of India" was reportedly used around 1200 to perfume the streets of Rome for a royal visit. In seventeenth- and eighteenth-century England, small silver personal nutmeg grinders became fashionable and permitted diners to grate fresh nutmeg over their meals. In this dish, nutmeg provides a subtle flavor for the scallops, which are best served with brown rice.

*2½ pound sea scallops, rinsed,
drained, and dried
5 tablespoons butter*

*2 medium shallots, diced
½ cup vermouth
½ fresh nutmeg, grated*

In a large skillet, sauté the scallops in 2 tablespoons of the butter over medium-high heat for about 3 minutes or until three-fourths cooked. Remove the scallops to a warm platter and discard the cooking liquid. Clean the pan.

Place the remaining 3 tablespoons of butter in the skillet and heat over medium-high heat until the butter is golden brown, about 1 or 2 minutes. Add the shallots and sauté for 30 seconds. Then add the vermouth and nutmeg and reduce until the sauce is thickened slightly. Add the scallops, toss to distribute the butter, and heat through. Serve immediately.

❖ Prawn and Scallop Brochettes ❖

Sheryl Benesch, Korbel Champagne Cellars
Accompanying champagne *Korbel Brut*

Serves 4

It takes less than thirty minutes to prepare these seafood brochettes, which pair well with pasta.

4 skewers, approximately 10
  inches long
16 large prawns, shells removed,
  leaving tails, and deveined
16 large scallops
Half a small onion, sliced thin

1/3 cup brut champagne
4 teaspoons fine unseasoned bread
  crumbs
4 tablespoons butter, melted
Dried thyme leaves

Heat the oven to 450° F.

Place the prawns and scallops on the skewers in the following manner. Pierce a prawn in the tail first and put it on the skewer. Then add a scallop and pierce the head end of the prawn, placing it on the skewer in a semicircle around the scallop. Repeat with 3 more prawns and scallops for each skewer.

Sprinkle the onion slices on a sheet pan or shallow baking dish. Lay the brochettes on the onion slices and pour the champagne over them. Sprinkle the seafood with bread crumbs and then drizzle melted butter over the crumbs. Place the pan on the top rack of the oven and bake for about 6 to 8 minutes. Prepare the Garlic Cream Sauce (recipe follows) while the brochettes are baking.

GARLIC CREAM SAUCE

1 tablespoon clarified butter
3 cloves garlic, minced
1/4 cup brut champagne
Dash of cayenne pepper
Dash of nutmeg

1/8 teaspoon salt
1 cup whipping cream
2 green onions, green tops only, cut
  into 2-inch thin julienne
1 tablespoon butter, chilled

Heat the clarified butter in an 8-inch sauté pan over medium heat, and sauté the garlic. Add the champagne, a dash of cayenne, a dash of nutmeg, and the salt. Turn the heat to medium-high and reduce the liquid by half. Add the cream and green onion tops. Again, reduce the sauce by half. Turn off the heat and whisk in the tablespoon of chilled butter. Serve over Prawn and Scallop Brochettes.

❖ Stuffed Lobster Tails ❖

Edna Tears, The Great Western Winery
Accompanying champagne *Great Western Blanc de Blanc*

Serves 4

Lobsters exist primarily in the Atlantic and are tastiest when they come from the cold waters off the coasts of Maine or Brittany. The spiny or rock lobster, which is clawless, is found in the warmer coastal waters of the Atlantic, Mediterranean, and Pacific. It is the source of the familiar rock lobster tails. These lobster tails are available frozen in the supermarket. In this recipe the lobster tail meat is cooked, put into the shells with onion, celery and green pepper, and then baked.

4 large rock lobster tails
8 tablespoons (1 stick) butter
3 tablespoons chopped onion
3 tablespoons chopped green pepper
2 celery stalks, chopped
1 cup fine bread crumbs
1/8 teaspoon dried thyme

1/2 teaspoon salt
1/2 teaspoon white pepper
2 tablespoons chopped parsley
1 teaspoon Worcestershire sauce
1/4 cup dry sherry
Grated Parmesan cheese

Poach the lobster tails until barely done. Split the shells in half and remove the meat, reserving the shells. Cut the lobster meat into bite-sized pieces.

Melt 4 tablespoons of the butter in a skillet, add the onion, pepper, and celery. Sauté the vegetables for a few minutes until crisp-tender and add to the lobster meat. Add the bread crumbs, thyme, salt, pepper, parsley, and Worcestershire sauce and mix. Melt the remaining 4 tablespoons of butter and pour, with the sherry, over the lobster mixture. Blend well. Place the lobster mixture into the shells and sprinkle with Parmesan cheese. Arrange the lobster tails on a baking sheet and cover with foil. Bake in a preheated 400° F. oven for 20 minutes, removing the foil for the last 5 minutes to let the tops brown.

❖ Poached Lobster ❖

Karen Mack, Chateau Ste. Michelle
Accompanying champagne *Domaine Ste. Michelle Blanc de Noir*

Serves 4

The tails of the Maine lobster, the most prized of the species, are use in this recipe. Live Maine lobsters are now available in many supermarkets throughout the country. In this recipe the tails are poached, removed from the shell, combined with a wine and cream sauce and then replaced in the shell for serving. If desired, the entire lobster may be cooked and the rest of the meat saved for a salad or another dish.

4 large Maine lobster tails
2 tablespoons unsalted butter
2 tablespoons lemon juice

½ cup blanc de noir sparkling wine
⅔ cup sour cream
Finely chopped fresh parsley

Thoroughly wash the lobster tails. Cut the undersides of the shells on both sides with kitchen shears to allow the meat to steam evenly. Place the lobster tails in a large flat pan. Add enough water to cover the tails and simmer, covered, just until the meat can be removed, about 7 to 9 minutes. The meat will not be fully cooked. Cut the tail down the middle of the back. Remove the meat and chop it coarsely.

Place the shells back in the water and steam them until they acquire the desired color. Then remove them and drain.

Melt the butter in a sauté pan. Add the lobster meat and lemon juice and gently sauté until the meat has finished cooking. Remove the meat and add the sparkling wine and sour cream to the pan. Gently simmer the mixture until it reduces. Replace the lobster meat just long enough to reheat it. Divide the mixture among the 4 shells, sprinkle with parsley, and serve.

❖ Chicken Breasts with ❖ Endive and Pears

Jamie Davies, Schramsberg Vineyards and Cellars
Accompanying champagne *Schramsberg Blanc de Noirs*

Serves 4

No one knows where pears originated. At the beginning of recorded history they were found growing wild and were being cultivated in Central Europe and Northeastern Asia. In Roman times there were about thirty species of cultivated pears; today there are about three thousand. One of the most popular varieties of dessert pear is the Anjou because it is juicy, firm, and very flavorful. In this recipe, the Anjou pear is combined with steamed endive and sautéed chicken breast. Bosc pears may also be used. To keep pears from turning brown after peeling, place them in water with a little lemon juice.

1½ cups champagne
8 small heads Belgian endive
1 tablespoon butter
1 tablespoon vegetable oil
4 half breasts of chicken, boned
   and neatly trimmed

2 Anjou pears, peeled and cut in
   quarters
½ cup crème fraîche
Minced parsley

In a medium saucepan, heat the champagne and cook the endive until tender, about 15 minutes. Drain the endive and set it aside. Reserve the champagne.

In a large skillet heat the butter and oil. Sauté the chicken breasts until lightly browned, about 4 minutes; remove them and keep warm. Add the pears (well drained if they were stored in water) to the skillet and sauté for 3 minutes. Pour in the reserved champagne, add the endive, and bring to a simmer. Cook uncovered for 5 minutes. Then return the chicken breasts to the sauce and stir in the crème fraîche. Cook just until warmed through.

Arrange the chicken, endive, and pears on warm serving plates. Garnish with minced parsley.

❖ Grilled Chicken with ❖ Raspberry Sauce

Tracy Wood Anderson, S. Anderson Vineyard
Accompanying champagne *S. Anderson Brut*

Serves 6

In this recipe for grilled chicken breasts served with a raspberry beurre blanc, the natural acidity of raspberries pairs well with a *brut* champagne. The more butter used in the sauce, the richer it is. Serve the grilled chicken with sautéed green beans or baby zucchini.

2 cups raspberries
1/3 cup wine vinegar
2 shallots
1/3 cup whipping cream

12 to 16 tablespoons (1 1/2 to 2 sticks) butter, softened
6 half breasts of chicken, boned and skinned

Combine 1/2 cup of the raspberries with the vinegar and mash them together to make a raspberry-flavored vinegar. Let this mixture sit for at least an hour.

Mince the shallots and put them in a small saucepan. Add the raspberry vinegar mixture and 1 cup of the fresh raspberries. Heat and cook until most of the liquid has boiled away. Add the cream and bring to a boil again. Simmer until the mixture is thick. Strain this sauce through a sieve and return it to the saucepan to heat once more. Reduce the heat to low and add the butter a little at a time, whisking until all is combined. Add as much butter as you wish for the desired richness of the sauce. Keep the sauce warm while grilling the chicken.

Grill the chicken breasts on an outside barbecue for 5 to 8 minutes on each side, or until done.

To serve, put a spoonful of the sauce on each plate and spread it to cover the plate. Cut each chicken breast into diagonal slices and fan over the sauce. Garnish with the remaining 1/2 cup of raspberries.

❖ Sautéed Chicken Breast with ❖ Champagne-Cream Sauce

Sheryl Benesch, Korbel Champagne Cellars
Accompanying champagne *Korbel Natural*

Serves 10

Writers agree that tarragon, a feature of this recipe, was one of the last herbs to reach Europe — in about the middle of the twelfth century. At a time when new foods were adopted more for their curative qualities than for their culinary value, tarragon was introduced in Europe by the invading Mongols who used it only as a flavoring. There are two varieties of tarragon. It is the French tarragon, not the Russian variety, that has the pungent leaves and is used in cooking.

This elegant chicken dish, served on a bed of steamed spinach, can be prepared in less than thirty minutes. A smooth velvety cream sauce flavored with tarragon is served over the chicken. Small red potatoes or wild rice and a green vegetable complete the main course.

5 tablespoons clarified butter
1/8 teaspoon salt
Dash of white pepper
5 chicken breasts, split, boned, and skinned
1/2 cup Natural champagne
Steamed Spinach (recipe follows)

1 tablespoon chopped shallots
12 sprigs fresh tarragon, each approximately 3 inches long
Dashes of cayenne pepper and nutmeg
1 cup whipping cream
1 tablespoon butter, chilled

In a large sauté pan, melt 4 tablespoons of the clarified butter. Lightly sprinkle salt and white pepper over the chicken breasts and sauté on medium-high heat until chicken is golden on both sides. Pour the champagne over the chicken and lay 1 sprig of fresh tarragon atop the side of the breast that was next to the skin. Cover the pan, turn heat to medium-low, and cook until the breasts are done, about 5 minutes. While the chicken breasts are cooking, prepare the Steamed Spinach.

Remove the chicken breasts to a warm platter. Pour out all pan juices and save. To the sauté pan add the remaining tablespoon of clarified butter and in it sauté the shallots until translucent. Add the reserved pan juices, the remaining tarragon, dashes of cayenne pepper and of nutmeg, and reduce the liquid to 1/4 cup. Add the cream and continue cooking until the cream thickens and is reduced by half. Whisk in the tablespoon of chilled butter.

Serve chicken breasts atop Steamed Spinach, with sauce poured over each serving.

STEAMED SPINACH

1 cup lightly salted water
Dash of nutmeg
2 tablespoons butter

4 bunches spinach, washed and stems removed

Bring the salted water to a boil in a large saucepan. Add the nutmeg and butter, then the spinach. Cover and steam for 3 to 5 minutes, stirring halfway through the cooking process. Do not overcook the spinach. Drain well, in order not to have any of the cooking liquid on the plates.

❖ Seafood-Stuffed Chicken Breasts ❖

Karen Mack, Chateau Ste. Michelle
Accompanying champagne *Domaine Ste. Michelle Blanc de Noir*

Serves 8

In this recipe chicken breasts are stuffed with either crabmeat or prawns and baked in a light almond coating. They may be prepared ahead and refrigerated until cooking time.

4 large chicken breasts, halved
8 fresh mushrooms, chopped
¹/₂ pound crab leg meat, or cooked
  prawns, lightly chopped
2 tablespoons parsley, chopped,
  plus extra for garnish

1 egg, well beaten
¹/₂ cup shredded Swiss cheese
1 cup almonds, finely chopped
8 tablespoons (1 stick) butter
Chopped parsley for garnish

Skin and bone the chicken breasts. Pound each half between sheets of waxed paper to make thin fillets.

Mix together the mushrooms, crab or prawns, 2 tablespoons chopped parsley, and cheese. Place a large spoonful of the seafood mixture on the inside of each piece of chicken. Roll it up and secure with toothpicks.

Dip each chicken roll in the beaten egg and then roll it in the almond crumbs.

Melt the butter in a large ovenproof frying pan. Brown the chicken breasts on all sides over medium heat. Place the entire pan in a preheated 350° F. oven for 15 to 20 minutes or until chicken is done. Serve, sprinkled with additional chopped parsley.

❖ Chicken Florentine ❖

Steve Wenger, Biltmore Estate
Accompanying champagne *Biltmore Estate Brut*

Serves 6

Featured at the Deerpark Restaurant on the Biltmore Estate, Chicken Florentine is sautéed breast of chicken served in a blanket of creamed spinach with a hint of Pernod, the French apéritif based on aniseed. Most of the preparation can be done ahead of time. Reheat the sauce and the spinach mixture while the chicken is sautéing.

CREAMED SPINACH

1 package (10 ounces) fresh spinach leaves, thoroughly rinsed
1 tablespoon Pernod
1½ teaspoons basil

1½ teaspoons thyme
1 cup water
½ cup Béchamel Sauce (recipe follows)

Place the spinach leaves in a large saucepan. Mix the Pernod, basil, and thyme in the cup of water and pour over the spinach. Cover and steam until done, about 3 minutes. Drain the spinach, cool it slightly, and then purée it. Add ½ cup of the Béchamel Sauce and set the mixture aside.

SAUTÉED CHICKEN

6 half breasts of chicken, boned and skinned
1 cup all-purpose flour
½ teaspoon salt

¾ teaspoon cayenne pepper
3 tablespoons butter
3 tablespoons olive oil
2 cloves garlic, peeled and crushed

Pound each chicken breast to a consistent thickness but do not flatten it out entirely. Mix the flour, salt, and cayenne pepper together. Dredge the chicken pieces in the seasoned flour. Melt the butter with the olive oil in a large sauté pan over medium-high heat. Add the garlic and sauté for a few seconds. Then add the chicken pieces, brown them on both sides, and cook just until done, but not dry. If done in 2 batches, keep cooked batch warm.

To serve, cover each chicken breast with some of the spinach mixture and top with a little Béchamel Sauce.

BÉCHAMEL SAUCE

Makes approximately 1½ cups
1½ cups milk
2 tablespoons chopped onion
3 tablespoons butter

3 tablespoons all-purpose flour
½ stalk celery, finely sliced
Salt and white pepper, to taste
Dash of ground nutmeg (optional)

Bring the milk to a gentle boil in a saucepan and add the onion and celery. Cook for a few minutes. Remove from heat and let the mixture stand for 15 to 20 minutes to blend the flavors. Strain the milk.

Melt the butter in a saucepan over medium heat. Add the flour and stir until well blended; do not brown the mixture. Add the milk and cook until the mixture is smooth, stirring constantly. Season with salt and pepper and a dash of nutmeg, if desired.

❖ Grilled Chicken Breast with ❖ Tomatillo Sauce

Sheryl Benesch, Korbel Champagne Cellars
Accompanying champagne *Korbel Brut*

Serves 6

Tomatillos, also known as Mexican green tomatoes, are not tomatoes but a type of gooseberry with a tart lemon-herbal flavor. They are sometimes called Chinese lantern plants because of the paper-thin covering around them. Cultivated since Aztec times in Mexico, tomatillos became well known in the United States in the early 1970s with the popularization of Tex-Mex cuisine. Tomatillos are now also grown in California. They are used in their unripe green state, with the papery skin removed, in *salsas*, sauces, enchiladas, and other Mexican dishes. Found in Mexican food markets and the produce section of many supermarkets, they keep for several weeks in the refrigerator.

Sheryl Benesch is very fond of Mexican cuisine. This chicken dish with Tomatillo Sauce is simple to prepare since the cooking is done on the barbecue.

3 chicken breasts, split and boned
Garlic powder, salt, and cracked
*   pepper, to taste*

Juice of 4 limes
¼ cup fresh cilantro, chopped

Season the chicken breasts with garlic powder, salt, and cracked pepper. Combine the lime juice and cilantro in a bowl and marinate the chicken pieces in the mixture for 3 to 4 hours.

Remove the chicken from the marinade and grill on the barbecue or a gas grill until done, 10 to 15 minutes. Serve with Tomatillo Sauce.

TOMATILLO SAUCE

1 pound fresh tomatillos, papery
*   skin removed and fruit washed*
*   and dried*
2 tablespoons olive oil
1 small onion, chopped
1 tablespoon garlic, minced

½ cup fresh cilantro, chopped
Juice of 1 lime
1 teaspoon sugar
Salt and white pepper, to taste

Grill the tomatillos on the barbecue or a gas grill until soft. Let them cool and blend them briefly in the food processor.

In a skillet, heat the olive oil and sauté the onions and garlic until translucent. Add the ground tomatillos and all of the other sauce ingredients. Cook for 10 to 15 minutes.

❖ Creamed Chicken with Avocado ❖

Edna Tears, The Great Western Winery
Accompanying champagne *Great Western Natural*

Serves 4

Chicken à la King was an American dish invented in the early 1900s. It became very popular and a great lunch favorite. There were other versions of the dish, such as Chicken à la Queen with pineapple chunks. The avocado gives another dimension to chicken in a cream sauce. Served with a tossed green salad, the dish makes a delightful main course for lunch or a light supper.

1 pound boned chicken breast
2 medium-sized ripe avocados
Lemon juice
1/4 cup chopped onion
2 tablespoons butter
2 tablespoons all-purpose flour
1/4 cup dry white wine

3/4 cup half-and-half
2 tablespoons snipped fresh parsley
1/4 teaspoon salt
Dash of white pepper
Dash of garlic powder
1 egg, slightly beaten
2 to 3 cups hot cooked rice

Cut the chicken into 1-inch cubes. Place in a saucepan, add enough water to cover, and cook until tender, about 3 to 5 minutes. Drain the chicken and set aside.

Halve the avocados lengthwise; remove the seeds and peel the halves. Brush the avocado halves with lemon juice and set them aside.

In a 1-quart saucepan cook the onion in butter until tender, but do not brown, about 5 minutes. Blend in the flour. Stir in the wine and the half-and-half. Cook and stir until the mixture thickens and bubbles, approximately 5 minutes. Add the chicken, parsley, salt, pepper, and garlic powder. Gradually stir about a third of the hot mixture into the beaten egg. Then return it to the remaining hot sauce and cook, stirring, until it bubbles again. Continue to cook on low heat for another minute or two.

To serve, spoon 1/2 to 3/4 cup of hot cooked rice on each serving plate and place an avocado half, hollow side up, on top of the rice. Spoon the chicken sauce over the avocado and serve.

❖ Le Poulet au Champagne ❖

Steve Wenger, Biltmore Estate
Accompanying champagne *Biltmore Estate Brut*

Serves 4

This chicken dish prepared in the classical French manner has an incomparable flavor. Fresh *shiitake* mushrooms may be substituted for the morels, or added to the dish, if desired. Small red potatoes and tender green beans complete the main course.

1 chicken (3½ to 4 pounds), cut into 8 pieces
8 tablespoons (1 stick) butter
3 dried morels, reconstituted and chopped
½ cup dry sherry

2 cups dry champagne
½ cup veal stock
6 tablespoons whipping cream
Salt and freshly ground pepper, to taste

In a large skillet sauté the chicken pieces in 4 tablespoons of butter for 30 minutes over medium heat. Turn the chicken frequently. It should be golden, not brown. Add the morels and sauté for 2 to 3 more minutes. Then add the sherry, champagne, and veal stock. Cover and cook on low heat for another 30 minutes or until the chicken is done.

Remove the chicken to a warm platter. Reduce the liquid by half, add the cream, and cook until slightly thickened. Whisk in the remaining 4 tablespoons of butter and adjust the seasonings. Pour the sauce over the chicken and serve immediately.

❖ Ten-Boy Chicken Curry ❖

Martha Culbertson, John Culbertson Winery
Accompanying champagne *Culbertson Brut*

Serves 6

While living in Singapore, the Culbertson family enjoyed this chicken curry, prepared by their Amah, every Sunday. The recipe uses authentic Southeast Asian ingredients, which do not include the familiar curry powder. The ingredients, however, have been translated into forms easily purchased in America, but the recipe is Norissah's. Ten-boy in the title refers to the number of condiments served with the curry. Traditionally each condiment was carried in by a serving boy — thus you could have five-boy curry or twenty-boy curry. Canned coconut milk may be found in the canned milk or gourmet section of the supermarket.

This recipe may also be made by substituting 1 cup of chicken broth for the coconut milk and omitting the yogurt. The dish then will have a different flavor, but will still be an excellent curry.

*1 frying chicken (3½ to 4 pounds),
   cut into serving-sized pieces*
4 tablespoons olive oil
1 onion, chopped
1 clove garlic, minced
*1 inch fresh ginger, peeled and
   minced*
1 tablespoon dried cilantro
1 teaspoon turmeric

*2 green chiles, seeds and membrane
   removed, then minced*
*2 tomatoes, blanched, peeled,
   seeded, and chopped*
½ teaspoon salt
1 teaspoon sugar
1 cup canned coconut milk
½ cup plain yogurt

Brown the chicken in the olive oil. Remove the chicken to a plate and drain the fat, leaving 2 tablespoons. Sauté the onion, garlic and ginger in the remaining oil. Add the cilantro and turmeric and continue sautéing for 30 seconds. Stir in the chiles, tomatoes, salt, sugar, and coconut milk. Cook for 5 minutes to blend. Add the chicken pieces and cook over low heat until the chicken is tender, 40 to 45 minutes. Stir in the yogurt, heat through, and serve with rice and the following condiments.

CONDIMENTS

*Shredded unsweetened coconut,
   toasted*
Chopped banana
Chopped cucumber
Raisins
Chopped mango

Diced avocado
Peanuts
Chopped apple
Chili sauce
Diced pineapple

❖ Chicken Pot Pie ❖

Martha Culbertson, John Culbertson Winery
Accompanying champagne *Culbertson Brut*

Serves 6

Chicken pot pies date back to colonial America. Not only did the early cooks use chicken in their pies, but other poultry, game, and meats as well. The vegetables to be included are up to the cook. In this recipe the snow peas add color as well as flavor. The elimination of a bottom crust ensures that none of the pastry will be soggy. Use individual casseroles for this recipe. The puff pastry, which may be found in the frozen food section of the supermarket, rises up on the bowls like a chef's *toque* and makes a magnificent presentation.

1 chicken (3 to 4 pounds), cut into pieces
2 tablespoons butter
½ cup sliced onions
1 bay leaf
½ teaspoon tarragon
1 tablespoon whole black peppercorns
½ teaspoon salt
1 cup brut champagne
Beurre manié (1 teaspoon butter and 1 teaspoon flour, kneaded together)

1 cup whipping cream
2 carrots, peeled, cut into 1 inch-dice and blanched until almost soft
½ cup frozen peas, thawed
1 cup sliced mushrooms
1 cup fresh snow peas, strings removed and blanched
1 pound puff pastry (can be purchased in the frozen food section)
1 egg beaten with 1 teaspoon water, to make an egg wash

In a large skillet brown the chicken pieces in the butter for 8 to 10 minutes. Add the onions, bay leaf, tarragon, peppercorns, salt, and champagne. Cover and cook until the chicken is tender, 40 to 50 minutes. Cool the chicken, remove meat from the bones, and cut into bite-sized pieces. Reduce the pan juices to 1 cup.

Whisk the beurre manié into the pan juices; bring to a boil, and simmer 5 minutes. Stir in the cream. Cook until blended.

Divide the carrots, peas, mushrooms, and snow peas among 6 individual baking dishes. Add the chicken pieces and mix lightly. Pour equal amounts of the sauce into each dish.

Roll the puff pastry ³/₈-inch thick and cut into circles 1-inch wider than the bowls. Brush the dough with the egg wash. Place the dough on top of the bowls, egg-side down. Pull the dough tightly across the bowl and press it firmly around the edges of the bowl. Brush the tops with the egg wash. Place the bowls on a cookie sheet and refrigerate for 20 minutes. Then bake the pies in a preheated 375° F. oven for 30 minutes or until top is puffed and brown.

This recipe may also be made in a large ovenproof terrine that is brought to the table for serving.

❖ Glazed Cornish Game Hens ❖

Steve Wenger, Biltmore Estate
Accompanying champagne *Biltmore Estate Brut*

Serves 2

Cornish Game hens are a cross between Cornish and White Rock chickens. Being small (they weigh between sixteen and twenty-two ounces), they have very delicate meat. This preparation of Cornish Game hens is enticing to the eye as well as to the palate. Filled with a nutty stuffing, the hens are roasted and served with a mandarin and cherry sauce. Fresh mandarins may be used when available and canned cherries may be substituted.

2 Cornish Game hens
2 small sweet potatoes, scrubbed
*   and pierced for baking*
¹/₂ cup pecan pieces

1 small can (11 ounces) mandarin
*   orange segments in light syrup*
2 tablespoons butter, melted

Remove the insides of the Cornish Game hens, rinse them, and pat them dry.

Microwave the sweet potatoes on high for about 5 minutes or until done, but firm; or cook the sweet potatoes in their skins until just tender, 20 to 25 minutes. Set them aside to cool.

Drain the mandarin oranges, reserving the syrup for the glaze. Peel the sweet potatoes, cut into ¹/₂-inch cubes, and place in a mixing bowl. Add ¹/₂ cup of the mandarin segments, the pecans, and the melted butter. Toss gently and stuff the hens with this mixture. Place in a baking pan and roast in a preheated 350° F. oven for approximately 1 hour or until done. During the last 10 minutes of baking, spoon over them a little of the Fruit Glaze (recipe follows), without any of the fruit.

When the hens are almost done, add the remaining orange segments and cherries to the glaze and heat.

To serve, place the hens on a serving platter, spoon some of the Fruit Glaze over them, and serve the rest of the sauce on the side.

FRUIT GLAZE

Fresh orange juice
1 tablespoon light brown sugar
1 tablespoon cornstarch

¹/₂ cup fresh Bing cherries, pitted
*   and halved*

While the hens are cooking, add enough fresh orange juice to the reserved mandarin syrup to make 1 cup of liquid. Place in a small saucepan and whisk in the sugar and cornstarch. Cook over medium heat, stirring constantly, until thickened. Set aside. Use some of the glaze for basting the hens, the rest as a sauce.

❖ Marinated Cornish Game Hens ❖ with Shiitake Mushrooms

Sheryl Benesch, Korbel Champagne Cellars
Accompanying champagne *Korbel Blanc de Noirs*

Serves 6

Star anise, an important ingredient in this recipe, is the dried fruit of an oriental evergreen of the magnolia family — a native of China and Japan. The reddish-brown star-shaped fruit is harvested when unripe and then dried in the sun. Star anise is used, whole or ground, as a spice in oriental cuisines. In this recipe it flavors a marinade for boned Cornish Game Hens served with sautéed *shiitake* mushrooms. To complete the oriental entrée, serve the game hens with steamed rice and stir-fried snow peas or asparagus. *Mirin* is available in an oriental grocery or the oriental section of the supermarket.

*6 Cornish Game hens, boned
    except for wings and legs
    (instructions below)*
4 dry shiitake mushrooms
1 cup boiling water
1 cup soy sauce
1 cup granulated sugar
3/4 cup mirin (Japanese rice wine)

4 whole star anise
1 teaspoon cornstarch
1 tablespoon water
*12 fresh shiitake mushrooms,
    stems removed, and sliced*
1 teaspoon peanut oil
1 teaspoon minced garlic
1/2 teaspoon fresh ginger, minced

To bone a Cornish Game hen, lay the bird on its side and, slicing along the side of the backbone, cut through the length of the hen. Place the hen flat, breast-side down. Cut through the cartilage above the breast bone and pull it out. Cut off the backbone. Take out the rib bones and collar bone by slicing down under the ribs first, then up to and through the top wing joint. Slice along the thigh bone to expose it. Slip the knife underneath the thigh bone and slice along the bone by cutting between the joint of the leg and the thigh bones. Remove the wish bone. Remove the end joint from the wings. Check the hen for any other bones that were missed.

Soak the dry *shiitake* mushrooms in the boiling water for 15 minutes. Then mix together the soaked mushrooms with their water, the soy sauce, sugar, *mirin*, and star anise. Reserve 1 cup of the marinade, pour the rest over the game hens, and refrigerate them overnight.

The next day remove the game hens from the marinade. Grill them for 10 to 15 minutes or until done, turning the hens every few minutes. Be careful; they can burn easily.

In a saucepan heat the reserved marinade. Mix the teaspoon of cornstarch with the tablespoon of water, add to the marinade, and bring to a boil.

Sauté the fresh, sliced *shiitake* mushrooms in the peanut oil with the garlic and ginger for 2 to 3 minutes.

To serve, sprinkle the sautéed mushrooms on the game hens and spoon some sauce along the edge of the hens.

❖ Poussin with Stuffing ❖

Jamie Davies, Schramsberg Vineyards and Cellars
Accompanying champagne *Schramsberg Blanc de Noirs*

Serves 6

Poussins are small chickens, weighing between one and two pounds. They are young chickens, but are old enough to have firm, well-flavored flesh. They are usually available in rural areas where there are poultry farms. Cornish Game hens or very small fryers, weighing between two and two-and-a-half pounds, may be substituted for poussins in this recipe. The stuffing of ham, black olives, bread and green onions blends well with the lemon-rubbed birds.

3 poussins or very small fryers
1 lemon
6 slices dry bread, crumbled
2 tablespoons butter, melted, plus
  extra, softened, for cooking
4 green onions, chopped
¼ cup ham, finely diced

¼ cup black olives, coarsely
  chopped
1 tablespoon chopped parsley
1 tablespoon lemon juice
1 egg, slightly beaten
½ cup chicken broth
Salt and pepper, to taste

Cut each poussin or small fryer in half and rub inside and outside of the bird with a cut lemon.

In a bowl combine the bread, melted butter, green onions, ham, olives, parsley, lemon juice, egg, and chicken broth. Toss lightly to mix and season with salt and pepper to taste.

Lightly rub a large, flat, ovenproof casserole or pyrex pan with butter. Place 6 mounds of stuffing in the pan, spaced far enough apart to permit a half of the poussin to be placed on top. Place the cut half of the poussin or fryer on top of each mound of stuffing. Rub the top of each bird half with softened butter. Roast in a preheated 350° F. oven for 40 to 60 minutes,, until done, depending on the size of the bird.

With a spatula ease each half bird with its stuffing onto serving plates. Keep warm while making the sauce, which is optional.

CHAMPAGNE SOUR CREAM SAUCE

1 cup chicken broth
1 cup champagne or dry white wine
4 tablespoon sour cream

Fresh herbs (chervil, thyme, chives), chopped

Deglaze the roasting pan with the chicken stock and pour into a saucepan. Add the champagne and reduce over high heat by one-third. Remove from heat, whisk in the sour cream, and sprinkle in the herbs. Pour some of the sauce over each bird.

❖ Grilled Poussin ❖

Marilouise Kornell, Hanns Kornell Champagne Cellars
Accompanying champagne *Hanns Kornell Brut*

Serves 6

For an easily prepared main course, poussins are butterflied, marinated, and grilled on the barbecue. Cornish Game hens may be used if poussins are not available.

6 poussins, ¾ to 1 pound each   *3 cups Champagne Marinade
                                                      (recipe follows)*

To butterfly a poussin, cut down the side of the backbone and open the back out flat. Cut down the other side of the backbone and discard it. Flatten the poussin by pressing firmly on the breastbone.

Marinate the poussins for at least 4 hours. Grill them over medium-hot coals on a covered barbecue or grill for about 20 minutes, basting every 5 minutes with the marinade. Be careful not to overcook the poussins.

CHAMPAGNE MARINADE
1½ cups brut champagne
*½ cup champagne, or white wine,
  vinegar*
1 cup olive oil
2 cloves garlic, crushed

*2 teaspoons chopped fresh
  rosemary (or 1 teaspoon dried
  rosemary)*
*Freshly ground black pepper, to
  taste*

In a bowl combine all of the marinade ingredients, whisking to mix well.

❖ Braised Quail on Polenta ❖
with Gorgonzola

Ruth Wiens, Mirassou Vineyards
Accompanying champagne *Mirassou Brut Reserve*

Serves 6

When the Europeans came to America there were neither quails nor partridges in the New World. There were, however, birds that were slightly larger, but similar in habit and habitat. These birds soon acquired the same names as their European counterparts. From New England to California they are called quail; in Louisiana the birds became known as partridges. Today quail are raised commercially and available in gourmet shops as well as in some supermarkets.

This quail dish can be assembled and refrigerated several hours before guests arrive. Bring it to room temperature before braising it in the oven. Snow peas, blanched or sautéed briefly in butter, are an excellent accompaniment.

1 recipe Polenta with Gorgonzola (see page 231)
12 quail, rinsed and dried
Salt and pepper, to taste
¼ cup olive oil
1 large onion, thinly sliced
4 cloves garlic, minced
2 tablespoons all-purpose flour
2 cups chicken broth

1 cup Mirassou Brut Reserve
¼ cup brandy
1 teaspoon dried oregano, crumbled
½ teaspoon salt
¼ teaspoon freshly ground black pepper
1 large red pepper, cut into fine julienne
2 tablespoons unsalted butter

Make the Polenta with Gorgonzola ahead of time, cutting it into 12 rounds, each about 3 inches in diameter.

Cut each quail down the center of the back from neck to tail. Spread the birds out, skin-side up, and press on the breast to break the rib bones so that the birds lie flat. Twist the wing tips under the shoulders. Season both sides with salt and pepper.

Heat the olive oil over high heat in a large sauté pan. Brown the quail on both sides and then transfer them to a large casserole or roasting pan. After all of the birds have been browned, add the onions to the pan and sauté for about 5 minutes, until golden brown. Add the garlic and sauté for 1 minute. Mix in the flour, cooking and stirring for 2 minutes. Stir in the chicken broth, champagne, brandy, oregano, salt, and pepper. Cook over high heat for 10 to 15 minutes, stirring often, until the mixture has the consistency of a sauce. Adjust seasonings, if necessary. Pour the sauce over the quail. Sprinkle red pepper over the top. Cover the casserole tightly and bake in a preheated 375° F. oven for 30 minutes.

To serve, melt the butter in a large sauté pan over medium-high heat and sauté the 12 polenta rounds on both sides. Place 2 on each heated serving plate and top each with a quail. Pour the sauce over the top.

❖ Quail Salad with Couscous ❖

Martha Culbertson, John Culbertson Winery
Accompanying champagne *Culbertson Blanc de Noir*

Serves 4

Couscous is a fine-grained pellet made from semolina flour and water — much like rice in shape. Used primarily in Middle Eastern cooking, couscous takes on the flavor and aroma of the ingredients with which it is cooked. Available in speciality food markets as well as some supermarkets, it can be used as an accompaniment to stews. This recipe, a specialty of Martha Culbertson's restaurant, was developed by one of her chefs, Jim Hill. Couscous is used as a stuffing for quail braised in the oven and then served on lettuce as a salad with a warm dressing. The dish makes an excellent luncheon or light supper entrée.

6 tablespoons clarified butter
1/3 cup minced red onion
1/3 cup minced red pepper
1/3 cup minced carrot
1/2 cup chopped parsley
5 cups chicken broth
1 cup couscous

4 quail
Salt and pepper, to taste
2 cups veal stock
2 cups blanc de noir champagne
A variety of lettuces
1 tablespoon balsamic vinegar
3 tablespoons olive oil

In a large sauté pan, heat 2 tablespoons of the butter over high heat. Add the onion, red pepper, carrot, and parsley and cook them for 3 minutes, stirring frequently. Lower heat and simmer for 2 more minutes. Remove the vegetables from the heat and set aside.

In a large saucepan bring 3 cups of the chicken broth to a boil. Place the couscous in a large container and pour the boiling chicken broth over it, mixing well so that all of the couscous is moistened. Cover the container and let it stand for 5 minutes. With a large fork mix up the couscous so that there are no lumps. Add 2 tablespoons of the butter and the sautéed vegetables, mixing well.

Stuff the quail with the couscous. Fold over the neck skin and secure it with a toothpick to close the opening. Fill the quail cavity with the couscous, packing it lightly. Do not overstuff the birds or they will burst while cooking.

In a large skillet heat the remaining 2 tablespoons of butter. Season the quail with salt and pepper and lightly brown them on both sides. Pour off any accumulated fat. Set aside while preparing the stock. If the skillet is not deep enough to hold the quail and about 1 1/2 cups of liquid, transfer them to another ovenproof pan.

In a saucepan combine the veal stock and the remaining 2 cups of chicken broth and reduce by half over high heat. Add the champagne and reduce further by one-third. Add the reduced stock to the pan with the quail and bring to a boil. Then place the quail in a preheated 350° F. oven for 10 to 12 minutes or until the quail are done.

To assemble the dish, place various types of lettuces on individual serving plates in an attractive pattern. Place one quail on each of the lettuce beds. Transfer the remaining stock from the baking pan to a small saucepan. Add the vinegar and olive oil. Heat, reduce if necessary, and serve warm over the quail.

❖ Grilled Breast of Duck ❖

Marilouise Kornell, Hanns Kornell Champagne Cellars
Accompanying champagne *Hanns Kornell Rouge*

Serves 4

Ducks have been hunted since the beginning of recorded time. Egyptians dried and salted them to have a constant supply on hand. The Chinese were the first to breed ducks for food and by the first century B.C. ducks had been domesticated in Europe. In this country, Long Island has been known for many years for its duck industry. Legend has it that all of the ducks raised on Long Island are descended from three ducks and a drake brought from China in a sailing ship around Cape Horn in 1873. This recipe, developed by Paula Kornell — Hanns Kornell's daughter and the marketing director of the winery — uses only the duck breast, which is marinated and then grilled on the barbecue.

2 cups puréed peaches
1 cup red wine
6 sprigs fresh rosemary

6 sprigs fresh thyme
2 whole duck breasts with the skin

In a bowl combine the peaches, wine, and herbs. Marinate the duck breasts in the mixture for 2 hours or overnight in the refrigerator.

Grill the duck on the barbecue or under a broiler for 8 minutes per side or until done to your liking.

❖ Champagne-Orange Duckling ❖

Edna Tears, The Great Western Winery
Accompanying champagne *Great Western Natural*

Serves 4

By the late eighteen hundreds ducks were raised not only on Long Island but also in Indiana, Kansas, Ohio, and in the Napa Valley in California. Today more than ten million ducks are consumed in this country every year. Ducks have been a favorite food in Europe and China for centuries and each country has its own way of preparing them. The French have an orange sauce, the Danes stuff theirs with apples and prunes, and the Chinese roast them crisply. In this preparation, homemade Champagne Orange Jelly is used to baste the duck.

1 duckling (4 to 5 pounds)
2 oranges, unpeeled and quartered
Salt and pepper, to taste

1 cup Champagne Orange Jelly
(recipe follows)

Wash and dry the duckling inside and out. Stuff the cavity with the orange quarters. Lightly sprinkle with salt and pepper and tie the legs together. Place on a rack in a shallow roasting pan. Cover and roast for 2 hours in a preheated 350° F. oven. Uncover, remove all fat and accumulated juices. Continue baking uncovered, basting every 10 minutes with the Champagne Orange Jelly, for 1 hour or until well done and well glazed. Untie the legs and discard the orange quarters.

To carve the duck, cut lengthwise and then crosswise to make 4 servings.

CHAMPAGNE ORANGE JELLY

Makes 4 eight-ounce glasses
1 cup orange juice
1 cup Extra Dry champagne

3 cups sugar
½ bottle fruit pectin

Combine the orange juice, champagne, and sugar in a medium-sized saucepan. Bring the mixture to a full rolling boil, stirring constantly. Add the fruit pectin and bring to a boil again. Remove from heat and skim off any foam that may have formed on the liquid. Pour into jelly glasses.

❖ Turkey with Pecan and ❖ Apple Stuffing

Tracy Wood Anderson, S. Anderson Vineyard
Accompanying champagne *S. Anderson Blanc de Noirs*

Serves 20

There is no better time to enjoy a turkey than at Thanksgiving with family and friends. The stuffing has become as important to the meal as the bird itself. In some parts of the country the turkey is not stuffed, but dressed. This means that the stuffing mixture is baked in a separate dish, basted with the turkey drippings and served alongside the turkey as an accompaniment. This method gives the hostess the opportunity to stretch the dressing with additional bread if unexpected guests arrive. This turkey stuffing pairs especially well with champagne.

4 cups bread cubes
8 tablespoons (1 stick) melted butter, plus extra butter for basting
2 onions, chopped
2 large apples, chopped
2 tablespoons butter
½ cup brandy

¾ cup chicken broth
2 cups toasted pecans
½ cup dried currants
2 tablespoons fresh chopped sage
Salt and pepper, to taste
1 turkey (15 to 17 pounds)
Melted butter

In a large bowl combine the bread cubes and 8 tablespoons of melted butter. Sauté the onion and apple in the 2 tablespoons of butter until soft. Add to the bread cubes along with the brandy, chicken broth, pecans, currants, sage, salt, and pepper. Toss lightly to mix.

Stuff the turkey, being careful not to pack the stuffing, and truss it. Season with salt and pepper. Place the turkey in a preheated 450° F. oven and immediately turn the heat down to 325° F. Roast the turkey for about 20 minutes per pound, basting with the pan juices and additional melted butter every 30 minutes.

GAME

❖ Rabbit with Wild Mushrooms ❖ and Grapes

Frederick Horton, Wente Bros. Sparkling Wine Cellars
Accompanying champagne *Wente Bros. Brut*

Serves 6

The rabbit reached America before the Europeans. The Aztecs had a rabbit god, while other Indian tribes in the Americas used rabbit for food. It also became a popular food for the colonial settlers. Thomas Jefferson was a particular fancier of rabbit. In one place where the settlers landed, they found rabbits so plentiful that they named the place for them — Coney Island. Coney, an old name for rabbit, is still used in the fur trade. Once hunted in the wild, rabbits are now bred commercially and are readily available in the supermarkets. Rabbit, which is primarily of white meat, and chicken are cooked in similar ways. In this recipe it is gently simmered in wine and garnished with wild mushrooms and grapes.

*1 rabbit (3 to 3½ pounds), cut into
    6 pieces
Salt and freshly ground pepper
½ cup all-purpose flour
6 slices bacon, chopped
2 onions, chopped
1 cup finely chopped celery leaves
Bouquet garni of 1 bay leaf, 3
    sprigs rosemary, 3 sprigs savory
    or chervil, tied together*

*1 cup brown stock or reduced beef
    broth
1½ cups Gewürztraminer wine
4 cups sliced wild mushrooms
2 cups seedless white table grapes
8 tablespoons butter
6 grape leaves, washed and dried,
    for garnish*

Wash the rabbit and pat it dry. Sprinkle the pieces lightly with salt and pepper. Coat the pieces with flour, shaking off the excess.

In a large skillet or Dutch oven, fry the bacon until brown and crisp. Add the rabbit and brown the pieces on all sides. Add the onions, celery leaves, bouquet garni, stock, and wine. Cover and simmer gently until the rabbit is tender, about 1 to 1½ hours. Remove the bouquet garni. The pan juices may be reduced or thickened, if desired, for a sauce.

Melt the butter in a sauté pan, add the mushrooms and grapes, and cook until the mushrooms are tender and the grapes still slightly crisp. Season with a little salt and pepper.

To serve, place the grape leaves on a large platter. Arrange the rabbit pieces on top of the leaves. Spoon the sautéed mushrooms and grapes over the rabbit.

❖ Venison Stew ❖

Marilouise Kornell, Hanns Kornell Champagne Cellars
Accompanying champagne *Hanns Kornell Rouge*

Serves 4

The word *venison* is derived from the Latin *venor* meaning to hunt. Originally venison referred to any game meat, but has come to mean only meat from the deer family. Venison is usually hunted in various parts of the country under strict laws. The meat is hung for several days to tenderize it. Red wine is used in cooking this stew, not only to add flavor, but also to act as a tenderizing agent. This Italian inspired stew is excellent served with polenta.

2 pounds venison, cut into cubes
2 tablespoons all-purpose flour
1/2 cup olive oil
1 large yellow onion, sliced
3 cloves garlic, chopped
1 large carrot chopped
2 large celery ribs, chopped
1/2 cup tomato purée

1 1/2 cups red wine (Zinfandel or
  Pinot Noir)
1 cup beef broth
1 bay leaf
1 teaspoon cumin
1/4 teaspoon dried oregano
Pinch of thyme
Salt and freshly ground pepper

Dredge the venison cubes in the flour. In a heavy skillet heat 1/4 cup of the olive oil. Add the meat and brown it on all sides. Transfer the meat to a casserole with a tight fitting lid.

Add the remaining oil to the skillet and sauté the onions, garlic, carrots and celery lightly over medium heat, stirring occasionally. The vegetables should not be brown. Transfer them to the casserole and discard the fat.

To the skillet add the red wine and scrape up the residue left in the pan. Boil over high heat for less than a minute and add to the casserole. Add the tomato purée, broth, bay leaf, cumin, oregano, thyme, and salt and pepper, to taste. Mix the ingredients to combine them. Cover the casserole and place it in the middle of a preheated 325° F. oven. Bake for 2 to 2 1/2 hours, stirring occasionally. If the liquid is absorbed before the meat is tender, add a little water, 1/4 cup at a time. Serve over or with polenta.

BEEF

❖ Tournedos of Beef with Red Wine ❖ and Blue Cheese Sauce

Frederick Horton, Wente Bros. Sparkling Wine Cellars
Accompanying champagne *Wente Bros. Brut*

Serves 4

Tournedos are the prized pieces of beef. They are the center slices of the fillet and are usually grilled or sautéed.

4 steaks from the center of the tenderloin, weighing 6 to 8 ounces each	3 tablespoons butter
	Salt
4 ounces blue cheese, crumbled	

Lightly salt the steaks. Heat the butter in a large frying pan until very hot. Add the steaks and cook over high heat for 4 to 6 minutes on each side, or to desired doneness. Lift the steaks out of the pan and keep them warm on a serving platter.

To serve, completely cover each steak with the Red Wine and Blue Cheese Sauce (recipe follows), and then garnish it with the crumbled cheese.

RED WINE AND BLUE CHEESE SAUCE

2 shallots, chopped	1 cup well-reduced beef broth
1 clove garlic, finely chopped	1 tablespoon arrowroot
1 bay leaf	2 tablespoons cold water
4 black peppercorns, crushed	4 ounces blue cheese
1 cup Cabernet Sauvignon (or other dry red wine)	

Boil the shallots, garlic, bay leaf and peppercorns in a small saucepan with the wine until the liquid is reduced by three-quarters. Add the beef broth and simmer for 20 minutes until somewhat further reduced.

Mix the arrowroot with the cold water. Pour the sauce into a pitcher, then strain it back into the pan. Mix a little hot sauce with the arrowroot paste, return it to the saucepan and cook for 1 minute. Whisk in the blue cheese and keep the sauce hot.

❖ Beef Tenderloin with ❖ Mustard-Cognac Sauce

Steve Wenger, Biltmore Estate
Accompanying champagne *Biltmore Estate Brut*

Serves 6 to 8

Ideal for a hot or cold buffet, this beef tenderloin is roasted in the oven and served with a creamy mustard and cognac mayonnaise.

*1 beef tenderloin, weighing about 3
   to 3½ pounds*
Freshly ground black pepper
¼ cup mayonnaise

¼ cup sour cream
½ cup Dijon mustard
3 tablespoons cognac

Preheat the oven to 350° F. Rub the beef with black pepper to taste. Place the beef in a shallow pan and roast in the preheated oven for approximately 30 to 40 minutes, to an internal temperature of 140° F., or to desired doneness.

Meanwhile, prepare the sauce by combining the mayonnaise, sour cream, mustard, and cognac. Blend thoroughly and refrigerate until ready to use.

When the meat is done, remove it from the oven and let it stand for a few minutes. Then slice it and serve with the Mustard-Cognac Sauce.

❖ Beef Supreme ❖

Edna Tears, The Great Western Winery
Accompanying champagne *Great Western Natural*

Serves 6 to 8

Beef Wellington, presumably a favorite of the Duke of Wellington, became popular in this country after the Second World War. Since then there have been several versions of it. This variation, which involves marinating the meat, is well worth the effort and makes a beautiful presentation.

1 cup dry red wine	*4 pounds rib eye of beef*
1 cup dry sherry	*Pastry (recipe follows)*
2 medium onions, quartered	*Mushroom filling (recipe follows)*
3 bay leaves	*2 eggs, beaten*
1 tablespoon Worcestershire sauce	*1 cup cold water*
1/2 teaspoon salt	*3 tablespoons flour*
1/8 teaspoon pepper	

Combine the wine, sherry, onions, bay leaves, Worcestershire sauce, salt, and pepper. Place the beef in a dish and pour the marinade over it. Marinate in the refrigerator for about 12 hours, turning the meat occasionally.

Prepare the mushroom filling; cover and chill.

Remove the meat from the marinade and reserve the juice. Place the meat in a shallow pan with enough of the marinade to cover the bottom of the pan. Roast in a preheated 425° F. oven for 60 to 70 minutes, or until a meat thermometer registers 130° F. The meat will be rare. Remove the meat; cool it for 20 minutes. Reserve the pan drippings for the gravy. Trim any remaining fat from the roast.

To prepare the crust, roll out the pastry on a lightly floured surface to a 14- by 12-inch rectangle, about 1/8-inch thick. Spread the pastry with the mushroom filling to within 1 inch of the sides and ends. Place the meat, top-side down, in the center of the pastry. Draw up the long sides to overlap. Brush with beaten egg to seal. Trim the ends, fold up and brush with a little more egg to seal.

Place the roast on a lightly greased baking sheet, seam-side down. Brush egg all over the surface. Bake in a preheated 425° F. oven for 30 to 35 minutes, or until the pastry is golden.

While the pastry is baking, combine 1 cup of the reserved marinade, the pan drippings, and 3/4 cup of the cold water. Blend the flour with the remaining 1/4 cup of cold water, add to the sauce mixture, and cook, stirring constantly, until thickened. Season to taste. Serve with the roast.

MUSHROOM FILLING

3 tablespoons butter
3/4 pound mushrooms, chopped
3/4 cup chopped onions
1/3 cup fine dry bread crumbs

4 tablespoons marinade
2 tablespoons chopped parsley
1/2 cup liver pâté

Heat the butter in a sauté pan and add the mushrooms and onions. Sauté the mixture over medium heat for about 10 minutes or until the onions and mushrooms are limp. Do not let them brown. Remove from heat and place in a bowl. Add the bread crumbs, marinade, parsley, and liver pâté. Mix thoroughly. Cover and chill for at least 1 hour.

PASTRY

2 cups all-purpose flour
1/2 teaspoon salt

2/3 cup shortening
About 1/2 cup very cold water

In a small bowl combine the flour and salt. Add the shortening and cut with a fork or pastry cutter until the mixture resembles small peas. Add the cold water, a tablespoon at a time, until the mixture is dampened and forms a ball. Wrap in plastic wrap and refrigerate for 30 minutes.

❖ Braised Beef in Cabernet ❖

Frederick Horton, Wente Bros. Sparkling Wine Cellars
Accompanying champagne *Wente Bros. Blanc de Noir*

Serves 6

Stews are a part of every nation's cuisine. At first meat was merely boiled with a bouquet of vegetables and served with a simple sauce. Then dumplings were added and later the meat was browned. Today stews are embellished with a wide variety of seasonings and liquids, such as the soy sauce, thyme, and red wine combined in this recipe. The meat is slowly braised in the oven and served with sautéed wild mushrooms. Rice, a green vegetable, and a seasonal salad would complete the main course.

2 tablespoons soy sauce
2 tablespoons all-purpose flour
2 pounds beef stew meat, cut into
  1 1/2-inch cubes
2 large onions, sliced
1 cup thinly sliced celery

2 cloves garlic, minced
2 cups Cabernet Sauvignon wine
1/2 teaspoon black pepper
1/2 teaspoon thyme
5 cups wild mushrooms, sliced
3 tablespoons butter

Blend the soy sauce with the flour in a 2- or 3-quart Dutch oven. Add the beef to the soy sauce mixture and toss to coat the meat. Add the onions, celery, garlic, wine, pepper, and thyme. Stir gently to mix. Cover tightly and bake in a preheated 325° F. oven for about 2 to 2 1/2 hours or until the meat and vegetables are tender.

Sauté the mushrooms in butter until limp. Place them on top of the braised beef and serve immediately.

❖ Fillet of Beef with Herbs ❖ and Sausage

Sheryl Benesch, Korbel Champagne Cellars
Accompanying champagne *Korbel Blanc de Noirs*

Serves 6

For this entrée, a fillet of beef is butterflied and filled with a spicy sausage and herb stuffing, marinated, and then grilled. The dish may be prepared ahead and cooked just before being served.

1 tenderloin of beef, "head"
  portion (approximately 3½
  pounds), trimmed of excess fat
  and silverskin
3 cloves garlic, minced
⅓ cup loosely packed chopped

fresh herbs, such as parsley,
  oregano, chives
1 pound spicy sausage, such as
  Italian or chorizo, cooked and
  drained of fat

Lay the tenderloin, fat-side down on a cutting board. Slice down the length of the fillet, cutting through approximately two-thirds of the meat. Flatten the meat to form a rectangle about 1-1/2-inches thick. It may be necessary to make additional small cuts in the center so that the meat will lie flat. If needed, cover the meat with a towel and pound the tenderloin to even out the thickness.

With the fat-side of the meat still down on the work surface, spread the minced garlic on the inside of the beef, then spread the herbs on top, leaving a 1-inch border along the edges of the meat. Lay the cooked sausage down the long center of the beef and bring the long sides of the meat up to cover the sausage. Overlap the meat by 1-inch to enclose the filling. Tie the meat into a roll with butcher's twine, squeezing the ends tightly to enclose the filling, creating a roulade.

Sprinkle the marinade (recipe follows) over the roulade and marinate the meat for a minimum of 3 hours, preferably overnight.

Grill the beef on a barbecue over direct heat for approximately 15 minutes, turning the meat regularly to keep it from burning. For medium rare, grill an additional 15 to 20 minutes, over indirect heat. Remove the meat from the grill and let it sit for 5 minutes before slicing.

MARINADE

1 teaspoon garlic salt
1 teaspoon garlic powder
2 teaspoons cracked pepper

1 tablespoon sugar
2 teaspoons Worcestershire sauce
2 tablespoons soy sauce

Combine all ingredients and sprinkle over the meat.

❖ Medallions of Veal with ❖ Pistachio Butter Sauce

Ruth Wiens, Mirassou Vineyards
Accompanying champagne *Mirassou Brut Reserve*

Serves 8 to 10

Members of the same family as the cashew nut, pistachios originated in the warmer parts of central Asia. They were reputed to have been a favorite food of the Queen of Sheba. In the first century A.D., pistachio trees were brought to Rome as a gift from the governor of Syria. Today the trees flourish all around the Mediterranean as well as in California, Texas, and Arizona. Pistachios are used in Middle Eastern as well as French desserts. They make delicious ice cream. Marcy Lessack, Mirassou Vineyards' chef, has created this dish.

> 2 tablespoons unsalted butter
> Salt and pepper
> 1 boneless veal loin (3 to 4
> pounds), trimmed and tied, at
> room temperature

Melt the butter in a heavy roasting pan. Season the veal with salt and pepper. Brown the meat on all sides over medium-high heat, for about 5 minutes. Place in a preheated 350° F. oven and roast for about 30 minutes, or until a thermometer inserted in the thickest portion registers 140° F. Baste with the butter several times during roasting. Remove the meat from the oven, cover loosely with foil and allow to rest in a warm place for 15 minutes before slicing. Slice into 1/4-inch thick medallions and serve with Pistachio Butter Sauce.

PISTACHIO BUTTER SAUCE

> 1/4 cup finely chopped shallots
> 1/2 cup champagne
> 1/4 cup white wine vinegar
> 1/2 cup water
> 1/4 teaspoon salt
> 1/4 teaspoon freshly ground white pepper
>
> 16 tablespoons (2 sticks) cold unsalted butter, cut into 16 pieces
> 1 clove garlic, peeled and mashed
> 1/2 cup coarsely chopped toasted pistachios

In a small, heavy saucepan, combine the shallots, champagne, vinegar, water, salt and pepper. Bring to a boil. Reduce the heat and simmer until the mixture is reduced to about 2 tablespoons. Cool it slightly. Over the lowest possible heat, begin whisking in the pieces of cold butter, one at a time. Do not add more butter until each piece has been incorporated. The sauce will have the consistency of heavy cream after all of the butter has been added. Whisk in the garlic and pistachios. Taste and adjust seasonings if necessary.

The sauce may be kept lukewarm in a double boiler. At serving time place over heat and whisk until hot. If the sauce is too thick, whisk in 1 teaspoon of cold water at a time until the desired consistency is reached.

❖ Veal Tenderloin in Morel Sauce ❖

Karen Mack, Chateau Ste. Michelle
Accompanying champagne *Domaine Ste. Michelle Blanc de Noir*

Serves 8

Veal, with its mild flavor, is a versatile meat that pairs well with various seasonings and accompaniments. In this recipe, veal tenderloin is roasted, sliced, and served with a mushroom cream sauce. It is simple to prepare and an elegant main course.

6 tablespoons butter
1 whole veal tenderloin,
    approximately 4 pounds
1 clove garlic, minced
¼ cup green onions, minced
⅓ pound morels, trimmed, washed,
    and coarsely chopped

½ teaspoon rosemary
½ teaspoon thyme
⅛ teaspoon white pepper
½ cup blanc de noir sparkling wine
1½ cups whipping cream

Melt 2 tablespoons of the butter in a large sauté pan over medium-high heat. Brown the veal on all sides, adding more butter as needed; about 8 to 10 minutes. Remove the veal to a roasting pan and set the sauté pan aside. Roast the meat in a preheated 325° F. oven for about 45 minutes; an internal thermometer should read 170° F. Fifteen minutes before the roast is done, reheat the sauté pan over medium heat. Add the remaining butter, the garlic, green onions, and mushrooms. Sauté lightly. Add the rosemary, thyme, and pepper and continue to sauté for 1 more minute. Add the sparkling wine and simmer 4 to 5 minutes, scraping the pan to loosen all the meat particles. Add the cream and continue to simmer and reduce the sauce.

To serve, slice the veal and serve 2 to 3 medallions per person. Serve the sauce over the meat.

❖ Veal Tournedos with Orange Sauce ❖

Tracy Wood Anderson, S, Anderson Vineyards
Accompanying champagne *S. Anderson Brut*

Serves 4

The best veal, known as milk-fed, is generally from calves two and a half to three month old that have been fed a diet entirely of milk or of milk and eggs. This results in a pale pink color of the flesh. The association of veal and milk goes back to Norman times when chefs prepared blancmange — veal cooked with milk and almonds. Over the years veal has become a mainstay of Italian, French, and Austrian cuisines. The mild taste of veal makes it an excellent vehicle for a great many sauces. In this recipe, veal slices are seared, finished in the oven and served with a tangy orange sauce.

2 tablespoons vegetable oil	Juice of 4 oranges
8 veal medallions, each about 3 ounces	Juice of 1 lemon
Salt and pepper	1 tablespoon sugar
¾ cup Chardonnay or other dry white wine	8 tablespoons (1 stick) butter, softened
	Orange slices for garnish

Heat the oil in a large frying pan over high heat. Sprinkle the veal slices with salt and pepper and sear them until brown on both sides. Then remove the slices to an ovenproof dish and place in a preheated 250° F. oven to finish cooking while making the sauce.

In the pan in which the veal was seared, add the wine and deglaze the pan over high heat. Reduce the liquid by three-quarters. Add the orange and lemon juices and the sugar and reduce by one-half. Strain the liquid into a small saucepan and, over low heat, whisk in the butter, 1 tablespoon at a time.

By this time the veal should be done. Serve 2 tournedos per person, top with the sauce, and garnish with orange slices.

❖ Veal Stew ❖

Martha Culbertson, John Culbertson Winery
Accompanying champagne *Culbertson Brut*

Serves 6

The mild flavor of veal is a perfect companion for champagne. This simple stew, with only a little thyme and bay leaf, brings out the full flavor of the meat. Carrots are cooked separately and added at the last minute. For an even richer sauce, cream may be added. Serve the veal stew with rice or boiled new potatoes.

1 tablespoon unsalted butter
2 tablespoons cooking oil
*3 pounds veal shoulder, cut into
   2-inch cubes*
1 large onion, chopped
3 tablespoons all-purpose flour
1½ cups brut champagne

1½ cups chicken broth
*¼ teaspoon dried thyme, or a
   generous sprig of fresh*
1 bay leaf
*6 carrots, peeled and cut into 2- by
   ½-inch pieces*
¼ cup whipping cream, optional

In a large saucepan heat the butter and oil. Add the veal cubes and brown them on all sides. Then remove the veal and sauté the onion until limp. Return the meat to the saucepan and sprinkle the flour over it. Stir until the flour is mixed into the meat. Add the champagne and chicken broth and bring to a boil. Cover and let the stew simmer for about an hour or until tender.

While the stew is simmering, cook the carrots in boiling water until tender. Keep them warm.

When the meat is tender uncover the pan and reduce the liquid to the desired consistency. Add the cream, mix well and reduce a little further, 1 or 2 minutes. Then add the warm carrots and serve.

❖ Veal Meat Loaf ❖

Martha Culbertson, John Culbertson Winery
Accompanying champagne *Culbertson Blanc de Noir*

Serves 6

This attractive meat loaf is simple to make. It may be prepared to the roasting point the day before, refrigerated and baked just prior to serving. The meat loaf can be served either hot or at room temperature, making it ideal for a picnic or tailgate party. If served hot, accompany the veal loaf with a tarragon hollandaise; if served cold, a red pepper purée or a tarragon mayonnaise goes well.

1 large red pepper	*1 cup toasted bread crumbs*
1½ pounds veal shoulder, ground	*Salt and pepper, to taste*
1½ teaspoons minced garlic	*3 tablespoons butter*
2 tablespoons chopped parsley	*2 tablespoons oil*
½ cup grated Parmesan cheese	*⅔ cup brut champagne*
1 egg	*Watercress, for garnish*

Roast the pepper over an open flame or under the broiler, place in a plastic bag for 10 minutes, and peel. Remove the seeds and membranes and slice the pepper vertically into ½-inch wide strips.

Mix the ground veal, garlic, parsley, cheese, egg, bread crumbs, salt, and pepper.

Tear off a piece of waxed paper 12 inches long. Dampen the paper on the bottom so that it does not slide, and on it pat out the veal mixture into a rectangle measuring 12 by 10 inches. Arrange the pepper strips in rows lengthwise on the meat loaf. Using the waxed paper to help roll the loaf, roll from one long side into a firm roll, measuring 12 inches by about 3½ inches. Pinch the seam closed.

Heat the butter and oil in a large ovenproof skillet. Once the loaf is browned, it is not delicate, but until then it does need some careful handling. Very carefully place the meat loaf in the skillet and brown on all sides, using a large spatula to roll the meat over.

Pour the champagne into the skillet and place it in a preheated 350° F. oven to bake the meat loaf for about 45 minutes or until done.

Allow the loaf to rest for 20 minutes and then cut into 1-inch thick slices. The red peppers will be exposed to make a colorful dish. Serve it on a platter garnished with fresh watercress.

❖ Bouchées de Ris de Veau ❖ au Champagne

Steve Wenger, Biltmore Estate
Accompanying champagne *Biltmore Estate Brut*

Serves 6

Sweetbreads are soft in texture and delicate in taste. Considered a luxury by some, they have long been everyday foods in many European countries. In this recipe, slices of veal sweetbreads are immersed in a cream and champagne sauce and served in puff pastry shells. The recipe is an old French one adapted for modern cooking by Martine Jourdain, who is married to Biltmore Estate's winemaker.

2 pounds veal sweetbreads	2 sprigs of parsley
11 tablespoons (1 stick plus 3 tablespoons) butter	1/4 teaspoon thyme
	2 cups champagne
1 medium onion, finely chopped	1/4 cup all-purpose flour
2 medium carrots, finely chopped	2 cups whipping cream
1 bay leaf	6 large puff pastry shells

Cover the sweetbreads with cold water and refrigerate for several hours. Drain and then place them in a saucepan, covered with salted water. Bring to a boil and cook over medium heat for 5 minutes. Drain and plunge the sweetbreads into cold water. Drain them again and trim away any gristle. Place the sweetbreads under a weighted board and refrigerate for 30 minutes.

Heat 8 tablespoons of the butter in a heavy casserole. Add the onion, carrots, bay leaf, parsley, thyme, and sweetbreads. Cover and cook over low heat for 20 minutes. Add 2/3 cup of the champagne and cook 15 minutes longer.

In a saucepan make a roux with the remaining 3 tablespoons of butter and the flour. Add the rest of the champagne (1 1/3 cups) and the cream to the roux and cook stirring constantly, over medium-low heat, until thickened. Cook over very low heat for a few minutes longer. Remove the sweetbreads from the casserole and keep them warm. Add the champagne sauce to the casserole. Stir to blend and adjust the seasonings, if necessary. Heat gently for 5 minutes. Slice the sweetbreads and serve in puff pastry shells with the sauce.

❖ Southern Comfort Food ❖

Jamie Davies, Schramsberg Vineyards and Cellars
Accompanying champagne *Schramsberg Reserve*

Serves 4

Sweetbreads were very popular in colonial America and were among the many dishes served at colonial dinners. They were often combined with oysters and mushrooms and served in a patty shell with a cream sauce. This recipe is an adaptation of an early colonial one brought up to date with the addition of sorrel and champagne. The sweetbreads may also be served on wedges of cornbread, waffles, or toasted French bread.

SWEETBREADS

3 cups water
Juice of 1 lemon
2 stalks celery with leaves, cut into chunks

3 sprigs of parsley
1 bay leaf
1 pair veal sweetbreads

Bring the water with the lemon juice, celery, parsley and bay leaf to a boil. Allow the mixture to simmer while washing the sweetbreads in several changes of cold water. Place the sweetbreads in the simmering water and continue to simmer for 20 minutes. Drain and place them in cold water for about 10 minutes. Then drain the sweetbreads again and clean them of tubes and membranes. Cover them and set aside.

OYSTERS

³/₄ cup chicken broth
2 cups sorrel leaves
1 teaspoon fresh marjoram or ¹/₂ teaspoon dry
1 cup half-and-half

1¹/₂ cups water
¹/₄ cup vermouth
20 medium oysters, shucked
Butter, for sautéing

Bring the chicken broth to a boil. Add the sorrel and cook 1 minute. Place in a food processor with the marjoram and purée. Strain and return the mixture to the food processor. Add the half-and-half and process to mix.

In a medium skillet bring the water and vermouth to a simmer. Add 8 of the oysters and poach them gently until their edges curl, about 1 minute. Remove the oysters and reserve the poaching liquid. Place the oysters in the food processor and purée with the sorrel and cream. Place this mixture in a small saucepan.

At serving time, sauté the sweetbreads in hot butter until golden. Bring the poaching liquid to a simmer and poach the remaining 12 oysters about 1 minute. Heat the sorrel mixture and add the poached oysters. Slice the sweetbreads and serve the slices with the oysters and sauce on wedges of cornbread, waffles, or toasted French bread.

❖ Calf's Liver with ❖ Country-Smoked Ham

Frederick Horton, Wente Bros. Sparkling Wine Cellars
Accompanying champagne *Wente Bros. Blanc de Noir*

Serves 4

Liver is about the only organ meat most Americans will eat. Calf's liver is preferred because of its tenderness. Aside from the varieties of liver pâtés available, the two most familiar liver dishes are liver and onions and liver and bacon. This recipe combines both flavorings in the form of mild shallots and smoked ham. The liver is served with a red wine sauce.

4 tablespoons butter
4 shallots, chopped
¼ pound country-smoked ham, cut
*   into medium-sized pieces*
2 pounds calf's liver, cut into 4
*   slices, membranes removed*

Salt and pepper
Flour for dredging
1 cup Petite Sirah wine
1 teaspoon fresh, chopped thyme

Heat the butter in a large frying pan and sauté the shallots and ham over medium heat until the shallots are translucent.

Salt and pepper the liver and lightly coat it with flour.

Add the liver slices to the pan and sauté until the liver is well browned, but still pink inside, about 5 minutes on each side.

Remove the liver to a warm platter. Add the wine and fresh thyme to the pan juices and boil for 1 minute over high heat to deglaze the pan. Pour the sauce over the liver and serve.

❖ Marinated Leg of Lamb ❖

Martha Culbertson, John Culbertson Winery
Accompanying champagne *Culbertson Cuvée Rouge*

Serves 10

Martha Culbertson learned this method of preparing a leg of lamb from her friend Julia Child. Both Martha and her husband, John, participate in the preparation of this entrée. John likes to grill the lamb outdoors over a grapevine fire to which fresh rosemary is added for the last 20 minutes of cooking. This gives the meat a smoky, herbal flavor. The lamb can also be roasted very successfully in the oven.

*1 leg of lamb (4 to 5 pounds),
    butterflied*
6 cloves garlic, sliced

4 tablespoons olive oil
2 tablespoons soy sauce
Juice of half a lemon

Lay the boned leg of lamb out flat on a cutting board. Make tiny slits all over the meat and insert the slivers of garlic into the meat. Combine the olive oil, soy sauce, and lemon juice and rub both sides of the lamb with the mixture. Let the meat marinate for at least 1 hour, preferably more.

Prepare the barbecue and when the coals are ready, place the leg of lamb on the grill. Barbecue about 20 minutes on each side or, for medium, a total of 40 minutes cooking time.

Place the cooked lamb on a carving board and let it rest for 10 minutes before slicing.

❖ Rack of Lamb with Mint Sabayon ❖

Tracy Wood Anderson, S. Anderson Vineyard
Accompanying champagne *S. Anderson Blanc de Noirs*

Serves 6

Sheep and goats have provided meat for mankind since antiquity. They predate cattle and pigs and were first domesticated in the Middle East, in northern Iraq. Sheep provide not only milk and meat, but also wool for clothing. In modern times meat has become more important. Lamb, the meat from sheep under a year old, provides small tender cuts. If older, it is mutton and tends to be tough. In this recipe, the racks of lamb are roasted in the oven and served with a light mint sauce.

2 racks of lamb (about 1½ to 2¼ pounds each), excess fat removed and the underside of the bones scraped clean

2 medium cloves garlic
Salt and pepper

Rub the racks of lamb with garlic and sprinkle them with salt and pepper. Place the lamb on a metal rack in a roasting pan and roast in a preheated 400° F. oven for about 30 minutes or to an internal temperature of 145° F. While the lamb is roasting, make the sauce.

MINT SABAYON

5 egg yolks
1 cup champagne

Salt and pepper, to taste
1 tablespoon freshly chopped mint

Combine the egg yolks, champagne, salt and pepper in a stainless steel or copper bowl. With a wire whisk, whip the mixture over simmering water until it triples in volume and becomes thick, about 10 minutes. Carefully stir in the mint.

To serve the dish, carve the lamb into chops and accompany with the sauce.

❖ Pork Tenderloin Roasted ❖ in Rock Salt

Steve Wenger, Biltmore Estate
Accompanying champagne *Biltmore Estate Brut*

Serves 6 to 8

Excavations have shown that the Chinese were probably the first people to roast pork. In the 1970s pork went out of favor because of the fat content of the meat. Today's pork is much leaner and is regaining popularity. The roasting technique used here of encasing the meat in rock salt ensures that the lean pork is moist and flavorful.

*4 pork tenderloins (approximately
  3 pounds in total weight)
2 tablespoons dried rosemary
Freshly ground black pepper*

*5 pounds rock salt
Riesling wine, in the dry style, for
  moistening*

Preheat the oven to 500° F. Sprinkle rosemary and pepper over the pork tenderloins. Place a sheet of foil in a roasting pan. The sheet should be large enough to enclose loosely the rock salt and all four tenderloins laid side by side.

Place a layer of rock salt on the foil and moisten it slightly with the wine. Place the seasoned roasts on the rock salt and loosely fold the foil up around them. Then pack wine-moistened rock salt around and over the pork. The rock salt should completely encase the meat. Do not seal the foil package at the top.

Insert a meat thermometer or oven probe into one tenderloin, removing a small amount of the rock salt around it to do so. Roast at 500° F. until the internal temperature of the meat is 155° F., approximately 20 to 30 minutes total cooking time. Let the meat stand at room temperature for 10 to 15 minutes, then crack and remove the rock salt. Slice the meat and serve.

❖ Pork Tenderloin with ❖ Mole Paste Stuffing

Jamie Davies, Schramsberg Vineyards and Cellars
Accompanying champagne *Schramsberg Blanc de Noirs*

Serves 4

Pigs were reputed to have arrived in America in the fifteen hundreds with Hernando de Soto and Cortez. Pork became the mainstay of the early American diet in both the Virginia and Massachusetts colonies. Pigs were easy to maintain, required no supervision, and were satisfied with scraps of all types. Their meat was cured and smoked for winter. Bacon and ham became staples for the pioneers during their migration west.

The *mole* used with pork in this recipe is a sauce of which there are several variations. The sauce dates back to Aztec times and the principal ingredient is chile pepper. The famous *mole poblano* is a rich dark brown sauce that owes its color to bitter chocolate. It is mostly used with pork and poultry. The *mole* paste is available in Mexican food markets and in the foreign food section of some supermarkets.

2 tablespoons mole paste
½ cup chicken broth
2 pork tenderloins (1½ to 2 pounds each)
4 small leeks, cleaned, trimmed, and chopped

2 tablespoons butter
3 slices bread, crumbled
4 slices bacon
Cilantro, for garnish

Combine the 2 tablespoons of *mole* paste and the chicken stock in a small saucepan and whisk over medium heat until smooth. Remove from the heat.

Butterfly the pork tenderloins by cutting almost through the length. Fold open and pound each side moderately to reduce thickness. Sprinkle with salt and pepper.

Sauté the leeks in butter, add the bread crumbs and toss. Mix in the *mole*. Spread the chopped leeks and bread mixture on the opened pork; close and tie in 3 places. Place, seam-side down, in a roasting pan and top each tenderloin with 2 bacon slices. Roast in a preheated 375° F. oven for 30 minutes. Then reduce the heat to 350° F. and continue roasting for another 20 minutes or until a meat thermometer registers 140° F. Remove the meat to a warm serving platter and make the sauce.

MOLE SAUCE

½ cup chicken broth
½ cup champagne or dry white wine
1 tablespoon mole paste

Beurre manié (1 tablespoon butter and 1 tablespoon flour kneaded together)

Deglaze the roasting pan with the chicken broth and wine. Whisk in enough beurre manié to make a sauce. Whisk in the *mole* paste. Strain the sauce and serve over the sliced pork tenderloin. Garnish with cilantro.

❖ Medallions of Pork with ❖ Champagne Mustard Sauce

Sheryl Benesch, Korbel Champagne Cellars
Accompanying champagne *Korbel Blanc de Noirs*

Serves 2 to 3

Pork tenderloin may be prepared in many ways, but it is best cooked in a moist heat in order to retain its juices. This cut of pork is readily available from your butcher or the supermarket. The dish can be prepared in less than 30 minutes. Serve the pork tenderloin with wild rice or Spätzle (page 227).

*1 pound pork tenderloin, cut into
    medallions about 1-inch thick*
Salt and pepper
Flour
1 tablespoon butter
¼ cup blanc de noirs champagne

¼ teaspoon dried rosemary
1 teaspoon Dijon mustard
1 teaspoon honey
*2 tablespoons demi-glace or
    heavily reduced beef broth*
4 tablespoons whipping cream

Sprinkle the pork medallions with salt and pepper and lightly dust them with flour. In a heavy sauté pan, melt the butter and sear the pork over medium-high heat. Cover the pan, turn the heat to low and cook until pork is done, about 10 minutes. Remove the medallions to warm plates.

Add the champagne and rosemary to the sauté pan, turn heat to medium-high and reduce to approximately 2 tablespoons. Add the mustard, honey, and *demi-glace* or beef broth. Mix well. Then add the cream. Bring to a boil and serve immediately over the pork medallions.

❖ Barbecued Spareribs ❖

Edna Tears, The Great Western Winery
Accompanying champagne *Great Western Natural*

Serves 4

Barbecued spareribs could be considered soul food — they go to the soul of the consumer and the heart of American cooking. Most barbecue sauces use ketchup for a base, but from there on it is everybody for themselves. The innovations are endless. Whatever strikes the cook's fancy — honey, brown sugar, mustard, spices, even tropical fruits. Regardless of the type of sauce, pork spareribs are at their best when they are cooked slowly, as they are in this recipe. The ribs may also be cooked over a slow charcoal fire.

3 pounds spareribs
Salt

2 cups Barbecue Sauce (recipe follows)

Place the ribs on a meat rack and sprinkle with salt. Place the rack in a shallow roasting pan and roast in a preheated 325° F. oven for 15 minutes. Then begin to brush the ribs with the barbecue sauce every 15 minutes for a total roasting time of 1¹/₂ hours or until no pink shows when a knife is inserted into the lean meat.

BARBECUE SAUCE

1 cup ketchup
¹/₄ cup white wine vinegar
¹/₄ cup Worcestershire sauce
¹/₂ cup dry red wine
1 tablespoon prepared mustard

1 tablespoon minced onion
2 teaspoons paprika
¹/₄ teaspoon Tabasco sauce
1 teaspoon sugar

Mix all of the sauce ingredients in a small saucepan and simmer for 10 minutes.

❖ Choucroute in Champagne ❖ with Smoked Pork Loin

Ruth Wiens, Mirassou Vineyards
Accompanying champagne *Mirassou Brut*

Serves 6

Choucroute is the French word for sauerkraut, which in this recipe is cooked in champagne. Juniper berries, bacon, and tart apples are added to the sauerkraut which surrounds smoked pork chops. This dish would have met with the approval of Justine Mirassou, wife of Peter Mirassou, the third-generation owner of the winery. In the early nineteen hundreds she came to America from Alsace where this entrée is famous.

4 pounds sauerkraut
1/4 pound bacon, chopped
2 large onions, chopped (about 4
    cups)
2 large tart apples, peeled, cored,
    and chopped
10 whole juniper berries
2 teaspoons caraway seeds

1 large bay leaf
1 1/2 teaspoons freshly ground black
    pepper
1 bottle brut champagne
6 smoked loin pork chops, cut
    3/4-inch thick
Boiled potatoes tossed with butter
    and chopped parsley

Place the sauerkraut in a colander and rinse well under cold running water. Drain well and squeeze dry.

In a large, 6-quart, heavy, ovenproof casserole or Dutch oven with a tight fitting lid, sauté the bacon until the fat is almost rendered, about 5 to 8 minutes over medium-high heat. Add the onions, lower the heat to medium, and sauté for about 15 minutes, stirring often until the onions are limp and golden in color. Stir in the sauerkraut, apples, juniper berries, caraway seeds, bay leaf, pepper, and champagne, mixing well. Cover the casserole and bake in a preheated 350° F. oven for 1 1/2 hours, stirring about every 30 minutes.

Remove the casserole from the oven and spoon half of the sauerkraut into a bowl. Arrange the pork chops, in a single layer if possible, over the top of the sauerkraut in the casserole. Cover with the sauerkraut in the bowl. Return to the oven and bake, uncovered, for 30 minutes. Sauerkraut should be moist, but not soupy. Serve with boiled potatoes that have been drizzled with melted butter, then tossed with chopped parsley.

❖ Leeks and Ham on ❖ Cornmeal Pancakes

Jamie Davies, Schramsberg Vineyards and Cellars
Accompanying champagne *Schramsberg Blanc de Noirs*

Serves 6

Leeks and ham top a cornmeal pancake that is napped with a Gruyère sauce and browned under the broiler for a light luncheon entrée.

18 small or 12 large leeks
4 cups chicken broth
6 thin slices ham
2½ cups Béchamel Sauce (page 169) or basic white sauce

½ cup grated Gruyère cheese
Cornmeal Pancakes (recipe follows)
Butter for cooking

Clean the leeks. Cut off the tops, leaving some tender green area, and cut them in half lengthwise. Poach them in the chicken broth until tender, drain, and set aside.

Make the Béchamel sauce and add the Gruyère cheese.

Before assembling the dish, heat the broiler. Place a warm pancake on a heat-resistant plate. Top with a slice of ham and a bunch of leeks. Spoon a strip of sauce over the pancake. Place under the broiler until the sauce bubbles and browns slightly.

CORNMEAL PANCAKES

1 cup yellow cornmeal
1 cup boiling water
1 teaspoon salt
1½ cups milk

2 tablespoons melted butter
2 eggs
½ cup all-purpose flour

Mix the cornmeal and salt. Add it to the boiling water, stir and let the mixture stand about 10 minutes. Mix in the milk and melted butter. Beat the eggs and add them along with the flour. Beat the batter until smooth.

Heat a crêpe pan with 1 teaspoon of butter. Put 2 to 3 tablespoons of the batter in the pan and swirl to make a thin pancake. Cook about 3 minutes on one side, turn, and cook another 2 minutes.

BILTMORE ESTATE

ON A VISIT TO WESTERN NORTH CAROLINA to enjoy the mountain air and mild climate George Washington Vanderbilt found an ideal spot to built a summer residence. The grandson of the shipping and railroad tycoon Commodore Cornelius Vanderbilt, he built the Biltmore House between 1890 and 1895 on a 125,000-acre estate in Asheville, North Carolina.

Two of the nation's most distinguished designers were engaged to plan and develop the estate. Richard Morris Hunt, the first American to receive an architectural degree from the École des Beaux Arts in Paris, was given the task of designing a French-style chateau, to be modelled after the great sixteenth-century chateaux of the Loire Valley. Frederick Law Olmsted was commissioned to lay out the gardens and parks that were to surround the house. It was also Olmsted who made the estate a working farm and a productive enterprise. He turned eroded farmlands into rich fields, imported fine animal stock, and managed the lumbering and reforestation operation in the outlying forest.

The name Biltmore for the house came from Bildt, the Dutch town from which the Vanderbilts immigrated, and *more*, an old English word meaning rolling countryside. Hundreds of local workers were employed for five years to construct the 250-room French Renaissance mansion. In addition, artisans from all over America and Europe came to carve the woodwork and fit the limestone, which was from Indiana. Brickworks and woodworking shops were set up on the property. A three-mile railroad spur was built from the present Biltmore station to bring supplies to the site.

The house incorporated the most modern technology of the times: central heating and plumbing, refrigeration, elevators, a dumb-waiter system, and a very sophisticated electrical system. Thomas Edison's first filament bulbs were used in the Biltmore House. The mansion employed eighty servants and there was a stable for forty horses.

There are many outstanding rooms in the Biltmore House. The Banquet Hall, which is seventy-two feet by forty-two feet, was designed to display five unique sixteenth-century Flemish wall tapestries. Although the ceiling arches are seventy feet high, the room has perfect acoustics. Two people sitting at opposite ends of the huge banquet table do not have to raise their voices to be heard. At one end of the hall is a massive marble fireplace over which is a carving by Karl Bitter entitled *The Return from the Chase*. At the opposite end of the hall, are more carvings by Bitter, including a scene from Wagner's opera, *Tannhauser*, which adorns the organ gallery.

Mr. Vanderbilt was well versed in many subjects and spoke eight languages. His library of twenty thousand volumes included histories, works on art, architecture, landscape gardening, classics, and novels. The walnut-panelled room also contains more carvings by Karl Bitter. A magnificent ceiling painting entitled *The Chariot of Aurora* is the work of Pellegrini and was brought to America by Mr. Vanderbilt from the Pisani Palace in Venice.

The Biltmore House became a favorite residence of the Vanderbilts and their only child, Cornelia. Upon her marriage to John Francis Amherst Cecil, it became the Cecils' residence. After Mr. Vanderbilt's death in 1914, a large part of the property was deeded to the United States government and became the nucleus of the Pisgah National Forest. Another part was developed into the Town of Biltmore Forest and a part was sold for the Blue Ridge Parkway. In 1930, Mr. and Mrs. Cecil opened the Biltmore House and its gardens to the public.

Today the Biltmore Estate, still privately owned and operated by Vanderbilt's grandson, William A.V. Cecil, is a prime tourist attraction, for visitors not only from North Carolina but also from the entire East Coast. The estate now consists of the 250-room mansion and eight thousand acres of cultivated flower gardens, fields, pasturelands, lakes, and woodland. Approximately 125 of the acres are planted in *vinifera* grape vines. Each year more of the house and gardens has been opened to the public. There is no one in residence in the mansion now.

The Biltmore Estate began experimenting with wine grapes in 1971 on a fifteen-acre plot below the mansion. French-American hybrid grapes were planted and did well. The climate and the 2,200-foot elevation were conducive to grape growing. Since it was the intention of Mr. Vanderbilt, according to his grandson, William Cecil, "to maintain a working estate in the European tradition," it was only fitting that a vineyard and winery operation be added to the estate, even though thishappened almost a hundred years later. William Cecil decided that a full-fledged winery operation needed an expert staff and proceeded to seek out the best possible help available. He went to France and engaged a well-experienced winemaker.

Phillipe Jourdain, born in Algeria of French parentage, comes from a family who have owned vineyards and made wine for many generations. He still owns and operates the family vineyard in Provence and was professor of viticulture and enology at the Lycée Agricole in Carcassonne. In 1977, Jourdain came to the Biltmore as a consultant for two years, after which William Cecil convinced him to make the Biltmore his home and take over the duties as chief winemaker.

Under Jourdain's supervision, the fifteen-acre vineyard of French hybrids near the mansion was phased out. He selected new areas for the vineyards, which now follow the rolling contours of the land. The soil was carefully prepared and properly fertilized for the planting of 125 acres of *vinifera* grapes. A dam was built and part of the French Broad River which runs through the property was diverted into a twenty-foot-deep lake. The lake helps warm the vineyards and protect them against frost. Each year more vineyards are being added. with a target of five hundred acres by 1992. "The ultimate goal is to have all of the grapes for the winery either estate-grown or grown in North Carolina," says Bill Cecil, Jr., son of William and Vice-President of Operations. Philippe Jourdain has created a nursery for the propagation of rootstock to be used in the Biltmore vineyards.

In May 1985, the Biltmore Estate winery officially opened to the public. The ninety-thousand-square-foot facility is located in buildings originally designed by Richard Morris Hunt as part of the Biltmore dairy operation. With the closing of the dairy, the buildings were renovated, expanded, and equipped with state-of-the-art winemaking equipment. In the grand tradition of many European wineries, the centerpiece of the building is a clock tower. Austrian in style, the winery includes eight stained glass windows designed by John LaFarge, the mentor of Louis Comfort Tiffany. The stained glass windows are to be found in the Welcoming Center, Tasting Room, and Retail Sales Area. There is a self-guided tour of the winery and tasting is available. In its first year of operation, the winery welcomed over four hundred thousand visitors.

The Biltmore Estate winery also produces a large range of premium varietal white and red still wines in addition to two *cuvées* of champagne. At present the production of still wine is about forty thousand cases a year, but will increase as more of the vineyards come into production and the market expands.

The grapes for the champagne *cuvée* are all hand picked into small lug boxes and transported to the winery for pressing. After the *cuvée* is blended, the second fermentation "is traditionally started during the last three days of the moon [that] begins in March," explained Philippe Jourdain. These "proper" days always fall between March 25 and April 29. It seems that at that time the natural temperatures in the winery increase sufficiently to allow a slow but complete fermentation.

After this second fermentation is completed, the champagne bottles are aged for between two and three years in a maze of underground tunnels that had existed under the dairy barn.

All of the champagne bottles are riddled by hand. After the plug of dead yeast is expelled from the neck of the bottle, a *dosage* of brandy and cane sugar is added to bring the champagne to the desired sweetness. Since the first release of champagne in 1982, there has been a steady increase in production. The goal is five thousand cases per year.

Also located on the Biltmore Estate is the Deerpark Restaurant. A set of outbuildings designed originally by Richard Morris Hunt in the 1890s for George Vanderbilt's farm operation has been renovated into an interesting restaurant. Continental as well as Southern specialities are offered. Located in a pastoral setting, the restaurant also features an open-air pavilion. Inside the restaurant there is exposed half-timbered woodwork and decorative brickwork, reminiscent of farm buildings a hundred years ago. The name Deerpark comes from an area nearby that George Vanderbilt had set aside as a deer preserve. The descendents of these deer can still be seen on the estate.

The Biltmore Estate winery produces champagne, under two labels, both by the *méthode champenoise:*

Chateau Biltmore ("reserve" champagne) — 100 percent Chardonnay: Brut; Dry
Biltmore Estate — a blend of Chardonnay and Pinot Noir: Brut; Dry (Sec)

Culinary Director: Steve Wenger

Steve Wenger received his practical training in the Colorado resort area where for five years he was employed in various culinary management positions. In 1982, Steve joined the staff of the Biltmore Estate, taking over the food service for the entire operation. This includes lunch service at the 600-seat Deerpark Restaurant, lighter food service at the Biltmore House Stable Café, and special events, such as wedding receptions, dinner functions at the Garden Courtyard of the Deerpark Restaurant and special dinners at the Biltmore mansion. In the summer there are numerous catered picnics.

Steve is also in charge of creating special dishes to complement the Biltmore Estate Winery's still wines and champagnes. In all of the food preparations Steve follows the Estate's European theme. He is also strongly influenced by the cuisine of the North Carolina mountains and relies on the availability of fresh ingredients.

Biltmore Estate Winery on the Biltmore Estate
One Biltmore Plaza
Asheville, North Carolina 28801
(704) 255-1776

Visits: Biltmore House, Gardens, and Winery, daily, 9:00 A.M. to 5:00 P.M.; admission charge covers self-guided tour of the Biltmore House, winery, and gardens
Principal: William A.V. Cecil
Varietal wines produced: Chardonnay, Sauvignon Blanc, Johannisberg Riesling, Chenin Blanc, Pinot Noir, and Cabernet Sauvignon
Champagnes produced: Brut and Dry (Sec)
1988 champagne production: 3,500 cases

VEGETABLES AND SIDE DISHES

VEGETABLES CAN PROVIDE CONTRASTS OF TEXTURE, color, and taste to the meat, poultry, or seafood that they accompany. Their purpose is to furnish variety and a balance of necessary nutrients. The side dishes mentioned are made principally from grains, rice, and wheat. One is made from cornmeal.

Although new varieties of vegetables are constantly being developed through cross-pollination and biotechnology, most of the familiar vegetables have been cultivated for centuries. Many common vegetables, such as corn, sweet potatoes, squashes, potatoes, and tomatoes were brought to Europe hundreds of years ago by explorers from the "new world" of the Americas. Potatoes and tomatoes became popular in Europe first, before being accepted as fit to eat in America; tomatoes were considered poisonous for many years by the early settlers.

To survive, the early American settlers learned to grow and eat many of the native American vegetables. Home gardens in colonial times had European beans and native corn growing side by side – the former using the latter for bean poles. When European immigrants came to America they not only brought their native cuisines with them, but also seeds for the vegetables used in their homelands. Recipes for these vegetables were soon melded into the cuisine of this country. Asian immigrants brought yet other types of vegetables along with a new method for their cooking – the stir-fry.

Until a decade ago, vegetable cookery in America was not very interesting. However, with the increased availability of fresh produce, the interest in vegetarianism and health foods, and the commercial development of boutique vegetables, side dishes have become culinary delights. Today there are three times as many vegetables in the produce section of our supermarkets than there were even fifteen years ago. Fast and less expensive transportation has made out-of-season vegetables available throughout the year. No longer do we have to plan our meals according to the seasonal availability of fresh vegetables. Although some of the more exotic vegetables, such as celery root, *chanterelle* mushrooms, and artichokes are still mostly seasonal, fresh broccoli, zucchini, and green beans, grown in California, Florida or Mexico, are now available all year round in most parts of the country.

In or near most urban areas, there are farmers' markets that specialize in seasonal fresh vegetables and fruits. These markets rely both on local products and on those flown in from far away places. Local produce farmers in many areas of the country have also started growing unusual vegetables. For example, Virginia, known for its peanuts, chickens, and Smithfield hams, is fast becoming a leading grower of *shiitake* mushrooms.

The vegetable and side dishes included in this book are not overpowering or heavily seasoned. There are recipes for traditional dishes as well as for new innovations. All of the recipes are compatible with the various champagnes recommended for the entrées. Some of the dishes may be served independently as a light luncheon entrée, or as a first course and, for those, suggestions have been made about the champagne that best accompanies them.

❖ Asparagus Sauté ❖

Steve Wenger, Biltmore Estate

Serves 6 to 8

Asparagus, a member of the lily-of-the-valley family, has been a favorite of Europeans for many centuries. Thought to be a native of the eastern Mediterranean, asparagus spread to the rest of Europe in Roman times. Even today, in May, there is a month-long celebration of asparagus in Germany. The white variety is found prepared in numerous ways on restaurant menus there. Early settlers in America brought roots of the vegetable with them and records show that Thomas Jefferson grew asparagus in his greenhouses at Monticello.

This Asparagus Sauté, a quick preparation, brings the fresh spring vegetable to the table in less than 15 minutes. Use a vegetable peeler to remove the tough outer layer from the lower stem of the asparagus.

1 pound asparagus, trimmed, and
    cut diagonally into 2-inch pieces
2 tablespoons butter

2 cloves garlic, crushed
Lemon wedges

Clean and trim the asparagus. Melt the butter in a large sauté pan over medium heat. Add the garlic and sauté for a minute. Then add the asparagus and sauté until crisp-tender. Remove garlic and discard. Serve individual portions of asparagus with a lemon wedge.

❖ Asparagus with Lemon Dill Sauce ❖

Frederick Horton, Wente Bros. Sparkling Wine Cellars

Serves 4

Dill has many uses — in pickles, potato salad, seasoning for fish — and is most often used in eastern European dishes. Combined with a lemon butter, it makes a pleasing sauce for fresh asparagus.

28 pieces fresh asparagus
16 tablespoons (2 sticks) butter
2 tablespoons lemon juice
2 teaspoons minced fresh parsley

2 tablespoons chopped fresh dill
2 tablespoons minced fresh chives
Toasted pine nuts for garnish

Blanch the asparagus. Arrange 7 pieces on each individual plate and keep warm.

In a heavy non-aluminum saucepan, melt the butter. Do not allow it to brown. Whisk in the lemon juice and remove from heat. Let the mixture cool slightly and add the parsley, dill, and chives. Spoon the sauce over the warm asparagus and garnish each plate with the toasted pine nuts.

❖ Black Beans with Tomatoes ❖ ❖ and Chiles

Martha Culbertson, John Culbertson Winery

Serves 6

This method of preparing dried black beans, influenced by Tex-Mex cooking, is similar to that used for chili but these beans are served as an accompaniment to meats and other Mexican-style dishes.

1 pound black beans
2 quarts water
2 medium onions, 1 sliced and 1 chopped fine
2 tablespoons shortening
2 large garlic cloves, chopped, plus 1 garlic clove, minced

1/2 teaspoon salt
2 tablespoons butter
3 medium tomatoes, peeled, seeded, and chopped
2 fresh green hot chiles, peeled, seeded, and chopped

Soak the beans overnight. The next day, drain the beans and place them in a large saucepan with the water, sliced onion, shortening, the 2 cloves of chopped garlic, and the salt. Bring to a slow boil and simmer until beans are tender, 1 1/2 to 2 hours. Drain liquid from beans and reserve it. Purée half of the beans and reserve the rest.

Sauté the chopped onion in the butter until transparent. Add the garlic, tomatoes, and chiles. Simmer for 20 minutes to blend flavors.

Return the puréed beans to the saucepan; add the whole beans and the tomato sauce, and mix well. If too dry add some of the reserved bean liquid. Season with salt and pepper to taste. Heat through, pour into a warm casserole dish, and serve.

❖ Green Beans with Almonds ❖

Marilouise Kornell, Hanns Kornell Champagne Cellars

Serves 6

Use either Blue Lake or Kentucky Wonder green beans for this easily prepared vegetable dish. It may accompany meat, poultry, or seafood.

2 pounds trimmed green beans
4 tablespoons butter
2 shallots, minced

1/2 to 3/4 cup slivered almonds, toasted
Juice of half a lemon

Steam the green beans until crisp-tender. Melt the butter in a large skillet over medium heat. Add the shallots and cook until they are tender, about 3 minutes. Add the beans and almonds and toss until heated through. Sprinkle beans with lemon juice and freshly ground pepper to taste. Serve hot.

❖ Green Bean Timbale ❖

Steve Wenger, Biltmore Estate

Serves 6

Originally a timbale was a small round drinking cup about the size of a present-day custard cup. Since these drinking cups were made of metal, they eventually became containers for chopped vegetables or meats either in a custard or in a sauce, mixtures that were steamed or baked in a water bath. Today timbales contain a variety of ingredients — vegetables, ground meat, fish, or cheese. Often the timbale itself may even be edible since the container is a prebaked pie crust or puff pastry. This Green Bean Timbale is served unmolded, warm or at room temperature, with Tomato Tarragon Mayonnaise.

*1 pound fresh green beans, cleaned
    and broken or cut into 2- inch
    pieces
2 tablespoons whipping cream*

*¼ cup fine bread crumbs
1 egg*

Grease and flour 6 miniature muffin tins or custard cups. Cook the green beans in lightly salted boiling water until tender. Drain and cool the beans for a few minutes before placing them in a food processor. Purée the beans and then add the cream, bread crumbs and egg. Process until thoroughly blended. Fill each of the 6 muffin tins, and bake in a water bath in a preheated 350° F. oven for about 30 minutes. Timbales will draw slightly away from the sides when done.

Cool on a rack for 15 minutes. Run a knife around each of the timbales, then invert onto a platter and remove any flour adhering to them. Serve with Tomato Tarragon Mayonnaise.

TOMATO TARRAGON MAYONNAISE

*¾ cup mayonnaise
2 teaspoons tomato paste*

1 teaspoon fresh snipped tarragon

Blend together the mayonnaise, tomato paste, and tarragon and refrigerate until ready to serve.

❖ Red Cabbage with Sautéed Apples ❖

Edna Tears, The Great Western Winery

Serves 6 to 8

One of the oldest cultivated vegetables, cabbage is believed to have originated in northern Europe. Several varieties of reddish purple cabbage are grown in New York State and Wisconsin. Different seasonings — nutmeg, caraway seeds, cloves, cinnamon — can be added. Apples are usually included. This simple version does not take long to cook, may be prepared ahead of time, and then placed in a casserole and reheated. Reheating the dish enhances the flavor. Red cabbage is most frequently served with duck, goose, venison, and other game.

4 medium tart apples
8 tablespoons (1 stick), plus 2 tablespoons, butter
1 to 2 teaspoons sugar
¼ teaspoon freshly grated nutmeg

Grated rind of 1 lemon
2 pounds red cabbage, coarsely shredded
½ cup red wine
Salt and pepper, to taste

Peel, core, and coarsely chop the apples. In a large skillet melt the 2 tablespoons of butter. Stir in the apples, sugar, nutmeg, and lemon rind. Sauté the apples over medium heat, turning them with a spatula occasionally so that they become lightly golden and soft, but not mushy. Set aside and keep warm.

While the apples are cooking, melt the remaining butter in a large saucepan. Stir in the shredded cabbage and mix well. Add the red wine and cover the saucepan tightly. Cook over medium-high heat until the cabbage is tender and the liquid has evaporated, about 8 to 10 minutes. If the liquid has not evaporated after the cabbage is tender, increase the heat to high and cook uncovered for a few more minutes. Season cabbage with salt and pepper to taste. Combine the sautéed apples with the cabbage and mix lightly.

❖ Purée of Carrot ❖

Martha Culbertson, John Culbertson Winery

Serves 6 to 8

This simple carrot purée is often mistaken for sweet potato or squash. Its color and mild flavor make it a good accompaniment to poultry and veal dishes.

4 pounds carrots, peeled and cut in large pieces
8 tablespoons (1 stick) unsalted butter, cut into 8 pieces

½ cup whipping cream
Salt and pepper, to taste

Cook carrots in boiling water until tender. Drain, place in a food processor, and purée until smooth. Add the butter, cream, and salt and pepper to taste and process 30 seconds until well blended. Keep in a pan over simmering water until served.

❖ Baked Carrots and Fruit ❖

Karen Mack, Chateau Ste. Michelle

Serves 6

The tartness of the apples contrasts well with the sweetness of carrots and grapes in this color-ful side dish. It is an excellent accompaniment to ham or pork. The carrots must be sliced very thin in order for them to be sufficiently tender when baked.

*10 to 12 medium carrots, peeled
    and sliced 1/4-inch thick*
*2 large crisp green apples, cored
    and sliced 1/3-inch thick*
2 tablespoons butter

1 teaspoon cornstarch
3/4 cup blanc de noir sparkling wine
*1/2 pound red seedless grapes,
    washed and cut in half*

In a 9- by 13-inch ovenproof casserole arrange alternating rows of carrot and apple slices. Melt the butter in a medium saucepan. Mix the cornstarch with 2 tablespoons of sparkling wine and whisk the mixture into the melted butter until well blended. Whisk in the remain-ing sparkling wine. Simmer the mixture for about 1 minute or until it just begins to thicken. Pour this glaze over the carrots and apples.

    Bake the casserole in a preheated 325° F. oven for 15 minutes. Place the grapes decora-tively across the top of the carrots and apples. Return to the oven for an additional 8 to 10 minutes.

❖ Stuffed Chard Leaves ❖

Jamie Davies, Schramsberg Vineyards and Cellars

Serves 4

Swiss chard, although it has no association with Switzerland, was originally a European vegetable. Often the stems and leaves are separated and prepared in two entirely different recipes. Its leaves are similar to spinach in color and texture. The slightly sweet, earthy taste of the Swiss chard is a good combination for the cauliflower filling used in this recipe.

*8 large Swiss chard leaves, green
    or red*
Half a medium cauliflower
1 clove garlic
1 3/4 cups chicken broth

1 egg yolk
*1 tablespoon grated Parmesan
    cheese*
Salt and pepper, to taste
1 tablespoon butter

Blanch the chard leaves in boiling salted water for 1 to 2 minutes. Immediately refresh them in ice water and drain them on paper towels. Remove the stem and most of the center rib, being careful not to split the leaf.

    Cook the cauliflower and garlic in 1 1/2 cups of the chicken broth until tender. Discard the garlic. In a food processor purée the cauliflower to a medium-coarse texture. Add the egg yolk, cheese, salt, and pepper. Overlap the center split of each chard leaf so that it forms one solid piece (the center will have a double thickness). Place 1 heaping tablespoon of the purée on each leaf. Roll into a packet, folding in the sides as you roll. In a large skillet, combine the butter and the remaining 1/4 cup chicken broth. Add the chard packets and steam, covered, about 5 to 7 minutes or until leaves are tender.

❖ Chiles Poblanos Pie ❖

Martha Culbertson, John Culbertson Winery

Serves 6

Chiles have been grown in the Americas for many centuries. The Indians of South and Central America cultivated them for seasonings long before Columbus arrived. The Europeans spread the growing of chiles to the rest of the world, including India, Africa, and Hungary where a pungent four-inch long red pepper is used for the making of paprika.

The *poblano* chile pepper, which looks like a slightly flattened and pointed dark green bell pepper, is usually very mild and tasty. This *Chiles Poblanos* Pie, similar to *Chiles Rellenos* in taste and texture, makes a beautiful presentation. Accompany it with grilled meats and Black Beans (page 213).

*1½ pounds (about 12) fresh chiles
    poblanos
6 eggs, beaten
¼ small onion, chopped
1 garlic clove, minced*

*¼ teaspoon salt
¾ cup sour cream
¾ cup whipping cream
½ pound Monterey Jack cheese,
    grated*

To char chiles, rub them with oil and then lay them directly on the electric burner of the stove turned on high or spear them and hold them, one at a time, over the flame of a gas stove. Keep turning the chiles as they char, which will only take a minute or so. The chiles may also be placed under the broiler to char the skins. After skins are blackened, place the hot peppers in a plastic bag or in damp paper towels for a few minutes to sweat so that the skins will slip off easily.

Butter a 9-inch pie pan. Line the pan with the chiles, leaving the points sticking up beyond the rim of the pan about ¾ inch. Cover the pan completely with the chiles.

In a bowl mix the eggs, onions, garlic, salt, sour cream, and whipping cream. Fold in the cheese. Pour the mixture over the chiles and bend the chile points over the pie. Bake in a preheated 350° F. oven for 50 minutes or until a knife inserted in the center comes out clean. Serve hot or at room temperature.

❖ Celery Root Soufflé ❖

Jamie Davies, Schramsberg Vineyards and Cellars
Accompanying champagne *Schramsberg Blanc de Noirs*

Serves 4

Celery root, also known as celeriac, is used extensively as a vegetable and in soup and salads in many European countries. It is a variety of celery that has been cultivated for its root rather than its stalks. Although small quantities of celery root have been available in this country since the nineteenth century, its gnarled, unappetizing appearance did not endear it to cooks other than those who had a European heritage. This light, tasty soufflé may be served as an accompaniment to poultry or as a first course. The slivers of smoked tongue or ham provide an additional flavor for the dish.

1 to 1½ pounds celery root
Juice of 1 lemon
3 tablespoons butter
3 tablespoons all-purpose flour
½ cup chicken broth
½ cup half-and-half

3 eggs, separated
1 tablespoon grainy mustard in the Dijon style
½ cup smoked tongue or ham, cut in julienne strips

Peel the celery root and cut it into large dice. Cook the pieces in water to cover with the lemon juice until they are tender but not mushy. (Celery root can get mushy quite quickly.) Drain, place the celery in a food processor and purée. Force the celery root purée through a sieve to eliminate rough fibers.

In a heavy saucepan melt the butter and add the flour. Cook, stirring for 1 minute. Remove from heat and gradually add the chicken broth and half-and-half, stirring constantly. Return the saucepan to the heat, simmering the mixture until the sauce is thick and smooth. Remove from heat and add egg yolks one at a time, whisking to prevent eggs from cooking. Mix in the celery root purée, mustard, and smoked tongue or ham. Beat egg whites until they are stiff but not dry and fold them into the sauce. Pour the mixture into a buttered 1-quart baking dish and bake in a preheated 350° F. oven for 35 to 40 minutes.

❖ Roasted Garlic and Leeks ❖

Karen Mack, Chateau Ste. Michelle
Accompanying champagne *Domaine Ste. Michelle Blanc de Noir*

Serves 6

Garlic becomes very sweet when roasted and loses most of its pungency. Leeks, with their mild flavor, are a good combination with the garlic since they belong to the same family. This dish will also serve 10 as an appetizer.

16 small leeks
6 whole heads of garlic
4 tablespoons unsalted butter

⅓ cup chicken broth
⅓ cup blanc de noir sparkling wine
Thin slices of crusty French bread

Thoroughly wash the leeks. Trim off the tough ends of the green stalks. Slice the leeks into ½-inch slices. Peel the garlic. Melt the butter in a 9- by 13-inch ovenproof pan. Arrange the leek slices and garlic cloves in alternate rows. Whisk together the chicken broth and sparkling wine and gently pour over the vegetables. Bake in a preheated 300° F. oven for 1 hour, basting with pan juices every 10 minutes. Remove the leeks and garlic from pan with a slotted spoon and serve hot with slices of French bread.

❖ Sautéed Mushrooms ❖

Tracy Wood Anderson, S. Anderson Vineyard

Serves 6

These dish is best when prepared with three different kinds of mushrooms and is a good accompaniment to grilled beef steak or lamb chops.

*¼ pound each oyster, shiitake, and
button mushrooms*
4 tablespoons butter
¼ cup raspberry vinegar

1 tablespoon sugar
⅛ teaspoon salt
⅛ teaspoon pepper

Cut the mushrooms in bite-sized pieces, if necessary. Melt the butter in a large frying pan over medium heat. Add the mushrooms and sauté about 3 minutes or until mushrooms are tender. Add the vinegar to deglaze the pan. Then add the sugar, salt, and pepper and reduce until syrupy. Adjust seasonings and vinegar to taste.

❖ Mushrooms in Tarragon Cream ❖

Ruth Wiens, Mirassou Vineyards
Accompanying champagne *Mirassou Brut*

Serves 4

Marcy Lessack, Mirassou Vineyards' chef, created this tasty mushroom side dish which can also be served as a first course. A combination of various kinds of fresh mushrooms such as *shiitake*, oyster, small white button, and *chanterelle* gives an even greater complexity to this dish. Serve the mushrooms in puff pastry shells (available in the frozen food section of the supermarket).

*8 tablespoons (1 stick) unsalted
    butter
1 pound mushrooms, cleaned and
    sliced (if larger than button
    mushrooms)
1/2 cup whipping cream*

*1/2 cup dry white wine
3 tablespoons fresh, finely chopped
    tarragon
Salt and pepper, to taste
4 puff pastry shells*

In a large sauté pan melt the butter. Add the mushrooms and cook until all liquid has been absorbed and mushrooms begin to sear very slightly. Add the cream and wine and cook over medium heat until the liquid is thickly coating the mushrooms, about 3 to 4 minutes. Add the tarragon and salt and pepper to taste. Simmer a few more minutes to blend flavors and serve hot in warm puff pastry shells.

❖ Potatoes Dauphine ❖

Martha Culbertson, John Culbertson Winery

Serves 8

This is a classic French preparation of scalloped potatoes. The dish may vary according to the ingredients and method of preparation. In American recipes, milk, cream, or a cream sauce may used as the liquid, the type of cheese varies, and onions and green pepper may be added. In this recipe, part of the liquid is absorbed by the potatoes during a boiling process, adding flavor to the dish.

*2 pounds boiling potatoes
2 cups milk
1 1/2 cups whipping cream
1 clove garlic, minced*

*1/4 teaspoon salt
1/8 teaspoon pepper
1/2 cup grated Swiss cheese*

Butter a gratin dish or shallow 2-quart casserole. Peel the potatoes and slice 1/8-inch thick. Put the potato slices, the milk, cream, garlic, salt, and pepper in a large saucepan. Bring to boil over medium heat, stirring to prevent scorching. When the potato mixture has reached a slow boil, pour it into the buttered gratin dish. Sprinkle the cheese over the top and bake in a preheated 400° F. oven for 1 hour. The potatoes are done when brown on top and easily pierced with a knife point. Let the dish sit for about 10 minutes before serving.

❖ Potato Fritters ❖

Sheryl Benesch, Korbel Champagne Cellars

Serves 8

These potato fritters go well with the Fillet of Beef with Herbs and Sausage (page 190). They are also a delicious accompaniment to breakfast. A wok or a deep pan may be used for the deep frying.

Approximately 5 potatoes, enough
to yield 4 cups when grated
2 to 3 tablespoons lemon juice
1 cup all-purpose flour
1 teaspoon cornstarch
1 teaspoon baking powder
½ teaspoon paprika

¼ teaspoon white pepper
1 teaspoon salt
⅛ teaspoon nutmeg
1 egg, lightly beaten
⅓ cup beer
6 green onions, diced
Oil for deep frying

Grate the potatoes into a bowl containing water and the lemon juice.

Combine the dry ingredients, including all the spices, into a bowl. Make a well in the center of the flour mixture and add the egg and half of the beer. Mix ingredients together until smooth, adding the remaining beer as you mix. Add the diced green onions.

Squeeze the grated potatoes dry and add them to the batter, mixing well.

To cook fritters, use a slotted spoon to lift out approximately ½ cup of potato batter per fritter and gently drop into the hot frying oil which should be at least 3 inches deep. Do not allow the oil to become too hot or the fritters will brown quickly but not cook in the center. They take approximately 8 to 10 minutes to cook.

Remove fritters from oil, drain on paper towels, and serve immediately.

❖ Pumpkin au Gratin ❖

Steve Wenger, Biltmore Estate

Serves 6 to 8

Pumpkin is often overlooked as a side dish since it is available fresh only during the fall. A similar squash such as the winter Golden Nugget, which looks like a miniature pumpkin, may be substituted in this recipe.

Half a medium sweet onion, sliced
2 tablespoons butter
4 cups cooked pumpkin, roughly
chopped

¼ teaspoon salt
4 ounces white Cheddar cheese,
shredded

Sauté the onion in butter until just translucent. Place 2 cups of the pumpkin in the bottom of a shallow casserole that has 2 tablespoons of water in it. Sprinkle with ⅛ teaspoon salt and distributed the onions evenly over the pumpkin. Spread a quarter of the cheese over the onions. Top with the remaining pumpkin and sprinkle with remaining ⅛ teaspoon of salt. Top with the rest of the cheese. Bake in a preheated 350° F. oven for approximately 30 minutes or until heated through and the cheese is golden brown.

❖ Spaghetti Squash with ❖ Fresh Tomatoes

Martha Culbertson, John Culbertson Winery
Accompanying champagne *Culbertson Blanc de Noir*

Serves 6

No one knows where spaghetti squash originated. It is believed that this variety of squash is an American native, but then probably traveled to China or Italy. Today this golden yellow, oval-shaped vegetable, which produces fibers like noodles, is grown in California as well as in most southern states. Spaghetti squash is fun to cook and provides the basis for a low calorie side dish. This dish may also be served as a luncheon or light supper entrée.

*2 pounds spaghetti squash, either
as a whole squash or in pieces*
½ cup olive oil
*2 cups peeled, seeded, and chopped
tomatoes*

½ cup basil leaves, minced
½ cup parsley leaves minced
*3 tablespoons grated Parmesan
cheese*

The squash may be either boiled or baked. To boil, place large pieces of squash, cut-side down, in a pan with sufficient water to cover. Bring to a boil and simmer for about 30 minutes or until squash is tender when pierced with a fork. To bake, place squash cut-side down in a shallow baking dish. Add 1 inch of water and bake in a preheated 350° F. oven for 1 to 1¼ hours or until it can be pierced with a fork. Do not overcook the squash since it tends to get watery and lose its sweetness.

After cooking the squash, cool it slightly. With a fork "comb" strands from each of the pieces until only the shell remains. These strands will resemble spaghetti in looks and texture.

While the squash is cooking, make the sauce. Heat the olive oil in a sauté pan and add the chopped tomatoes. Cook over medium heat about 5 minutes or until slightly thickened. Add the basil and parsley, and heat through. Pour sauce over the strands of spaghetti squash, toss, and sprinkle with the Parmesan cheese.

❖ Twice-Baked Sweet Potatoes ❖

Steve Wenger, Biltmore Estate

Serves 6

The sweet potato, a perennial vine of the morning glory family, is a native American vegetable. The American Indians cultivated them long before the settlers arrived. Sweet potatoes became a staple food in the Southern states where they were known as the "potato" and the white potato became known as the "Irish potato." The sweet potato is often confused with the yam, which it resembles. The two are of different botanical origins, but today are used interchangeably.

Twice-Baked Sweet Potatoes is a grand accompaniment to baked ham. To speed up the preparation, microwave the sweet potatoes on high for seven minutes or until done. Proceed with the rest of the recipe and then reheat the potatoes in the microwave for one or two minutes. Even if he potatoes are baked in the oven, they may be reheated in the microwave. The recipe may be prepared ahead to the reheating stage.

*6 medium sweet potatoes,
  scrubbed and pierced
3 small oranges, peeled, seeded,
  and diced*

*6 tablespoons chopped dates
3 tablespoons honey
1/4 teaspoon ground cinnamon*

Bake the sweet potatoes in a preheated 350° F. oven for 1 hour or until done. Cut off the top of the sweet potatoes and carefully scoop out the pulp, reserving the skins. Mash the pulp. Combine the orange pieces, dates, honey, cinnamon, and mashed potatoes and mix thoroughly. Stuff the potato shells with the mixture. Bake in a preheated 350° F. oven for 20 to 30 minutes or until heated through.

❖ Baked Spinach ❖

Edna Tears, The Great Western Winery

Serves 6

A light accompaniment to meats, this dish may be prepared with either the fresh or frozen spinach.

*6 cups fresh, chopped, lightly
  cooked spinach, well drained; or
3 packages (10 ounces each)
  chopped, frozen spinach, thawed
6 eggs, well beaten
1 cup half-and-half*

*1/4 cup medium-dry white wine
2 tablespoons butter, melted
1/2 teaspoon salt
1 cup grated Cheddar cheese
5 strips bacon, crisply fried and
  crumbled*

In a large bowl mix together the spinach, eggs, cream, wine, butter, salt, and cheese. Pour the mixture into a well buttered 10-inch ovenproof skillet. Bake in a preheated 350° F. oven for 25 to 30 minutes. Just before serving sprinkle with the crumbled bacon.

❖ Garden Casserole ❖

Edna Tears, The Great Western Winery
Accompanying champagne *Great Western Blanc de Blanc*

Serves 8 to 10

This fresh vegetable combination can also be served as a luncheon entrée. It goes well with broiled meats or chicken.

*4 medium potatoes, peeled and
  sliced thin*
2 onions, cut into rings
*1 medium zucchini, halved, seeds
  removed, and cut into small
  cubes*
4 tomatoes, cut into cubes

3 carrots, peeled and sliced thin
1 cup dry white wine
Salt and pepper to taste
1 cup white bread cubes
4 tablespoons butter, melted
2 cups grated Cheddar cheese

Place the sliced potatoes in the bottom of a medium-sized casserole and place the onion rings on top. Then add the cubes of zucchini in an even layer and top with the cubes of tomatoes. Finally add the carrot slices. Pour the wine over the mixture and add salt and pepper to taste. Cover the casserole and bake in a preheated 375° F. oven for 45 minutes to 1 hour, or until vegetables are just tender. Remove from oven.

Mix the bread cubes with the melted butter until they are well coated. Sprinkle the bread cubes and the grated cheese over the casserole. Return it to the oven and bake uncovered for another 15 minutes.

❖ Summer Stir-Fry ❖

Tracy Wood Anderson, S. Anderson Vineyard

Serves 6

Japanese eggplants, sweeter and smaller than regular eggplants, are a recent addition to the produce section of the markets. Popular in the orient, these small black-purple eggplants add an interesting texture to a stir-fry. This stir-fry of summer vegetables is a welcome addition to grilled meat or seafood entrées.

2 tablespoons butter or oil
1 small onion, diced
*3 medium zucchini, sliced in
  rounds*
*2 Japanese eggplants, sliced in
  rounds*

3 medium tomatoes, diced
2 medium cloves garlic, minced
*1 teaspoon each of fresh chopped
  thyme, oregano and marjoram*
Salt and pepper, to taste

Melt the butter in a large skillet over medium high heat. Add the onions and sauté until soft. Then add the zucchini and sauté for 1 minute. Add the eggplant and sauté until the mixture begins to brown. Add the tomatoes, garlic, herbs, and salt and pepper to taste. Sauté until vegetables are tender, but not overcooked.

❖ Grilled Vegetables with ❖ Champagne Vinaigrette

Frederick Horton, Wente Bros. Sparkling Wine Cellars

Serves 4

Any fresh vegetable may be used in this recipe. Select tiny ones to grill whole on skewers, or slice larger vegetables into bite-sized pieces

12 tiny pattypan squashes
12 cherry or yellow pear tomatoes
12 mushrooms
12 Brussels sprouts
2 red bell peppers

2 green bell peppers
2 sweet onions
Olive oil
Salt and pepper
Thyme, optional

Wash the vegetables, but do not peel them. Cut the peppers and onions into 1-inch strips. Thread the vegetables onto skewers, brush with olive oil, and season with salt, pepper, and dried thyme. Grill on a barbecue over moderate heat until the onions and peppers are soft, but not charred. Remove from skewers and place in a bowl. Toss with Champagne Vinaigrette and serve.

CHAMPAGNE VINAIGRETTE

1/3 cup champagne vinegar
1/2 teaspoon salt
1/2 cup walnut oil

12 tablespoons fresh chopped sweet basil leaves
1/2 teaspoon pepper

Combine the vinaigrette ingredients and pour over the grilled vegetables.

❖ Vegetable Trio ❖

Jamie Davies, Schramsberg Vineyards and Cellars

Serves 4

In Egyptian, Greek, and Roman times, leeks were used as both a vegetable and medicine. The Roman Emperor Nero ate great quantities of leeks to improve his singing voice. No one knows exactly where the plant originated, although the Mediterranean region seems to have been its early home. Leeks have been a symbol of strength and victory in Wales since the sixth century when the Welsh defeated the Saxons. Before the battle the Welsh had adorned their helmets with leeks to give them strength, and to distinguish themselves from the enemy. Through the years, leeks have become a favorite vegetable or soup ingredient in many European countries. Combined with colorful carrots and red peppers in this recipe, leeks are enhanced by a mustard cream sauce.

1 cup whipping cream
1 teaspoon whole mustard seeds,
  crushed coarsely with a mortar
Pinch of cumin
2 leeks, trimmed, washed, and cut
  in thin julienne strips

2 carrots, peeled and cut in thin
  julienne strips
2 red peppers, seeded and cut in
  thin julienne strips

Reduce the cream by half in a small saucepan. Add the crushed mustard seeds and the cumin. Set aside and keep warm.

Bring 3 cups of water to a boil. Cook each vegetable separately until just done, the leeks first, then the carrots, and then the peppers, removing them from the water with a slotted spoon. Group the vegetables in separate stacks on individual serving plates. Top with a little mustard cream.

❖ Zucchini Frittata ❖

Sheryl Benesch, Korbel Champagne Cellars
Accompanying champagne *Korbel Brut*

Serves 12 to 16

Frittata, the Italian version of the French omelet, differs greatly from its French cousin. It is flat in shape, firm but not heavy, and is cooked over low heat or baked in the oven. An omelet is cooked quickly over high heat, is creamy and moist, and is folded into an oblong shape. This Zucchini Frittata may be served as a vegetable accompaniment or as a luncheon entrée. It may also be cut into 2-inch squares and served as an hors d'oeuvre. Other firm vegetables, such as broccoli or cauliflower, may be substituted for the zucchini, but should be blanched before being added to the batter.

5 eggs
¼ cup olive oil
¼ cup all-purpose flour
1 teaspoon baking soda
1 teaspoon baking powder

1 cup grated Cheddar cheese
½ cup grated Parmesan cheese
1 medium red onion, sliced
6 cups sliced zucchini

Grease and flour a 9- by 13-inch baking pan. In a bowl mix all of the ingredients except the sliced zucchini. Then add the zucchini and pour the mixture into the prepared pan, spreading the mixture evenly. Bake in a preheated 350° F. oven for 25 minutes or until golden brown. Serve warm or cold.

❖ Spätzle ❖

Sheryl Benesch, Korbel Champagne Cellars

Serves 6

Spätzle are small dumplings that originated in southern Germany, Austria, and Hungary. Depending on where they come from, the dough may be made thick enough to roll out and cut into slivers, or thin enough to push through a colander. *Spätzle* are usually served with a sauce or gravy, however, in this recipe, they are sautéed before serving. They provide a delightful accompaniment for Pork Medallions (page 203).

3 eggs
1½ cups all-purpose flour
⅓ cup milk

Dash each of salt, pepper, and
  nutmeg
3 tablespoon butter

In a bowl combine the eggs, flour, and milk to form a thick batter. Add the salt, pepper, and nutmeg. Bring lightly salted water to a boil in a large pot. When the water is boiling, add 1 tablespoon of the butter.

Use a colander with large holes to create the *spätzle*. Holding the colander a few inches above the boiling water, pour the dough into colander and press it through the holes using a rubber spatula. Short pieces will form and fall into the water. When the *spätzle* rise to the surface, cook for an additional minute or two. With a slotted spoon remove them from the water to a plate to dry.

To serve, melt the remaining 2 tablespoons of butter in a sauté pan; add the *spätzle* and sauté until light golden brown, about 3 minutes.

❖ Mexican Rice ❖

Sheryl Benesch, Korbel Champagne Cellars

Serves 8 to 10

Rice is an ancient grain, believed to have been first cultivated between 3,000 and 2,000 B.C. Today rice, one of the chief sources of food for half of the world, is grown primarily in the southeastern United States, California, and the Orient. Its exact origin is not known. The most accepted theory is that rice growing started in Thailand and spread to Southeast Asia, China, and Japan. As soldiers and travelers to India and Southeast Asia brought seeds back, Europeans became familiar with rice which was eventually to be cultivated in southern Europe. In the United States rice was first grown in the swamps along the coast of South Carolina. Rice has an advantage over wheat in that it goes directly from grain to mouth and does not have to be ground before it can be consumed.

In Mexican cooking, rice is typically enhanced with vegetables and spices. Tomatoes and green peppers are an integral part of the combination. Serve this Mexican Rice with the Chicken with Tomatillo Sauce (page 170).

2 tablespoons butter
2 tomatoes, finely chopped
1/2 cup finely chopped carrots
1 green pepper, finely chopped
1/2 cup finely chopped zucchini
1/2 cup finely chopped onion
2 cloves garlic, minced

1/4 teaspoon oregano
1/2 teaspoon thyme
1 teaspoon cumin
Dash of nutmeg
Salt to taste
4 cups cooked rice

Melt the butter in a sauté pan. Add the chopped vegetables and garlic, and cook until soft. Add the spices and continue cooking for 5 minutes. Add rice and mix well. Heat through and serve.

❖ Risotto ❖

Marilouise Kornell, Hanns Kornell Champagne Cellars

Serves 4 to 6

This traditional Risotto with the addition of saffron is a flavorful companion to poultry dishes. Cook until all the moisture is absorbed but the rice is still al dente.

1 onion, chopped
2 tablespoons butter
2 tablespoons olive oil
2 cups Italian Arborio rice
1/2 cup brut champagne

1/4 teaspoon salt
1 quart chicken broth
Pinch of saffron
5 tablespoons grated Parmesan cheese

Sauté the onion in butter and olive oil in a large heavy saucepan. Add the rice and sauté until golden. Add champagne and cook over medium-low heat until liquid is absorbed. Stir in the salt and 2 cups of the chicken broth to which the saffron has been added. Simmer until broth is almost absorbed. Continue adding the remainder of the broth by half cupfuls until it is all absorbed, stirring occasionally. When rice is done, remove from heat and add the cheese. Cover saucepan and let stand 5 to 10 minutes before serving.

❖ Porcini Risotto with Red ❖ and Yellow Peppers

Ruth Wiens, Mirassou Vineyards
Accompanying champagne *Mirassou Brut*

Serves 8

Risotto, often confused with rice pilaf, is the result of a unique Italian method of cooking rice. The method is a slow one in which hot liquid is added a little at a time to cooking rice. This allows the rice to swell and attain a creamy texture, yet the grains of rice remain separate. Almost any ingredient may be added to the risotto — bits of meat, shellfish, vegetables, herbs or cheese. Creamy risottos are so delicious that the extra effort required to make them is well worth it. This version is rich and full of flavor and can easily be served as a separate course. Italian Arborio rice, a short, thick-grained rice, is available in gourmet shops.

If dried *porcini* mushrooms are not available, any other dried mushrooms may be substituted. The flavor, however, will be slightly different. This recipe may also be prepared with four ounces each of *shiitake* and domestic white mushrooms. If doing so, proceed with the recipe by sautéing the mushrooms with the pepper strips and substitute chicken broth for the mushroom liquid.

1½ ounces dried porcini mushrooms
4½ to 5 cups hot chicken broth
8 tablespoons (1 stick) unsalted butter
1 cup julienned red bell pepper
1 cup julienned yellow pepper
1 cup chopped sweet red onion
2 large cloves garlic, minced

2 cups Italian Arborio rice
1 cup brut champagne
½ teaspoon freshly ground black pepper
1 cup whipping cream
1 cup freshly grated Parmesan cheese
Salt to taste, if needed

Place the *porcini* mushrooms in a small saucepan and cover with 2 cups of the chicken broth. Bring to a boil. Remove from heat, cover saucepan, and let stand for 30 minutes. Strain the liquid through a fine cloth, reserving it for later. Coarsely chop the *porcini*.

Melt 4 tablespoons of the butter in a large heavy pot over medium heat. Add the red and yellow peppers and the mushrooms; sauté for 2 minutes. Remove with a slotted spoon and set aside. Melt the remaining butter in the same pot. Add the onion and garlic and sauté for about 3 minutes until the onion is translucent. Mix in the rice, stirring for about 2 minutes until the rice is well coated with the butter.

Stir in the mushroom liquid, 2 more cups of the chicken broth, champagne, and freshly ground pepper. Cook uncovered over low heat until the liquid is almost absorbed. Stir occasionally. Continue adding chicken broth, half a cup at a time, until the rice is almost al dente. Stir in the cream and continue cooking and stirring until the mixture is thick and creamy. The rice will take a total of about 30 to 35 minutes to become tender. Stir in the vegetables and cheese and adjust seasonings, if necessary. The finished risotto will be creamy.

❖ Wild Rice with Sautéed Spinach ❖

Karen Mack, Chateau Ste. Michelle

Serves 4 to 6

Wild rice is not a rice but the grain of a wild grass originally used for food by the Indians living in the Great Lakes region. This grain, named "crazy oats" by the French explorers, was a staple food of the Indians. Like regular rice, wild rice grows in shallow water. According to Waverley Root, in China the solid stems but not, apparently, the grains were eaten. Production of wild rice has expanded in this country and it is no longer considered a luxury food.

8 ounces wild rice
1 tablespoon butter
1 medium onion, finely sliced
1 clove garlic, minced
1/4 teaspoon salt
1/4 teaspoon white pepper

1 cup chicken broth
1 1/2 cups blanc de noir sparkling wine
1/2 pound fresh spinach
2 tablespoons olive oil

Wash the rice. Melt the butter in a 1 1/2-quart ovenproof casserole. Add the onion and garlic and cook until the onion is tender. Stir in the wild rice. Add the salt, pepper, chicken broth, and sparkling wine. Bake uncovered in a preheated 450° F. oven for 50 minutes or until liquid is absorbed and the rice is tender. Add more sparkling wine if needed.

Wash the spinach, drain and shred it. Just before rice is done, heat the oil over medium heat in a deep sauté pan. Add the spinach all at once and sauté rapidly, stirring constantly until barely tender. Remove from heat.

To serve, place a portion of hot spinach on each serving plate and make an indentation in the center, like a nest. Fluff the rice and place a large spoonful into each nest.

❖ Polenta with Gorgonzola ❖

Ruth Wiens, Mirassou Vineyards

Serves 6

Polenta, a porridge of coarse cornmeal, is a staple food in Italy and there ranks in popularity with pasta and risotto. Similar to American cornmeal mush, polenta is cooked for a long time. Its flavor may be enhanced by the addition of cheese, sun dried tomatoes or sautéed mushrooms. The coarse cornmeal known as polenta is packaged and available in the supermarket.

Traditionally, polenta is served informally. The cooked porridge is turned out on a wooden board and then cut into serving pieces. It also may be spooned into a baking dish, left to cool, then cut into fancy shapes and reheated. Polenta is served with a gravy or sauce. This Polenta with Gorgonzola is delicious served with Braised Quail (page 179). Any leftover polenta may be topped with a fresh tomato sauce and baked until hot.

2 quarts chicken broth
1½ teaspoons salt (omit if broth is salted)
2 cups polenta (coarsely ground cornmeal)

4 tablespoons unsalted butter
8 ounces Gorgonzola cheese, crumbled

Bring the chicken broth to a boil in a heavy 4 quart saucepan. Add the salt, if necessary. Keeping the broth at a rolling boil, pour in the polenta in a slow, steady stream, stirring constantly with a wire whisk to avoid lumps. Reduce the heat and simmer the polenta, stirring almost constantly for about 30 minutes. When done, the polenta leaves the sides of the pan and is thick enough to support a spoon in an upright position. Remove from heat.

Stir in 2 tablespoons of butter and all of the cheese, mixing well. Spoon the polenta evenly into an ungreased 10- by 15- inch jelly roll pan. Smooth the top surface, cover tightly, and refrigerate until firm and cold. Cut into desired shapes, or into 12 rounds about 3 inches in diameter.

To serve, melt the remaining 2 tablespoons of butter in a large sauté pan over medium heat. Sauté the polenta shapes or rounds on both sides. Top each piece with meat or sauce.

JOHN CULBERTSON WINERY

JOHN AND MARTHA CULBERTSON FIRST BECAME INTERESTED in wines while John's firm was exploring for oil off the coast of Australia in 1967. Their interest in wine deepened in 1971 when the family, which by then included two small sons, moved from Australia to Singapore. The move permitted John and Martha to extend their knowledge of wines to those of Bordeaux, Burgundy, and Champagne, having become thoroughly familiar with Australian wines. Both John and Martha found that the sparkling wines of Champagne complemented Martha's gourmet cooking. The Culbertsons began to dream of owning a winery when they returned to the States — and of, perhaps, even producing champagne.

Upon returning to Houston, John enrolled in winemaking courses, made wines in his cellar as a hobby, and won several medals with his wines in amateur tastings. He also did some research work, in conjunction with Texas A & M University, on grape growing in Texas. Martha continued to develop her expertise in gourmet cooking. Frequent trips to Europe further intensified the couple's interest in fine wine and food.

In 1975, the Culbertsons purchased an eighty-acre avocado ranch near Fallbrook, California — 20 miles north of San Diego. Since they were both natives of the San Diego area, the Culbertsons planned eventually to make the ranch their permanent home. The next year they decided to move from Houston to Fallbrook and built a home on the property, which they named Rancho Regalo del Mar — meaning gift from the sea. This reference to the sea was in recognition of the successful deep-sea diving company, Martech, that John had started in Houston after World War II. From 1976 until recently, when John sold his company, the Culbertsons commuted to Houston from Fallbrook each week.

A cellar was excavated in the basement of the new home for John's winemaking experiments. After taking several extension courses from the University of California at Davis, John began making champagne at home. By 1981 Martha and John decided to build a winery and to make only champagne using the traditional *méthode champenoise*. From this small beginning, the John Culbertson Winery became a reality. It moved from the basement to a series of construction trailers in the avocado grove below the house, then to a small permanent building, to which an underground cellar was subsequently added. They also took out twenty acres of avocado trees and replaced them with a Chardonnay vineyard. These vines yielded their first crop in 1986.

This expansion did not happen overnight or without its ups and downs. The first release of Culbertson champagne was declared the best sparkling wine of the year in 1983 by the *Wine and Spirits Buying Guide*. In 1983, however, the winery's refrigeration unit malfunctioned and two-thirds of the bottles of aging champagne exploded. Many people would have given up the project at that point, but John was determined to make the winery work. He redesigned the winery and added an underground cellar with a series of bays. The cellar was constructed in the hillside to take advantage of natural cooling. Each bay is ten feet high and holds twenty thousand bottles. While the winery was being rebuilt and the cellars added, ten thousand bottles were temporarily stored at a neighboring winery.

While the winery was growing, Martha Culbertson continued her interests in food as well as wine. In 1982 she and a friend opened a take-out gourmet shop, which eventually turned into a very successful restaurant called the Fallbrook Grocery.

By the 1985 crush, John Culbertson realized that the winery was too small. There was no room for expansion and storage space had to be rented. Production was growing, and Culbertson champagne was being sold in eighteen states. Also the winery was rather inaccessible for visitors, tour groups, and distributors. A major decision had to be made. John and Martha finally decided to move both the winery and restaurant to Temecula, twenty miles away, in the heart of the Southern California wine country.

In the spring of 1987, the Culbertsons purchased twenty acres on the south side of Rancho California Road across from the Callaway Winery. Construction of the new winery and restaurant complex and the planting of the vineyards began immediately. The style of the winery complex, situated on a hill overlooking the vineyards, is Mediterranean. The buildings are grouped around a plaza with a bubbling fountain. At present there are two buildings, the winery and a new restaurant, called Café Champagne. There is also a beautiful picnic area on the shore of a small lake. The Culbertsons' plans for the future include a sixty-room inn.

The winery, at the top of the plaza, has aging cellars tunnelled into the hillside to provide natural cooling at a constant temperature. It has a production capacity of fifty thousand cases annually. In the winery building are a tasting bar, a gift shop and a dining room, called the Vineyard Room, for special events. At present it is used for special meetings and parties, but will eventually be open to the public for dining on weekends. There is also a teaching kitchen which Martha uses for cooking seminars given by visiting chefs. Free tours of the winery are available for visitors.

Café Champagne is a bistro-type café featuring foods that complement champagne. The café also provides a changing menu of *tapas*, which are served complimentarily at the tasting bar with the purchase of a glass of champagne. Martha researched the recipes used by the *tapas* bars of Spain and adapted them for the tasting bar. The buildings, the food, and the setting are all designed around a Mediterranean theme, which blends well with the Southern Californian ambience.

There have been other changes in the Culbertson Winery operation. Jon McPherson, formerly the assistant winemaker at Culbertson assumed the position of winemaker in 1987. He comes from a winemaking family. His father started Llano Estacado Winery in Lubbock, Texas. Jon has a degree in food science and chemistry from Texas Tech. In mid-1987, John Quinonis, a graduate in enology from the University of California at Davis became the assistant winemaker. The oldest Culbertson son, John Tyler, also joined the staff of the winery. His first assignment had been to oversee the construction of the new facility and he is now involved in marketing.

With the opening of Café Champagne, Martha Culbertson has closed her Fallbrook Grocery. Even though there is a full-time chef and manager at the Café Champagne, Martha continues to supervise the food facility at the new winery, and plans the menus and cooking programs.

John Culbertson thoroughly enjoys creating new champagne *cuvées*. One of the most interesting is the Cuvée de Frontignan — a blend of Muscat di Canelli, Chenin Blanc, and Pinot Blanc. It is a wonderful accompaniment to desserts since it contains 3 percent sugar and also has a good acid balance. The newest Culbertson champagne is Cuvée Rouge, a sparkling burgundy. It brings back memories of Singapore for both John and Martha. While they were living there, they became very fond of a sparkling burgundy produced by a famous French champagne maker. The wine was light and fruity, perfect for the picnics and light meals so typical in that warm climate. When John and Martha could not find this sparkling wine in the United States, John vowed to make one someday. This he has now done. The Cuvée Rouge consists of 80 percent Pinot Noir that has been lightly fermented on the skins. The balance of the *cuvée* is Pinot Blanc and Chenin Blanc.

The Culbertson champagnes are aged on the yeast for a minimum of eighteen months, and depending on the *cuvée* for up to four years. Although some of the riddling is still done by hand, gyropallets — automatic riddling machines imported from France — are being used. Bottles of champagne are put into a large crate and a machine turns the crate according to a predetermined computerized program. This technique was developed in France to cut costs and is now used in the larger champagne cellars throughout the world.

The twenty acres of vineyards on the ranch in Fallbrook are not nearly enough to supply the winery. Additional vineyards have been planted at the new Temecula winery, but at present most of the grapes are purchased. The whites — Pinot Blanc, Sauvignon Blanc, Chenin Blanc, and Chardonnay — are from the Temecula Valley near the winery. The Pinot Noir grapes come from San Luis Obispo. All of the grapes are hand picked into small boxes and then transported to the winery in half-ton gondolas for pressing.

Each harvest and each *cuvée* bring new challenges and new innovations for the Culbertsons. Martha is constantly experimenting with new food combinations to complement the Culbertson champagnes and John is always refining the product.

The John Culbertson Winery produces six styles of champagne:

Natural — a blend of Pinot Blanc, Chardonnay, Chenin Blanc, and Sauvignon Blanc; finished dry, with no *dosage* added

Brut — also a blend of Pinot Blanc, Chardonnay, Chenin Blanc, and Sauvignon Blanc in different quantities from those used in the Natural; finished dry (0.75 percent sugar)

Brut Rosé — a blend of 90 percent Pinot Noir and the rest Chardonnay and Pinot Blanc; finished very dry (0.5 percent sugar)

Blanc de Noir — a blend of Pinot Noir with a small amount of Pinot Blanc and Chardonnay; finished dry

Cuvée de Frontignan — a blend of Muscat di Canelli with Chenin Blanc and Pinot Blanc; finished semisweet

Cuvée Rougue — a blend of 80 percent Pinot Noir with Pinot Blanc and Chenin Blanc; finished off-dry

Culinary Director: Martha Culbertson

Born in San Diego, Martha Culbertson attended San Diego State University and received a Bachelor of Arts degree in education. While in college, she married her high-school sweetheart, John Culbertson. She and John have two sons, John Tyler, who has joined the winery, and Scott Charles, who is attending Northern Arizona University in Flagstaff.

After the Culbertsons returned from Southeast Asia in the early 1970s, Martha became a serious student of food, its preparation, and its combination with wines. She refined her cooking techniques by taking classes from such renowned food authorities as Julia Child, Jacques Pépin, and Simone Beck. She also taught cooking classes, both in Fallbrook and Houston.

In 1982, Martha and a friend decided to open a carry-out deli, with a few tables on the patio, specializing in pâtés, cold salads, and other gourmet foods. They called the new venture the Fallbrook Grocery. Martha recalls that "the Grocery was an instant success, but there was a drawback. The customers would not leave, choosing to eat on the premises. Before long the Grocery had turned into a full-service restaurant." At first Martha did much of the cooking, but eventually a chef and manager were hired and Martha supervised only on weekends when she was in Fallbrook. In a few years this restaurant had grown into one of the most fashionable eating establishments between San Diego and Los Angeles.

Martha now supervises the food service at the Café Champagne and the planning and scheduling of food-related activities at the winery. She is a founder of the American Institute of Wine and Food, of which she is now a director. She is also a member of the International Association of Cooking Professionals.

Martha Culbertson has been the subject of numerous newspaper and magazine articles in Los Angeles, San Diego, and Houston. Well-traveled and knowledgeable, she is in constant demand as a speaker and an honored guest at national and international food functions.

John Culbertson Winery
32575 Rancho California Road
Rancho California, California 92390
(714) 699-6002

Visits: Daily, 10:00 A.M. to 4:00 P.M
Principals: John and Martha Culbertson
Champagnes produced: Natural, Brut, Brut Rosé, Blanc de Noir, Cuvée Rouge, and
    Cuvée de Frontignan
1988 Production: 30,000 cases

BREADS

BREAD IS ONE OF OUR OLDEST FOODS. Primitive man had learned to make beer from barley and wheat grains. This beer, mixed with crudely ground wheat grains, became the first bread dough. From these rough loaves, to the leavened bread of the Egyptians, who invented the oven, to the commercial bakers of Rome, to the bakers' guilds in the Middle Ages, and to the improved flours and ovens of the nineteenth century, bread has always played an important part in the life and times of most countries of the world.

Every nation has its own special bread. In Russia, eastern Europe, and Scandinavia, rye bread and dark pumpernickel fill the bread box since the soil is poor and rye grows better than other bread grains. American Indians taught the early settlers to use the native corn to make a great variety of corn breads. In England the "cottage loaf", originated to conserve space in the oven, is still being baked. It consists of two round loaves of unequal sizes, with the smaller one baked on top of the larger. Unleavened breads, known as flat breads, have also survived through the ages since the time when the first barley cakes were made by primitive man. Flat breads include the tortilla, Indian johnny cake, the Chinese pancake, and matzoh. The latter came into being when the Jews left Egypt in Biblical times. It is still baked today, particularly at Passover.

Bread making has not changed very much since ancient Egyptian times. Ground grain is mixed with a liquid and a leavening agent to form a dough that is then allowed to double or triple in bulk before being placed in the oven. The first breads were baked on a stone which the ancient Egyptian replaced with an oven. It contained both the coals and the bread dough, which was stuck to the walls of the oven to be baked. The oven, first of clay, then of brick, and now of metal, with modern temperature controls, is still the principal facility for bread baking.

At one time the color of flour and of the resulting bread was a status symbol. White breads were the most prized since they signified that the flour used was free of dirt and contamination. In Roman society, the person who had white bread was affluent and influential. The peasants and poor had only dark bread. Bakers in Roman times occasionally added chalk to make the dough white, thereby enabling them to charge a higher price for the bread.

Bread played a crucial role in American history. During the Civil War, the Senate wing of the Capitol was turned into a bakery to provide bread for the Union army. More than ten thousand loaves of bread were produced every day. Some say it was the most productive period of our national legislature.

Bread making is a rewarding experience. It involves working with a living organism — yeast — or some other leavening agent. For many, kneading the dough is both soothing and satisfying. Then the scent of bread baking permeates the air with a heavenly aroma — a smell evocative of security and tranquillity.

Today, bread is still an integral part of many of our meals. There is a great variety from which to choose — yeast breads, quick breads, sweet and fruit breads, and breads from other countries. A small sampling of some of these breads, all of which are enhanced by champagne, are included in this section.

❖ Sparkling Bread ❖

Karen Mack, Chateau Ste. Michelle

Makes 1 loaf

The combination of self-rising flour and the fermentation of the sugar reacting with the sparkling wine creates bread that is extremely easy to make. This recipe works best with properly stored and chilled sparkling wine opened just before it is used. If the wine is at all flat, add 3 teaspoons of baking powder to the recipe.

> *3 cups self-rising flour*
> *1/3 cup sugar*
>
> *1 1/2 cups blanc de noir sparkling wine*
> *Melted butter*

In a large bowl combine the flour, sugar, and sparkling wine. Cover with plastic wrap and let stand in a warm place until it begins to rise, about 30 minutes. Place the dough in a buttered loaf pan and let it continue to rise for another 30 minutes. Drizzle melted butter on top of the loaf. Bake in a preheated 350°F. oven for 50 to 60 minutes or until golden brown.

❖ Cornmeal White Bread ❖

Martha Estes, Wente Bros. Sparkling Wine Cellars

Makes 2 loaves

This basic white bread is enriched with eggs, butter, and for additional flavor — cornmeal. An electric mixer can be used for the mixing as well as the kneading. If the mixer has no paddle attachment, simply use the dough hook at a very low speed for the mixing. This avoids unnecessary air bubbles forming in the dough.

> *1 tablespoon dry yeast*
> *1 1/4 cups warm water*
> *1/2 cup, plus 2 tablespoons, sugar*
> *6 cups bread flour*
> *1/2 cup butter, softened*
>
> *1 tablespoon salt*
> *1/2 cup milk*
> *2 eggs, plus 1 egg yolk*
> *1 cup cornmeal*
> *Melted butter, for glazing*

In a medium-sized bowl mix together the yeast, warm water, the 2 tablespoons of sugar, and 1 1/2 cups of the flour. Cover the bowl, set it in a warm place, and let this sponge mixture rise until doubled in size, about 30 minutes.

In a large bowl mix together the softened butter, the 1/2 cup sugar, salt, milk, eggs, and egg yolk. Add the risen sponge and mix well. Then mix in the cornmeal and the remaining 4 1/2 cups of flour, 1 cup at a time. Knead the dough until smooth and elastic. Transfer the dough to an oiled bowl, cover, and let the dough rise in a warm place until doubled in bulk.

Grease 2 loaf pans (9- by 5- by 3-inch). Punch down the dough and cut it in half. Form each half into a loaf and place a pan. Cover the pans and let the dough rise until doubled in size. Remove cover and bake in a preheated 350°F. oven for 35 to 40 minutes. If the bread is browning too fast, lay a piece of aluminum foil on top of the bread. After the loaves have been removed from the oven, glaze them with melted butter.

❖ Honey Brown Bread ❖

Martha Culbertson, John Culbertson Winery

Makes 2 two-pound loaves

Martha Culbertson has been baking this bread for many years. When she opened her restaurant, The Fallbrook Grocery, she adjusted the recipe so that it could be made commercially. The bread, with its wonderful combination of oats, wheat, and honey flavors, contains neither shortening or eggs. It is also good toasted.

1½ tablespoons dry yeast
3 cups lukewarm water
½ cup honey
½ cup brown sugar
1 cup rolled oats

1 teaspoon salt
5 cups whole wheat flour
2 cups all-purpose flour
½ cup sunflower seeds

In the bowl of a mixer dissolve the yeast in ½ cup of the lukewarm water. Then add the honey, brown sugar, rolled oats, the remaining 2½ cups water, and salt. Mix and then add the whole wheat flour, followed by the all-purpose flour. Beat together and mix in the sunflower seeds.

Put the dough hook on the mixer and knead for 10 minutes. (This step can also be done by hand.)

Place the dough into an oiled bowl, cover with plastic wrap, and let rise in a warm place until doubled in bulk, about 1½ hours.

Punch the dough down, form into two round loaves, and place them on a greased baking sheet. The dough may also be divided and placed into two greased loaf pans. Let the formed dough rise until double.d

Bake in a preheated 350°F. oven for about 30 to 35 minutes or until the loaf sounds hollow when tapped. Turn out on a rack to cool.

❖ Focaccia ❖

Martha Culbertson, John Culbertson Winery

Serves 8

Focaccia, derived from the Latin word, *focus,* meaning hearth, is a round Italian flat bread that was originally cooked on a hearth. Because of the olive oil, the bread needs no butter. It can be topped with olives, fresh herbs, cheeses, or coarse salt. *Focaccia* is delicious on the day it is made, but can be frozen and reheated. Try it toasted the day after baking. The bread is also ideal for picnics because it travels well.

*2 envelopes (2½ teaspoons each)
  active dry yeast*
1 cup lukewarm water
3 teaspoons salt
3½ cups all-purpose flour
⅓ cup mashed potatoes

7 tablespoons olive oil
¼ pound oil-cured black olives
*¼ pound California goat cheese,
  crumbled*
*1 tablespoon fresh rosemary,
  chopped*

Dissolve the yeast in the lukewarm water in a large bowl. Add the salt and set aside until the mixture bubbles.

Gradually add the flour and mashed potatoes, mixing until the dough forms a sticky ball. Add 1½ tablespoons of the olive oil. (To this point the ingredients may be combined in a mixer with a paddle attachment.)

Coat a bowl with 2 tablespoons of the olive oil. Place the dough in the bowl and turn to coat. Cover with a piece of plastic wrap and let rise in a warm place for 30 minutes. Punch down the dough and place it on a baking sheet that has been coated with ½ tablespoon of the olive oil. Shape the dough into a ½-inch thick round.

Press olives into the dough and sprinkle with the remaining 3 tablespoons of olive oil, crumbled goat cheese, and rosemary.

Let the dough rest for 20 minutes. Bake in a preheated 400°F. oven for 30 minutes or until golden brown. Cut into wedges like a pizza.

❖ Homemade Pan Bread with ❖ Fresh Herbs

Sheryl Benesch, Korbel Champagne Cellars

Serves 8 to 12

This pan bread has an Italian heritage. It does not need butter and is best cut into squares and eaten shortly after it has emerged from the oven. It is excellent with vegetable soups.

2 cups warm water
1 tablespoon dry yeast
3 tablespoons sugar
6 to 7 cups all-purpose flour
1 tablespoon salt
½ cup olive oil

1 tablespoon dry Italian seasonings
2 tablespoons minced fresh garlic
¼ cup chopped fresh basil leaves
2 tablespoons chopped fresh oregano

Combine the water, yeast, sugar, and approximately 2 cups of the flour to make a thick paste. Mix thoroughly and let stand a few minutes until bubbles rise to the surface.

Combine the salt with the remaining flour; add gradually to the yeast mixture, until it will absorb no more flour. Knead the dough until the texture is smooth and not sticky to the touch; about 5 to 10 minutes. Place the dough in an oiled bowl and let it rise in a warm place until it has doubled in bulk. Punch dough down, place on a lightly floured surface, and knead for another minute. Let dough rest for 5 to 10 minutes.

Brush a 9- by 13-inch sheet pan with ⅓ of the olive oil. Sprinkle the pan with ½ tablespoon of the dry Italian seasonings and 1 tablespoon of garlic. Roll the bread dough out to line the pan.

Lay the dough into the pan, brush with the remaining olive oil, sprinkle with the remaining garlic and Italian seasonings, and then the fresh herbs. (At this point the bread may be prepared a day ahead and kept in the refrigerator, on the prepared pan, to rise.)

Let the dough rise for about 45 minutes to 1 hour. Bake in a preheated 350°F. oven for 20 to 25 minutes or until golden brown.

❖ Tecate Bread ❖

Martha Culbertson, John Culbertson Winery

Makes 1 large loaf

Tecate Bread, also known as Mexican Village Bread, is similar to the famous fruit breads served on Twelfth Night in Mexico. *Tecate* Bread, however, is not as sweet, does not contain as much fruit, and does not have the traditional china doll baked into it. This attractively braided loaf may be served to accompany a meal. The dough may be partially made one day, refrigerated, and the process completed the next day.

1 envelope (2½ teaspoons) dry
    yeast
¼ cup warm water
3½ cups all-purpose flour
½ cup sugar
1½ teaspoons salt
¼ cup milk, at room temperature

5 eggs, at room temperature
1 cup unsalted butter, cut into
    cubes
½ cup raisins, slivered almonds,
    and pieces of dried apricots,
    mixed together

Sprinkle the yeast over the warm water in a medium-sized bowl. Stir ½ cup of the flour into the yeast mixture and mix until smooth. Cover the bowl with plastic wrap and let the dough rise in a warm place for 2 hours.

Put the remaining 3 cups of flour, the sugar, and the salt into a mixer with a paddle attachment. Add the yeast mixture, milk, and eggs and beat until smooth. Beat in the butter, 1 cube at a time, and continue beating until dough is smooth and shiny. Cover the bowl with plastic wrap and let rise in a warm place until tripled in volume. (The dough can be made up to this stage, securely wrapped in plastic and put into the refrigerator overnight.)

Punch the dough down and divide into 3 equal pieces. Flatten and roll each piece into a 3- by 20-inch rectangle. Sprinkle fruit mixture over each piece and roll up, jelly-roll fashion. Pinch the edges to seal and braid the three small rolls together.

Place the bread on a lightly greased baking sheet, cover and let rise until doubled, about 2 hours. Bake in a preheated 400°F. oven for 15 minutes. Then reduce heat to 375°F. and bake 25 to 30 minutes more. Cool the bread on a rack.

❖ Harvest Bread ❖

Edna Tears, The Great Western Winery

Makes 2 loaves

A good way to use up the last of the zucchini from the garden is this moist, spicy bread. It may be served at brunch, with a mild salad for lunch, or as a dessert with fresh fruit. After baking, this quick bread may be frozen.

3 cups grated raw zucchini
2 eggs
2 cups sugar
1 cup salad oil
¼ cup dry white wine
1 teaspoon vanilla extract
1 teaspoon cinnamon

1 teaspoon nutmeg
1 teaspoon salt
3 teaspoons baking soda
1 teaspoon baking powder
3 cups all-purpose flour
1½ cups pecan pieces
1½ cups raisins

Cut the zucchini in half, remove the seeds, grate it, and set aside.

In a large bowl, beat the eggs until light colored and fluffy; add the sugar gradually and beat thoroughly. Add the oil, wine, vanilla, cinnamon, nutmeg, salt, baking soda, and baking powder, and mix well. Add the flour alternately with the grated zucchini. Fold in the nuts and raisins. Pour into 2 greased 9-inch bread pans and bake in a preheated 325 °F. oven for 50 to 55 minutes.

❖ Smoked Salmon Scones ❖

Ruth Wiens, Mirassou Vineyards
Accompanying champagne *Mirassou Brut*

Makes 24 small scones

These versatile, delectable scones can be served hot from the oven as appetizers or split and filled with cream cheese for brunch. They may also be served with salads at lunch or they may accompany homemade soups at a light supper. If neither of the varieties of canned salmon is available, five ounces of sliced smoked salmon may be substituted and should be drained, patted dry with paper towels to remove excess oil, and then cut into small pieces.

1 can (6 ¾ ounces) alder-smoked salmon (sockeye salmon may be substituted)
2 cups all-purpose flour
1 tablespoon baking powder
Pinch of salt (check the saltiness of the salmon before adding)
1 tablespoon grated lemon zest

2 tablespoons finely chopped chives
4 tablespoons cold unsalted butter, cut in small pieces
2 eggs, lightly beaten
½ cup whipping cream
1 egg beaten with 1 teaspoon water, for egg wash

Drain the canned salmon well, remove bones and skin, flake, and set aside. Sift the flour, baking powder, and salt together. Mix in the lemon zest and chives. Using a pastry blender, cut in the butter until it is the size of rice kernels. Combine the eggs and cream. Add to the flour mixture along with the salmon and use a fork to mix lightly, just until the flour is absorbed. Do not overmix.

Turn the dough onto a lightly floured board. Knead lightly for 2 or 3 minutes. The dough will be a little sticky. Pat into a ¾-inch-high rectangle measuring 6 by 8 inches. Cut into 12 two-inch squares. Flour the knife between cuts. Cut each square in half crosswise to form triangles. Arrange the scones on a buttered baking sheet and brush tops with egg wash. Bake in a preheated 425°F. for 15 to 18 minutes until golden brown.

S. ANDERSON VINEYARD

ACTUALLY BOTH A VINEYARD AND A WINERY, S. Anderson Vineyard is a family enterprise in which Dr. Stanley Anderson, his wife Carol, their son, John, and his wife, Tracy, are all involved. The Andersons started their vineyards in 1971 and added a small winery in 1978. Production of the winery has grown steadily every year and the Anderson champagnes are now recognized among the premium United States champagnes made by the traditional French *méthode champenoise*.

Dr. Stanley Anderson, for many years a practicing dentist in Southern California, became enamored with the Napa Valley while attending dental school at the University of Pacific in San Francisco. "At the time I was not a connoisseur of fine wines, but did enjoy the free tastings," he says. After Stan and Carol were married, they began to enjoy and appreciate fine champagnes and have continued to do so over the years. "We have had a bottle of champagne with a meal every day since we were married twenty-six years ago," adds Carol.

Competitive yacht racing was Stan's hobby for many years. Being a highly motivated person, he found this sport relaxing from the day-to-day stress of his dental practice. However, after receiving twenty-two awards in international yacht racing, Stan was ready for a new challenge. He was also seeking something to interest him and keep him busy when he eventually retired.

In 1971, the Andersons found just what "the doctor ordered" – a thirty-acre prune orchard in Napa Valley. They did not want to grow prunes but did want to grow grapes and maybe eventually to produce champagne. The property the Andersons purchased had been planted with vineyards in the 1860s, but by the turn of the century it had become an orchard.

Commuting twice a month from the Los Angeles area, Stan and Carol planted twenty of the acres with vineyards, primarily Chardonnay. The soil was particularly well suited to that variety of grape. They also renovated the sixty-year old farmhouse on the property. After the initial planting, the Andersons continued their bimonthly commute to take care of the vineyard. Starting in 1975, with the first harvest, the Andersons sold their grapes to the premium wineries in the Napa Valley. However, each year they would hold back a small part of the crop for their own experiments. In 1978, the Andersons purchased an additional twenty acres and the following year twelve of the acres were planted with Pinot Noir and Chardonnay vines.

Stan became a home winemaker shortly after the Andersons purchased their Napa property. Carol, who had a full-time professional career as a dental hygienist, decided to go back to school to study enology. She took all of the prerequisite courses at a local junior college in Southern California so that she could still work at the office and take care of their teenaged children. To finish her degree, at the age of forty-two, she enrolled as a student in the fermentation science program at the University of California at Davis. Carol was there at the same time as the Andersons' two daughters were undergraduates. In 1978, when she received her degree, it was time for Stan and Carol to establish a winery. From that point on, life became very hectic for Stan and Carol.

Stan practiced dentistry in his Pasadena office from Monday through Thursday. Thursday afternoon the Andersons would drive 400 miles to Napa, arriving in the middle of the night, and would work at the winery Friday through Sunday. Late on Sunday afternoon it was time to drive the 400 miles back to Southern California so that Stan could be in the office at 9 A.M. on Monday. They led double lives, maintained two homes, and had two sets of friends. For over five years the Andersons drove fifty thousand miles a year up and down Interstate Highway 5.

Unfortunately, life got a little too hectic and Stan suffered a heart attack in 1985. Forced to choose between his two professions – dentistry or winemaking – Stan decided to retire from dental practice. The Andersons moved to Napa Valley and now live in the remodeled farmhouse on their property. Both Stan and Carol work full-time in the winery. Carol is the official winemaker; Stan is the cellar master in charge of the winery. John, the Andersons' son, and his wife, Tracy, joined the winery staff in 1987. John is in charge of marketing. Tracy is the culinary and special events director. The Andersons also employ a full-time vineyard manager.

Until 1987, all of the Chardonnay was from the estate vineyard, but with the growth of production of both their champagne and Chardonnay wine, the Andersons are buying grapes, primarily from the Carneros district of Napa Valley. The Pinot Noir grapes for the Blanc de Noirs champagne are also bought from selected growers. Great care is taken to choose the proper grapes for champagne.

In the S. Anderson vineyards, the vines are spaced more closely than is typical of California vineyards. This results in less tonnage per acre but produces a more flavorful grape. The vines are not irrigated or fertilized. The Andersons feel that dry farming gives the resulting wine more intensity.

Carol and Stan Anderson have always loved champagne and had done quite a bit of experimental work on producing champagne before they established the winery. They knew the techniques required and wanted to produce champagne in the French tradition – a slow and labor-intensive process of aging. As Stan says, "We are not in a hurry to produce champagne. After all Michelangelo didn't make his painting with a roller." To age their champagne properly, the Andersons needed a cellar, or better yet, underground caves similar to those in the Champagne district of France.

On the Anderson's fifty-acre property there are two hills of solid rock. Stan decided to tunnel into the rock to build his champagne cellar. He contracted with the person who had the most experience at building tunnels – Alf Burtleson. Not only had Alf dug tunnels for other wineries and San Francisco city projects, but also he had helped build the underground rapid transit system, BART, in San Francisco. For the tunneling job at S. Anderson Vineyard, Alf Burtleson used a Welsh coal-mining machine to get through the solid rock and build the caves. Although expensive to build, underground caves for wine and champagne aging have advantages. The cool temperature never varies by more than one or two degrees and the humidity is constant. "In the long run, it costs less to build caves than to pay monthly utility bills," says Stan Anderson.

The Anderson champagne cave, with three separate chambers for aging, is a showpiece in itself. The middle chamber has a cathedral ceiling, candelabras attached to the walls, and a natural raised ledge resembling a stage. This stage has been the setting for concerts and formal dinners are served in the cave on special occasions.

All of the S. Anderson champagnes are hand-riddled. Stan believes in using the traditional French methods of champagne production and shuns the highly mechanized procedures used by some of the larger wineries. He and Carol like to handcraft their wines and give them individual attention. The results have been award-winning champagnes. Even the first release of Blanc de Noirs received a three-star rating from a reputable wine publication. To aid in the champagne making process, a French wine consultant comes over every fall to offer advice at crush and fermentation time.

At present, there are three *cuvées* of Anderson champagne on the market – Blanc de Noirs, Brut, and Tivoli. These champagnes spend anywhere from eighteen months to three years on the yeast, depending on the *cuvée*. The shorter time is for the Tivoli and the longer for the Brut. The Brut is held for an additional six months on the cork after disgorging to allow the flavors to gain more complexity. All of the S. Anderson champagnes are vintage-dated.

In due course, the Andersons will be releasing two more champagnes: a Blanc de Blancs, which is entirely Chardonnay from estate-grown grapes; and a Rosé, which is made of Pinot Noir grapes with some red Pinot Noir wine added at the second fermentation. They are also experimenting with a special *cuvée* that will receive considerably longer aging on the yeast.

It has been a family effort for the Andersons since the inception of the winery. At one time or another the entire family, including the two daughters, has participated – whether it be picking, crushing, bottling, marketing, or hosting tasting parties. This concerted effort that has produced some of the premium American champagnes.

S. Anderson Vineyard produces three types of champagne, all with a brut finish on the drier side:

Blanc de Noir – 100 percent Pinot Noir

Brut – 60 percent Pinot Noir and 40 percent Chardonnay

Tivoli – usually 85 percent Pinot Noir and 15 percent Chardonnay, the percentage varies with each harvest

Culinary Director: Tracy Wood Anderson

A recent graduate of the California Culinary Academy in San Francisco, Tracy gained professional experience as a chef at the Domaine Chandon Restaurant in Napa Valley. She recently left that position to take over the duties of Culinary Director and Director of Special Events for S. Anderson Vineyard. To enhance Anderson champagne, she creates recipes that use fresh ingredients and are designed for the lifestyle of the eighties. A working wife and homemaker, she focuses her recipes on meals that are simple to prepare.

S. Anderson Vineyard
1473 Yountville Road
Napa, California 94558
(707) 944-8642

Visits: By appointment only
Principals: Stanley B. and Carol G. Anderson
Varietal wine produced: Chardonnay
Champagnes produced: Blanc de Noirs, Brut, and Tivoli
1988 champagne production: 4,000 cases

SALADS

SALADS ARE VERSATILE AND OFTEN STIMULATE and showcase a cook's imagination. They may be served at the beginning of the meal to whet the appetite, as a side dish to contrast with heavy entrées, or after the main course to cleanse the palate. In warm weather or for luncheons a salad may be the entire meal. A salad may be as casual a dish as a bowl of various types of lettuces with a dressing or as elaborate as a carefully composed seafood salad.

The earliest salads were probably mixtures of greens sprinkled with salt: the word *salad* is derived from the Latin *herba salata*, meaning salted greens. Salted in early times probably also meant pickled because salt was used to preserve greens and vegetables. By Roman times, dressings of vinegar, oil, and dried herbs were used on greens, as well as on cooked and raw vegetables. Through the years, salads have been regarded as a symbol of summer and a way bringing of part of the garden to the table.

The structured, or more formal, salad came into being in the eighteenth century. An early reference to this type of salad was given in an English cookbook, first published in 1747, and much used in America, entitled *The Art of Cookery, Made Plain and Easy* by Hannah Glasse. In her recipe for Salamongundy (later spelled *salmagondi* and *salmagundy*), Mrs. Glasse gave precise instructions for making a salad. First the lettuce leaves were placed to line a bowl, then slices of chicken interspersed with anchovies were laid on the lettuce. The salad was topped with diced chicken leg meat, a lemon, diced cooked egg yolks, and chopped parsley. A circle of boiled small white onions garnished the dish. An oil and vinegar dressing was poured over the salad. Although the word *salamongundi* eventually denoted a hodgepodge, this salad was formally structured, with the dressing poured over. It was not tossed.

Several salads were either originated or perfected in America and are a part of our cuisine. Coleslaw was brought to America by Dutch settlers, although through the years it has seen numerous changes. Originally a salad of only cabbage with a dressing, it now includes carrots, celery, green and red peppers, and even crushed pineapple. Waldorf Salad, an American invention of apples and mayonnaise, has also had many additions over the years. The gelatin or molded salad gained popularity when a Pennsylvania housewife in the early 1900s won a national prize for her jellied salad. This American innovation may contain meat, seafood, vegetables, fruits, and nuts. It may even consist of different layers, each of a different color and flavor. In the mid-fifties, molded salad concoctions were very popular.

Today we have a wide selection of salads. Recently pasta salads have become popular. Warm salads, of sautéed meat or seafood served with various lettuces, are now featured as luncheon entrées and first courses by many restaurants and hostesses. With the development of rapid transportation and the availability of previously little known salad ingredients, the choice of ingredients for salads has become much wider. *Radicchio*, fennel, yellow bell peppers, and Belgian endive, for example, are available in many local produce markets.

The salads offered in this section are diverse. They include the simple green salad, as well as pasta, chicken and seafood salads. Although many of the salads were designed to follow the main course, it is up to the hostess to decide on their place on the menu. Several of these salads may be served as luncheon entrées. The dishes have been carefully designed to be served with champagne and so are not overpowering in acidity. Most of the recipes include a suggestion for an accompanying champagne. Since cider vinegar does not go well with wines, lemon or lime juice, wine or fruit vinegars, or champagne are used.

❖ Spring Greens with Hazelnut ❖ Champagne Dressing

Ruth Wiens, Mirassou Vineyards
Accompanying champagne *Mirassou Brut*

Serves 6

The flavors of sweet hot mustard, hazelnut oil, and toasted hazelnuts used in this salad go well with the tartness of watercress. This is a tasty light salad to serve after a meat course.

*2 to 3 bunches tender lettuce
(Limestone, Butter) washed,
dried and torn into bite-sized
pieces*
*1 bunch watercress, cleaned, dried,
and coarse stems removed*
¼ cup brut champagne
1 tablespoon hot, sweet mustard

¼ teaspoon salt
*¼ teaspoon freshly ground white
pepper*
¼ cup hazelnut oil
¼ cup vegetable oil
*1 cup hazelnuts, lightly toasted
and coarsely chopped*

Combine the lettuces and watercress in a large bowl. In a small mixing bowl, whisk together the champagne, mustard, salt, and pepper. Slowly whisk in the oils until well blended. Adjust seasonings, if necessary. Pour the dressing over the salad and toss well. Arrange on serving plates and sprinkle each salad with chopped hazelnuts.

❖ Fallbrook Salad ❖

Martha Culbertson, John Culbertson Winery
Accompanying champagne *Culbertson Brut*

Serves 8

A popular dinner salad at Martha Culbertson's Fallbrook Grocery restaurant, it can also be served as a light summer luncheon entrée.

*2 heads Romaine lettuce, washed
and torn into bite-sized pieces*
House Dressing (recipe follows)
*4 ounces Gruyère or Swiss cheese,
cut into ¼-inch cubes*
4 ounces feta cheese, crumbled

1 avocado, cut into cubes
*8 tablespoons Parmesan cheese,
grated*
16 cherry tomatoes
16 Niçoise olives

In a large bowl combine the lettuce with the dressing. Divide the dressed lettuce among 8 salad plates. Sprinkle the Gruyère, feta, avocado, and lastly the Parmesan on top. Place cherry tomatoes and olives attractively on the plates.

HOUSE DRESSING

¾ cup olive oil
¼ cup champagne vinegar
2 tablespoons capers
Salt and pepper, to taste

2 garlic cloves, minced
*1 teaspoon chopped fresh herbs,
such as tarragon, thyme,
oregano and parsley*

Place all of the dressing ingredients in a jar, cover, and shake thoroughly.

❖ Warm Goat Cheese Salad ❖

Karen Mack, Chateau Ste. Michelle
Accompanying champagne *Domaine Ste. Michelle Blanc de Noir*

Serves 4

Goat cheese, from the milk of the animal known as the poor man's cow, is one of the world's most expensive cheeses because the milk production of a goat is about one-sixth that of a cow and there are fewer goats around, at least in America and Europe. Goat cheeses, also known as *chèvre*, are more common in France than in the United States, where cow's milk is added in the production of some goat cheeses. In this recipe goat cheese is the basis of the warm dressing that adds a tangy element to the green salad.

1 small head Bibb lettuce
2 small heads Butter lettuce
1 small bunch watercress
1 medium English cucumber

1 egg yolk
8 ounces goat cheese
¼ cup blanc de noir sparkling wine
2 tablespoons olive oil

Wash and trim the lettuces and watercress. Tear into bite-sized pieces and keep each variety separate. Slice the cucumber lengthwise into quarters. Remove any seeds. Using a carrot peeler, slice the pieces of cucumber lengthwise. This will give long, paper-thin strips edged in green.

Place the egg yolk, goat cheese, and sparkling wine in a blender. Mix well on low speed. Gradually add the oil. Continue blending until well emulsified. Pour the dressing mixture into a medium saucepan and gently bring to a simmer, stirring constantly.

To assemble, place concentric circles of greens on each salad plate; start with the watercress in the center, then make a ring of Butter lettuce, and then a ring of Bibb lettuce. Place the cucumber slices in a gentle pile on top of the greens. Top with the warm dressing and serve immediately.

❖ Green Bean Salad ❖

Marilouise Kornell, Hanns Kornell Champagne Cellars
Accompanying champagne *Hanns Kornell Blanc de Noirs*

Serves 6

Grated ginger and toasted sesame oil impart an oriental flavor to this green bean salad. It may be served on lettuce leaves, if desired.

1 pound fresh green beans
1 tablespoon grated fresh ginger
¼ cup slivered almonds, lightly toasted
2 teaspoons Chinese mustard or Colman's dry mustard

1 teaspoon cold water
1½ teaspoons sugar
½ teaspoon salt
2 tablespoons toasted sesame oil
2½ tablespoons rice vinegar

Wash, trim, and string the beans. Break or cut them into uniform lengths. Drop the beans into boiling water and cook until crisp tender. Drain the beans immediately and plunge them into cold water to stop the cooking. Drain and dry the beans carefully and place them in a bowl. Add the grated ginger and almonds and toss.

Mix the dry mustard with the water to form a smooth paste. Add the sugar, salt, sesame oil, and vinegar. Mix well. If too thick add 1 tablespoon water. Pour the dressing over the beans and mix well to coat them. Serve at room temperature.

❖ Sliced Tomatoes And Basil ❖

Marilouise Kornell, Hanns Kornell Champagne Cellars
Accompanying champagne *Hanns Kornell Blanc de Noirs*

Serves 6 to 8

In this simple salad of Italian origin, the tomatoes may be used either peeled or unpeeled.

4 large red ripe tomatoes
1 red onion
1 cup coarsely chopped fresh basil leaves
½ cup extra virgin olive oil

Dash of red wine vinegar
Whole basil leaves, for garnish
Salt and freshly ground pepper, to taste

Thinly slice the tomatoes and onion and arrange on a platter. Sprinkle the chopped basil over the top. Pour the olive oil over the mixture and add a dash or two of the vinegar. Garnish with the whole basil leaves. Let stand at room temperature for 30 minutes before serving. Just before serving, season with salt and freshly ground pepper.

❖ Salade des Îles ❖

Steve Wenger, Biltmore Estate
Accompanying champagne *Biltmore Estate Brut*

Serves 6

Hearts of palm are derived from the variety of palm known as *Sabal palmetto*. In order to obtain the heart, an entire a tree is cut, stripped, and then only the ivory colored interior used. The small tree, also known as swamp cabbage, grows abundantly in Florida and Brazil. Heart of palm is rarely obtainable fresh, but is available canned. It has been precooked and is packed in water. This salad be prepared early in the day, wrapped in plastic, and refrigerated until serving time.

*Romaine lettuce and curly endive
   to dress salad plates
6 spears hearts of palm
1 medium red bell pepper, julienned
6 medium mushroom caps, sliced*

*Dressing (recipe follows)
1 small can (8 ounces) pineapple
   chunks in juice, drained, for
   garnish*

Trim Romaine to fit and line 6 salad plates with the leaves. Slice each spear of palm from one end almost to the other, in very thin strips. Center one spear on each plate and gently fan the cut ends. Garnish the uncut end with a small amount of curly endive. Place a piece of red pepper between each strip of the heart of palm. Arrange the mushroom slices above the heart of palm and red pepper strips to crown the spear.

    Just before serving, drizzle dressing over the arrangement and garnish with a few pieces of pineapple.

DRESSING

*1 cup mayonnaise
1/2 cup sour cream
1/3 cup buttermilk
1/2 teaspoon dried tarragon*

*1/8 teaspoon dried basil
1/8 teaspoon dried marjoram
1/8 teaspoon garlic powder
1/8 teaspoon white pepper*

Combine all of the dressing ingredients and mix well. Chill for an hour before using.

❖ Greek Salad ❖

Martha Culbertson, John Culbertson Winery
Accompanying champagne *Culbertson Cuvée Rouge*

Serves 6

Olives are the fruit of civilization and have a long and colorful history. Olive trees originated in the Mediterranean region thousands of years ago. There they provided essential fats needed for the daily diet, since dairy products were virtually nonexistent. Only war destroys olive trees, and from this comes the symbol of peace — the olive branch.

The poor soil of Greece, which was not conducive to many crops, provided ideal growing conditions for olive trees. In the ancient world, the oil from Greek olives was considered superior and Greece became a powerful country trading olive oil for grain and other necessities. The Kalamata olive is named after a Greek port from which the oil was shipped.

3 tomatoes, cut into chunks
1 green pepper, cut into slices
1 red pepper, cut into slices
1 medium onion, cut into slices
1/2 cup Kalamata olives
1/2 pound feta cheese, cut into
*   1/4-inch dice*

8 large basil leaves, cut into
*   shreds, or 1 tablespoon dried*
*   basil*
Salt and pepper, to taste
1/4 cup olive oil
2 tablespoons red wine vinegar

In a large bowl combine the vegetables, olives, cheese, and seasonings. Then combine the olive oil and vinegar and pour over the salad. Toss gently to mix. Let the salad sit at room temperature for one hour to meld the flavors.

❖ Classic Chicken Salad ❖

Martha Culbertson, John Culbertson Winery
Accompanying champagne *Culbertson Brut*

Serves 6

This salad was the most popular item on the menu of Martha Culbertson's restaurant, The Fallbrook Grocery, and is being offered at the new Culbertson Winery restaurant. Each day, twenty-four chickens are cooked for the salad, and the rich stock that results is used for soup. Any fresh herbs may be used in the recipe. The chicken salad may be used for sandwiches, served on a bed of lettuce, or used as a filling for an avocado half.

3 pounds boneless chicken breasts
*   or 2 whole chickens*
Chicken broth or water
2 sprigs fresh tarragon
2 celery ribs, cut into small dice
1 bunch green onions, sliced into
*   1/4-inch slices*

Salt and pepper, to taste
3 tablespoons chopped fresh herbs,
*   such as tarragon, thyme, and*
*   marjoram*
1/2 cup sour cream
1/2 cup homemade or good quality
*   commercial mayonnaise*

Poach the chicken breasts in chicken broth with the 2 sprigs of tarragon. If using whole chickens, cut into serving pieces and cover with water to cook. Add the tarragon sprigs to the water. Cool the poached chicken and cut or pick into bite-sized pieces.

Combine the chicken pieces with the celery, onions, salt, and pepper and herbs. Combine the sour cream and mayonnaise and toss with the chicken mixture.

❖ Tortellini Salad ❖

Sheryl Benesch, Korbel Champagne Cellars
Accompanying champagne *Korbel Natural*

Serves 6 to 8

Tortellini are half-moon-shaped, small individual pastas stuffed with meat or cheese. Legend says that they were modeled after the navel of Venus. Previously only homemade, tortellini may now be bought fresh as well as dried. Golden plum tomatoes are similar in size to cherry tomatoes, but are elongated and yellow in color.

8 ounces fresh tortellini (meat or cheese filling)
1 tablespoon balsamic vinegar
¼ cup olive oil
1 teaspoon cracked black peppercorns
1 clove garlic, minced
1 teaspoon dried oregano
2 tablespoons chopped fresh parsley

1 tablespoon chopped fresh basil
2 tablespoons chopped green onions
10 cherry tomatoes
10 golden plum tomatoes
½ cup pitted black olives
2 tablespoons toasted pine nuts (optional)

Cook the tortellini according to the package directions and cool slightly. In a bowl combine the balsamic vinegar, olive oil, peppercorns, garlic, herbs, and green onions. Add the tortellini, tomatoes, and olives. Sprinkle with the toasted pine nuts, if desired. Refrigerate for a few hours or overnight to let the flavors mix.

❖ Spinach and Bay Shrimp Salad ❖

Frederick Horton, Wente Bros. Sparkling Wine Cellars
Accompanying champagne *Wente Bros. Brut*

Serves 4

The pretty white and pink poppies are the source of the seeds used in cooking. The familiar blue-grey seeds have a nutty flavor that complements the honey mustard vinaigrette, the shrimp, and the spinach in this salad. If walnut oil is not available, peanut oil may be substituted but the flavor of the salad will be slightly different.

3 bunches fresh spinach
8 ounces bay shrimp
1 egg yolk
3 tablespoon rice vinegar

1 tablespoon Dijon mustard
1 tablespoon honey
⅓ cup walnut oil
1 tablespoon poppy seeds

Wash and stem the spinach and set aside to drain well. Pick over shrimp to remove any pieces of shell.

Put the egg yolk, vinegar, mustard, honey, and oil into a blender and process until smooth and emulsified. Place spinach in a bowl and toss with the dressing. Divide the spinach among 4 salad plates and arrange a quarter of the shrimp meat on each. Garnish with the poppy seeds.

❖ Smoked Trout on Various Greens ❖

Jamie Davies, Schramsberg Vineyards and Cellars
Accompanying champagne *Schramsberg Blanc de Blancs*

Serves 4

The slightly acid flavor of the *enoki* mushrooms used in this salad pairs well with the smoked trout. Well known in Japan, the long, tiny capped, white *enoki* mushrooms are now cultivated in this country. They are available fresh and may be found packaged in the produce section of the grocery or at the oriental market. Smoked trout is available at the delicatessen.

Red-leaf or green-leaf lettuce
Other greens as might be
available, such as arugula,
mâche, watercress, or sprouts
1 smoked trout

1 package (3 to 4 ounces) enoki
mushrooms
Champagne Dressing (recipe
follows)

On 4 individual salad plates make a base of red- or green-leaf lettuce. Toss together a combination whatever other greens are available and mound on the plates. Skin and break the trout into "chevrons" and distribute on the greens. Arrange bundles of *enoki* mushrooms on the side and spoon the dressing on the salad.

CHAMPAGNE DRESSING
1/2 cup olive oil
1/2 cup champagne

2 tablespoons chopped chives

Mix the dressing ingredients just before serving.

❖ Shrimp Salad ❖

Steve Wenger, Biltmore Estate
Accompanying champagne *Biltmore Estate Brut*

Serves 6

This simple shrimp salad is best when allowed to marinate in the refrigerator overnight. Artichoke hearts are available canned or frozen. Do not used the canned artichoke hearts that are marinated.

8 ounces artichoke hearts
1 pound shrimp, cooked, shelled,
and deveined
10 medium mushrooms, quartered
1 small onion, diced fine
2/3 cup olive oil
1/3 cup red wine vinegar

1/2 teaspoon dried oregano
1/2 teaspoon dried rosemary
1/2 teaspoon dried parsley
1/4 teaspoon freshly ground black
pepper
Juice of 1 lemon

In a bowl combine the artichoke hearts, shrimp, mushrooms and onion. Whisk together the oil and vinegar. Add the herbs, pepper, and lemon juice and pour over the shrimp mixture. Marinate in the refrigerator overnight and arrange each serving on a bed of lettuce leaves.

❖ Endive with Dilled Prawns ❖

Sheryl Benesch, Korbel Champagne Cellars
Accompanying champagne *Korbel Brut*

Serves 4

Chervil is used in this recipe as an edible garnish to impart an additional flavor to the salad. A small delicate plant similar to parsley, chervil is used primarily in French cookery for soups, omelets and salads. It is always included in the classical mixture, *fines herbes*. This dish may be served as a salad or as a first course. It is light and refreshing for a summer day, and takes only 15 to 20 minutes to prepare.

½ teaspoon dill weed
2 tablespoons rice vinegar
1 pound prawns, peeled and deveined
3 lemons, 2 squeezed to yield approximately ⅓ cup juice, the other sliced thin for garnish
1 tablespoon fresh cracked black peppercorns

½ teaspoon sugar
¾ teaspoon dry dill weed or 1½ teaspoons chopped fresh dill
½ cup olive oil
Salt to taste
2 Belgian endives
Fresh chervil, for garnish

Bring 2 quarts water to a boil and add the ½ teaspoon dill weed and the rice vinegar. Bring back to a boil, add the prawns and poach them for about 3 minutes for larger prawns, 2 for smaller ones. Drain the prawns and place them in a bowl. Add the lemon juice, cracked peppercorns, sugar, the ¾ teaspoon dry dill weed or the chopped fresh dill, olive oil, salt, and lemon slices. Toss well and refrigerate for at least 1 to 2 hours, mixing occasionally.

To serve, julienne the endive and arrange half an endive in a semicircle on each of 4 salad plates. Arrange the prawns and lemon slices on the center of each plate. Drizzle a little of the marinade over the endive and prawns. Garnish with fresh chervil.

❖ Scallop and Endive Salad ❖

Karen Mack, Chateau Ste. Michelle
Accompanying champagne *Domaine Ste. Michelle Blanc de Noir*

Serves 4

The sweet hazelnut dressing complements the scallops in this recipe and is a good contrast to the slightly bitter flavor of the Belgian endive.

1 pound sea scallops
2 to 2½ cups, plus 2 or more
    tablespoons, blanc de noir
    sparkling wine
2 cloves garlic, crushed
1 teaspoon liquid smoke

2 Belgian endives
1 small bunch cilantro
1 cup hazelnuts, finely ground
2 tablespoons lemon juice
1 egg yolk

Place the scallops, 2 to 2½ cups of the sparkling wine, garlic, and liquid smoke into a 2-quart saucepan. The scallops should barely be covered with the sparkling wine. Bring mixture to a simmer and cook for 1 minute or until the scallops are just done. Do not overcook or the scallops will become rubbery. Remove the scallops, drain, and chill them.

Wash and separate the leaves of the endives and the cilantro. Drain well.

For the dressing, combine the hazelnuts, lemon juice, and 2 tablespoons sparkling wine to reach a smooth consistency. If too thick add a little more sparkling wine. Blend in the egg yolk and mix well.

To serve, fan the endive leaves out on 4 salad plates. Sprinkle with some cilantro leaves. Place the poached scallops on the leaves. Drizzle with the dressing.

❖ Warm Lobster Salad ❖

Tracy Wood Anderson, S. Anderson Vineyard
Accompanying champagne *S. Anderson Brut*

Serves 6

Warm salads have only recently become fashionable in this country, although they are regularly on menus in France. Shrimp, lobster, crayfish, chicken liver, small pieces of chicken, or sweetbreads may be served in a warm salad. Simply sautée any of these main ingredients, some of which may have been precooked, and serve on lettuce greens. A reduced warm dressing consisting of pan juices, wine, and a little lemon juice is the accompaniment. This salad will also serve four as a luncheon entrée.

2 heads Butter lettuce	*1 bay leaf*
1 head red-leaf lettuce	*1 teaspoon white peppercorns*
1 head curly endive	*1 teaspoon salt*
1 ripe avocado sliced	*2 live lobsters (about 2½ pounds*
12 cherry tomatoes, quartered	*each)*
1 tablespoon, plus 1 to 2	*4 tablespoons butter*
teaspoons, lemon juice	*1 cup champagne*
2 lemons, cut in half	*Salt and white pepper, to taste*

Wash and dry the lettuces and curly endive and arrange them on 6 large salad plates. Arrange the avocado slices and tomatoes around the outside of the lettuce. Lightly sprinkle 1 tablespoon of lemon juice on the avocado slices to keep them from turning color. Refrigerate the salad plates while preparing the lobsters.

Squeeze the juice of the two halved lemons into 1½ gallons boiling water and then add the lemon halves. Add the bay leaf, white peppercorns, and salt. Plunge the lobsters, head first, into the water and boil for 5 minutes. Then plunge them into ice water to stop the cooking. If they are not completely cooked, they will finish cooking later. Remove the tail and the claw meat. Slice the tail meat.

In a medium frying pan, melt the 4 tablespoons of butter over high heat. Sautée the lobster pieces long enough to heat through and finish cooking, if necessary. Remove the lobster to a warm dish, leaving the butter in the pan.

Add the champagne to the pan and heat to boiling over high heat. Reduce the liquid slightly and add 1 to 2 teaspoons lemon juice and salt and pepper to taste.

Quickly place the lobster in the center of each salad and pour a little sauce over each. Serve immediately.

❖ Grilled Breast of Chicken ❖ with Grilled Pineapple

Martha Culbertson, John Culbertson Winery
Accompanying champagne *Culbertson Brut*

Serves 8

Serve this warm salad as a luncheon entrée. The slightly sweet dressing is a nice complement to the chicken and the pineapple.

4 whole chicken breasts, boned and skinned
4 slices fresh pineapple, 1-inch thick
2 tablespoons olive oil
1 head Romaine lettuce, washed and torn into bite-sized pieces

1 head Butter lettuce, washed and torn into bite-sized pieces
1 head red-leaf lettuce, washed and torn into bite-sized pieces
Sunflower seed sprouts
Honey Mustard Dressing (recipe follows)

Grill the chicken breasts and the pineapple slices, brushing them with the olive oil as they cook. Remove from heat and slice the chicken and pineapple into 3-1^1/$_2$- by 1-inch pieces.

Toss the lettuces with the Honey Mustard Dressing.

On each of 8 salad plates, arrange some of the dressed greens and put a few sprouts on top. Divide the chicken among the plates and garnish each with half a slice of pineapple. Serve at room temperature.

HONEY MUSTARD DRESSING
^{1}/$_3$ cup fresh lime juice
^{1}/$_3$ cup honey

1 tablespoon Dijon mustard
1 cup salad oil

Place all of the dressing ingredients in a jar and cover tightly. Shake thoroughly to combine.

❖ Chinese Chicken Salad in ❖ Radicchio Cups

Frederick Horton, Wente Bros. Sparkling Wine Cellars
Accompanying champagne *Wente Bros. Brut*

Serves 4 to 6

Radicchio, with its beautiful deep red color and its delicate bitter taste, has become a popular enhancement to the American salad bowl in recent years. Most *radicchio* is still imported from Italy. The leaves of this cabbagelike lettuce, a member of the chicory family, make a perfect container for this chicken and blanched vegetable salad. This is an excellent luncheon entrée. Long green beans are available in the produce section of the grocery or in oriental food markets.

> ³/₄ cup snow peas, cut in bite-sized
>   pieces
> ³/₄ cup Chinese long green beans,
>   cut in bite-sized pieces
> 1¹/₂ cups cooked, julienned chicken
> ³/₄ cup bean sprouts

> 3 heads radicchio
> Oriental Dressing (recipe follows)
> 2 tablespoons poppy seeds, for
>   garnish
> 2 tablespoons toasted sesame
>   seeds, for garnish

Blanch the snow peas and the green beans separately for a few minutes until each is crisp-tender.

Place the chicken, snow peas, long green beans, and bean sprouts in a large bowl. Add the dressing and mix well. Refrigerate for at least an hour before serving.

To serve, pull the leaves off the *radicchio* to make cups. Arrange 3 cups per plate and put some chicken salad in each. Garnish each salad with poppy and sesame seeds.

ORIENTAL DRESSING

> 2 tablespoons sesame seed paste or
>   peanut butter
> 2 tablespoons finely chopped green
>   onions
> 2 tablespoons sesame oil
> 3 tablespoons rice vinegar
> 3 tablespoons light soy sauce

> 1¹/₂ tablespoons finely chopped
>   garlic
> ¹/₂ teaspoon salt
> 2 teaspoons sugar
> 3 tablespoons rice wine or dry
>   sherry
> 1 tablespoon chopped cilantro

In a blender combine all of the dressing ingredients and blend until smooth.

❖ Wild Rice and Duck Salad ❖

Ruth Wiens, Mirassou Vineyards
Accompanying champagne *Mirassou Brut*

Serves 6

Coriander and cilantro, both used in this recipe, come from the same plant. Cilantro, also known as Chinese parsley, is the leaf of the plant; coriander is the seed. The intriguing blend of flavors and textures in this salad are complemented by the effervescent crispness of a *brut* champagne. To save time, buy a whole duck from a Chinese market or restaurant. If roasted duck is not readily available, chicken or turkey, preferably smoked, may be substituted.

1 cup uncooked wild rice
2 cups chicken broth
1/2 teaspoon salt
1/2 cup finely minced sweet onion
1 can (8 ounces) water chestnuts, drained and sliced
2 cups seedless grapes, halved if large

1 whole roasted duck (3 to 4 pounds), breast and leg meat cut into slivers; should yield about 3 cups of meat.
1 cup chopped pecans, toasted at 350° F. for 10 to 12 minutes
1/2 cup loosely packed fresh cilantro leaves

DRESSING

3/4 cup mayonnaise
1/4 cup brut champagne
2 teaspoons ground coriander
2 teaspoons grated orange rind

1/2 teaspoon freshly ground black pepper
Bunches of grapes and extra cilantro, for garnish

Rinse the rice well and drain it. Combine it with the chicken broth and salt in a heavy pot and bring the mixture to a boil. Cover and simmer over low heat for 1 to 1¼ hours, until all of the liquid is absorbed and the rice is tender. Cool. In a large bowl combine the rice, onion, water chestnuts, grapes, duck, pecans, and cilantro.

In a small bowl, whisk together the mayonnaise, champagne, coriander, orange rind, and pepper. Pour this dressing over the salad and toss to blend. Adjust seasonings, if necessary. Place the salad on a serving platter and garnish with bunches of grapes and bouquets of cilantro.

❖ Fuyu Persimmon and Kiwi Salad ❖

Marilouise Kornell, Hanns Kornell Champagne Cellars
Accompanying champagne *Hanns Kornell Blanc de Noirs*

Serves 6

Often thought to be of Japanese origin, the persimmon is a native of China and was brought to Japan. Some wild varieties of the fruit were found by the early explorers in Florida and the southern states. However, it was not until the middle of the nineteenth century when Commander Perry's expedition brought back some small persimmon trees from Japan that the fruit became popular in the United States. Today the fruit is grown in California and the southeast. The Fuyu variety is light in color and shaped like a tomato. Tannin-free, it is usually eaten when still crisp. In this recipe the sweetness of the persimmon is a good contrast to the kiwi.

6 Fuyu persimmons
6 kiwi fruit
1 head Butter lettuce
1/2 cup olive oil

1/4 cup raspberry vinegar
1 teaspoon sugar
Salt and pepper, to taste

Peel and slice the persimmons and kiwis into 1/4-inch slices. Place alternate slices of persimmon and kiwi on a bed of Butter lettuce. Whisk together the oil, vinegar, sugar, salt, and pepper. Drizzle over the salad and serve chilled.

❖ Waldorf Rosé Salad ❖

Edna Tears, The Great Western Winery
Accompanying champagne *Great Western Blanc de Blanc.*

Serves 6 to 8

Waldorf Salad was originally created by Oscar Tschirky, maître d'hôtel of the Waldorf-Astoria, for a party of fifteen hundred guests honoring the opening of the hotel in 1893. Since then there have been many variations of the original recipe which included only three ingredients — apples, celery, and mayonnaise.

2 cups diced tart apples
1 teaspoon sugar
1/2 teaspoon lemon juice
Dash of salt
1/4 cup rosé wine
1/2 cup diced celery

1/2 cup broken walnuts
1/2 cup miniature marshmallows
1/3 cup seedless raisins
1/4 cup mayonnaise
1/2 cup whipping cream, whipped

In a bowl combine the apples, sugar, lemon juice, salt, wine, celery, walnuts, marshmallows, and raisins. In another bowl fold the mayonnaise into the whipped cream and gently fold the combination into the apple mixture. Chill and serve on lettuce leaves.

❖ Fennel and Apple Salad ❖
with Calvados Mayonnaise

Tracy Wood Anderson, S. Anderson Vineyard
Accompanying champagne *S. Anderson Tivoli*

Serves 6 to 8

Fennel, a plant similar to celery, is not eaten very much in America, although it is grown in California. Throughout history this plant, with its subdued licorice flavor (like anise), has been a prominent herb. It is yielded one of the four hot seeds of medieval medicine and was one of the five appetite-stimulating roots. In Italy, where the plant is thought to have originated, the variety known as Florence fennel is considered a vegetable. In France the leaves are added to salads, and, in England, dried fennel is used in fish cookery. In the orient dried fennel seeds are used in curries and it is one of the ingredients in the famous Chinese five-spice powder. In America, where it is also known as sweet anise, it is served cold in salads or as an appetizer, like celery. This tart and spicy salad goes well with roasted meats and baked ham.

2 medium fennel bulbs
4 pippin or Granny Smith apples
Juice of 1 lemon
1/2 cup coarsely chopped cranberries

1 cup peeled pistachios
Calvados Mayonnaise (recipe follows)

Quarter the fennel bulbs and slice them thinly. Quarter and core the apples and slice them 1/4-inch thick. In a large bowl, combine the fennel, apples, lemon juice, cranberries, and pistachios. Toss to cover the apples with the lemon juice. Add the Calvados Mayonnaise until all ingredients are well coated. Serve cold.

CALVADOS MAYONNAISE
2 whole eggs
1 egg yolk
1 tablespoon Dijon mustard
1 tablespoon lemon juice
Pinch of salt

2 cups vegetable oil (more or less)
1/4 cup Calvados or applejack brandy, or to taste
1 tablespoon sugar, or to taste

In a food processor, combine the eggs, egg yolk, mustard, lemon juice and salt. While the machine is running, add the oil in a thin stream until the mixture is a very thick mayonnaise. Add the Calvados and sugar. This will make the mixture a bit more runny. Taste and adjust the lemon juice, sugar, or Calvados, as needed.

WENTE BROS. SPARKLING
WINE CELLARS

FOURTH-GENERATION WENTES, Eric, Philip, And Carolyn, along with their mother, Jean, celebrated the family winery's hundredth anniversary in 1983 with the release of their first *méthode champenoise* sparkling wine. It was an historic event for many reasons, not least of which was the opening of the newly created Wente Bros. Sparkling Wine Cellars. Once known as the Cresta Blanca Winery, the facility has been designated by the state as a historic landmark. About two miles from the Wente Bros. Winery, it is an entirely separate complex devoted to the production of sparkling wine. Also included in the Spanish-style setting is the Wente Restaurant, which has become known throughout the country for its cuisine.

Over a hundred years old, Wente Bros. is one of the oldest continuously operated family-owned wineries in California. It all began in the eighteen hundreds when C.H. Wente, the second son of a north German farmer discovered that farms in Germany were traditionally inherited by the oldest son. Being the second oldest, he decided to emigrate to the United States in 1870 to seek his fortune. His journey took him across America to Lake County in California. There he worked in the vineyards and later moved to St. Helena, in Napa Valley, to work in the wine cellar at the Charles Krug Winery. As C.H. learned more about winemaking, he realized that he wanted to own his own vineyards and winery.

While in St. Helena, C. H. met his bride, Barbara Trautwein, who was also a German immigrant. She encouraged her husband's ambition to become a vintner because she, too, was interested in winemaking. Barbara was well versed in the subject having worked in her family's vineyards and cellars in Alsace-Lorraine.

The young couple decided in 1883 to move to the Livermore Valley. With two silent partners, they bought fifty acres from Doctor George Bernard. The plot contained a twenty-eight acre vineyard, which Dr. Bernard had planted four years earlier. Today the winery stands on that original piece of property on Tesla Road just outside the town of Livermore. The gravelly soils of the Livermore Valley proved well suited to vineyards, particularly to the cuttings of Sémillon and Sauvignon Blanc that Wente had imported. He soon became sole owner of the vineyards, expanded them to three hundred acres and built a winery. The young couple was happy in the valley and there they raised their family of seven children.

When C. H. considered retiring, after thirty-five successful years of being a vintner, he remembered the unfair German custom that had forced him to seek his living elsewhere. He decided to divide his estate among his seven children. As a result, two sons, Ernest and Herman formed Wente Bros. in 1918. The third son, Carl, choose banking over winemaking and eventually became president of the Bank of America.

Ernest, who had studied at the College of Agriculture at the University of California at Davis, took over the vineyards. Herman, after studying enology at the University of California at Berkeley, became the winemaker. He soon became famous as a winemaker and is still regarded as one of the greatest California has ever known. Since white wine sold for four times as much as red, Herman decided to specialize in white wines. Today Wente still concentrates primarily on white wines. Ernest aggressively improved the vineyards and the brothers soon gained a reputation for their fine wines. They sold their entire output in bulk, mainly to the Napa & Sonoma Wine Company in San Francisco, of which they were part owners.

During Prohibition Herman and Ernest produced altar wines and sold grapes to home winemakers in the local area as well as on the East Coast. Believing that Prohibition would not be permanent, they turned to cattle raising. This provided the necessary funds to maintain the vineyards and winery.

After the repeal of Prohibition, the Wentes led the industry by becoming the first to produce varietal wines and label them as such, rather than use generic names such as Chablis, Burgundy, and Sauterne. The first varietal wine they made, Sauvignon Blanc, won the Grand Prix at the Paris International Exhibition and, in 1939, the grand prize at the San Francisco Golden Gate International Exposition. Although the wines were sold under the Valle de Oro (Valley of Gold) label, the producer, Wente Bros., became known throughout the United States.

In 1949, Karl, Ernest's son, joined the winery and continued the innovative practices of his father and uncle. Under his leadership the vineyards were greatly expanded. Since land was scarce and very costly in the Livermore Valley, a new three-hundred-acre vineyard was planted in Monterey County in the early 1960s. This Arroyo Seco Vineyard has since been expanded to eight hundred acres, about half the size of the Livermore acreage cultivated today. The federal government approved Arroyo Seco as a viticultural appellation and the Wentes have added the term "vintner grown" to their Monterey County wines.

After Herman Wente's death in 1961, Karl became president of the winery. When Karl died unexpectedly in 1977 at the age of forty-nine, the fourth generation of Wentes took over the winery. Guided by their mother, Jean, twenty-five-year-old Eric, twenty-four-year-old Philip, and twenty-one-year-old Carolyn followed in the footsteps of their famous ancestors. Again there are two Wente brothers operating the winery. Eric, a graduate of Stanford University with a Bachelor of Science degree in chemistry, became president. He also received a Master's degree in enology from the University of California at Davis. Although Eric creates the wines, the entire family is involved. Philip, who has a degree in agricultural science and management from the University of California at Davis, took over the management of the vineyards. Carolyn became vice-president in charge of public relations and marketing, although she, like the rest of the family, is involved in every aspect of the winery.

The Wente Bros. winery has become the twenty-fifth largest in California and now produces about 350 thousand cases annually. The company produces fourteen varietals and about 90 percent of its grapes are estate-grown. As in the past, the emphasis remains on white wines.

In 1982, the Wentes purchased the historic Cresta Blanca Winery and vineyards that had been founded by Charles Wetmore in the late eighteen hundreds. Wetmore, a reporter for the San Francisco newspapers, had become interested in wines when he was in France covering the Paris Exposition. After Prohibition, the Cresta Blanca Winery was owned by Wetmore's younger brother and later by the chief salesman of the company, Lucien B. Johnson, who in turn sold it to Schenely. Although some innovative wines were made at Cresta Blanca, the firm was unable to stay in business. In 1965 the winery closed and the name was sold to the Guild Wine Company in Lodi, California.

Shortly after the Wentes purchased the Cresta Blanca property, they replanted the vineyards and refurbished the winery as a sparkling wine facility. The caves, which had been dug into the adjoining hillside by Chinese workers in the late eighteen hundreds were perfect for the aging of sparkling wine. The caves are very long and originally went through the hill to the next valley. Tradition says that, during Prohibition, wine was transported "out the back door" so to speak, through the caves to the neighboring valley without the knowledge of the federal agents.

Wente Bros.' *méthode champenoise* sparkling wines are made from a combination of Chardonnay, Pinot Blanc, and Pinot Noir grapes, all from the estate vineyards in Monterey County. The grapes are mechanically harvested at night so that they stay cool and are whole-berry pressed in the vineyard. For the Pinot Noir, the press is carefully adjusted so that the grape skins are barely cracked. This prevents any color from being extracted from the grapes. The juice is kept cool and transported to the winery for fermentation.

The sparkling wine remains on the yeast and ages for between three and four years, depending on the *cuvée*. After the aging has been completed, the bottles of sparkling wine are placed in A-frames to be hand riddled. No mechanical riddling machines are used at Wente Bros. The Brut sparkling wine was the first released and is the most readily available. Two other *cuvées* — Blanc de Blanc and Blanc de Noir — are now available in limited quantities.

In addition to the refurbished Cresta Blanca winery, there are several other buildings, all in the Spanish style — white stucco with red tiled roofs — at the Wente Sparkling Wine Cellars. The Conference Center is used for meetings, special dinners, and as a hospitality center with a wine bar for free tastings of sparkling wine. Tours of the winery originate from there every hour on the hour.

Another focal point of the complex is the beautifully designed restaurant, which features American cuisine. Most of the produce is locally grown; seafood is from the San Francisco Bay Area, and beef is raised on the nearby Wente ranch. Many of the dishes are designed to showcase Wente Bros.' wines. Since its opening in 1986, the Wente Restaurant has been featured in numerous articles and has gained a national reputation. It was included in the 1987 — 88 edition of *The Best Restaurants in America* with a recommendation as "one of the finest restaurants in California."

The Wentes have succeeded in presenting to the public not only a quality *méthode champenoise* sparkling wine but also an elegant setting for this newest addition to their wines. Producing sparkling wine in the traditional French *méthode champenoise* has become an integral part of this hundred year old winery.

Wente Bros. produces three styles of sparkling wine, all in the *brut* or off-dry style:

Brut — a blend of 50 percent Chardonnay, 30 percent Pinot Noir, and 20 percent Pinot Blanc

Blanc de Blanc — 100 percent Chardonnay

Blanc de Noir — 100 percent Pinot Noir

Chef: Frederick Horton

Frederick Horton joined the Wente Restaurant at its inception. He worked very closely with the *chef de cuisine*, Robert Baird, and helped create many of the dishes that became known at the Wente Restaurant as "new American fare." Fred received most of his culinary training at the famous restaurant, Narsai's, in Kensington, California, and subsequently held a number of positions in San Francisco restaurants. He is a master at creating unusual flavor combinations that pair well with champagne.

Pastry Chef: Martha Estes

Martha Estes, a native of Oklahoma, has enjoyed cooking and baking since the age of six when she received a Betty Crocker cookbook. At the California Culinary Academy in San Francisco, she was one of three students chosen to be a pastry apprentice. While going to school, she became an assistant pastry chef at the Fairmont Hotel in San Francisco. Upon graduation from the Culinary Academy, Martha attended a two month course in pastry making given by Gaston Le Nôtre in Plaisir, France. After her return from France, Martha Estes assumed the position of executive pastry chef at the new Ramada Renaissance Hotel in San Francisco. From there she was recruited to become pastry chef at the new Wente Restaurant. Now she is a freelance chef, but the recipes included in this book are among those she developed while at the Wente Restaurant.

Wente Bros. Sparkling Wine Cellars
5050 Arroyo Road
Livermore, California 94550
(415) 447-3023

Visits: Daily, 11:00 A.M. to 5:00 P.M.; tours every hour on the hour
Principals: Eric Wente, Philip Wente, Carolyn Wente, and Jean Wente
Varietal wines produced: Grey Riesling, Sémillon, Sauvignon Blanc, Chardonnay, Gamay Beaujolais, Zinfandel, Cabernet Sauvignon, Petite Sirah, and Johannisberg Riesling,
Sparkling wines produced: Brut, Blanc de Blanc, and Blanc de Noir
1988 sparkling wine production: 30,000 cases

Wente Sparkling Wine Restaurant
Open Wednesday through Sunday
Lunch: 11:30 A.M. to 3:00 P.M.
Dinner: 5:30 P.M. to 10:00 P.M.
Sunday Brunch: 10:30 A.M. to 2:30 P.M.
Reservations advised: (415) 447-3696

DESSERTS

DESSERTS, MORE THAN ANY OTHER PART of the meal, are designed solely for the pleasure of eating. Like the happy ending of a good novel, the last chords of a symphony, or the tranquil ending of a good day, desserts are the crowning point of the meal. They appeal to the eye as well as the palate. There is a great variety of dessert recipes ranging from simple family favorites to the exotic creations of the world's leading chefs.

The one ingredient prevalent in almost all desserts, however, is sugar. Without it most desserts would not have their appealing taste. The development of the great variety of modern desserts paralleled the availability of sugar throughout the world. Although in recent years the use of sugar has been reduced for health reasons, few dessert recipes manage to avoid it entirely.

Sugar was used in India and the Muslim world as early as the fourth century B.C., but it did not reach Europe until the Moors conquered the Iberian peninsula in the ninth century. Until then, the Europeans sweetened their foods with honey. For many centuries only the wealthy and nobility could afford sugar. Widespread use of sugar did not occur in Europe and the American colonies until after the Spanish colonized the Caribbean and started cultivating sugar cane on a large scale.

In colonial days in America and up until the beginning of the twentieth century, sugar came in the form of hard cones or slabs. Today, it is available in many forms: granulated, fine, superfine, confectioners', and light and dark brown. All to make desserts more tasty.

Records from Colonial Williamsburg indicate that desserts were an important part of the colonial meal and were made in great variety — cakes, pies, stewed fruits and syllabubs. Some colonial communities, such as the Pennsylvania Dutch and the Quakers, shunned desserts because they thought them unhealthy and consequently evil. In other parts of Pennsylvania, especially where there was a German influence, desserts were always served: without them a man did not feel that he had eaten a proper meal. As immigrants came to America in the nineteenth century, they brought with them recipes for their native desserts. As sugar became more generally available and less expensive in America, desserts were used to stretch a lean meal when money and more nutritional food was scarce.

Desserts fit a wide range of occasions. A cake may be ideal for a birthday; fresh fruit with a champagne sabayon perfect for a summer day; or a light dessert, such as a soufflé or mousse, to end a heavy meal. The dessert should complement the main course and may also be used to supply a missing nutritional link in the meal, such as eggs, milk or fruit.

The variety of desserts is great and ranges from puddings to custards, soufflés, mousses, crêpes, fresh, stewed and baked fruits, pies, tarts, cakes, and cookies. Hostesses, as well as professional chefs, take great pride in producing tasty and appealing desserts. Desserts, which were avoided because of weight consciousness, have once again became popular in American cuisine. Dessert carts, which had all but disappeared in the 1970s, are again in evidence in most restaurants and a large selection of cookbooks on the subject are now available.

The desserts included in this section range from those made with fresh fruit, to soufflés, custards, tarts, and cakes. None of the recipes is overabundant in sugar, although some are not for the calorie conscious. All have been designed to be served with champagne and, for several, a specific dessert champagne has been suggested.

❖ Three-Berry Compote ❖

Sheryl Benesch, Korbel Champagne Cellars
Accompanying champagne *Korbel Extra Dry*

Serves 4 to 6

This quick and easily prepared dessert is a refreshing way to end a summer meal. Other berries, such as blueberries, may be substituted or added to this recipe.

¼ cup Extra Dry champagne
1 tablespoon brandy
2 tablespoons strawberry, or Triple Sec, liqueur
2 tablespoons currant jelly

1 cup each fresh strawberries, raspberries, and blackberries, washed and stemmed
2 tablespoons unsalted butter, chilled
1 to 1½ pints vanilla ice cream

In a 10-inch sauté pan heat the champagne, brandy, liqueur, and currant jelly to a boil. Add the strawberries and ignite the brandy with a long match, tossing the strawberries until the alcohol is burned off. Add the remaining berries, and cook for 1 minute. Turn heat down to medium; add the butter, shaking the pan until the butter is incorporated. Remove the compote from the heat.

Spoon the compote into serving bowls or bowl-shaped champagne glasses and place a scoop of vanilla ice cream in the center of each.

❖ Fruit with Cheese ❖

Steve Wenger, Biltmore Estate
Accompanying champagne *Biltmore Estate Dry*

Serves 6

Fruit and cheese to finish a meal is an old tradition and this is a new approach. Saga is a semi-soft blue veined cheese from Denmark. Any blue cheese, such as Roquefort, may be substituted.

1 pint strawberries, with caps if possible
1½ pounds large seedless green grapes, cut in half

¼ pound Saga cheese, softened
1 cup Crème Fraîche (recipe follows)

Pipe a small quantity of the Saga cheese onto the grape halves. Place the *Crème Fraîche* in a small bowl in the center of a serving platter. Arrange the strawberries around it. Arrange the grape halves around the strawberries.

CRÈME FRAÎCHE

2 cups whipping cream   *½ cup buttermilk*

Combine the whipping cream and buttermilk in a saucepan and heat over medium heat until warm (should be less than body temperature). Place the mixture in a jar, cover, and let it sit at room temperature for between 10 and 12 hours or until thickened. Store in the refrigerator where it will keep for up to 2 weeks.

❖ Fresh Figs with Champagne ❖ Sabayon

Ruth Wiens, Mirassou Vineyards
Accompanying champagne *Mirassou Brut*

Serves 6

Sabayon is the French name for the dessert sauce or light dessert that the Italians call *zabaione*. It usually consists of sugar, egg yolks, and wine. Sabayon makes an elegant and versatile dessert that can be whipped up quickly and served hot or cold. In this recipe it is used as a sauce over fresh figs, but it is equally delicious over any fresh fruit, especially berries.

CHAMPAGNE SABAYON

6 egg yolks
⅓ cup sugar

1 cup brut champagne

In the top of a double boiler set over simmering water, whisk the egg yolks and sugar together until foamy. (The water must not touch the top pot.) Add the champagne, a little at a time, whisking constantly until the mixture is thick and is the consistency of softly whipped cream, about 10 minutes. The sabayon should never get so hot that you cannot put your finger in it. Remove from heat.

FRUIT

2 to 3 ripe, fresh figs per person

1 tablespoon chopped, candied ginger per serving (optional)

Cut the figs in quarters and arrange them on plates. Drizzle with the sabayon and sprinkle with the chopped candied ginger, if desired.

❖ Bananas Flambé ❖

Marilouise Kornell, Hanns Kornell Champagne Cellars
Accompanying champagne *Hanns Kornell Extra Dry*

Serves 4

The spirits most frequently used for flaming (described as *flambé* in French) are brandy, rum, and kirsch. However, any strong alcoholic liquid, including flavored extracts, can be flamed. The alcohol evaporates completely in the burning, leaving only the flavor behind.

2 tablespoons butter
4 bananas, halved lengthwise
2 tablespoons brown sugar
1 teaspoon grated orange zest
½ teaspoon cinnamon

2 tablespoons Extra Dry champagne
2 tablespoons cognac
1 pint vanilla ice cream

Melt the butter in the top of a double boiler. Add the bananas, which have been sprinkled with the brown sugar, and the orange zest, cinnamon, and champagne. Cover and simmer for 20 minutes. Pour the cognac over the bananas and ignite with a long match. When the flames die down, serve one banana per person and top with a scoop of vanilla ice cream.

❖ Mexican Vanilla Ice Cream ❖ with Poached Peaches

Tracy Wood Anderson, S. Anderson Vineyard
Accompanying champagne *S. Anderson Tivoli*

Serves 8

Mexican vanilla has a distinctively different taste from that of our usual vanilla extract and makes a wonderful ice cream. This is served with a peaches poached in champagne and topped with fresh raspberries. If Mexican vanilla is not available, Suzy's Vanilla Extract may be substituted. If that is not available, use the best quality you can find.

ICE CREAM

4 egg yolks
1 cup sugar
1 quart half-and-half

1 tablespoon Mexican vanilla
extract
Pinch of salt

In a metal bowl combine the egg yolks and sugar. Bring the half-and-half to a boil. Whisk it into the egg mixture quickly and return it to medium heat, stirring constantly until thick. Do not allow the custard to boil. Cool the mixture and add the vanilla and salt. Freeze in an ice-cream maker according to the manufacturer's directions.

POACHED PEACHES

1 cup sugar
1½ cups water
4 large ripe peaches

2½ cups champagne
1 piece vanilla bean, about
2-inches long

Combine the sugar and water in a small saucepan and bring to a boil. Gently cook until it reaches a syrupy consistency, then cool. Plunge the peaches into boiling water for a few seconds, then place them in ice water immediately. Peel the peaches and put them in a medium saucepan. Add the champagne, sugar syrup, and vanilla bean. Bring to a boil over low heat, then simmer gently for 5 minutes. Remove the peaches from the liquid and let them cool to room temperature.

GARNISH

1 pint fresh raspberries

To assemble, cut the peaches in half and remove the pits. Serve each person half a peach and a scoop of the vanilla ice cream, garnished with a handful of raspberries.

❖ Chocolate-Covered Strawberries ❖

Martha Culbertson, John Culbertson Winery
Accompanying champagne *Culbertson Cuvée de Frontignan*

Serves 4

Simple to make, these strawberries may either be served as the dessert itself or as an accompaniment to a fruit tart.

8 ounces white chocolate, chopped
*8 ounces semisweet dark
    chocolate, chopped*

*16 large strawberries with long
    stems*

In separate small dishes over simmering water melt the white and dark chocolates. Holding each strawberry by the stem, dip 8 of the strawberries into the white chocolate and 8 into the dark, placing them on an oiled cookie sheet to harden.

These strawberries may be refrigerated for a few hours before serving.

❖ Loganberry Meringue ❖

Karen Mack, Chateau Ste. Michelle
Accompanying champagne *Domaine Ste. Michelle Blanc de Noir*

Serves 8

Meringue shells, of egg white and sugar, make an elegant dessert when filled with fruit and cream. *Larousse* cites unnamed historians of cookery who hold that meringues were invented by a Swiss chef in 1720 in the small town of Mehrinyghen. Some say the town was in Germany, others have it placed in Switzerland. The name *meringue* is a variation of the name of the town. Meringues became very popular at the courts of Europe. Marie Antoinette is reputed to have made them herself.

Loganberries, a cross between a raspberry and a blackberry, are popular in the Northwest. If they are unavailable, raspberries may be substituted.

MERINGUE
6 egg whites
1¹/₂ cups sugar

*1 tablespoon blanc de noir
    sparkling wine*

Beat the egg whites until foamy and gradually add the sugar. Beat until the sugar is dissolved and soft peaks form. Beat in the sparkling wine. Spread as a smooth layer in a well-greased 9-inch springform pan. Bake in a preheated 250° F. oven for 1 to 1¹/₂ hours. Meringue should look dry, but not brown. Cool completely; the center will fall.

FILLING
*1 pint fresh loganberries (or
    raspberries)*
1 pint whipping cream

*¹/₄ cup Whidbeys Liqueur (a
    loganberry liqueur)*

Wash the berries, drain them well, and cut them in half. Whip the cream, gradually adding the liqueur as the cream thickens. Fold in the berries, reserving a few for garnish. Fill the center of the meringue and chill overnight.

Just before to serving, remove the springform pan and serve in pie wedge slices garnished with the remaining berries.

❖ Apple Meringues ❖

Jamie Davies, Schramsberg Vineyards and Cellars
Accompanying champagne *Schramsberg Crémant Demi-sec*

Serves 4

Champagne-poached apples are stuffed with dried fruit and topped with a meringue that is browned in the oven just before serving.

POACHED APPLES

4 large apples, preferably Rome
   Beauty
1½ cups champagne

1½ cups water
½ cup sugar

Lightly score the skin and peel three strips from the sides of apples, making a decorative pattern. Remove the cores.

For the poaching liquid, combine the champagne, the 1½ cups water, and the ½ cup of sugar in a large saucepan. Add the apples and bring to a simmer. Cover and cook until the apples are just soft when pierced with a knife. Remove the apples to a plate, cover with plastic wrap, and chill. Reduce the poaching liquid to 1 cup.

STUFFING

Zest from 1 large orange, coarsely
   chopped
¾ cup water

¼ cup sugar
8 dates, seeds removed, and
   chopped

Blanch the orange zest by covering it with water, bring to a boil, and drain. Do this once more. Combine the ¾ cup of water and the ¼ cup of sugar, bring to a boil, and add the orange zest. Simmer for about 20 minutes. Remove the zest with a slotted spoon and add the orange liquid to the poaching liquid. Stir together the orange zest and the chopped dates. Stuff each apple with the mixture.

MERINGUE

2 egg whites

1 tablespoon sugar

Beat the egg whites until foamy. Add the 1 tablespoon of sugar gradually and beat until the egg whites are stiff, but not dry.

Put the apples on a cookie sheet and top with the meringue. Bake in a preheated 350° F. oven until meringue begins to brown, about 5 to 8 minutes. Watch closely.

GARNISH

Fresh mint leaves

Place one apple on each serving plate and spoon some poaching liquid around the base. Garnish the meringue with mint leaves.

❖ Lime Angel Pie ❖

Marilouise Kornell, Hanns Kornell Champagne Cellars
Accompanying champagne *Hanns Kornell Extra Dry*

Serves 8

This lime pie, as light as a cloud, is served in a meringue shell. It must be chilled overnight before being served.

MERINGUE

4 egg whites
¼ teaspoon cream of tartar

1 cup sugar

Beat the egg whites with the cream of tartar until soft peaks form. Gradually add the sugar and beat until stiff peaks form. Line the sides and bottom of a 9-inch springform pan with brown paper. Spread the meringue on the sides and bottom. Bake in a preheated 275° F. oven for 1 hour. Let the meringue cool completely and then remove it from the pan, discarding the paper. To help keep the shape of the pie, return the meringue to the springform pan and add the filling. Remove the ring of the pan just before serving.

LIME FILLING

1 tablespoon (1 envelope)
* unflavored gelatin*
⅓ cup cold water
4 eggs, separated
1 cup, plus 2 tablespoons, sugar
⅔ cup lime juice

Grated zest of 1 lime
1 teaspoon butter
1 pint whipping cream
1 teaspoon vanilla extract
Thin slices of lime, for garnish

Soften the gelatin in the water. In the top of a double boiler beat the egg yolks. Add ½ cup of the sugar and the lime juice. Cook over boiling water, stirring constantly, until thickened. Add the lime zest, butter, and unflavored gelatin. Stir until the gelatin is dissolved. Cool the mixture. Beat the egg whites until foamy and gradually add the remaining ½ cup of sugar. Beat until the egg whites are stiff and fold them into the gelatin mixture.

Beat the whipped cream in a chilled bowl until stiff, adding the remaining 2 tablespoons of sugar and the vanilla gradually. The cream will double in bulk.

Spread the bottom of the cooled meringue shell with half of the whipped cream. Add the lime filling, spreading it evenly. Top with the remaining whipped cream. Chill overnight before serving. Garnish the pie with thin slices of lime.

❖ Brandy Flan ❖

Sheryl Benesch, Korbel Champagne Cellars
Accompanying champagne *Korbel Blanc de Blancs*

Serves 6

Flan is the name of a baked custard, as well as of a French pastry tart. The former is considered to be a staple dessert in Spanish-speaking countries. This recipe is enhanced by the addition of brandy.

CARAMEL

½ cup sugar   3 tablespoons water

Heat the sugar and water over medium-low heat, stirring occasionally, until golden brown. Pour approximately 2 tablespoons into each of 6 custard cups.

FLAN

2 cups milk   3 whole eggs
1 teaspoon vanilla   2 egg yolks
1 tablespoon brandy   ¼ teaspoon nutmeg
½ cup sugar   ⅛ teaspoon salt

Mix the milk, vanilla, and brandy together and warm. In a small bowl mix the sugar, eggs, egg yolks, nutmeg, and salt. When the milk mixture is warm, slowly and carefully add it to the egg mixture. Strain to remove any solid egg particles that may have formed. Pour into 6 caramel-lined custard cups, dividing mixture evenly. Place the cups in a baking pan and fill the pan with hot water two-thirds of the way up the sides of the custard cups. Bake in a preheated 350° F. oven for about 1 hour or until a knife inserted in center comes out clean.

❖ Champagne Syllabub ❖

Steve Wenger, Biltmore Estate
Accompanying champagne *Biltmore Estate Dry*

Serves 10 to 12

Syllabub, a frothy dessert, is thought to have originated in Elizabethan England. There are as many spellings of the word as there are stories of its origin. The most prevalent of these is that syllabub is a combination of *sill,* a type of wine made in the French Champagne district, and *bub,* which meant a bubbling drink, usually a frothy cream. At the height of their popularity, syllabubs were served as refreshments at balls, card parties, and public entertainments. Serve this Champagne Syllabub after a roasted entrée.

1¼ cups confectioners' sugar, sifted   3 tablespoons grated orange zest
5 ounces flat champagne   2 tablespoons fresh orange juice
3 tablespoons Grand Marnier   10 cups whipping cream, whipped
   liqueur   Orange zest curls, for garnish

Mix together the sugar, champagne, liqueur, orange zest, and orange juice in a large bowl. Stir and let the mixture stand for 10 minutes, then beat until blended. Fold in the whipped cream. Serve in champagne flutes with orange curls for garnish.

❖ Orange Crème Caramel ❖

Tracy Wood Anderson, S. Anderson Vineyard
Accompanying champagne *S. Anderson Brut*

Serves 4

Baked caramel custard is known by different names in various European countries. In Spain it is known as *flan,* in France as *crème renversée au caramel,* and in Italy as *crema caramella.* Regardless of the name, it is simply a custard that has been baked in a caramel-lined mold. In this recipe the caramel is made with sugar and champagne instead of the more usual sugar and water. Baked custards are always cooked in a *bain-marie* (water bath).

CARAMEL

1 cup sugar	*¼ cup champagne*

In a small saucepan or skillet, heat the sugar and champagne over medium-high heat until they turn a caramel color. Divide the caramel among 4 individual custard cups.

CUSTARD

2 cups milk	*3 egg yolks*
1 vanilla bean, 3- to 4-inches long, slit open and tiny seeds removed	*½ cup sugar*
2 whole eggs	*Zest of 1 orange*

Bring the milk and vanilla seeds to a boil. In a medium-sized bowl, whisk together the eggs, egg yolks, and sugar. Slowly add the hot milk to the eggs, stirring constantly, but not whisking air into the mixture. Add the orange zest and pour into the custard cups.

Place the custard cups in a baking pan and add water up to half the height of the custard cups. Bake in the water bath in a preheated 325° F. oven for 45 to 50 minutes or until the custard is round on top and a small knife inserted in the center comes out clean. Remove the baking pan from the oven and let the custard cups cool in the water bath. Chill for at least 2 hours before serving.

To remove the custard, run a knife around the inside of the cup, then invert it onto the serving dish. With a short snap forward, the custard should come out.

❖ Little Custards with ❖ Poached Nectarines

Jamie Davies, Schramsberg Vineyards and Cellars
Accompanying champagne *Schramsberg Crémant Demi-sec*

Serves 4

So-called baked custards may be cooked over hot water on top of the stove or in a water bath in the oven. This recipe uses the oven method. The custard is sweetened with honey and flavored with chopped ginger, a pleasing contrast to the slight tartness of the stewed nectarines. Peaches may be substituted for the nectarines.

CUSTARDS

2¼ cups milk
1-inch piece of vanilla bean, split in half
4 slices (each ¼-inch thick) fresh ginger

3 whole eggs
1 egg yolk
½ cup mild honey
Pinch of salt

Preheat the oven to 325° F. Butter 6 custard cups. Place a baking pan large enough to hold the cups in the oven and fill with about 1 inch of hot water.

Put the milk in a medium-sized saucepan, add the vanilla bean and ginger, and scald. Beat the eggs together just to mix and stir in the honey. Slowly whisk the hot milk into the egg mixture and add the salt. Strain the custard mixture through a sieve into a pitcher and fill the custard cups. Place the cups in the baking pan and bake in the preheated 325° F. oven for 45 minutes. The custard is set when a knife inserted into the center comes out clean. Cool on a rack. Cover custards and chill in the refrigerator until serving time.

POACHED NECTARINES

1 cup champagne
1½ cups water
Juice of half a lemon
¼ cup honey

6 nectarines, peeled and sliced
Zest of half an orange, cut into julienne strips

Combine the champagne, water, lemon juice, and honey in a large skillet or sauté pan, and bring to a boil. Add the nectarine slices and poach gently until they are soft, about 3 to 4 minutes. With a slotted spoon, remove the slices to a bowl. Add the orange zest to the poaching liquid and reduce the liquid over high heat until 1 cup is left. Set aside to cool. When cool, the poaching liquid may be combined with the nectarines and placed in the refrigerator until served.

To assemble, cut around the edges of the custards and unmold on individual serving plates. Arrange the nectarine slices around the custards, and spoon the poaching syrup and zest over the top.

❖ Orange Soufflé with ❖ Strawberry-Rhubarb Sauce

Steve Wenger, Biltmore Estate
Accompanying champagne *Biltmore Estate Dry*

Serves 6

Soufflés are special. They are as light as air and are considered by many to be the finest of the French-inspired desserts. The basis of a dessert soufflé is either a custard sauce or a fruit purée to which beaten egg whites have been added. It is the expansion of these egg whites during baking that causes the soufflé to rise and makes it light. Soufflés cannot be hurried in preparation or baking time, but they must be served immediately when they are ready.

This Orange Soufflé was created by Steve Wenger's wife, Reni, and uses a purée for its base. Frozen rhubarb and strawberries may be used when fresh fruit is not in season.

STRAWBERRY-RHUBARB SAUCE

1 rib rhubarb, peeled and diced
(about ¾ cup)
¼ cup sugar

1 cup orange juice
8 to 10 fresh strawberries

Place the rhubarb, the ¼ cup of sugar, and the orange juice in a saucepan and bring to a boil. Reduce the heat and simmer until the sauce is reduced to ⅔ cup, about 15 to 20 minutes. Remove from heat and set aside.

Ten minutes before the soufflé is done, add the strawberries to the rhubarb sauce and cook gently over medium-low heat.

SOUFFLÉ

12 ounces cream cheese, softened
3 egg yolks, at room temperature
5 tablespoons sugar
¼ cup Cointreau liqueur
1 teaspoon grated orange zest
¼ teaspoon ground cardamom

½ piece vanilla bean, 2- to
3-inches long
4 egg whites, at room temperature
Pinch of salt
1 teaspoon orange juice

Preheat the oven to 350° F. Butter and lightly sprinkle with sugar a 1½-quart soufflé dish. In a food processor, mix the cream cheese, egg yolks, sugar, liqueur, orange zest, cardamom, and the seeds of the vanilla bean. Process until smooth and completely blended. Pour mixture into a large bowl and set aside.

In a large mixing bowl, beat the egg whites with a pinch of salt until soft peaks form. Add the orange juice and continue beating until stiff.

Add one-third of the egg whites to the cream cheese mixture and blend well. Carefully fold in the remaining egg whites only until blended. Pour the mixture into the prepared soufflé dish. After gently leveling the top of the soufflé, make a shallow groove by running a knife around the top about 1 inch in from the edge. Bake in a preheated 350° F. oven for about 30 minutes or until the top is golden. As soon as it is done, serve the soufflé with the hot sauce.

❖ Lemon Pudding Soufflé ❖ with Champagne Sabayon

Tracy Wood Anderson, S. Anderson Vineyard
Accompanying champagne *S. Anderson Tivoli*

Serves 6

The pudding soufflé is different from the classic soufflé in that it may contain fewer egg whites and is cooked in the moist heat of a water bath. As a result it does not expand as much as the classic soufflé, but neither does it fall as much when it cools. These individual soufflés will hold their shape when removed from their molds and they should be served warm.

PUDDING SOUFFLÉS

8 tablespoons (1 stick) butter
½ cup sugar
1 cup all-purpose flour

1⅓ cups milk
5 eggs, separated
Zest of 1 large lemon

Combine the butter, sugar, and flour in a saucepan. In another saucepan, bring the milk to a boil and add it to the flour mixture. Bring this mixture to a boil, stirring constantly until it thickens a little. Remove from heat and add egg yolks, one at a time. Mix in the lemon zest. Beat the egg whites to stiff peaks and fold into the egg yolk mixture. Pour into 6 individual well-buttered molds or large custard cups.

Place the molds in a baking pan with 1 to 1½ inches of water. Bake in a preheated 375° F. oven until puffed and starting to brown, about 20 to 25 minutes. Remove the pudding soufflés from the oven and turn them out of the molds. They will fall slightly. Serve immediately with Champagne Sabayon.

CHAMPAGNE SABAYON

9 ounces sugar
6 egg yolks

1¼ cups champagne

Place the sugar and egg yolks in a stainless steel bowl and whip to a ribbon consistency. Add the champagne and whisk over hot water until thick. Serve immediately.

❖ Raspberry Soufflé with ❖ Chantilly Cream

Martha Culbertson, John Culbertson Winery
Accompanying champagne *Culbertson Cuvée de Frontignan*

Serves 4 to 6

Plan the meal so that this elegant soufflé can be served the minute it comes out of the oven. Martha Culbertson says that this type of soufflé, with a custard base, may be prepared up to two hours in advance, left at room temperature with a bowl over it, and baked just before serving. This is a technique she learned from several French chefs.

RASPBERRY SOUFFLÉ

1 cup crushed raspberries, fresh or
    frozen
1 tablespoon raspberry liqueur
7 tablespoons sugar
2 tablespoons butter
1½ tablespoons all-purpose flour

½ cup scalded milk
5 egg yolks
7 egg whites
Pinch of cream of tartar
Confectioners' sugar, for garnish
Chantilly Cream (recipe follows)

In a small bowl mix together the crushed raspberries, the raspberry liqueur, and 2 tablespoons of the sugar.

Melt the butter in a skillet, add the flour, and cook, stirring constantly, until the mixture just starts to turn golden. Do not let it brown. Add the scalded milk and cook the sauce over medium heat, stirring constantly, until it has thickened. Then gently cook for 5 more minutes and remove from heat. Beat the egg yolks with 4 tablespoons of the sugar and combine them with the sauce. Add the raspberry purée and mix to blend.

Beat the egg whites with a pinch of cream of tartar until stiff; add the remaining tablespoon of sugar at the end. Gently fold the egg whites into the raspberry mixture.

Pour the batter into a buttered and lightly sugared soufflé dish and bake in a preheated 400° F. oven for about 20 minutes, or until puffed and nicely browned. Sprinkle confectioners' sugar on top and serve immediately with Chantilly Cream.

CHANTILLY CREAM

1 pint whipping cream
¼ cup confectioners' sugar
2 tablespoons Culbertson Cuvée de

Frontignan or other sweet
champagne

Beat the whipping cream with the confectioners' sugar until it is the consistency of custard (do not whip into peaks). Stir in the champagne.

❖ Hazelnut Praline and Pear Soufflé ❖

Ruth Wiens, Mirassou Vineyards
Accompanying champagne *Mirassou Blanc de Noir*

Serves 8

The combination of pear and hazelnut flavors makes this an unusual cold soufflé. A most impressive dessert, it is well worth the effort it takes. It may be prepared in stages: the praline a day or two ahead and the soufflé a day ahead. Since it uses dried pears, this Pear Soufflé can be made at any time of the year. The Hazelnut Praline can be stored for several days in an airtight container. Williams Pear Brandy is available in miniature bottles.

SOUFFLÉ

12 ounces dried pears, core
    remnants removed, and coarsely
    chopped
¹/₂ cup Williams Pear Brandy
¹/₂ cup blanc de noir champagne
Vegetable oil
1 tablespoon unflavored gelatin

¹/₄ cup water
1 cup milk
4 eggs, separated
¹/₂ cup sugar
1¹/₂ cups whipping cream
Hazelnut Praline (recipe follows)

Combine the chopped dried pears and the pear brandy in the bowl of a food processor fitted with the steel blade and purée the mixture until it is very smooth. Add the champagne and process for about 1 minute, scraping the bowl as needed. Set aside to macerate for 30 minutes before proceeding.

Fold a long strip of heavy aluminum foil in half lengthwise and rub one side with vegetable oil. Secure it tightly with string or a heavy rubber band around a 6-cup soufflé mold, with oiled side facing in. You should have a collar standing about 3 inches above the top of the dish. Set it aside.

Sprinkle the gelatin over the ¹/₄ cup of water and allow it to soften. Heat the milk in the top of a double boiler. In a bowl, combine the egg yolks and sugar and beat until thick and yellow in color. Slowly add the hot milk, beating well. Return the mixture to the top of the double boiler. Whisking constantly over hot but not boiling water, cook until the mixture is thick and creamy. Remove it from the heat; add the gelatin mixture, stirring until completely dissolved. Cool. Whisk in the pear purée. Refrigerate the mixture until it begins to thicken.

Whip the cream until it holds a soft peak and fold it into the pear mixture. Refrigerate again until it begins to set. Beat the egg whites until they are stiff but not dry and fold them gently into the pear mixture.

Fill half of the mold with the pear soufflé mixture. Level the top and sprinkle it with ¹/₂ cup of the praline. Add the soufflé mixture until it is level with the top of the mold. Smooth the top and sprinkle with another ¹/₂ cup of the praline. Place the mold in the freezer (keeping the remaining soufflé mixture in the refrigerator) for 15 minutes. Remove both and spoon the last of the pear mixture into the collar section of the mold, pressing the purée down all around to eliminate air bubbles. Level the top. Refrigerate for 3 to 4 hours or until it is set.

Just before serving, carefully remove the collar. Pat the remaining praline around the exposed sides of the soufflé and sprinkle some on the top.

HAZELNUT PRALINE

Makes about 1³/₄ cups
1 cup hazelnuts
¹/₂ cup sugar

2 tablespoons water
1 teaspoon vanilla extract
1 tablespoon unsalted butter

Preheat the oven to 350° F. Toast the hazelnuts on a baking sheet for 8 to 10 minutes, shaking the pan several times. Cool the nuts slightly. Rub the nuts against one another in a kitchen towel to remove the skins.

In a heavy, medium-sized saucepan, slowly heat the sugar and water. Continue heating without stirring until the sugar is completely melted and begins to caramelize. If the mixture begins to smoke, remove it from the heat and cool slightly before continuing. When the syrup is a light caramel color, stir in the vanilla and the nuts, using a wooden spoon. Continue to cook just until the syrup is runny again. Remove from the heat and stir in the butter.

While it is still hot, spread the praline mixture evenly on an oiled pan to cool. When completely cold, break the praline in pieces and pulverize coarsely in a food processor fitted with the steel blade. Store the chopped praline in an airtight container.

❖ Chateau Orange Soufflé ❖

Karen Mack, Chateau Ste. Michelle
Accompanying champagne *Domaine Ste. Michelle Blanc de Noir*

Serves 12

A chilled soufflé is not a soufflé that has been baked and then chilled; it is more like a mousse. Many chilled soufflés have an egg base and their fluffiness comes from beaten egg whites or whipped cream. Often gelatin is added to help the mixture keep its shape. Like a hot soufflé, it is served from a soufflé dish. This rich Orange Soufflé, which gets its lightness from whipped cream, is served very cold, since it has been previously frozen.

2 tablespoons (2 envelopes)
unflavored gelatin
1¹/₂ cups blanc de noir sparkling
wine
¹/₄ cup boiling water
¹/₂ cup fresh orange juice

6 egg yolks
1¹/₂ cups sugar
¹/₃ cup orange liqueur
2 cups whipping cream, whipped
Orange sections, for garnish

In a bowl soften the gelatin in ¹/₂ cup of the sparkling wine. While it is softening, prepare an oiled collar for a 7-inch soufflé dish (see page 279 for directions).

Stir the boiling water into the softened gelatin mixture until the gelatin is completely dissolved. Beat the orange juice with the egg yolks. Beat in the sugar, the remaining cup of Blanc de Noir, and the orange liqueur. Then stir in the gelatin mixture. Beat until the mixture starts to thicken. Fold in the whipped cream, blending carefully. Pour into the prepared soufflé dish and freeze for 4 hours or longer.

Remove the soufflé from the freezer 30 minutes before serving. Just before serving, remove the oiled paper collar. Garnish with orange sections.

❖ Champagne Mousse ❖

Marilouise Kornell, Hanns Kornell Champagne Cellars
Accompanying champagne *Hanns Kornell Muscat Alexandria*

Serves 6

Mousse, from the French word meaning froth, is a dessert usually made frothy with beaten egg whites or whipped cream. The classic cold mousse is chilled but not frozen. A cold mousse may be prepared from a custard or fruit base. Mousses are wonderful summer desserts. This Champagne Mousse may be served with fresh fruit.

*1 tablespoon (1 envelope)
  unflavored gelatin
1/4 cup Hanns Kornell Muscat
  Alexandria champagne
2 eggs, separated
1/2 cup sugar*

*1/4 teaspoon salt
1 cup milk
1 cup whipping cream
1 teaspoon almond extract*

Soften the gelatin in cold champagne. Beat the egg yolks, sugar, and salt until pale and creamy. Heat the milk in the top of a double boiler and slowly addd the egg mixture, whisking constantly. Cook until the consistency of custard. Add the gelatin and stir to dissolve it. Cool the custard mixture thoroughly.

Whip the cream and the egg whites, separately. Add the almond extract to the custard mixture, then fold in the cream and the egg whites. Pour into a mold that has been rinsed in cold water and dried. Chill for at least 4 hours before serving.

❖ White Chocolate Mousse in ❖ Almond Cookie Shells with Dark Chocolate Sauce

Martha Culbertson, John Culbertson Winery
Accompanying champagne *Culbertson Cuvée de Frontignan*

Serves 6 to 8

This elegant dessert is a chocolate lover's delight. Much of the three-part dessert can be prepared ahead and assembled at serving time. The chocolate sauce can easily be made just before serving.

MOUSSE

6 ounces white chocolate
1½ cups whipping cream
8 egg whites

⅛ teaspoon cream of tartar
¾ cup confectioners' sugar

Melt the chocolate in a double boiler. Whip the cream until it stands in stiff peaks. In another bowl, beat the egg whites with the cream of tartar until frothy. Beat in the confectioners' sugar, a little at a time, and beat until the egg whites stand in stiff peaks.

Stir about one-third of the chocolate into the cream and then gently fold in the remaining two-thirds of the chocolate. Fold in the egg whites. Refrigerate the chocolate mixture until it is firm.

ALMOND COOKIES

1 cup finely ground almonds
¾ cup granulated sugar
6 tablespoons soft butter

4 teaspoons all-purpose flour
2 tablespoons milk

Combine all of the cookie ingredients into a smooth paste.

Cut parchment paper into 6-inch squares and place on a cookie sheet. Place 1 tablespoon of the dough on each square and smooth it out into a circle about 3 inches wide.

Bake in a preheated 350° F. oven for 12 minutes. Watch the cookies closely. Take them out of the oven and let them sit for about 1 minute. Remove each pice of parchment with its cookie from the baking sheet and invert it over a small Pyrex bowl (about 3 inches in diameter). Mold the cookie into a little shell and remove the paper.

Bake only two cookies at a time until you become very adept. If the cookie sits too long on the baking sheet, it will become too brittle to form a shell.

CHOCOLATE SAUCE

4 ounces dark sweet chocolate, chopped
2 ounces unsweetened chocolate, chopped

2 tablespoons water
⅔ cup whipping cream, scalded

Combine the two kinds of chocolate and the water in the top of a double boiler over simmering water. Melt the mixture, stirring until smooth. Add the hot cream and cook, stirring constantly until heated through and smooth. Serve hot or at room temperature.

To assemble the dessert, place a cookie shell on a dessert plate. Put a scoop of the mousse inside the shell and spoon some chocolate sauce over the top.

❖ Chocolate Mint Sorbet ❖
in Cookie Cups

Martha Estes, Wente Bros. Sparkling Wine Cellars
Accompanying champagne *Wente Bros. Blanc de Noir*

Serves 8

The chocolate in this creamy sorbet is melted in mint tea with crème de menthe, frozen, and served in a delicate cookie cup. The cookie cup is made by cooling warm and still pliable cookies over a buttered mold. For the molds use wooden dowels, rolling pins, or any tall narrow container. The diameter of the mold should be between one and a half and two inches.

CHOCOLATE MINT SORBET

4 tablespoons, or 4 tea bags, mint tea

1 quart water

1½ cups sugar

6 tablespoons cocoa powder

4 ounces semisweet chocolate, chopped finely

2 tablespoons crème de menthe liqueur

1 egg white

In a saucepan combine the mint tea, water, sugar, and cocoa powder. Cook over medium-low heat until the sugar is melted and the mixture forms a syrup. Stir in the chopped chocolate. Simmer until very smooth and not grainy, 20 to 25 minutes. Do not let the mixture boil. If not using loose tea, strain the mixture through a fine sieve. If using tea bags, remove them but do not strain the mixture. Cool the chocolate mixture and add the crème de menthe.

Place the sorbet mixture in metal ice-cube trays and freeze until mushy, about 45 minutes. Whip the egg white until soft peaks form. Place the sorbet in a bowl and fold in the beaten egg white. Return the sorbet to the freezer and freeze to desired consistency.

If using an ice-cream maker, add the beaten egg white after adding the crème de menthe and then follow manufacturer's directions for freezing. Serve the sorbet inside the cookie.

COOKIE CUPS

⅔ cup sugar

3 egg whites

6 tablespoons flour, sifted

3 tablespoons unsalted butter, melted and cooled

2 cups finely sliced blanched or natural almonds

½ teaspoon grated lemon zest

1 teaspoon vanilla extract

In a large bowl whisk the sugar into the egg whites and continue whisking for 1 minute. Stir in the flour, butter, almonds, lemon zest, and vanilla.

Line baking sheets with lightly buttered parchment paper. Place mounds of batter, each about 1 tablespoon, on the baking sheets, about 4 inches apart. Flatten each mound with a spatula into a 3-inch round that is ¹/₁₆-inch thick. The almonds should be well spread out in one layer. Bake only one sheet of cookies at a time because they cool quickly and must be shaped while still warm.

Bake the cookies in a preheated 350° F. oven until they are light brown all over, about 10 to 12 minutes. Meanwhile butter the molds. Remove the cookies from the oven and allow them to cool for 5 seconds. One at a time, place them over the molds to make U-shaped cookies that resemble taco shells. If the cookies harden on the cookie sheet, return them to the oven until soft enough to bend easily.

When the cookie shells are cool and crisp, transfer them to an airtight container. They will keep for several days in dry weather, but will absorb moisture and go limp in wet weather.

❖ Crêpes with Fresh Berry Sauce ❖

Edna Tears, The Great Western Winery
Accompanying champagne *Great Western Natural*

Serve 4 to 6

A *crêpe*, the French word for a very thin pancake, may have various fillings and be rolled into different shapes. It becomes a dessert crêpe when sugar is added to the batter. To make delicate and tender crêpes, allow the batter to rest for a time. This gives the protein in the flour an opportunity to relax and, consequently, tiny air bubbles develop in the batter.

CRÊPES
(Makes about twelve 6- to 7-inch crêpes)

3 eggs
⅔ cup all-purpose flour
¼ teaspoon salt
1 tablespoon sugar

1 tablespoon cream sherry
1 cup milk
Melted butter, for cooking

Beat the eggs in a large mixing bowl. Combine the flour, salt, and sugar and, in a separate bowl, combine the sherry and milk. Gradually add the dry ingredients to the eggs, alternately with the milk mixture. Beat until smooth. Let the batter stand, covered with plastic wrap, for 30 minutes.

Heat a crêpe pan over moderate heat and lightly brush with melted butter. When butter is hot, add just enough batter to cover the bottom of the pan, tilting the pan and distributing the batter to make a very thin crêpe. Cook until brown underneath and quickly turn and cook the other side. Continue cooking crêpes until all of the batter is used, brushing pan with butter as necessary.

FRESH BERRY SAUCE

1 quart fresh blueberries,
    raspberries, or strawberries,
    cleaned, washed and lightly
    crushed
Sugar

¼ cup cream sherry
Vanilla ice cream
Whipped cream

Reserve ¼ cup berries for garnish. In a bowl combine the berries with sugar to taste. Add the sherry and mix lightly.

To serve, fill each crêpe with a small scoop of vanilla ice cream and 2 tablespoons of the sauce. Fold the crêpe into the desired shape and top with a small dollop of whipped cream. Garnish with a fresh berry.

❖ Lavender Rose-Petal Cheesecake ❖

Tracy Wood Anderson, S. Anderson Vineyard
Accompanying champagne *S. Anderson Brut*

Serves 10 to 12

Lavender adds a flavor of mint to this creamy cheesecake, which is garnished with crystallized rose petals. Lavender is available dried in health food stores and in the spice section of gourmet shops. Silver pearls are available in supermarkets.

CHEESECAKE

*1 cup Late Harvest Chardonnay,
   or other sweet white wine*
2 tablespoons dried lavender
*1½ pounds cream cheese, softened
   and at room temperature*
½ cup, plus 2 tablespoons, sugar
4 large eggs

*Prepared Shortdough (recipe
   follows)*
1 cup sour cream
*Rose petals, crystallized (recipe
   follows)*
Silver pearls

In a small saucepan combine the wine and lavender. Heat the mixture and reduce to the consistency of marmalade. Strain the liquid and chop the lavender finely, if you plan to add it to the cheesecake; otherwise, discard it.

In the bowl of a mixer combine the cream cheese and the ½ cup of sugar, mixing at low speed. Beat in the eggs one at a time. Add the strained wine and the lavender, if desired.

Place the shortdough in the bottom of a 9-inch springform pan. Pour the cream cheese mixture into the pan and bake in a preheated 325° F. oven for 45 minutes. Remove the cake from the oven and let it sit at room temperature for 30 minutes. Combine the sour cream and the 2 tablespoons of sugar, or more to taste, and spread evenly over the top of the cheesecake. Bake in a preheated 400° F. oven for 5 minutes. Cool the cake and chill for 3 hours before serving.

Garnish the cake with the crystallized rose petals, putting one on each slice of cake, and sprinkle some silver pearls around the petals.

SHORTDOUGH

1¼ cups all-purpose flour
1 tablespoon sugar
⅛ teaspoon salt

*8 tablespoons chilled butter, cut
   into 1-inch pieces*
3 to 5 tablespoons ice water

In a bowl combine the flour, sugar and salt. Add the butter pieces and with a pastry blender work the mixture until it resembles coarse meal. With a fork mix the ice water, 1 tablespoon at a time, into the dough until it forms a ball. Knead the dough lightly for a few seconds, re-form it into a ball, and chill it for an hour. Roll out on a floured board.

CRYSTALLIZED ROSE PETALS

1 egg white
Rose petals

Sugar

Beat the egg white until frothy and brush it onto each rose petal. Sprinkle some sugar over the petals and let them dry.

❖ Blueberry Shortcake with ❖ Warm Crème Anglaise

Tracy Wood Anderson, S. Anderson Vineyard
Accompanying champagne *S. Anderson Brut*

Serves 8

An old-fashioned biscuitlike shortcake is the base for fresh blueberries and a soft custard sauce. Raspberries, blackberries, or small strawberries may also be used in this recipe.

SHORTCAKE

1¾ cups all-purpose flour
¼ teaspoon salt
3 teaspoons baking powder

¼ cup sugar
5⅓ tablespoons (⅔ stick) butter
½ cup milk

Combine the flour, salt, baking powder, and sugar in the bowl of a food processor. Add the butter and mix until crumbly. Add the milk and quickly mix into a soft dough. Place the dough on a floured board and, with floured hands, pat it out to a thickness of about 1 inch. Cut biscuits with a 3-inch biscuit cutter. Place biscuits on a nonstick or parchment-lined cookie sheet. Bake in a preheated 375° F. oven until golden brown, about 15 minutes.

CRÈME ANGLAISE

1 cup milk
1 cup half-and-half
5 egg yolks

⅔ cup sugar
1 teaspoon vanilla extract
⅛ teaspoon salt

In a small saucepan bring the milk and the half-and-half to a boil. In a bowl mix the egg yolks, sugar, and vanilla. While stirring, add half of the milk to the egg yolks, and then add this mixture back to the milk in the saucepan. Continue cooking over low heat until the sauce starts to thicken. Be careful not to overcook it.

BERRIES

¾ cup sugar
½ cup water
Zest of 1 lemon

1 pint blueberries
2 tablespoons cornstarch
3 tablespoons water

Combine the sugar, water, and lemon zest in a saucepan and boil for 5 minutes. Add half of the blueberries, reserving the rest for garnish, and simmer another 5 minutes, stirring occasionally. Mix the cornstarch with the 3 tablespoons of water and add to the berries. Cook until the mixture thickens.

GARNISH

1 cup whipping cream, whipped

To assemble the dessert, cut each shortcake in half. Pipe a mound of whipped cream onto the bottom half of each cake. Put a spoonful of the cooked berry mixture on the cream and sprinkle with some fresh berries. Pipe another small mound of whipped cream over the berries. Place the top of the shortcake on the cream, and pour some Crème Anglaise over it. Garnish with fresh berries.

❖ Rhubarb Crumble with ❖ Cardamom Crème Fraîche

Martha Estes, Wente Bros. Sparkling Wine Cellars
Accompanying champagne *Wente Bros. Brut*

Serves 6

For this crumble, fresh rhubarb is macerated overnight with orange juice, cinnamon, and brandy. The fruit is then baked with a crunchy topping and served with a cardamom-flavored *crème fraîche* that has been made ahead.

RHUBARB

6 cups sugar
2 tablespoons grated orange zest
1 tablespoon grated lemon zest
1 cup brandy

3 cups freshly squeezed orange juice
4 pounds fresh rhubarb, cut into 1-inch pieces
1/4 cup cornstarch

The day before serving, combine in a large bowl the sugar, orange rind, lemon rind, brandy and orange juice. Add the rhubarb, toss well, and let the mixture stand overnight.

On the following day, drain the rhubarb and place the juice in a saucepan. Add the cornstarch to the juice, whisking the mixture over medium heat until thickened. Put the rhubarb into a large well- buttered soufflé dish or deep baking dish, and pour the thickened juice over it. Set aside while preparing the topping.

TOPPING

1/3 cup all-purpose flour
1/2 teaspoon allspice
1/2 teaspoon nutmeg
1/4 teaspoon cinnamon
1/4 teaspoon salt
1/2 cup regular or quick-cooking oats

1/2 packed cup dark brown sugar
8 tablespoons (1 stick) cold unsalted butter, cut into 1-inch pieces
1/3 cup coarsely chopped walnuts

In a bowl combine the flour, spices, salt, oats, and sugar. Cut in the butter until coarse crumbs form. Stir in the walnuts. Scatter the topping evenly over the fruit in the baking dish. Bake in a preheated 350° F. oven for 40 to 50 minutes or until topping is golden brown. Let the crumble cool on a rack for about 15 minutes before serving. Serve with cold Cardamom Crème Fraîche.

CARDAMOM CRÈME FRAÎCHE

2 cups (1 pint) whipping cream
1 cup (1/2 pint) buttermilk

1/4 teaspoon freshly ground cardamom

Stir together the cream and buttermilk in a saucepan. Heat gently until the mixture is no longer cold, but is still cooler than body temperature. Pour into a glass container and partially cover. Leave at room temperature for 8 hours or overnight until thickened and slightly acid in taste. (On a hot day, the cream may thicken faster.) Stir the cream, add the cardamom, cover, and refrigerate. The Crème Fraîche will keep in the refrigerator for several days.

❖ Tiny Fruit Tarts ❖

Martha Culbertson, John Culbertson Winery
Accompanying champagne *Culbertson Blanc de Noir*

Makes 24 two-inch tarts

These tiny, jewel-like tarts make wonderful finger food and can be easily transported to a pot luck supper or taken on a picnic. They need no refrigeration.

1¼ *cups all-purpose flour*
8 *tablespoons (1 stick) unsalted*
  butter, cut into bits
⅛ *teaspoon salt*
¼ *teaspoon sugar*
3 *tablespoons cold water*

⅓ *cup currant jelly, melted*
24 *or more pieces of fresh fruit:*
  strawberries, raspberries, pitted
  cherries, peach slices, mandarin
  orange slices, grapes, etc.
Mint leaves, for garnish

Place the flour, butter, salt, and sugar into the bowl of a food processor. Process until the flour mixture looks like meal. Add the cold water until the dough forms a ball on the blade.

Roll out the dough ¼-inch thick. Cut out rounds to fit tiny tart shells. Press the dough down firmly in the shells, place on a baking sheet, and pierce bottom of tart shells with a fork. Bake in a preheated 400° F. oven 12 to 15 minutes or until lightly browned.

Remove the shells from the oven and cool them. Melt the currant jelly and brush the shells with it. Place the fruit in the tart and brush again with the lukewarm jelly. A piece of fresh mint tucked alongside the fruit looks pretty and tastes good.

❖ Lemon Tarts ❖

Sheryl Benesch, Korbel Champagne Cellars
Accompanying champagne *Korbel Brut Rosé*

Makes 24 small tarts

The differences between a pie and a tart are that the former is served from a pie pan and the latter is freestanding and that pie dough does not contain sugar, but tart dough may contain not only sugar, but also egg. These simple-to-make individual tarts contain graham cracker crumbs in addition to flour for extra texture and flavor.

TART SHELLS

1½ cups all-purpose flour
¼ cup fine graham cracker crumbs
8 tablespoons (1 stick) unsalted

butter, chilled and cut into
pieces
¼ cup whipping cream

Mix the flour and graham cracker crumbs and cut in the butter until the mixture has the consistency of cornmeal. Add the whipping cream gradually (you may not need all of it) and mix until the dough holds together, but do not overmix. Roll out the dough and use a circular cutter 3- to 4-inches in diameter to cut out the dough. Line ungreased muffin tins or tart tins with the dough, prick it with a fork, and bake in a preheated 375° F. oven until golden, about 8 to 10 minutes. Let the tart shells cool before filling.

LEMON FILLING

3 egg yolks
1 can (16 ounces) sweetened
*   condensed milk*
2 tablespoons lemon zest

½ cup of lemon juice
Whipping cream, whipped, for
*   garnish*

In a mixing bowl, beat the egg yolks with an electric mixer until light and fluffy. Add the condensed milk, mixing well. Turn the mixer to low speed and add the lemon juice and 1 tablespoon of the lemon zest, mixing until well blended, about 1 minute. Fill the cooled tart shells. Garnish with whipped cream rosettes and sprinkle with a little of the reserved lemon zest. Serve at once.

❖ Queen's Tarts ❖

Jamie Davies, Schramsberg Vineyards and Cellars
Accompanying champagne *Schramsberg Crémant Demi-sec*

Makes 10 to 12 tarts

These small pastry packets are not shaped like tarts at all, but are served in the same way. Filled with a mixture of dates, currants and lemon, they are a reminiscent of an old fashioned dried fruit tart.

PIE CRUST

1¹/₂ cups all-purpose flour	*¹/₂ cup shortening, part butter*
¹/₈ teaspoon salt	*3 to 4 tablespoons ice water*

Mix the flour and salt. Cut in the shortening with a pastry blender and work until the mixture resembles crumbs. Add the water, a little at a time, stirring until the mixture forms a ball and cleans the side of the bowl. Wrap the dough in plastic and rest it in the refrigerator while preparing the filling.

FILLING

1 lemon	*¹/₄ cup sugar*
³/₄ cup pitted dates	*1 egg*
³/₄ cup dried currants	*1 teaspoon cinnamon*

Cut the lemon into large pieces. Grind the lemon, dates, and currants in a food grinder or pulse to a coarse texture in a food processor. Beat together the egg and sugar and add to the date mixture.

To make the tarts, roll the pie crust thin. Cut into 4-inch squares — there will be between 10 and 12 squares. Place 1 heaping tablespoon of filling in the center of each square. Lightly moisten the corners with cold water and draw up the dough, as if it were a handkerchief or scarf, into "hobo" packets, pinching the corners to seal the top. Place the packets on an ungreased cookie sheet and bake in a preheated 425° F. oven for 15 to 18 minutes or until lightly brown.

❖ Pecan Toffee Tart ❖

Ruth Wiens, Mirassou Vineyards
Accompanying champagne *Mirassou Blanc de Noir*

Serves 12

Marcy Lessack, Mirassou Vineyards' chef, created this rich pecan tart. Unlike the traditional Southern pecan pie, this dessert consists of a sweetened tart shell and a creamy pecan filling.

PASTRY

2 cups all-purpose flour
3 tablespoons sugar
12 tablespoons (1½ sticks)
    unsalted butter, in 1-inch pieces

½ teaspoon grated orange zest
2 egg yolks

In a food processor, combine the flour, sugar, butter, and orange zest and process until blended and the consistency of crumbs. Add the egg yolks and process until the dough holds together. With your fingers press the dough into a 10- or 12-inch tart or springform pan. Bake in a preheated 325° F. for 15 minutes. While the tart shell is baking, prepare the filling.

PECAN FILLING

1 cup sugar
1½ cups whipping cream
1½ teaspoons grated orange zest
⅛ teaspoon salt

2 cups pecan halves
Lightly sweetened whipped cream
    flavored with Grand Marnier
    liqueur, for garnish

In a saucepan, combine the sugar, cream, orange rind and salt. Bring to a boil, stirring until the sugar is dissolved. Reduce the heat to medium and cook 5 to 6 minutes longer. Remove from heat and fold in the pecans, stirring until they are well coated with the syrup. Pour the filling into the baked tart shell and bake in a preheated 375° F. oven until golden brown, about 35 to 40 minutes.

Serve with lightly sweetened whipped cream flavored with Grand Marnier.

❖ Hot Apple and Sour Cherry ❖ Tarte Tatin

Martha Estes, Wente Bros. Sparkling Wine Cellars
Accompanying champagne *Wente Bros. Brut*

Serves 8

There are several stories about the origin of the famous Tarte Tatin, an upside-down confection usually made with apples. One version is that the tart originated at a hotel outside Paris owned by the Tatin sisters. They had no oven in which to bake and devised the method of putting the fruit, sugar, and butter in the bottom of a pan and covering it with a dough. This pan was placed on top of the stove, under a metal hood and baked. The tart was then inverted and served.

In this recipe, apples and pitted sour cherries, spiced with cinnamon and sugar, are baked with puff pastry. The fruit is caramelized after the tart has been baked. Puff pastry sheets are available in the freezer section of the grocery.

> 1 ten-inch circle of puff pastry, ⅛-inch thick
> 6 to 8 large Golden Delicious apples, peeled, cored, and quartered
> 1 pound fresh sour cherries (pitted, canned cherries, well-drained, may be substituted)

> 1½ cups sugar, plus extra for the caramel
> 1 tablespoon cinnamon
> 3 tablespoons lemon juice
> 8 tablespoons (1 stick) unsalted butter

Prepare the puff pastry circle and prick it all over. Refrigerate it until ready to use.

Place the apples, cherries, 1 cup of the sugar, cinnamon, and lemon juice into a bowl. Toss to coat apples and let the mixture sit for 1 hour.

Use a deep, heavy-bottomed, 9-inch pan with an ovenproof handle for the tart. Cut the butter into small chunks and place in the bottom of the pan. Sprinkle the remaining ½ cup of sugar evenly over the butter. Making 2 layers of fruit, arrange the apple pieces in tight circles in the pan. Put the apples as close together as possible and place the cherries in the crevices. The fruit should be packed tightly because it shrinks during baking.

Place the puff pastry on top of the fruit, tucking it in around the edges. Bake in a preheated 350° F. oven until the crust is browned, 40 to 50 minutes. Remove the tart from the oven and let stand for 5 minutes. Place a round platter over the top of the pan and carefully invert it, leaving the pan in place, still covering the tart. After 5 minutes, remove the pan. If the apples fall, rearrange them neatly. Pour any juices over the top.

To caramelize the tart, heat a heavy skillet until quite hot. Dust the tart with sugar and hold the bottom of the hot skillet just above the tart to sear the sugar. Repeat this process three more times. A caramel crust should form on top of the tart. Serve hot with vanilla ice cream.

❖ Chestnut Roll ❖

Jamie Davies, Schramsberg Vineyards and Cellars
Accompanying champagne *Schramsberg Crémant Demi-sec*

Serves 6

Native chestnut trees were once abundant in the eastern part of the United States. They were killed in the first half of this century, however, by a fungus that came with some saplings imported from the Far East and planted on Long Island. Today most of the chestnuts used in this country come from the European variety of trees and are known as Italian chestnuts. These large sweet nuts come primarily from groves in California and the Pacific Northwest. They are available from early November to Christmas. This cake log is filled with a fresh chestnut cream and served with strawberries.

5 eggs, separated
½ cup brown sugar
1 teaspoon vanilla extract
¾ cup cake flour
¾ teaspoon baking powder

Pinch of salt
Chestnut Filling (recipe follows)
Confectioners' sugar
Fresh strawberries

Grease a 10- by 15-inch jelly roll pan and line it with buttered waxed paper.

In a bowl beat the egg yolks until light. Gradually add the sugar and continue beating until the mixture falls back into the bowl in a ribbon when the beaters are lifted. Add the vanilla. Sift together the flour, baking powder, and salt and gradually stir them into the egg yolks, blending well. Beat the egg whites until stiff but not dry. Gently fold them into the egg yolk mixture. Spread the batter into the prepared pan and bake in a preheated 375° F. oven for 10 to 12 minutes, or until a toothpick inserted in the center comes out clean. Invert the cake onto a tea towel that has been sprinkled with confectioners' sugar. Remove the waxed paper and roll up the cake from the long side. Let it cool still rolled up in the cloth.

To assemble the cake, gently unroll it and spread the filling in the center. Re-roll, sprinkle the top with confectioners' sugar, and serve with fresh strawberries.

CHESTNUT FILLING

1½ cups whipping cream
⅓ cup sugar
1 tablespoon brandy or rum

¾ cup ground chestnuts
(instructions follow)

Whip the cream, gradually adding the sugar. Add the brandy or rum and fold in the ground chestnuts.

CHESTNUTS

2 cups Italian chestnuts

With a sharp knife cut a lengthwise slit in the flat part of each chestnut. Place the nuts in a saucepan and cover them with water. Bring to a boil and simmer for 20 to 25 minutes. Drain and remove the shells and skins. Force the chestnuts through a potato ricer or use a food processor to grind them coarsely.

❖ Almond Torte with ❖ Pineapple Sorbet

Karen Mack, Chateau Ste. Michelle
Accompanying champagne *Domaine Ste. Michelle Blanc de Noir*

Serves 8

This almond torte is served warm and topped with fresh pineapple sorbet.

ALMOND TORTE

1 medium, fully ripe, fresh
    pineapple
1 cup whole natural almonds
16 tablespoons (2 sticks) unsalted
    butter

¾ cup sugar
2 eggs
2 cups sifted all-purpose flour

Peel and core the pineapple. Purée the pulp in a food processor until smooth.

Spread the almonds on a cookie sheet and roast in a preheated 350° F. oven for 8 to 10 minutes. Cool the nuts and then grind them in a food processor.

Butter an 8-inch springform pan.

In a bowl cream together the butter and sugar. Beat the eggs until foamy and add them to the sugar mixture. Beat in the ground almonds and 2 tablespoons of the pineapple purée. Stir in the flour and mix well. Press the dough into the prepared pan and bake in a preheated 350° F. oven for 30 minutes. Serve warm with Pineapple Sorbet.

PINEAPPLE SORBET

1 cup blanc de noir sparkling wine
¼ cup sugar
¼ cup water

1 tablespoon lemon juice
1 cup fresh pineapple purée

In a medium saucepan combine the sparkling wine, sugar, and water and simmer for 5 minutes, stirring constantly. Remove from the heat and add the lemon juice and pineapple purée. Blend well. Process in an ice-cream maker until frozen. (Alternatively, freeze the mixture in ice-cube trays. When frozen, place it in a blender and blend until fluffy. Then put the sorbet into a bowl and refreeze.)

✦ Chocolate Almond Torte ✦

Martha Culbertson, John Culbertson Winery
Accompanying champagne *Culbertson Cuvée de Frontignan*

Serves 8 to 10

The term *torte* has several meanings. In Austria and Germany it denotes a layered cake with fillings. In other countries, it means a cake made with many eggs and ground nuts or bread crumbs and usually covered with a rich glaze. This Chocolate Almond Torte fits the latter description. The ground almonds take the place of the flour and the coffee-soaked raisins add another dimension to the cake.

TORTE

¼ cup raisins
¼ cup hot coffee
10 ounces semisweet chocolate
12 tablespoons (1½ sticks) butter
4 large eggs, separated

⅔ cup sugar
⅔ cup ground almonds
4 tablespoons sifted cake flour
1 teaspoon vanilla extract
½ teaspoon almond extract

Butter and flour a 9-inch torte or springform pan.

Soak the raisins in hot coffee. Melt the chocolate and beat it together with the butter. Beat the egg yolks and the sugar together. Add the raisins and coffee to the egg mixture. Stir in the ground almonds, cake flour, and vanilla and almond extracts. Then blend in the chocolate mixture. Beat the egg whites until stiff and fold them into the batter.

Pour the batter into the prepared pan and bake in a preheated 375° F. oven for 25 minutes, or until top springs back when lightly touched. Cool, then glaze the cake.

GLAZE

6 tablespoons butter
3 tablespoons corn syrup
3 tablespoons brandy

4 ounces semisweet chocolate
Slivered almonds, for garnish

Bring the butter, corn syrup, and brandy to a boil. Remove from the heat and add the chocolate. Gently pour the glaze over the cake. Some of the glaze will run down the sides. Decorate the top of the cake with slivered almonds.

❖ Chocolate Decadence with ❖ Raspberry Sauce

Sheryl Benesch, Korbel Champagne Cellars
Accompanying champagne *Korbel Brut Rosé*

Serves 12

Chocolate and raspberries are a natural combination and make this rich chocolate dessert with a raspberry sauce a splendid finale for a meal.

CHOCOLATE CAKE

1 pound semisweet chocolate
10 tablespoons (1¼ sticks)
*   unsalted butter*
2 tablespoons brandy

4 eggs, separated
1 tablespoon granulated sugar
2 tablespoons all-purpose flour

Place a sheet of parchment or waxed paper on the bottom of an 8-inch springform pan and lightly butter and flour it.

Melt the chocolate and butter together in a saucepan. Add the brandy and let the mixture cool.

In a mixing bowl, beat the egg whites until frothy. Add the sugar and beat until firm peaks hold. In a separate mixing bowl, whip the egg yolks until lemon-colored. Add the flour slowly and beat until thickened. Fold the egg yolks into the whipped egg whites. Then fold in the chocolate mixture.

Pour the batter into the prepared pan. Place on the center rack of a preheated 425° F. oven for 15 minutes. Turn off the oven and leave the cake in the oven for an additional 5 minutes. Remove the cake from the oven and let it cool in the pan. When cake is cool, remove it from the pan, and place upside-down on a platter. Pour the Chocolate Glaze over the cake and serve it with Raspberry Sauce.

CHOCOLATE GLAZE

4 ounces semisweet chocolate
4 tablespoons unsalted butter

2 tablespoons corn syrup
2 tablespoons whipping cream

Melt the chocolate, butter, and corn syrup in a small saucepan on low heat. Blend in the cream. Pour warm glaze over the cake.

RASPBERRY SAUCE

Makes ¾ cup
1 cup fresh or frozen raspberries

¼ cup rosé champagne
3 tablespoons currant jelly

In a saucepan combine the raspberries, champagne, and currant jelly. Bring to a boil and cook for 2 to 3 minutes. Push the sauce through a sieve to extract as many seeds as possible. (Make sure that you scrape the sieved raspberry pulp from the bottom of the sieve.) Mix the sauce well and chill before serving.

❖ Pineapple Upside-Down Cake ❖

Martha Culbertson, John Culbertson Winery
Accompanying champagne *Culbertson Cuvée de Frontignan*

Serves 6

Pineapple Upside-Down Cake is an American classic. This recipe was given to Martha Culbertson by her mother. It is delicious served warm with whipped cream. Canned pineapple may be substituted for the fresh.

12 tablespoons (1½ sticks) butter	*1 egg*
¾ cup brown sugar	*1 teaspoon vanilla extract*
4 slices fresh pineapple, about ½ inch thick, halved	*1½ cups all-purpose flour*
	1½ teaspoons baking powder
¼ cup walnuts	*¼ teaspoon salt*
½ cup granulated sugar	*½ cup milk*

In either a 9-inch square pan or a 10-inch cast iron skillet, melt 4 tablespoons of butter and scatter the brown sugar over it. Arrange the pineapple and walnuts in a pattern over the sugar and butter.

Cream the remaining 8 tablespoons of butter with the ½ cup granulated sugar and beat in the egg. Add the vanilla extract. Combine the flour, baking powder, and salt and stir into the egg mixture alternately with the milk. Pour the batter carefully over the pineapple. Bake in a preheated 350° F. oven for 30 to 35 minutes, or until a toothpick inserted in the middle comes out clean.

Let the cake stand for 5 minutes and invert onto a cake plate. The syrup will run down the sides.

❖ Apple Cake ❖

Marilouise Kornell, Hanns Kornell Champagne Cellars
Accompanying champagne *Hanns Kornell Extra Dry*

Serves 10 to 12

This Apple Cake is an old family recipe that originated in Europe. The moist cake needs no frosting and keeps well for several days.

16 tablespoons (2 sticks) butter	*1 teaspoon cinnamon*
2 cups sugar	*½ teaspoon salt*
3 eggs, lightly beaten	*4 cups diced apples*
1 cup all-purpose flour	*1 cup chopped walnuts or pecans*
1 cup whole wheat flour	*1 cup raisins, lightly floured*
2 teaspoons baking soda	*Confectioners' sugar, for garnish*
1 teaspoon nutmeg	

Cream the butter and sugar until smooth. Add the beaten eggs and mix until creamy. Sift together the flours, soda, nutmeg, cinnamon, and salt, and add to the egg mixture. Fold in the apples, nuts, and raisins. Pour the batter into a well-greased 10-inch tube pan and bake in a preheated 325° F. oven for 1¼ hours. When cool remove from pan and dust with confectioners' sugar.

❖ Orange Blossom Chiffon Cake ❖

Ruth Wiens, Mirassou Vineyards
Accompanying champagne *Mirassou Blanc de Noir*

Makes 1 ten-inch cake

The delicate scent of orange blossoms lends an exotic touch to this light and fluffy old favorite. Part of the secret of a good chiffon cake is the use of oil rather than butter or shortening. The oil makes the cake rich, but light. Orange blossom water is available in gourmet shops and Middle Eastern food stores.

CAKE

2¼ cups cake flour
1 cup sugar
1 tablespoon baking powder
½ teaspoon salt
½ cup vegetable oil
*½ cup frozen orange juice
    concentrate, thawed*
¼ cup orange blossom water

6 egg yolks
3 tablespoons grated orange zest
8 egg whites
½ teaspoon cream of tartar
*Whipping cream whipped with
    sugar and an orange liqueur,
    such as Grand Marnier or
    Cointreau, for garnish*

Sift the flour, sugar, baking powder, and salt into the large bowl of a mixer. Add the oil, orange juice concentrate, orange blossom water, egg yolks, and orange zest. Beat at medium speed until very smooth. Combine the egg whites and cream of tartar in a clean large bowl. Beat at high speed until stiff peaks form. Gradually and gently, fold the batter into the egg whites with a large spatula. Pour into an ungreased 10-inch tube pan and smooth the top. Bake in a preheated 325° F. oven for 55 minutes, or until a cake tester inserted in the center comes out clean.

Remove the cake from the oven and invert the pan immediately so that it rests on the center core only, with the remaining surfaces of the pan and cake free of the counter top. Allow the cake to hang until it is completely cool. Loosen the cake by running a knife around the inside edges of the pan and the tube. Invert onto a cake plate and spoon Orange Glaze over the top, allowing it to trickle down the sides of the cake. Serve each slice topped with a dollop of sweetened whipped cream flavored with orange liqueur.

ORANGE GLAZE

1 cup sifted confectioners' sugar
4 teaspoons orange blossom water

2 teaspoons grated orange zest

Combine the sugar, orange blossom water, and orange rind in a small bowl. Mix until smooth.

❖ Gingerbread with ❖ Apricot-Sherry Glaze

Edna Tears, The Great Western Winery
Accompanying champagne *Great Western Natural*

Serves 10 to 12

Gingerbread was served in America in colonial times and recipes for it are included in many early American cookbooks. It was Martha Washington's favorite dessert. This moist gingerbread is topped with an apricot-sherry glaze.

GINGERBREAD

1/2 cup sugar	1/2 cup dark molasses
1/4 teaspoon salt	1 teaspoon baking soda
1/2 teaspoon ginger	1/4 cup boiling water
1/4 teaspoon cinnamon	1/4 cup cream sherry
1/4 teaspoon cloves	1 1/4 cups all-purpose flour
1/4 teaspoon nutmeg	1 egg, beaten
1/2 cup cooking oil	

Combine the sugar, salt, and spices in a bowl. Stir in the oil and molasses, blending well. Mix together the soda and the boiling water and stir into the sugar mixture. Then add the cream sherry and pour in the flour in a gradual stream, stirring constantly to prevent lumps. Add the beaten egg and mix well. Pour into a well-greased 8- by 8-inch pan and bake in a preheated 350° F. oven for 30 to 35 minutes.

Spoon the Apricot-Sherry Glaze over the warm cake and serve.

APRICOT-SHERRY GLAZE

1 cup apricot jam	1 teaspoon grated orange zest
1/3 cup water	2 tablespoons cream sherry
1 teaspoon sugar	1/2 cup chopped walnuts

Combine the apricot jam, water, sugar, and orange zest in a small saucepan. Bring to a boil and simmer for 5 minutes, stirring constantly. Remove from the heat and stir in the sherry and walnuts.

THE GREAT WESTERN WINERY

BY THE MID-1850S, THE EUROPEAN SETTLERS of the Finger Lakes region of New York found growing conditions so favorable for their grapes that there was an overabundant supply for home use. On March 15, 1860, Charles Davenport Champlin and twelve local businessmen in Hammondsport on the shores of Lake Keuka consolidated their vineyard holdings and drew up a business agreement for the "Manufacture of Native Wines." With a capitalization of $10,000, these businessmen built the first winery in the region, The Hammondsport and Pleasant Valley Wine Company. It was designated as "Bonded Winery #1" in the state and federal annals.

The winery was built on a slope overlooking the Pleasant Valley two miles south of Hammondsport. The land was originally owned by Mr. Champlin whose adjacent properties, after the construction of the winery, increased in value from ten dollars an acre to one hundred dollars an acre in one decade. Today the original wood and stone winery building and some other Great Western buildings are listed on the National Register of Historic Places. All of the buildings are still being used for winery operations.

Two brothers, Jules and Joseph Masson, noted French-born winemakers, were engaged by the Hammondsport and Pleasant Valley Wine Company. Both had previously worked in the champagne cellars in Cincinnati. During the first year, eighteen tons of Isabella and Catawba varieties of native American grapes were harvested and crushed. This first crush yielded 220 gallons of wine per ton. The first recorded shipment of 100 gallons of wine left the winery on August 17, 1862. Although there were labor shortages and transportation difficulties brought about by the Civil War, business thrived. There had been sufficient profit made by 1865 that the company could invest in champagne making equipment. That year twenty thousand bottles of Sparkling Catawba were made. Two years later this champagne was awarded an honorable mention at the Exposition Universelle in Paris. In 1873, the Pleasant Valley champagne won its first European medal in Vienna.

After the Civil War the Finger Lakes wine industry expanded rapidly. Gold Seal Vineyards was founded in 1865 by another group of businessmen from Hammondsport and farmers from Urbana Township. The Taylor Wine Company was founded in 1880 by Walter Taylor, a cooper who, with his bride, had come to the area to make wine barrels. Smaller wineries, owned primarily by Swiss and German immigrants, sprang up along the shores of the Finger Lakes. The region became one of the prime producers of American wines.

With the international recognition for its champagne and because of the similarities of climate and soil between the Hammondsport area and the Champagne district of France, the area became known as the "Rheims of America." When the United States Postal service opened a branch at the winery, it used the postmark, "Rheims, N. Y." This continued until rural delivery service replaced the facility in 1945.

In March 1871, Mr. Champlin sent a case of champagne to his friend Marshall P. Wilder, a well-known wine connoisseur in Boston. The *cuvée*, a new blend made by the Masson brothers, contained the native American grapes, Delaware and Catawba. Upon tasting it Wilder declared the champagne to the "great champagne of the West." By West, he meant the entire continent, the whole New World. From then on the Pleasant Valley Wine Company's champagne was named Great Western. Shipping records indicate that such prestigious restaurants as the Palmer House of Chicago and the Parker House of Boston as well as retail outlets and distinguished individuals purchased Great Western champagnes.

In 1875 Mr. Champlin and the area businessmen built a nine-mile single-track railroad from Hammondsport to the rail center at Bath in order to combat increasing prices of canal transportation. Known as the "Champagne Trail," this successful business venture not only carried wine to market, but also brought tourists to the area to ride the Keuka Lake steamers for ten cents a ride. The slogan of the railroad was "Not as long as the others, but just as wide."

In March of 1893, the Pleasant Valley Wine Company was registered as a New York corporation with the Champlin family and the Masson brothers as the majority stockholders. On July 4, 1908, the area again gained renown when Glenn Curtiss made the first pre-announced airplane flight on the Pleasant Valley flats directly below the winery entrance. Today there is a museum dedicated to his flying endeavors.

In the first six months of 1919, the Pleasant Valley Wine Company sold more champagne than it had in any previous year. This increase in business was short-lived with the enactment of Prohibition on July 1. At that time the winery had an inventory of seventy thousand cases of champagne and substantial quantities of still wine. The company managed to survive Prohibition by selling wine for sacramental purposes. The permit to sell sacramental wine did not extend to the winery's principal product, champagne. Government officials insisted that champagne was not a wine. Charles Champlin II, grandson of the winery's founder, filed a suit against the government in order to sell the champagne. Rather than fight the suit, the government granted the company special permission to sell champagne to the clergy. Two years later, other wineries made such a fuss about the monopoly that the government relented and conceded that all bubbly wine might be sold as sacramental wine. With their monopoly broken, Pleasant Valley managed to survive Prohibition by also selling grape juice to home winemakers.

After the repeal of Prohibition, the Pleasant Valley Wine Company grew steadily. Charles Champlin II, considered the dean of American champagne makers at the time, managed the company until his death in 1950. The Champlin family retained control of the winery until 1955 when it was sold to a company operated by Marne Obernauer, a businessman from New Jersey. He renamed the winery the Pleasant Valley Division of Great Western Producers. For many years the owners of the neighboring Taylor Wine Company had their sights on the Pleasant Valley Winery. When the opportunity presented itself in 1961, they purchased the controlling stock and made Great Western wines a division of Taylor.

In the early 1960s, the Taylor Wine Company went public, but the family retained the controlling stock until the death of the last of the three Taylor brothers in 1976. In the following year, the Taylor Wine Company, with its Great Western Division, was purchased by the Coca-Cola Company. In 1983, Coca-Cola sold its wine interests to the Seagram Wine Company who, after two years, sold its interests to an American group of investors, Vintners International Company, Inc.

While it was part of the Taylor Wine Company, Great Western added varietals to its production of generic still wines. The first varietal wines were made from Delaware, Diamond, and Isabella — all American grapes. In 1964, Great Western introduced the first Finger Lakes varietal wines made from new French-American hybrid grapes. Some of these hybrid varietal table wines are still made today, along with the European *vinifera* varietals.

Due to rising production costs, Great Western discontinued making champagne by the *méthode champenoise* in 1954 and switched to the transfer method. In the early 1980s, the management decided once again to make the premium *méthode champenoise* champagne for which the winery had been famous. The first release was made in 1985 with a Natural champagne. The following year Blanc de Blanc was added and, in the fall of 1988, a Blanc de Noir will be released. No *dosage* is added to the Natural or Blanc de Blanc, creating an off-dry champagne, with the Natural being the driest. Some French-American hybrid grapes are used in the Natural *cuvée*.

This time, however, time-and money-saving devices were added to the *méthode champenoise* production. Some of the grapes are harvested mechanically. A gentle whole-berry pressing is used to obtain a more delicately flavored champagne. Only the free run is taken from the first pressing for the champagne *cuvée*. The remainder of the pressing goes into the still wines. The Blanc de Blanc grapes are picked by hand into small lug boxes. After a ten-to fourteen-day fermentation, the bottles of champagne are aged from eighteen months to three years. Riddling is done in huge, specially designed square wooden boxes. Each box holds 352 cases of champagne and is computer-controlled.

The Great Western Winery is the oldest winery in the historic New York Finger Lakes area and produces a variety of table wines, fortified wines, and champagnes. By again producing *méthode champenoise* champagne it has returned to its heritage.

Great Western Winery produces the following champagnes, all in an off-dry style:

Natural — a blend of 30 percent Aurora, 30 percent Seyval Blanc, and 40 percent Chardonnay

Blanc de Blanc — 100 percent Chardonnay

Blanc de Noir — primarily Pinot Noir with some Chardonnay; to be released in the fall of 1988

Culinary director: Edna Tears

Edna Tears is a native of the Hammondsport, New York, area. She has been interested in cooking since she was a teenager. For fifteen years she worked in the area's restaurants in various capacities from chef to manager.

In the late 1970s, Edna joined the staff of Great Western. She is in charge of all winery food functions, preparing menus for special luncheons and dinners. All of her menus are planned to complement the Great Western wines and she relies heavily on the availability of local food products. Edna was also instrumental in the compilation of the winery cookbook, published by Taylor, entitled *Favorite Recipes*.

Great Western Winery
Hammondsport, New York 14840
(607) 569-2111

Visits: April through October, daily, 10:00 A.M. to 5:00 P.M.
Principals: Vintners International Company, Inc.
Varietal wines produced: Aurora, Seyval Blanc, Dutchess, Vidal Blanc, Rosé of Isabella, Baco Noir, Chardonnay, Johannisberg Riesling, and Cabernet Sauvignon
Champagnes produced: Natural, Blanc de Blanc, and Blanc de Noir (fall, 1988)
1988 champagne production: 20,000 cases

BRUNCHES

LTHOUGH AN AMERICAN-SOUNDING WORD USED TO DESCRIBE an American style of meal, the word brunch actually first appeared in London in 1896. An article in Punch magazine is reported to have stated, "To be fashionable nowadays, we must 'brunch', [a term] introduced last year by Mr. Guy Beringer, in the now defunct *Hunter's Weekly*, and indicating a combined breakfast and lunch." The term did not appear in this country until 1941 when a New York hotel advertised a "Sunday strollers' brunch, $1 per person, served from 11:00 A.M. to 3:00 P.M." It has since become a popular form of home entertaining on Sundays and holidays. Many restaurants also feature champagne brunches.

A meal that is neither breakfast nor lunch, brunch is an informal meal, eaten in leisure, and frequently accompanied by champagne. The food, too, is casual, more elaborate than food served at breakfast, but lighter than luncheon food. Many dishes may be prepared ahead or at the last minute while guests watch and join the conversation in the kitchen.

Brunch dishes usually feature eggs or egg-related dishes, although these are more elegant than plain bacon and eggs. They are transformed into quiches and soufflés. Vegetables, salads, and soups are typically not included, but appetizers of melon, berries, or grapefruit halves, and light desserts frequently are. Depending on the entre, a wide variety of breads may be served, including popovers, croissants, English muffins, and homemade bread.

In this section there are recipes for entreés and desserts suitable for brunch. The entreés vary from those made with eggs, to those of ham, cheese, or chicken. All may be accompanied by champagne and most have suggestions for appropriate champagnes.

❖ Souffléd Eggs ❖

Tracy Wood Anderson, S. Anderson Vineyard
Accompanying champagne S. Anderson Brut

Serves 4

Eggs have been called the basis of all cookery; cheese has been referred to as milk that has been immortalized. In many dishes the two go hand-in-hand. In this dish, the eggs are first poached and then baked in a very light cheese soufflé mixture.

8 poached eggs

SOUFFLÉ

3 tablespoons butter	*3 ounces Swiss cheese, grated*
¹/₃ cup all-purpose flour	*2 ounces Parmesan cheese, grated*
2 cups boiling milk	*5 egg whites, at room temperature*
3 egg yolks	*Salt and white pepper, to taste*

Melt the butter in a medium saucepan over medium heat. Add the flour and stir a few minutes, making a roux. Add the hot milk, stirring vigorously. Reduce the heat to low and let the mixture simmer for 10 minutes, then remove it from the heat.

In a small bowl lightly beat the egg yolks, then add a little of the hot milk mixture to temper, then add the yolks to the pan with the milk mixture. Mix well. Stir in the cheeses, a little at a time, until they are melted. Transfer the mixture to a bowl and let it cool to room temperature.

Add a pinch of salt to the egg whites and beat them until medium-stiff peaks form. Fold the egg whites, one-third at a time, into the cheese mixture.

Spread a quarter of the soufflé mixture on the bottom of a 9- by 13-inch flat casserole dish. Bake for 10 minutes in a preheated 400° F. oven. Remove from the oven and lay the poached eggs on top in a pattern that will make serving easy. Spread the remaining soufflé mixture over the eggs and return the casserole to the oven. Bake until puffed and golden brown, about 15 to 20 minutes. Serve immediately.

❖ Sparkling Eggs Benedict ❖

Karen Mack, Chateau Ste. Michelle
Accompanying champagne *Domaine Ste. Michelle Blanc de Noir*

Serves 4

There are conflicting stories about the origin of Eggs Benedict. One is that Mr. and Mrs. Benedict, frequent customers at Delmonico's Restaurant in New York, tired of the lack of variety in the restaurant's menu and came up with the idea of toast, ham, poached egg, and hollandaise sauce. Another story is that a Mr. Benedict, a New York stockbroker, always ordered this same egg dish, which he claimed to have invented, as a cure for a hangover. Oscar of the Waldorf-Astoria Hotel admired this breakfast concoction, but made his own variations — English muffin instead of toast, ham instead of bacon. Karen Mack has enhanced the recipe with a sparkling wine.

2 English muffins
4 slices ham
1 tablespoon butter
½ cup blanc de noir sparkling wine

4 eggs
Hollandaise Sauce (recipe follows)
Fresh parsley, for garnish

Split the English muffins, toast, and butter them. Keep them warm in the oven. Sauté the ham slices (add butter if necessary) and place on the muffin halves. Melt the butter in a small skillet, add the sparkling wine, and bring to a gentle boil. Drop the eggs in carefully and cover the pan, poaching the eggs until the whites glaze over.

Place the poached eggs on top of the ham slices, spoon Hollandaise Sauce on top. Garnish with sprigs of fresh parsley.

HOLLANDAISE SAUCE

3 egg yolks
2 tablespoons blanc de noir
*   sparkling wine*

1 tablespoon lemon juice
16 tablespoons (2 sticks) butter,
*   cut into slices*

Place the egg yolks, sparkling wine, and lemon juice in a small saucepan over low heat. Whisk briskly until egg yolks start to thicken. Add the butter, one slice at a time, stirring constantly. Continue adding the remainder of the butter slowly and stirring until the sauce has thickened. Remove from heat and set the pan in a bowl of warm water to keep the sauce warm until assembling the dish.

❖ Eggs in Cheese Sauce ❖

Martha Culbertson, John Culbertson Winery
Accompanying champagne *Culbertson Blanc de Noir*

Serves 6 to 8

This dish of stuffed hard-boiled eggs in a light cheese sauce may be prepared the night before, brought to room temperature, and then broiled.

6 hard-boiled eggs	¼ cup whipping cream
¼ cup minced parsley	¼ teaspoon salt
2 cloves garlic, minced	¼ teaspoon freshly ground pepper

Cut the eggs in half and place the yolks in a bowl. Mash the yolks until smooth. Mix in the parsley, garlic, cream, salt, and pepper. Fill each half egg white with the yolk mixture.

SAUCE

5 tablespoons unsalted butter	1 cup milk
2 tablespoons chopped onion	1 cup whipping cream
3 tablespoons water	2 ounces Swiss cheese, grated
6 tablespoons all-purpose flour	Salt and pepper, to taste
1 cup chicken broth	

Melt the butter in a saucepan, add the onion and water, and cook over moderate heat for about 2 minutes, or until the water has evaporated. Stir in the flour and cook over low heat, whipping constantly with a wire whisk for 3 minutes. Add the chicken broth and bring to a boil, whipping constantly; add the milk and bring to a boil again. Reduce the heat and simmer for 5 minutes. Stir in the cream and bring to a boil again, and cook until smooth. Season to taste with salt and pepper.

Place the egg halves in a buttered baking dish, yolk side up, and pour the sauce over the eggs. Sprinkle with the cheese and put the dish under a preheated broiler for 8 to 10 minutes, until nicely browned. Watch carefully so that it does not burn.

❖ Eggs Schramsberg ❖

Jamie Davies, Schramsberg Vineyards and Cellars
Accompanying champagne *Schramsberg Cuveé de Pinot*

Serves 4 to 6

Scrambled eggs is a favorite breakfast dish that has many variations. In this recipe a round loaf of French bread forms the crust for a tasty scrambled egg, sausage, and spinach combination.

*2 packages (10 ounces each) frozen
  spinach
1 cup sour cream
1 round loaf French bread
2 tablespoons butter*

*4 Italian fennel sausages
6 green onions, chopped
1 small red pepper, chopped
10 to 12 eggs
¼ cup water*

Preheat oven to 300° F.

Thaw the spinach and cook it in a small quantity of water for about 2 minutes. Drain the spinach well and squeeze out as much water as possible. Mix it with the sour cream and set aside in a small saucepan over low heat.

Cut the top off the bread and pull out the inside dough, making a 2-inch-deep shell. Spread the inside with 1 tablespoon of the butter. Replace the top and place in the oven to crisp and warm.

In a large skillet brown the sausages, cut them in diagonal pieces, and keep them warm.

Remove any fat from the skillet. Melt the remaining 1 tablespoon of butter in the skillet and sauté the onions and peppers for about 1 minute. Beat the eggs with a fork to break them up and add the water. Add the eggs to the skillet, then slowly and gently scramble them. Add the sausage pieces and continue cooking until the eggs are softly set.

Spoon half of the egg mixture into the bread and cover with the spinach. Top with the remaining eggs and put the top on the bread. Cut in wedges and serve.

❖ Delicate Pancakes with ❖ Blueberry Sauce

Sheryl Benesch, Korbel Champagne Cellars
Accompanying champagne *Korbel Brut Rose*

Serves 3 to 4

In a different approach to a traditional brunch entreé, very thin pancakes are rolled like crêpes and served with a fresh blueberry sauce.

PANCAKES

1 cup all-purpose flour
¼ teaspoon salt
1 teaspoon baking powder
1 teaspoon cornstarch
2 eggs, slightly beaten

1½ cups milk
1 teaspoon vanilla extract
Butter, for cooking
Blueberry Sauce (recipe follows)

In a bowl mix together the flour, salt, baking powder, and cornstarch. Add the eggs, milk, and vanilla extract, blending all ingredients well. Do not overmix. Refrigerate the batter while preparing the Blueberry Sauce.

To cook the pancakes, heat an 8-inch nonstick sauté pan on medium heat. Melt approximately 1 tablespoon of butter and add about ⅛ cup of batter. Brown each side of the pancake, roll up, and place on a warm platter. Continue cooking pancakes until all of the batter has been used. Serve with Blueberry Sauce.

BLUEBERRY SAUCE

½ cup rosé champagne
1 orange, zested and juiced
1 cinnamon stick

1 teaspoon cornstarch mixed with
  1 teaspoon water
2 cups fresh or frozen blueberries

Bring the champagne, orange zest and juice, and cinnamon stick to a boil. Turn heat to medium and cook for 1 minute. Add the cornstarch mixture and bring to a boil. When the mixture has thickened, add the blueberries and toss for 1 minute (longer if blueberries are frozen) until the berries are heated through. Serve over the pancakes.

❖ Strawberry Crêpes ❖

Karen Mack, Chateau Ste. Michelle
Accompanying champagne *Domaine Ste. Michelle Blanc de Noir*

Serves 4 to 6

Thomas Jefferson, after his stay in France, was probably the first to introduce crêpes to the New World. In this recipe thin crêpes are filled with fresh strawberries that have been very lightly tossed in a cream sauce.

CRÊPES
(Makes 12 to 15 crêpes)

1¼ cups cold blanc de noir
    sparkling wine
1¼ cups sifted all-purpose flour
4 eggs

1 cup milk
3 tablespoons melted unsalted
    butter
¼ teaspoon salt

Combine all of the ingredients in a mixing bowl and beat with an electric beater on medium-high for 60 seconds, stirring the sides of the bowl often. Cover and refrigerate the batter for 1 hour.

To make the crêpes, pour ⅓ cup of batter onto a hot buttered crpe pan or griddle. Cook over medium-high heat until the surface is bubbly, flip, and cook the other side (approximately 30 seconds). Remove from heat, stack and keep warm until ready to use.

STRAWBERRY FILLING

½ cup light brown sugar
½ cup whipping cream
½ cup blanc de noir sparkling wine

2 quarts fresh strawberries,
    washed, hulled, and well drained
Whipped cream or confectioners'
    sugar, for garnish

Melt the brown sugar in a medium saucepan over low heat. Gradually stir in the cream and the sparkling wine, stirring until well blended. Bring to a simmer and continue simmering until the mixture thickens and reduces by a third. Remove from heat and stir in the strawberries.

To assemble, place a large spoonful of the filling in the middle of each crêpe. Roll and garnish with whipped cream or confectioners' sugar. Serve warm.

❖ Poppy Seed Cheese Blintzes ❖

Sheryl Benesch, Korbel Champagne Cellars
Accompanying champagne *Korbel Blanc de Blancs*

Serves 4

Blintzes are the Jewish version of the French crêpes, although their origin is attributed to Russian cookery. These Poppy Seed Blintzes with a light cheese filling may be prepared several days ahead of serving and stored in the refrigerator. They may served with the Rosé Currant Sauce or simply with sour cream and jam.

FILLING

½ pound ricotta cheese
1 cup dry cottage cheese
1 egg yolk
2 tablespoons sugar

¼ teaspoon vanilla extract
⅛ teaspoon cinnamon
Dash of nutmeg

Combine all of the ingredients and place in the refrigerator while making the blintzes.

BLINTZES

(Makes 16 blintzes)

1 cup all-purpose flour
¼ teaspoon salt
Dash of nutmeg
1 tablespoon poppy seeds

2 eggs, lightly beaten
1 cup milk
2 tablespoons butter, melted

Mix the flour, salt, nutmeg, and poppy seeds in a bowl. Make a well in the center of the dry ingredients and add the eggs, milk, and melted butter. Mix all of the ingredients together. Some lumps may remain.

Heat a 7-inch nonstick sauté pan on medium-high heat. The pan is ready when a few drops of water flicked on its surface sizzle. Ladle ⅛ cup of batter into the pan; tilt the pan to spread the batter evenly. Cook until the blintz is golden brown on one side (it is not necessary to cook both sides). Place cooked-side down on a plate or towel.

To assemble, place approximately 2 tablespoons of filling on the center of the browned side of each blintz. (The filling may easily be piped through a pastry bag.) Fold up two sides first, then roll from end to end. At this point the blintzes may be cooked or stored, tightly covered, in the refrigerator for several days.

To cook, fry the blintzes on medium-high heat in a little butter until brown on both sides. Serve with Rosé Currant Sauce (recipe follows).

ROSÉ CURRANT SAUCE

¾ cup rosé champagne
1 stick cinnamon
1 slice lemon zest
2 tablespoons sugar

½ cup currants
1 teaspoon cornstarch
2 teaspoons water
1 tablespoon chilled butter

Bring the champagne, cinnamon stick, lemon zest, and sugar to a boil. Cook for 2 minutes; remove the cinnamon stick and lemon zest. Add the currants, and cook on low heat for 5 minutes. Mix the cornstarch with water, add to the sauce, and bring to a boil. Remove the sauce from the heat and whisk in the butter. Serve with Poppy Seed Cheese Blintzes.

❖ Blue and White Enchiladas ❖

Tracy Wood Anderson, S. Anderson Vineyard
Accompanying champagne *S. Anderson Blanc de Noirs*

Serves 6

Enchiladas are the Mexican version of a filled pancake. In this recipe the pancakes are prepared with blue cornmeal, filled with chicken and cream cheese, and are served with a white cumin-flavored sauce. They may be assembled the day before serving and stored in the refrigerator. At serving time, make the sauce, pour it over the enchiladas, and bake. Blue cornmeal is available in Mexican markets and specialty stores. If unavailable, yellow cornmeal may be used.

BLUE CORN PANCAKES
(Makes 12 pancakes)

1 cup blue cornmeal
¼ teaspoon salt
3 eggs

1 cup milk
1 tablespoon oil
1 tablespoon butter, for cooking

In a medium bowl, combine the cornmeal, salt, and eggs, whisking until smooth. Add the milk, a little at a time, to make a thin batter. Then add the oil. Strain the mixture and let it stand for 30 minutes.

Heat a small, well-seasoned or nonstick frying pan over moderately high heat. Melt the butter in the pan. Using about 3 tablespoons of the batter for each pancake, coat the bottom of the pan quickly and cook about 1 minute per side. Cool the pancakes, then keep them covered.

FILLING

1½ pounds boneless chicken breast
1 quart chicken broth or water
   seasoned with salt, peppercorns,
   and garlic

1 pound cream cheese
2½ cups grated Monterey Jack
   cheese

Poach the chicken in the simmering broth or water for 15 to 20 minutes or until done. Remove the chicken and cool. When the chicken is cool enough to handle, shred it.

Cut the cream cheese into 12 long pieces. Reserve ³/₄ cup of the Monterey Jack cheese to top the enchiladas.

SAUCE

2 tablespoons butter
2 tablespoons all-purpose flour
1 tablespoon ground cumin
2½ cups milk, warmed

¼ teaspoon salt
Juice of half a lemon
1 large clove garlic, minced

In a medium saucepan over medium heat, melt the butter. Add the flour and cumin, stirring to blend. Cook for a few minutes. Add the warm milk, whisking quickly. Reduce the heat to low, then add the salt, lemon juice, and garlic. Let the mixture simmer on the lowest heat possible for 10 minutes, stirring occasionally so that the sauce does not scorch. Add more milk if the sauce becomes too thick.

To assemble the enchiladas, moisten the chicken with a little sauce, then divide among the 12 pancakes. Add a piece of cream cheese and some Monterey Jack cheese to each one and roll it up. Place the enchiladas, seam-side down, in a buttered 13- by 9-inch ovenproof dish. Pour the sauce over the casserole and sprinkle the reserved ³/₄ cup grated cheese on top. Bake in a preheated 325° F. oven for 20 to 30 minutes, or until heated through.

❖ Pithiviers with Ham and Chard ❖

Ruth Wiens, Mirassou Vineyards
Accompanying champagne *Mirassou Brut*

Serves 6

Pithiviers, a dessert tart of puff pastry normally filled with almond cream, is a specialty of the town of Pithiviers, forty miles south of Paris. Filled with ham, chard, and cheese, this version makes a delectable brunch entreé that may be made ahead and served warm or cold.

1 bunch red or green Swiss chard,
cleaned and de-ribbed
½ pound cooked ham, diced (about
1½ cups)
4 ounces tangy goat cheese,
crumbled

3 whole green onions, finely sliced
¼ teaspoon freshly ground pepper
3 large eggs
1¼ pounds puff pastry, or 1
package (17¼ ounces) frozen
puff pastry sheets

Steam chard until tender. Cool and squeeze dry. There should be about 1 cup. Chop the chard finely and combine it with the ham, cheese, onions, pepper, and 2 beaten eggs. Mix well.

Roll puff pastry ¼-inch thick. (Pre-rolled sheets can be used as they are.) Cut out 2 pastry circles, each 9 inches in diameter. Place 1 on a cookie sheet and spread the chard filling evenly in the center, leaving an inch uncovered all around the edge. Beat the remaining egg and brush the uncovered part of the pastry circle with some of the egg wash. Top with the second pastry circle and seal it all the way around. Using the blunt-sided tip of a knife, pull the pastry edge in about ½ an inch at 1-inch intervals to create a scalloped edge all around. Brush the tart with beaten egg. Cut a ½-inch-round vent hole in the center and, using the point of a knife, make a pattern of spiral lines from the edges toward the center, cutting into the dough about 1¹/₁₆ of an inch.

Refrigerate the tart for at least 2 hours. Bake in a preheated 375° F. oven for about 30 minutes, or until puffed and golden brown.

❖ Quiche ❖

Edna Tears, The Great Western Winery
Accompanying champagne *Great Western Blanc de Blanc*

Serves 6 to 8

Quiche is a baked custard tart that originated in Lorraine, an eastern province of France, although the neighboring province of Alsace also claims its origin. The word comes from the French-German dialect spoken in these provinces and can be traced to the German word *kuchen* meaning cake. Never a dessert tart, quiche today is still a custard-cheese tart with various flavorings and can include bacon, ham, or vegetables. This Quiche is similar to the traditional Quiche Lorraine.

1 pie crust (10-inch), unbaked
10 slices crisp fried bacon,
    crumbled
2 cups grated Swiss cheese
3 eggs
1¼ cups whipping cream

¼ cup delicate dry white wine
¼ teaspoon salt
¼ teaspoon white pepper
Dash of cayenne
½ teaspoon dry mustard

Sprinkle the bacon and grated cheese into the unbaked pie shell. Beat together the eggs, cream, wine, and seasonings. Pour the mixture over the cheese. Bake in a preheated 375° F. oven for 45 minutes or until firm and brown. Remove from the oven, cut into wedges, and serve warm.

❖ Chicken Sauté in Puff Pastry ❖

Steve Wenger, Biltmore Estate
Accompanying champagne *Biltmore Estate Brut*

Serves 6

This delicate chicken sauté is very simple to prepare when frozen puff pastry shells are used. At the Biltmore Winery's grand opening ball, this was one of the dishes served for the midnight breakfast.

1½ pounds boned chicken breast,
    cut into 1-inch pieces
4 tablespoons butter
½ pound mushrooms, sliced
1 medium leek, sliced
¾ cup whipping cream

¾ cup half-and-half
2 teaspoons fresh snipped parsley
Salt and freshly ground pepper, to
    taste
6 puff pastry shells, baked

In a large skillet, sauté the chicken pieces in 3 tablespoons of the butter over medium heat for about 5 minutes or until just cooked. Remove the chicken to a warm plate. Add the remaining tablespoon of butter to the skillet and gently sauté the mushrooms and leeks for about 5 minutes. Do not let them brown. Add the cream, half-and-half, and parsley and cook until the sauce coats the back of a spoon. Return the chicken pieces to the sauce to heat. Add salt and pepper to taste. Divide the chicken mixture among the 6 baked puff pastry shells and serve.

❖ Oysters at Brunch ❖

Jamie Davies, Schramsberg Vineyards and Cellars
Accompanying champagne *Schramsberg Blanc de Blancs*

Serves 4

This unusual brunch dish features a baked potato shell filled with eggs delicately scrambled with oysters and topped with bacon and chives.

2 large baking potatoes
1 cup White Sauce (recipe follows)
3 tablespoons butter
½ cup dry white wine
3 shallots, minced
12 small oysters

6 eggs
1 tablespoon water
Chopped chives
3 slices bacon, cooked and
  crumbled

Bake the potatoes. While the potatoes are baking, make the White Sauce.

After the potatoes are baked, cut them in half lengthwise. Scoop out about 2 tablespoons potato from each half and reserve for another use. Loosen remaining potato with a fork. Keep the potatoes warm.

In a medium skillet, melt 1 tablespoon of the butter and sauté the shallots for 2 minutes. Add the wine and bring to a simmer. Add the oysters and poach them until the edges begin to curl. Remove the oysters from the pan and keep them warm.

Break the eggs into a bowl. Add the water and beat lightly with a fork. Melt the remaining 2 tablespoons of butter in a large skillet. Scramble the eggs over medium heat until soft curds form. Gently mix in 1 cup of the White Sauce and the oysters. Divide the egg mixture and place into the warm potato halves. Sprinkle with chopped chives and bacon. Serve immediately.

WHITE SAUCE

2 tablespoons butter
2 tablespoons all-purpose flour

1½ cups milk
2 teaspoons prepared mustard

Melt the butter in a small saucepan. Add the flour and cook, stirring, about 2 minutes. Gradually add the milk and mustard, stirring constantly until the sauce thickens and comes to a boil. Remove from the heat and cover the surface of the sauce with plastic wrap to prevent a skin from forming on the top.

❖ Tomates Farcies ❖

Steve Wenger, Biltmore Estate
Accompanying champagne Biltmore Estate Brut

Serves 6

A delightful spring or summer brunch on its own, these stuffed tomatoes may also accompany a light omelet for a heartier meal. The tomatoes are stuffed with smoked trout, baked, and topped with sour cream.

6 ripe medium-sized tomatoes, skinned	*8 ounces sour cream*
2 to 3 tablespoons olive oil	*3 ounces black caviar*
2 cups flaked smoked trout	*6 lemon wedges, for garnish*

Preheat the oven to 350° F. Slice the tops off the tomatoes; scoop out and discard the pulp. Sprinkle a little olive oil into each tomato. Place 1/3 cup of smoked trout into each tomato. Bake for 10 minutes and then cool slightly.

To serve, place 2 tablespoons sour cream on each tomato. Sprinkle with a tablespoon of caviar, and garnish with a lemon wedge.

❖ Popovers ❖

Martha Estes, Wente Bros. Sparkling Wine Cellars

Makes 16 popovers

A popover is a hollow, light, muffin-type of quick bread made from a rich egg batter. Popovers must be baked in a hot oven in order to activate the egg protein which allows the batter to expand and produce a light, crunchy puff. These popovers are served with an Herb Butter.

POPOVERS

2 cups all-purpose flour	*2 tablespoons butter, melted and cooled*
1/2 teaspoon salt	
2 cups milk	*4 eggs*

Preheat the oven to 450° F. Generously oil popover pans, cups or tins and preheat them for a few minutes. Beat all of the ingredients together until just smooth, being careful not to over-beat. The batter should be the consistency of heavy cream. Fill prepared pans one-half to two-thirds full.

Bake the popovers in the preheated oven for 15 minutes. Then, without opening the oven door, lower the temperature to 350° F. and bake another 15 minutes until the popovers are firm and golden brown. Remove them from the oven and make slits in the bottom to release the steam. Serve hot with Herb Butter (recipe follows).

HERB BUTTER

16 tablespoons (1 stick) butter, at room temperature	*1/4 cup chopped chives*
	1/8 cup chopped basil
1/4 cup chopped parsley	

Cream the butter and blend in the parsley, chives, and basil. Press the butter into a serving dish or a mold. Cover and refrigerate. Serve with hot Popovers.

❖ Bread Pudding Soufflé with ❖ Sabayon Sauce

Martha Culbertson, John Culbertson Winery
Accompanying champagne *Culbertson Cuve de Frontignan*

Serves 8

This soufflé can be made ahead up to the addition of the egg whites. Whip the egg whites just before baking and gently fold them in. The bread pudding can also be made ahead and served as a dessert, with the leftovers being used in this Bread Pudding Soufflé. The soufflé can be served either as the entreé or the dessert at brunch.

SOUFFLÉ

6 egg yolks
1/2 cup granulated sugar
2 1/2 cups Bread Pudding (recipe follows)

6 egg whites
1/2 cup confectioners' sugar

Mix the egg yolks and granulated sugar and whip over simmering water until frothy and shiny. Mix the egg yolks with the Bread Pudding.

Beat the egg whites, adding the confectioners' sugar gradually until the whites stand in stiff peaks. Fold the egg whites into the Bread Pudding mixture.

Butter and sugar a 1 1/2-quart soufflé dish. Fill the dish with the soufflé and bake in a preheated 375° F. oven for 35 to 40 minutes. Bring the soufflé dish to the table and serve the Sabayon Sauce (recipe follows) on the side.

BREAD PUDDING

1 cup sugar
8 tablespoons (1 stick) butter, at room temperature
5 eggs, beaten
2 cups whipping cream

1/4 teaspoon cinnamon
1 tablespoon vanilla extract
1/4 cup raisins
12 slices (each 1-inch-thick) white bread

Cream together the sugar and butter. Add the eggs, cream, cinnamon, vanilla and raisins. Mix well.

Arrange the bread slices in a 9-inch square baking dish and pour the egg mixture over them. If necessary, turn the bread slices so that they are thoroughly covered with the egg mixture.

Set the baking dish in another pan containing water (a *bain-marie*) and cover with foil. Bake in a preheated 350° F. oven for 45 minutes, uncovering the pudding for the last 10 minutes to brown.

SABAYON SAUCE

1/2 cup sugar
6 egg yolks

1 cup Culbertson Cuveé de Frontignan champagne

Place all of the ingredients in a the top of a double boiler (do not use aluminum). Cook over simmering water, whipping with a whisk constantly, for 8 to 10 minutes. The sauce should never get too hot to allow you to put your finger in it. Whip to the consistency of a light custard and serve.

❖ Fresh Fruit Medley with ❖ Champagne Custard Sauce

Ruth Wiens, Mirassou Vineyards
Accompanying champagne *Mirassou Brut*

Serves 6 to 8

A wonderfully easy sauce tops fresh fruit for a light brunch dessert. The sauce may be made ahead and served warm or at room temperature.

6 to 8 cups assorted fresh fruit, cut up. For best flavor and color choose a wide variety from the following: seedless grapes, nectarines, papaya, kiwi fruit,

pears, oranges, pineapple, melon, strawberries, and raspberries
½ cup brut champagne

Combine the fruit in a large bowl, add the champagne, and toss gently. Cover tightly and refrigerate until ready to serve. Spoon the fruit salad into glass dessert bowls or large wine glasses and top with Champagne Custard Sauce.

CHAMPAGNE CUSTARD SAUCE

Makes 3 cups
1 package (3⅛ ounces) vanilla pudding and pie filling (not instant)

1 cup whipping cream
½ cup milk
1 cup chilled brut champagne

Combine the pudding mix with the cream and milk. Cook and stir over medium heat until mixture thickens. Whisk in the champagne and continue cooking until sauce comes to a boil. Remove from heat. Serve warm or at room temperature over the fruit.

❖ Strawberry Dip ❖

Edna Tears, The Great Western Winery
Accompanying champagne *Great Western Blanc de Blanc*

Serves 4 to 6

Strawberries with a dip of ginger, cream cheese, and orange juice make this a different version of a fruit and cheese dessert.

*1 package (8 ounces) cream cheese,
   softened*
2 tablespoons sugar
½ teaspoon ground ginger
⅓ cup fresh orange juice

3 tablespoons dry white wine
1 teaspoon fresh chopped parsley
*1 quart ripe fresh strawberries
   with stems, washed and drained*

In a bowl combine the cream cheese, sugar, ginger, orange juice, wine, and parsley. Blend until very creamy.

Set the bowl of dip in the middle of a round platter and surround it with the long-stemmed strawberries.

BIBLIOGRAPHY

Numerous books and articles were consulted in writing this book.
The following ones were especially helpful.

Food

Ackart, Robert. *Soufflés, Mousses, Jellies and Creams.* New York: Atheneum, 1980.

Bailey, Adrian. *Cook's Ingredients.* Edited by Elizabeth L. Ortiz. New York: William Morrow, 1980.

Beard, James. *American Cookery.* Boston: Little, Brown, 1972.

Beard, James. *James Beard's Theory and Practice of Good Cooking.* New York: Knopf, 1977.

Boxer, Arabella, Jocasta Innes, Charlotte Parry-Crooke, and Lewis Esson. *The Encyclopedia of Herbs, Spices and Flavorings.* New York: Crescent Books, 1984.

Carcione, Joe. *The Greengrocer Cookbook.* Millbrae, California: Celestial Arts, 1975.

Famularo, Joe, and Louise Imperiale. *The Joy of Pasta.* Woodbury, N. Y.: Barrons, 1983.

Hazan, Marcella. *The Classic Italian Cookbook.* New York: Knopf, 1983.

Jones, Evan. *American Food.* New York: Vintage Books, 1981.

Jones, Judith, and Evan Jones. *The Book of Bread.* New York: Harper & Row, 1982.

Langseth-Christensen, Lillian, and Carol Sturm Smith. *The Complete Kitchen Guide.* New York: Grosset and Dunlap, 1968.

Marquis, Vivienne, and Patricia Haskell. *The Cheese Book.* rev. ed. New York: Simon and Schuster, 1985.

Merinoff, Linda. *The Glorious Noodle: A Culinary Tour Around the World.* New York: Poseidon Press, 1986.

Montagné Prosper. *Larousse Gastronomique.* Edited by Charlotte Turgeon and Nina Froud. New York: Crown, 1965.

Morris, Joanna, ed. *The Encyclopedia of Cooking.* New York: Exeter Books, 1985.

Pappas, Lou S., and Jane Horn. *The New Harvest.* San Francisco: 101 Productions, 1986.

Radecka, Helena. *The Fruit and Nut Book.* New York: McGraw-Hill, 1984.

Root, Waverley. *Food: An Authorative and Visual History and Dictionary of the Foods of the World.* New York: Simon and Schuster, 1980.

Schneider, Elizabeth. *Uncommon Fruits and Vegetables: A Commonsense Guide.* New York: Harper & Row, 1986.

Tighe, Eileen, ed. *Woman's Day Encyclopedia of Cookery.* 12 vols. New York: Fawcet Publications, 1966.

Whitman, Joan, comp. *Craig Claiborne's "The New York Times" Food Encyclopedia.* New York: Times Books, 1985.

Wine and Champagne

Adams, Leon D. *The Wines of America.* 3d. ed. New York: McGraw-Hill, 1985.

Amerine, Maynard A., ed. *Wine Production Technology in the United States.* Washington, D. C.: American Chemical Society, 1981.

Balzer, Robert Lawrence. *The "Los Angeles Times" Book of California Wines.* New York: Abrams, 1984.

De Groot, Roy Andries. *The Wines of California, The Pacific Northwest and New York.* New York: Summit Books, 1982.

Domaine Chandon. "A User's Guide to Sparkling Wine." Yountville, Ca: Domaine Chandon, 1985.

Forbes, Patrick. *Champagne, The Wine, The Land, and The People*. London: Reynal; New York: William Morrow, 1967.

Johnson, Hugh. *The World Atlas of Wine*. 3d ed. New York: Simon and Schuster, 1985.

Lichine, Alexis, in collaboration with Samuel Perkins. *Alexis Lichine's Guide to the Wines and Vineyards of France*. 3d ed., rev. New York: Knopf, 1986.

Muscatine, Doris, Maynard A. Amerine, and Bob Thompson, eds. *The Book of California Wine*. Berkeley and Los Angeles, Calif.: University of California Press; London: Sotheby Publications, 1984.

Simon, André L. *The History of Champagne*. London: Octopus Books, 1971.

Stevenson, Tom. *Champagne*. London: Philip Wilson for Sotheby Publications, 1986.

Teiser, Ruth, and Catherine Harroun. *Winemaking in California*. New York: McGraw-Hill, 1983.

Wasserman, Sheldon, and Pauline Wasserman. *Sparkling Wine*. Piscataway, N.J.: New Century, 1984.

INDEX

A

Almond(s)
  cookie shells (cups), 285, 286
  green beans with, 213
  torte, 297, 298
Anderson, Tracy Wood, 247
Apple(s)
  cake, 300
  and goat cheese, in phyllo, 53
  meringue, 274
  and pecan stuffing, 183
  poached, 274
  salad, 263, 264
  sautéed, with red cabbage, 215
  soup, with onion, 106
  tart, with sour cherries, 295
Apricot, glaze, with sherrry, 302
Artichoke, hearts, canned, with
  seafood, 49
Asparagus
  in chicken terrine, 73
  with lemon dill sauce, 212
  with linguine, 141
  sauté, 212
Aspic, 70
Avocado
  with creamed chicken, 171
  salad, with smoked oysters, 78

B

Bananas, flambé, 271
Basil
  in pesto, 67
  sorbet, 131
  in soup, 111, 115
Beans
  black
    chili, 140
    sauce, with ginger, 153
    with tomatoes and chiles, 213
  Chinese long green, 261
  green
    with almonds, 213
    salad, 252
    timbale of, 214
Beef
  rib eye, in pastry (Beef Supreme), 188
  stewing, braised in wine, 189
  tenderloin
    with herbs and sausage, 190
    roast, with mustard-cognac sauce, 187
    tournedos of, with red wine and blue
      cheese sauce, 186
Bell pepper
  red
    with leeks and carrots, 226
    purée of, with kale, 150

in risotto, 229
  salad dressing of, 80
  yellow, in risotto, 229
Benesch, Sheryl, 36–37
Biltmore Estate, 207–9
Bisque. *See* Soup
Blackberries
  in compote, 270
  with shortcake, 289
Blinis, buckwheat, and caviar, 40
Blintzes, poppy seed and cheese, 313
Blueberry
  sauce, 287, 312
  shortcake, with crème anglaise, 289
Bollinger, 21
Brandy, flan, 276
Bread, 237
  cornmeal white, 238
  harvest, 243
  homemade pan, with herbs, 241
  honey brown, 239
  pudding, 320
  sparkling, 238
  Tecate (Mexican village), 242
Broth. *See* Soup
Butter
  herb, for popovers, 319
  sauce, with pistachios, 191

C

Cabbage, red, with apples, 215
Cake
  apple, 300
  chestnut roll, 296
  chocolate, decadence, with raspberry
    sauce, 299
  gingerbread, with apricot-sherry glaze,
    302
  orange blossom chiffon, 301
  pineapple upside-down, 300
Calvados, in mayonnaise, 263
Canapé, bay shrimp, 50
Cantaloupe, in salad, with seafood, 81
Caramel, for custard, 276, 277
Cardamom, in *crème fraîche*, 290
Carrot(s)
  baked with fruit, 216
  purée, 116, 215
  soup
    chilled, 107
    curried, 107
Casserole, vegetable, 224
Cauliflower
  in crab soup, 103
  in stuffed chard, 216
Caviar
  with angel hair pasta, 83

with buckwheat blinis, 40
  eggplant as, 44
  mold, 41
  mousse d'or, 42
  and potato pancakes, 43
Celery root (celeriac), souffle, 218
Centre Vinicole de la Champagne, 25
Champagne
  American, 26–32
  court bouillon of, 149
  French, 11–25
  mousse, 284
  and orange jelly, 182
  production methods of, 5–8
  serving, 10
  storage of, 10
  styles of, 8–10
  syllabub, 276
  vinaigrette, 225
Chard, Swiss
  in pithiviers, 316
  roulade of, with smoked mussels, 90
  stuffed, 216
Charles Heidsieck, 18
Chateau Ste. Michelle, 133–35
Cheese
  Asiago, 48
  blue, sauce of, for tournedos, 186
  Brie, 102
    baked in phyllo, 65
    crisps of, 54
    and wild mushroom gratin, 64
  Camembert, crisps of, 54
  Cheddar, 221, 223, 224
    puffs of, with bacon, 54
    soup, 108
  cottage, dry, 313
  cream, 41, 139, 315, 322
    herb (Rondelé), 50
    soufflé, 279
  Danish Blue, mold of, 64
  farmer's, 41
  feta, 250, 254
  goat
    salad, 74, 75
    sauce, for pasta, 142
    tartlets, 55
  Gorgonzola, 231
    sauce, for pasta, 142
  Gruyère, 55, 66, 250
  Monterey Jack, 217, 315
  Mozzarella, 67
  ricotta, 67, 313
    ravioli of, 147
  Roquefort, sauce, 68, 69
  Saga, 270
  Stilton, mold of, 64
  Swiss, 250, 310, 317
  tartlets, savory, 55
Cheesecake, lavender rose-petal, 288

sauce, 154, 162
Gazpacho, 118
Ginger
    and black bean sauce, 153
    in cream cheese dip, 322
Gingerbread, with apricot-sherry
    glaze, 302
Glaze
    apricot-sherry, 302
    chocolate, 298, 299
    fruit, for Cornish Game hens, 175
    for mushroom tarts, 63
Grapefruit, sorbet, 129
Grapes
    with baked carrots, 216
    with cheese, 270
    in duck salad, 262
    with rabbit, 184
    varieties of, used in champagne, 22–23,
        31–32
Gratin, wild mushroom and Brie, 64
Gravlax, 46
Great Western Winery, 303–5

H

Ham
    and leek pancakes, 206
    in pâté, 70, 71
    in pithiviers, 316
Hanns Kornell Champagne Cellars,
    57–59
Hazelnuts
    praline, 283
    in salad dressing, 250, 258
Heidsieck & Co. Monopole, 18
Hens, Cornish Game
    glazed, 175
    marinated, with *shiitake* mushrooms, 176
Herb(s)
    butter, 319
    in pan bread, 241
Honey
    in brown bread, 239
    and mustard dressing, 260
Horton, Frederick, 267

I

Ice cream, Mexican vanilla, 272

J

Jacquart. *See* Co-opérative Régionale
Jelly, champagne and orange, 182
John Culbertson Winery, 233–36

K

Kale, purée of, with red peppers, 150
Kiwi fruit
    salad, with persimmons, 263
    sorbet, 130
Korbel Champagne Cellars, 34–37

Kornell, Marilouise, 59
Kornell. *See* Hanns Kornell
    Champagne Cellars

L

Lamb
    leg of, marinated, 199
    rack of, with mint sabayon, 200
Lanson Père et Fils, 18, 30
Laurant Pommery & Co., 21
Laurent Perrier, 30
Lavender, in cheesecake, 288
Leek(s)
    and clams, 92
    and ham pancakes, 206
    roasted, with garlic, 219
    soup, with potatoes, chilled, 122
Lemon
    pudding soufflé, 280
    sauce, 92, 212
    tarts, 292
Lettuce, packages of, for oriental salad,
    77
Lime, angel pie, 275
Liver, calf's, with ham, 198
Loganberry, meringue, 273
Louis Roederer, 17–18, 30

M

Mack, Karen, 134–35
Marinade
    for beef tenderloin, 190
    champagne, 47, 178
    for Cornish game hens, 176
    for lamb, 199
Marne et Champagne (producer), 25
Mayonnaise
    Calvados, 263
    herb, 62
    oregano, 56
    tomato-tarragon, 214
Meringue
    apple, 274
    for lime angel pie, 275
    loganberry, 273
Mint
    and chocolate sorbet, 286
    sabayon, 200
Mirassou Vineyards, 97–99
Moët et Chandon, 16–17, 30
Mold, blue cheese, 64
Mole sauce, 202
Mousse
    caviar, 42
    champagne, 284
    chocolate, white, in almond cookie shells,
        with dark chocolate sauce, 285
    smoked salmon, 45
Mumm, G.H., & Co., 21, 30
Mushroom(s)
    consommé, jellied, 119
    and corn, in crêpe pouches, 138
    filling of, for Beef Supreme, 189

sautéed, 219
soup, chilled, 119
spread, for tartlets, 62
stuffed with crab, 50
in tarragon cream, 220
timbale of, 95
wild, 143, 184, 189
    gratin, with Brie, 64
Mustard
    and honey dressing, 260
    sauce, 187, 203

N

Nasturtiums, stuffed, 51
Nectarines, poached, 278
Noodles, bean-thread, in salad, 77

O

Onion soup, with apple, 106
Orange
    cake, chiffon, 301
    crème caramel, 277
    glaze, 301
    jelly, with champagne, 182
    sauce, 182, 193
    sorbet, with lemon, 128
    soufflé, 279, 283

P

Palm, hearts of, in salad, 253
Pancakes
    cornmeal
        blue, 315
        with leeks and ham, 206
    delicate, with blueberry sauce, 312
    potato, and caviar, 43
Papaya, soup, cold, 120
Paper, parchment, cooking salmon in,
    157
Papillotes, salmon, 157
Pasta
    angel hair (capellini)
        with caviar, 83
        with prawn sauce, 85
        salad of, with tomato sauce, 82
        with truffles, 84
    capellini. *See* Pasta, angel hair
    fettuccine
        with goat cheese and Gorgonzola
            cream sauce, 142
        with wild mushrooms, 143
        spinach, with prawns and oyster
            mushrooms, 144
    fusilli, salad, with seafood, 80
    homemade, 85, 147
    linguine, with asparagus, 141
    ravioli, homemade ricotta, with sage, 147
    salad, 80, 255
    shells, crab-filled, 146
    spaghettini
        with prawn sauce, 85
        with shrimp, crab, and scallops, 145

Stew
   oyster, 158
   veal, 194
   venison, 185
Stir-Fry, summer vegetable, 224
Stock
   fish (fumet), 152
   veal, 119
Strawberries
   with cheese, 270
   chocolate-covered, 273
   in compote, 270
   and cream cheese dip, 322
   in crêpes, 312
   sauce, 279, 287
   with scallops, in champagne sauce, 91
   with shortcake, 289
Sweet potatoes, 22, 175
Syllabub, champagne, 276

T

Taittinger, 16, 30
Tarragon, mayonnaise, with tomato, 214
Tarte tatin, hot apple and sour cherry, 295
Tarts
   fruit, tiny, 291
   lemon, 292
   mushroom, 62–63
   Queen's, 293
   smoked salmon, 66
Tart (*see also* Quiche)
   apple and sour cherry (*tarte tatin*), 295
   pecan toffee, 294
   pithiviers, with ham and chard, 316
Tears, Edna, 305
Terrine, chicken, 73

Timbale
   green bean, 214
   mushroom, with truffle sauce, 95
Tomatillo, sauce, 170
Tomato(es)
   mayonnaise, with tarragon, 214
   salad, with basil, 252
   sauce, fresh, for pasta, 82
   soup, with basil, 115
   with spaghetti squash, 222
   stuffed with smoked trout, 319
Torte
   almond, with pineapple sorbet, 297
   chocolate almond, 298
Truffle(s)
   with pasta, 84
   sauce, for mushroom timbales, 95
Turkey, with pecan and apple stuffing, 183

V

Vanilla
   Mexican, in ice cream, 272
   pudding and pie filling, for custard sauce, 321
Veal
   bones, for stock, 119
   calf's liver, with ham, 198
   and ham *pâté en croûte*, 70
   leg, for *vitello tonnato*, 72
   loin (tenderloin)
      medallions of
         with orange sauce, 193
         with pistachio butter sauce, 191
      in morel sauce, 192
   meat loaf, 195
   in pâté, 70, 71
   stew, 194
   sweetbreads

      with oysters, 197
      in puff pastry shells, 196
Vegetables
   casserole of, 224
   grilled, with champagne vinaigrette, 225
   soup, Spring, 114
   Summer stir-fry of, 224
   trio of, 226
Venison, stew, 185
Veuve Clicquot-Ponsardin, 17
Vichysoisse, 122
Vinaigrette
   champagne, for vegetables, 225
   for warm goat cheese salad, 75
Vin mousseaux, 25
Vitello tonnato, 72

W

Watercress, in salad, 74, 75, 250, 251
Wenger, Steve, 209
Wente Bros. Sparkling Wine Cellars, 265–68
Wiens, Ruth, 99
Wine
   beef braised in, 189
   sauce
      with blue cheese, 186
      with garlic, 154
Wonton, pesto, 114

Z

Zucchini
   in bread, 243
   frittata, 227
   soup, cream of, 116